MW01406124

Clout City

Clout City

THE RISE AND FALL OF THE

CHICAGO POLITICAL MACHINE

Dominic A. Pacyga

THE UNIVERSITY OF CHICAGO PRESS
Chicago and London

The University of Chicago Press, Chicago 60637
The University of Chicago Press, Ltd., London
© 2025 by The University of Chicago
All rights reserved. No part of this book may be used or reproduced in any manner whatsoever without written permission, except in the case of brief quotations in critical articles and reviews. For more information, contact the University of Chicago Press, 1427 E. 60th St., Chicago, IL 60637.
Published 2025
Printed in the United States of America

34 33 32 31 30 29 28 27 26 25   1 2 3 4 5

ISBN-13: 978-0-226-73370-8 (cloth)
ISBN-13: 978-0-226-73384-5 (e-book)
DOI: https://doi.org/10.7208/chicago/9780226733845.001.0001

Library of Congress Cataloging-in-Publication Data

Names: Pacyga, Dominic A. author
Title: Clout city : the rise and fall of the Chicago political machine / Dominic A. Pacyga.
Other titles: Rise and fall of the Chicago political machine
Description: Chicago : The University of Chicago Press, 2025. | Includes bibliographical references and index.
Identifiers: LCCN 2025008158 | ISBN 9780226733708 cloth | ISBN 9780226733845 ebook
Subjects: LCSH: Democratic Party (Chicago, Ill.) | Chicago (Ill.) — Politics and government | Bridgeport (Chicago, Ill.)
Classification: LCC F548.52 .P33 2025 | DDC 977.3/11 — dc23/eng/20250326
LC record available at https://lccn.loc.gov/2025008158

♾ This paper meets the requirements of ANSI/NISO Z39.48-1992 (Permanence of Paper).

Authorized Representative for EU General Product Safety Regulation (GPSR) queries: **Easy Access System Europe**—Mustamäe tee 50, 10621 Tallinn, Estonia, gpsr.requests@easproject.com
Any other queries: https://press.uchicago.edu/press/contact.html

In memory of

Arnold R. Hirsch, Raymond Mohl, Paul Barrett,
Perry Duis, and Peter McLennon.

Five of the Finest Friends and Observers of
the American City. I miss you all.

Contents

INTRODUCTION
The Sacred and the Profane in Chicago's Politics 1

1
THE GREAT FIRE, AN ASSASSINATION,
AND THE SEEDS OF CHANGE 19

The Day Everything Changed 20 "Our Carter" 23

2
BRIDGEPORT AND DE LA SALLE INSTITUTE:
THE BIRTH OF THE MACHINE 41

Bridgeport 42 The River and the Bridgeport Stench 43
Rum, Riot, and Romanism 45 The Working-Class Response 47
The Bridgeport Way 50 De La Salle Institute:
The Cradle of Clout 52 Communal Catholicism and Clout 60
Patron Saints and Patronage 64

3
THE COMMUNAL WEB 67

The Priest, the Minister, and the Rabbi 68
The Saloon 80 The Ward Boss 82 The Gangster 91

4
THE MACHINE'S GROWING PAINS 97

Roger Sullivan and John Hopkins 99 Demographic and Technological Change 107 Young Carter 109 Patronage and the Traction Issue 113

5
A REPUBLICAN PROTESTANT PROTO-MACHINE 125

William Hale Thompson 126 The Blond Boss 127 Mayor Thompson 128 A Democratic Reformer 139 The Return of Big Bill 142 Thompson's Last Hurrah! 1927–1931 144

6
BOHEMIAN RHAPSODY: A NEW ETHNIC ALIGNMENT 147

Bohemia in Chicago 148 Anton Cermak: The Early Years 151 The United Societies for Local Self-Government 153 The Growth of a Communal Political Machine 158 Cermak Rising 166 Mayor Cermak 167

7
BRIDGEPORT'S VICTORY 171

Frank J. Corr: A De La Salle Graduate 172 Mayor Edward Kelly: A South Side Irish Catholic Mayor 174 Kelly, the Policy Wheel, and the Growth of the Democratic Machine 179 Dawson, Clout, Community, and the Emerging Black Democratic Majority 181 Labor, Ethnic, Class Conflict and the Kelly–Nash Machine 186 Wartime Mayor 191

8
CLOUT AND COMMUNALISM TRIUMPHANT 197

Kennelly: A Bridgeport Reformer 198 A True Bridgeport Mayor 205 The Church Triumphant 214 A Battle Between the Sacred and Profane 219

9

FRAGMENTATION: CLOUT AND COMMUNALISM IN DECLINE 223

The Racial Divide: The Sacred and Profane in Conflict 224
Racial Clashes 232   The Chicago Freedom Movement 235
Coming Apart: The Democratic Convention 241   Dark Days 244

10

CHANGING TIMES 255

Let the Chaos Begin! 257   The Democratic Civil War
Begins: Bilandic, Byrne, Daley, and Washington 262
The Church Dispirited 275

11

NOT YOUR FATHER'S MACHINE 281

Restoration? 283   A New Machine? 285   A Neoliberal Machine 293
The Daley Family 296   The End of the Daley Era 302

12

AFTER THE DALEYS 309

Emanuel Takes Control 310   The Sacred vs. the Profane in
Englewood 313   A Second Emanuel Administration 315
The Last Gasp of the Old Machine: Burke and Madigan 319
A Progressive Interlude: The Lightfoot and Johnson
Administrations 325   Conclusion: The End of the Communal
Machine 330

Acknowledgments 333
List of Abbreviations 335
Notes 337
Index 377

Introduction

The Sacred and the Profane in Chicago's Politics

> What is inherently wrong with the word "politician" if the fellow has devoted his life to holding public office and trying to do something for his people?
>
> RICHARD J. DALEY[1]

Despite its use by journalists, pundits, political scientists, historians, and politicians themselves, the phrase "machine politics" is frequently misunderstood, often misused, and much maligned. In recent decades, "political machine" has been used to describe almost any political faction that successfully won an election and exercised power—or in the Chicago parlance, "clout." In 2023, Chicago political journalists cast the indictment of former Alderman Ed Burke as signaling the defeat of the old Democratic political machine, while announcing the rise of a new progressive political machine led by the Chicago Teachers Union that aided Mayor Brandon Johnson's election.[2]

But the new formation is not a machine. The "Chicago Machine" was a particular and distinctive institution that emerged in a specific time and place, shaped by historical context, to hold power for several generations. While weak remnants of it survive, that machine eventually fell victim to corruption, reformism, and a constellation of demographic, economic, and cultural changes. This book will trace the historical origins, development, victory, and final defeat of tradi-

INTRODUCTION

tional machine politics in Chicago—the last of the big city machines to develop and the last to fall.*

Clout City covers the period from 1870 to 2023 in an attempt to show the long evolution of what has come to be known as the Chicago way of politics. It further emphasizes the religious, specifically Judeo-Christian, communal roots of Chicago's political machine and the eventual withering of those roots over time, including the impact of the Vatican II Ecumenical Council. My argument emphasizes the political machine's deep foundation in Irish Catholic and East European Jewish neighborhoods. Since I argue that both Jewish and Catholic communalism played a central role in the creation of machine politics, I believe delving into this interwoven social and cultural history is essential for understanding Chicago politics. Given the often simplistic and ahistorical perspective many people have about Chicago's political life, I believe it is necessary to cover events during that wide-ranging period, and I argue that you cannot fully and accurately understand today's politics without seeing the larger (and indeed, longer) picture—the growth of the machine and its decline over time. In fact, a purpose of this book is to demonstrate that the origins of Chicago's clout-based approach to politics is not only intertwined with its social and cultural history, but also predates the Richard J. Daley era. Ultimately, this is a book that seeks to anchor the reader's experience in deep historical territory.

Chicago's political history is a long and storied one. Much has been written about political legends such as Big Bill Thompson, Anton Cermak, Ed Kelly, and of course the Daley family. Chicago's well-known political corruption has long been a favorite topic as well. The goal of this book is to look beyond headline-making scandals and partisan maneuverings to explore the religious and sociocultural roots of the city's politics. What were the precursors to the Democratic Party machine in Chicago? How and why did this machine come to be? What were its roots? How did Chicago's immigrant "cultures shape it? How did race transform the machine? How did

---

*Like other observers of Chicago politics, I use the terms "political machine," "the machine," and "urban machine politics" interchangeably.

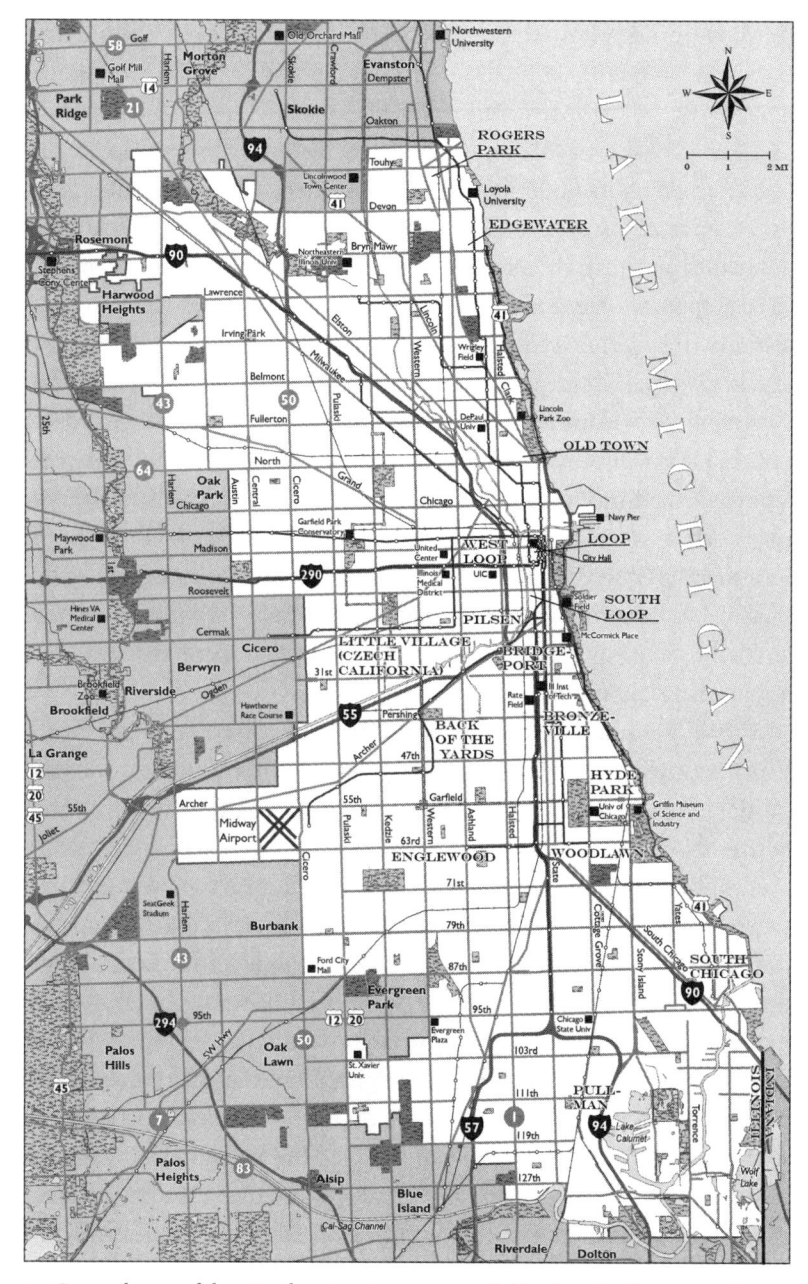

1.1 General map of the city showing important neighborhoods. Courtesy of Parker Otto.

this governing system thrive, and how did it change over time? And finally, what factors contributed to the machine's decline in the last decades of the twentieth century?

Clout City surveys Chicago's political history from the Great Fire (1871), through its flourishing and decline as an industrial city, to its emergence as a global city in the early twenty-first century. It concentrates on those cultural, economic, and demographic elements that shaped the Democratic Party machine and its predecessors. It also focuses on those elements that transformed the Regular Democratic Organization of Cook County and led to its decline in the twenty-first century. The more contemporary period of Chicago politics is given only modest treatment because the quintessential Chicago machine reached its apex during the period from 1930 to 1965. While political events, persons, and scandals are not ignored, I argue that Chicago's politics is understood best as a mixture of the sacred and the profane, a combination of cultural and religious roots and more worldly pursuits. Chicago is a secular, capitalist city, but one with a religious core.

While cathedrals—sacred architecture—dominated medieval European cities, skyscrapers—secular architecture—dominated modern American cities, and no place more so than the birthplace of the skyscraper, Chicago. And no matter how much you stretch the metaphor of a skyscraper reaching to the heavens, there's nothing sacred about a corporate office building. If there are sacred spaces in the industrial capitalist city, they are in the neighborhoods, with their many houses of worship of every possible denomination. For many Chicagoans, the neighborhood itself was a sacred space where families lived among friends and neighbors. It was a communal setting with institutions that served residents, but also connected them to the larger city. Most Chicagoans defined the neighborhood against downtown, "us" against the industrial giants that dominated local economies, such as meatpacking, steel, or the garment industry.

Catholicism, especially the immigrant peasant version first brought over by the Irish in the mid-nineteenth century, shaped Chicago politics. At the height of Catholic power in the region, more than 400 Roman Catholic parishes and parochial schools in the archdiocese created a largely Catholic sacred place. Even non-Catholics often identified with the local parish. Neighborhoods became shared spaces largely defined by communal Catholicism. These, in turn, spawned other neighborhood institutions. Out of this sacred cultural grounding was born the Democratic machine as well as countless fraternal organizations and other institutions that provided support, services, and spiritual nourishment to residents from "cradle to grave." That did not mean that all went well or that there was no crime or injustice, since the sacred and profane often collided and sometimes merged in the neighborhoods and in politics.

There is a common belief that simply cleaning streets, fixing streetlights, and filling in potholes made up the social contract between voters and politicians in Chicago. If local politicians met those needs, then residents voted for them. Certainly, providing basic municipal services was a fundamental responsibility of local elected officials. But the social contract between voters and politicians in Chicago came to depend on many other factors. Constituent favors and jobs were key for politicians, but so too were a myriad of public service efforts. Patronage and preferential treatment for some existed alongside economic and social welfare programs for many. It should be no surprise that the great urban machines supported progressive measures such as Social Security, unemployment compensation, food stamps, welfare relief, and funding for public schools and public transit. Local elected officials recruited police officers and firefighters from the various ethnic and racial groups, and they supported churches and charities through donations or through government aid.

These officials were not selfless. If someone took a little graft (or a lot) on the side, that was all right as long as he or she took care of their constituents. Where some saw corruption, others saw tribute to community leaders, much like the peasant clan leaders of the past. They attended wakes and funerals, dropped off turkeys and hams on holidays, showed up at charitable events, and offered help in times of need. When a family could not afford to pay for the delivery of coal, aldermen delivered it. They often did not ask if there was real need, instead adopting a "social services" mentality. Politicians became friends and protectors to many in their communities. In this way, communalism was the foundation for clout and its effective use. Without a local politician's support, it could be nearly impossible to get things done. In return for this kind of personal service, the politician asked for loyalty in the form of a vote and possibly a campaign donation. Yet this was not a simple transactional relationship. There was an internal contradiction that often crossed the line between communal advancement—the sacred—and transactional corruption—the profane.

By the end of the twentieth century, the communally based political machine exercising clout had largely broken down in Chicago. It dissolved under the impact of deindustrialization, socio-religious changes, assimilation, federal programs, upward mobility, suburbanization, demographic change, and technological advances that transformed all of America. To some extent the very successes of the political machine contributed to its demise. As it promoted upward mobility for many Chicagoans, it also promoted assimilation and buying into the American idea of individualism.

Modern Chicago was born out of disaster. The Great Fire of October 8, 1871, destroyed roughly one-third of the city, and changed it forever. This defining event marked the rise of Chicago's first modern politician and mayor, Carter H. Harrison III (1825–1893). It also launched the expansion of municipal government.[3] But another, less traumatic transformation shaped urban political power as well.

In 1872, Illinois inaugurated cumulative voting for the State House of Representatives. Under this reform, each voter had three votes that could be divided up among several candidates, in an attempt to ensure minority party representation. Even if a district voted largely Republican, it was likely that at least one legislator would be a Democrat. This was an ingenious way of assuring that all citizens were represented in the state legislature. At the same time, voters could bundle their votes for one candidate, which allowed racial and ethnic groups to come together behind a candidate.[4] As a result, the state legislature became a sort of farm club for rising Chicago politicians.[5]

Nevertheless, the array of ethnic groups made it difficult for Harrison and the Democrats to create a citywide political organization. In other cities, like New York, a single ethnic group would dominate the political structure at any one time. But Chicago's population was not dominated by one ethnic group in the same way. The Irish emerged as political brokers in Chicago, as they did in other cities, but they had strong competition from German immigrants, as well as Swedes, Poles, Jews, and Italians. A Czech-born Democrat, Anton Cermak, created the Democratic Organization, known as the House for All Peoples, in 1931 as immigrants from southern and eastern Europe and African Americans emerged as powerful forces in the Party. Once a sort of ethnic peace could be established, along traditional peasant communal lines, the Democratic political machine emerged.

The career of Richard J. Daley (1902–1976) embodies much of this part of the history. Born in the working-class neighborhood of Bridgeport adjacent to the Union Stock Yard, Daley came of age in the culture and place that gave birth to the machine. In 1889, the French Christian Brothers (the LaSallians) organized De La Salle Institute at 35th Street and Wabash Avenue, just to the east. The school became a political incubator for some of the city's most important Democratic politicians, including Daley. Eventually five mayors graduated from the Institute along with Cook County Board Presidents Dan Ryan (1894–1961) and George W. Dunne (1913–2006), and countless other politicians, judges, and city officials. The school gave a start to numerous businesspeople, police officers, firefighters, and a host of city workers, many of whom wielded political clout. The virtues learned at De La Salle Institute included loyalty: to the Catholic Church, Chicago, classmates, the neighborhood, and (unofficially) the Democratic Party. The Catholic school also taught the meanings of sin and of hierarchy. The informal folk Catholicism of Chicago's streets and the teachings at De La Salle Institute shaped the city's Democratic machine in distinctive ways. De La Salle Institute is where the sacred learned to coexist with the profane. That tenuous relationship is at the heart of a certain understanding and definition of clout.

When the cornerstone of De La Salle Institute was laid in 1889, Father Maurice Dorney prophesied that it would be an instrument for Catholic power in the city and the nation. He could not have imag-

INTRODUCTION

ined how correct he was. De La Salle shaped the lives of many of the city's future leaders. The way of thinking learned at the school influenced the city for decades. Indeed, Catholic communalism, more than the individualism often celebrated by American mythmakers, influenced urban Democratic political machines across the country. By the 1930s, it also shaped the national Democratic Party and President Franklin Roosevelt's New Deal. This communalism was largely misunderstood by outsiders and reformers, like Jane Addams and those who came after her, who never understood or appreciated the institutional and cultural intricacies of immigrant neighborhoods.

The power of this communalism was not to last. By the time Richard J. Daley's eldest son, Richard M. Daley, also a De La Salle graduate, won the mayoralty in 1989, Chicago had undergone tremendous change. The stockyards had closed, the steel industry had all but left the city, and the industrial base that had provided income to the city's huge workforce had largely disappeared. A new city emerged in the years after the Vietnam War. Newcomers, primarily from Mexico and Puerto Rico but also from across Latin America and Asia, emerged as vital political forces. Other interest groups appeared, especially organized LGBTQ+ groups and young urban professionals. Importantly, the American Catholic Church also changed. After the Second Vatican Council in the early 1960s, Latin disappeared from the liturgy, the old immigrant Catholic cultural walls came down, and the Church ceased to foster the type of communalism that had been its hallmark.[6]

Today, the cultural and demographic foundations of the traditional Democratic political machine have weakened, while the spirit of reform has effectively challenged the old politics. *Clout City* aims to plot the historical development of the city's politics from Carter Harrison in the nineteenth century to the administration of Lori Lightfoot, the city's first Black and LGBTQ+ mayor, in the early twenty-first century. By tracing this history, I hope to demonstrate that while the traditional political machine effectively responded to historical conditions, those same ideas and practices became inadequate for governing the emerging global city.

I graduated from De La Salle Institute in 1967. The LaSallian Christian Brothers shaped much of my early intellectual life and made me aware of certain cultural, social, economic, and political forces. One of my English teachers assigned Edwin O'Connor's novel *The Last Hurrah* (1956), which depicts what the author saw as a passing age of urban machine politics, albeit in Boston. In Chicago, machine politics lasted much longer than O'Connor might have imagined. Revisiting the novel while I was writing this book shed light on how politics was practiced in urban America during much of the period covered here.

The Chicago of my youth was marked by Catholic communalism. I grew up in the 14th Ward on the South Side, and later lived in the 13th Ward. The Democratic organizations of these wards, dominated for decades by Alderman Ed Burke and State Representative Mike Madigan, were part of everyday life. Precinct captains visited neighbors, talked with them, assisted them with problems, and helped to create a communal web.

I now live in the 19th Ward, supposedly known for its machine politics, yet I have not seen a precinct captain in years. Aldermen no longer play a crucial role in the everyday life of typical Chicagoans. In the spring of 2022, Alderman Patrick Daley Thompson, the grandson of one mayor and the nephew of another, was found guilty of federal income tax evasion. Traditional machine politicians such as Madigan and Burke have been indicted on various charges. While Democrats still rule, Chicago's political world has shifted. The machine of Anton Cermak, Ed Kelly, and Richard J. Daley is long gone. Edwin O'Connor is correct in this particular as well.

The flaws of Chicago's machine politics existed side by side with an approach to political governance that derived from and centered the communalism of Chicago's immigrant and working-class communities. *Clout City* therefore examines the socioeconomic and cultural foundations of the political machine. I make the case that the very socioeconomic and cultural factors that fed the machine's success also led to its gradual decline.

Chapter 1 briefly reviews the political history of pre-fire Chicago and discusses early social and cultural developments dominated by migrants from New England and New York. The initial settlement stood on the western edge of the frontier in 1833. Visitors described it as a wild place dominated by hustlers, traders, and others seeking their fortunes. This became even more true with the arrival of the canal and the railroads in 1848. The city's politics were dominated by business interests and the emergent Yankee culture of the Upper Midwest, eventually giving birth to the Republican Party. Even at this time, Chicago politicians and boosters called for vigorous federal investments. Already a "type" of political behavior was emerging in the city.

Many were attracted to the city, including Carter H. Harrison III, the scion of a slave-owning family in Clifton, Kentucky. He counted two presidents as relatives and claimed English noblemen as his ancestors. In 1855, he married Sophonisba Preston and eventually came to Chicago, where he invested in real estate. In 1870, he ran for the lower house of the Illinois state legislature.

After the Great Fire, the rebuilding city took advantage of the technological changes remaking America. These changes created the need for franchises to provide public transportation, gas, and electricity, as well as telegraph and telephone lines. For many individuals, Chicago's rebuilding needs also created a chance to make politics a career path. Franchises provided a source of graft and wealth for many.

Harrison was among the first to understand the change that gripped what had been a Yankee-dominated city. While, strictly speaking, he did not invent ethnic politics, he quickly recognized the emerging ethnic nature of Chicago's population, as well as the rise of Catholic immigrant groups. His own background made him friendly toward the Irish, Germans, Poles, Czechs, Jews, and others who came to dominate the working-class wards. He understood and appreciated Catholic culture. This would not be lost on his son, Carter H. Harrison IV, who attended St. Ignatius College, married a Catholic woman, and, while not himself a member of any particular denomination, raised his children as Catholics. He, too, became mayor.

The Harrisons displayed an uncanny ability to connect with various immigrant communities. As a result, the people of Chicago elected both Harrisons to five terms each as mayor. The elder Harrison often supported labor unions, looked the other way as gamblers and prostitutes plied their trades downtown, and rarely enforced Sunday blue laws. This gave him what we would call clout, and it made the patronage he offered supporters invaluable. Perhaps ironically, in 1893, at the height of his success, a mad and disappointed patronage seeker assassinated Harrison.

Chapter 2 looks at the Chicago neighborhood of Bridgeport and De La Salle Institute. The district was first settled largely by Irish canal workers and quickly became known for corrupt politics. Bridgeport's Irish saw the whole city as a political plum ripe for the picking, and they quickly joined the Democrats in their struggle against the Republicans, who enjoyed the support of the native-born and the upper classes. Out of the Bridgeport hardscrabble, and many other such places, emerged a political machine obsessed with ethnicity, class, and political spoils. The Irish knew that it was all about jobs, favors, and upward mobility. They had learned that from their British tormentors, and they taught these lessons to their new allies, the hundreds of thousands of immigrants who joined them on Chicago's streets.

The chapter also distills the history of De La Salle Institute, founded in 1889. The new school stood in the prestigious Douglas neighborhood but was close enough to attract the working-class boys of Bridgeport, Canaryville, and Back of the Yards, giving them something to aspire to. The Brothers believed that while humans were perfectible in the next life, "the child is not born good" and has strong inclinations toward evil.[7] Simply put, humans sinned. In this context, the school promoted Catholic attitudes toward hierarchy, fairness, duty, and sin.

In addition, the development of popular Catholicism, including the cult of the saints, had an added impact on the city's culture and politics. Understanding the role of these spiritual patrons and of folk religion goes a long way toward explaining the creation of secular patronage as an outgrowth of religion: everybody needs a friend, a patron. The folk religion of Chicago's Catholic neighborhoods proved vital for understanding the communal nature not only of Catholicism, but of the powerful political machine that rested on its foundation.

Chapter 3 explains the communal web and the role played by the priest, minister, and rabbi as well as the saloonkeeper, the ward boss, and the gangster in the collective network that created the political machine. Chicago's neighborhoods operated as small towns. The local house of worship, whether Protestant, Catholic, or Jewish, helped to establish an institutional base for community-building. This communalism protected immigrant ethnic groups against the dominant White Anglo-Saxon communities that often favored individualism. Communalism sheltered immigrants in a hostile urban and capitalist environment. Distinctive economic engines gave a particular identity to each neighborhood. Stockyards, steel mills, tanneries, and sweatshops each provided a symbolic base for their surrounding neighborhoods. So did universities and other upper-class institutions.

Chapter 4 deals with early attempts to build a citywide Democratic political organization. Four years after his father's death, "Young Carter" Harrison won the mayoralty. Like his father, he understood the yearnings of Catholic immigrants. By following in his father's footsteps, Young Carter helped establish a tradition of political dynasties in Chicago.

Both Harrisons and their Democratic rivals, Roger Sullivan and John P. Hopkins, attempted to take control of the party and establish their domination over the large, growing, rambling city. These attempts at unifying and centralizing control failed, although they did set down a foundation for later success. Much like the city, the Democrats were divided, whether by social class, ethnicity, neighborhood loyalties, or even monetary policy. Eventually these divisions would be overcome.

Ironically, it was a Republican, William H. "Big Bill" Thompson, the subject of chapter 5, who first partially succeeded in creating a citywide political machine. Coming from an august lineage, Thompson grew up on the affluent West Side and was a star athlete. He was everything the Bridgeport Irish were not. In 1900, he ran for the City Council as a reform candidate. Voters elected Thompson mayor in 1915 as World War I raged in Europe. Playing the demagogue, he wooed Chicago's Irish and German communities by taking an anti-British stance while also inviting socialists and anti-war groups to rally in the city. He also promised the return of White Anglo-Saxon Protestant rule to the unruly city of immigrants, while at the same time courting the expanding African American community. This odd coalition even included older immigrant-ethnic groups such as the Swedes, Norwegians, and Dutch, but it did not go unchallenged. A similarly centralizing Democratic machine, led by Anton Cermak and the Southwest Side Czech communities of Pilsen and Czech California (Little Village), soon emerged.[8]

Chapter 6 discusses the rise of new immigrant groups and of Cermak, who became the first and only foreign-born mayor of the "City of Immigrants." Cermak began his political career as a precinct captain, and in 1902 was elected to the Illinois House of Representatives. In 1909 he became alderman of the 12th Ward; in 1922 he was elected president of the Cook County Board and six years later chairman of the Cook County Democratic Party. Three years later, in 1931, Cermak's coalition of eastern and central European ethnic groups, along with a large and important group of South Side Irish, swept him into the mayoralty.

Cermak's organization had a distinctive blue-collar edge to it. He brought Czechs, Jews, Poles, Italians, and others together and eventually began to coax African Americans into the Democratic Party. When he became mayor, Cermak gave the chairmanship of the local Democratic Party to a West Sider, Patrick Nash, who brought along the Bridgeport Irish. After Cermak was assassinated in 1933, Nash maneuvered his ally, Edward J. Kelly, originally from Bridgeport, into the mayor's office. The Kelly–Nash Democratic machine stayed in power until 1947, consolidating the Stockyard Irish's political control.[9]

Chapter 7 details the ascendancy of Kelly and Bridgeport politicians to real power in the city. Kelly presided over the city during the Great Depression and World War II. If Cermak was the George Washington of the Chicago Democratic machine, Kelly might have been its Andrew Jackson. He expanded the reach of the Democratic Party

INTRODUCTION

and brought unions into it. Yet as we will see, in 1947 the Democratic Party dumped Kelly and chose a reform candidate, Martin H. Kennelly, for mayor. Kennelly was also born in Bridgeport, but unlike Kelly, he graduated from De La Salle Institute.[10]

Chapter 8 begins with the Kennelly administration and also marks the rise of Richard J. Daley, who graduated from De La Salle Institute in 1919 and entered the workforce as a clerk in the Union Stock Yard shortly thereafter. The future mayor learned much from Bridgeport Alderman Joseph McDonough and Mayor Anton Cermak. He also absorbed the art of national politics from Mayor Kelly, who made himself indispensable to President Franklin D. Roosevelt. Later Daley learned from Martin Kennelly not to give others power over his political future. He would control the Democratic party and the mayor's office for more than two decades until his death in 1976. While Daley studied politics under Cermak and Kelly, he learned his moral and religious worldview from the Christian Brothers at De La Salle Institute. These included a communal response to social problems.

Even though Daley is often portrayed in conservative terms, he actually embraced the New Deal and liberal ideals concerning civil rights and labor unions. Relationships formed at De La Salle and in Bridgeport informed his sense of loyalty and his understanding of urban politics. Daley remained steadfastly loyal to De La Salle Institute, the neighborhood, and the Catholic Church. The old-line WASP families might have had the elite downtown clubs and sent their children to Harvard or Yale, but Daley had De La Salle Institute, the Hamburg Athletic Association, the corner tavern, and the loyalty of everyday Chicagoans.[11]

By this time, the Democratic machine reached well beyond the mayor, aldermen, and city workers. Judges, state politicians, precinct captains, and commissioners, as well as union members, police officers, firefighters, and teachers, also played parts. The machine even had clout in the private sector. Businesses need favors too, and the machine counted on them to provide funds for political campaigns and private-sector jobs for party regulars and those who aspired to clout. This social contract reached beyond City Hall to the smallest precincts and created a vast hierarchy of political influence and patronage. Daley used the power of the system masterfully to control the city. He also had a bearing on national politics, as he could deliver the vote for senators, members of Congress, and even presidents.[12]

Chapter 9 traces the initial decline of the machine during the final years of the first Daley's rule. The year 1968 proved pivotal in weakening the Regular Democratic Organization. The Tet Offensive in Vietnam eventually led to the end of Lyndon Johnson's presidency and to the catastrophe of the Democratic Convention in Chicago. The assassination of Dr. Martin Luther King Jr. provoked riots across the city's Far West Side. In the aftermath of these events, Daley lost power in the national party, culminating in his exclusion from the 1972 Democratic Convention. Perhaps more importantly, those events contributed to the rise of independent Democrats led by Alderman William Singer, Reverend Jesse Jackson, and maverick Governor Dan Walker. The federal indictments of many of Daley's allies and investigations of Daley himself put untold pressure on the mayor, who then suffered a stroke. Daley won a sixth term in 1975, but signs of the machine's decline were evident.[13]

Chapter 10 begins with the 1976 election and, shortly thereafter, the death of Richard J. Daley. As president pro tempore of the City Council, Wilson Frost, an African American, declared himself acting mayor, but Democratic politicians maneuvered Michael A. Bilandic into the job. The new mayor, also from Bridgeport and a graduate of De La Salle Institute, had previously served as alderman of Daley's 11th Ward. But Bilandic found it difficult to control the vast political machine that had lost the only leader it had known for more than two decades.

Jane Byrne ran against Bilandic in the 1979 Democratic primary as a reformer, and she shocked the city by winning. It seemed as if the Democratic machine had ground to a halt. It had not. Byrne soon dismissed her reform-minded advisors and turned to an alliance with the City Council's leadership, especially the "two Eddies," Vrdolyak and Burke, along with Alderman Fred Roti of the 1st Ward. This resulted in the temporary continuation of the traditional political order and of the still powerful, if weakened, communal response to urban and especially ward-based politics.

INTRODUCTION

As the 1983 election approached, candidate Harold Washington quickly energized the Black community, revealing the power of African American voters. As Richard M. Daley and Byrne split the White ethnic vote, Washington, backed by Blacks, many Hispanics, and lakefront liberals, became the first African American mayor of Chicago. Many Black Chicagoans now called for their community to have a larger share of the political pie. They declared their right to clout.

The White ethnic community, who had been in power for so long, greeted this with deep consternation. White ethnic politicians still held considerable power on the City Council. Led by Vrdolyak and Burke, they blocked most of Washington's program. It took a court-ordered redrawing of ward boundaries for Washington to gain control of the City Council in 1986. Unfortunately, he died shortly thereafter, igniting a spectacular political battle between the Washington forces and machine diehards, which included several Black aldermen.[14]

The machine was indeed not dead. Chapter 11 tackles the election in 1989 of Richard M. Daley, another graduate of De La Salle Institute, and his lengthy administration. The younger Daley had previously followed in his father's footsteps and served in the Illinois Senate from 1972 until 1980. Once in office, this Daley went on to serve for twenty-two years, surpassing his father's record. This so-called restoration depended on several factors, including political fractures in the Black community.

Daley attempted to run the political organization as his father had. But the city was changing. Court decisions known as the Shakman decrees removed the majority of patronage jobs once under the control of the mayor and the City Council. In addition, the Catholic Church's presence in the city had changed. The reforms of the Second Vatican Council and the decline of religious orders transformed Catholic Chicago and led to the decline of Catholic communalism. Traditional Catholic values of hierarchy and fidelity to the Church, but also to friends and neighborhood, shifted. During a time of significant assimilation and White flight, the archdiocese abandoned neighborhoods.

Equally important, the traditional relationship between ward bosses and their neighbors changed. Since the New Deal a growing federal government had come to provide many of the services originally offered by local politicians. Social Security and other social programs slowly transformed and undermined the Democratic machine.[15]

Demographic change continued apace. The growth of the Hispanic and Asian populations, and the LGBTQ+ community, along with the continued decline of the White ethnic community, created a new landscape. Many older ethnic groups lost influence. The growth of a so-called independent voting bloc also had a huge impact on the traditional Democratic machine and its exercise of clout.[16]

The communal system created by the Irish and other immigrant groups floundered under the pressures of assimilation, upward mobility, globalism, deindustrialization, suburbanization, federalization, and the forces unleashed by the Second Vatican Council. All of this meant a political adjustment for the city and its political organization. It meant a shift in the traditional system of clout, which no longer seemed to serve the larger public. Corruption persisted, but it could no longer be tolerated.

In the twenty-first century, the old system ground to a halt. Chapter 12 deals with the 2011 election of Rahm Emanuel, Rich Daley's handpicked successor and Chicago's first Jewish mayor, which marked a fundamental shift—even as Daley's backing echoed the old system of favors and paybacks.[17] During Emanuel's two terms, pillars of the old Democratic machine rooted in the neighborhoods disappeared. Often referred to as "Mayor 1%," Emanuel courted large companies and helped to grow investments in the central business district. But the neighborhoods came to feel neglected, and it wasn't clear anymore where Emanuel's Democratic constituents were or what they wanted. After botching an attempt to conceal the video of the 2014 killing of Laquan McDonald by a Chicago police officer, Emanuel chose not to run for a third term. Arguably, the machine was no longer even on the ballot.

The election of Lori Lightfoot as mayor in 2019 seemed to represent a major break with the past. An African American woman, a member of the LGBTQ+ community, and a political outsider, Lightfoot promised to drive a stake into the clout-based system. The trials and tribulations of Edward Burke and Michael Madigan became symbolic of the disrepair in the old-line machine. The election of several Democratic Socialists to the City Council, along with Lightfoot's overwhelming victory in all fifty wards, implied a shift in attitudes. Chicago's politics had transformed, the result of tremendous economic, cultural, demographic, and technological changes spanning decades.

Yet Lightfoot did not make good her promises, and she was defeated in 2023 by a coalition that backed the boldly progressive Brandon Johnson, just as I was completing this book. This underscored the end of the traditional citywide machine — an event long in coming, and often heralded — as it finally died with a whimper, here. Politics, however, remains Chicago's favorite sport.[18]

1

The Great Fire, an Assassination, and the Seeds of Change

> First in violence, deepest in dirt, lawless, unlovely, ill smelling, irreverent, new. An over-grown gawk of a village—the tough among cities, a spectacle for the nation.
> LINCOLN STEFFENS, *The Shame of the Cities*, 1905[1]

Carter H. Harrison III, Chicago's World's Fair mayor, rested at home on the night of October 28, 1893. Earlier in his busy day, Harrison had given a rousing speech at the fair to the nation's mayors. The Columbian Exposition had proven to the world that Chicago had fully recovered from the disastrous fire of 1871. No longer simply a wild western cow town, it might soon be the nation's leading city. The mayor had big plans for his fifth administration and was looking forward to his imminent third marriage.

Just before 8:00 p.m., Patrick Eugene Prendergast rang the doorbell of the Harrison residence on Ashland Avenue. The housekeeper, Mary F. Hansen, answered the door. At the time, politicians often received their constituents at their homes, as did Harrison. Hansen went to rouse Harrison. When he stepped from the parlor into the hall, Prendergast drew a pistol and shot him in the stomach. He fired two more shots. One hit Harrison in the heart and the other shattered a knuckle. Harrison's coachman ran into the house and fired three times at the assailant as he fled. Prendergast fired back and ran north on Ashland Avenue.

Harrison started toward the dining room, but he reeled and fell into the butler's pantry. His son Preston ran to his side. The mayor said, "I am shot, Preston, and cannot live." The young man chased after the assassin, stopping to tell neighbors, Mr. and Mrs. W. J. Chalmers, what had happened. They ran into the mayor's home. Chalmers made a pillow of his overcoat and placed it under Harrison's head. Carter H. Harrison became unconscious and died at 8:27 p.m.

Prendergast ran to the Desplaines Street Police Station and gave himself up, proclaiming that he had killed Harrison. He maintained that the mayor had broken his promise to appoint him the city's corporation counsel. Officers brought him to the central police station downtown. Shortly after 11:00 p.m., word of Harrison's death had spread, and a crowd of perhaps 500 people stood outside and threatened Prendergast's life. After getting reinforcements, the police took him to the Cook County Jail. Subsequently, a jury found him guilty, despite the plea of insanity filed by his lawyer, Clarence Darrow. On July 13, 1894, after receiving the last rites of the Catholic Church, the Irish-born murderer was hanged. Ironically, a job seeker, an immigrant, and a Catholic killed the mayor most favored by those very groups.

THE DAY EVERYTHING CHANGED

Carter Harrison III emerged on Chicago's political scene as a result of the catastrophe that began on the night of Sunday, October 8, 1871. The fire that began in the O'Leary barn on DeKoven Street moved quickly to the northeast. Flames soon leapt over the South Branch of the Chicago River and swept toward downtown. The conflagration consumed the Chicago Tribune Building, the new Palmer House, and the Marshall Field Building; then it crossed the main branch of the river and made its way north, eventually dying out in the rain in Lincoln Park. Fully one-third of the city's population was made homeless by the fire, and more than three hundred Chicagoans had died. Many feared that even more would die from cold and starvation. Survivors felt they had lived through an apocalypse. Over 21,000 acres lay in ruins and 17,420 buildings had been destroyed. The "Burnt District" included over twenty-eight miles of streets and over 120 miles of sidewalks. Financial losses amounted to close to $200 million (nearly $5 billion in 2023), or roughly a third of the city's valuation. City and county records had been destroyed, the collection of public revenues was in chaos, tax receipts had disappeared, and no courthouse or jailhouse survived. Everything seemed to have been swept away by the conflagration.

Yet the *Chicago Tribune* immediately announced that "Chicago Will Rise Again." Roughly 200,000 Chicagoans still had homes on the South, West, and Northwest Sides of the city. The downtown railroad stations lay destroyed, but the rail lines still connected Chicago to the rest of the country. Many lumberyards, packinghouses, and factories went untouched. Boosters proclaimed that the city remained a good place for investment. Within roughly eighteen months, the city had largely recovered.

Anti-Catholic and anti-immigrant feelings boiled as many blamed the West Side Irish for the disaster. Rumors spread that the Catholic Irish had not only started the fire, but had raped Protestant women, sacked the homes of the wealthy, and in general benefited from the chaos. The fact that two Irish Catholic churches near the fire zone, Holy Family and St. Patrick's, survived intact spurred on the conspiracy theories. Nativist and anti-Catholic sentiments ran high.[2]

The basic organization of Chicago's government had been laid down well before the fire, but the crisis had a profound impact on the role of government and on politics. A marked extension of municipal activities occurred, strengthening the power of the mayor and placing the executive at the head rather than at the tail of the municipal organism. Chicagoans elected Joseph Medill, the publisher of the *Chicago Tribune*, on the Fireproof ticket. The so-called Mayor's Bill passed by the state legislature in March 1872 vastly increased the powers of city government. During the next few years, supporters and opponents of expanded municipal government battled in the City Council, in petition drives and civic groups, at the ballot box, and in the courts. By 1875, "the pestiferous relic of the Medillian Era," as expanded mayoral power was called, became the accepted basis for Chicago's reincorporation.[3]

Before the Civil War, a Protestant eastern elite, many from New

England or upstate New York, ruled Chicago. Parlor politics were central. Families such as the Kinzies, Newberrys, Ogdens, and others decided policy questions in the refined setting of their social circle. These movers and shakers of early Chicago had great political, financial, and social power, created an early public sphere, and saw themselves as city builders. These families literally ran the city, and businessmen exerted a tremendous amount of influence. Ogden, the first mayor of the city, raised money for the Illinois and Michigan Canal, as well as the Galena and Chicago Union Railroad. As proponents of the Whig Party, they tapped into federal patronage and investment. While women could not vote, they took part in these parlor meetings and voiced their opinions, influencing their husbands, brothers, and sons. Once the Whig Party declined, Juliette Kinzie and her husband John joined other Whigs, including their friend Abraham Lincoln, to organize the Republican Party in Illinois.[4]

By the Civil War, the City Council had become the focal point of government with the mayor a presiding officer with few legislative functions. During this time, often known as the "Feudal Period" or "Era of the Gray Wolves," the City Council had vast powers, and powerful aldermen reigned. Corruption ran rampant as politics provided wealth and power to the members of the ruling body. The low pay of aldermen did not attract the most able and honest candidates. Only the wealthy and those willing to take part in bribery, payoffs, patronage, or favors were attracted to the office.[5]

The structure of city government changed after the fire, but its nature did not. This period also saw technological and demographic transformations that called for quick responses from city government. These changes included the development of mass production industries and city franchises which affected not only the economic life of the city, but also social class and political relationships. Hallmarks of late nineteenth-century urban development such as streetcars, telegraph, and later, telephone lines, gas pipes, and electric wires all used publicly owned city streets and alleys. Each had to get a permit or franchise from the City Council. Industries needed rail lines, paved streets, and a plentiful supply of water. All came to the aldermen with hats in hand and often envelopes filled with cash.

Suddenly aldermen became rich, as the new corporations needed their votes to access the public byways. In addition, the city began to employ legions of men and women to provide new services. The expansion of the police force and establishment of the Chicago Fire Department in 1869 increased the payroll of the city government and, with that, the possibility of patronage. Various other departments evolved, including garbage pickup, street cleaning, the water department. These too held out the possibility of jobs and contracts, which gave politicians a permanent base of funds and voters. These developments transformed Chicago's politics.

Demographic change played a role too. Chicago became a magnet for Irish, German, and other immigrants. They brought with them different customs, religions, and ideologies. Catholic, Jewish, Orthodox Christian, and Protestant in faith, immigrants often stood in contrast to the native-born Protestants who ruled the city's economic, social, and political life. The Irish and then the Germans dominated the immigrant population, but Scandinavians also arrived in large numbers, as did Dutch, British, and Scottish newcomers. By the time of the fire, Czechs, Poles, and eastern European Jews had made their way into the city's rapidly expanding industries.

The old business elites found themselves first sharing political power and then losing it to these new groups. The 1870 Illinois constitution stipulated cumulative voting for the State House, opening the doors of political power to ethnic groups. Under this system, each citizen had three votes. Blocs could split or bundle ballots in various manners. Since three office holders represented each district, the cumulative voting system often allowed ethnic communities to elect one of their own to the State House.[6] One of the major early beneficiaries of this was Carter H. Harrison III. And he created the foundation of a political organization that would come to dominate Chicago.[7]

"OUR CARTER"

Carter H. Harrison III was born on February 15, 1825, near Lexington, Kentucky. The family lineage went back to the earliest days of

1.1 Carter Harrison, a familiar figure in Chicago, is pictured here with his slouch hat. Author's Collection.

British settlement in Virginia. Related to a signer of the Declaration of Independence, two presidents, and many important members of the Virginia planter class, Harrison grew up in a slaveholding family. As a boy, Harrison studied under Dr. Lewis Marshall, the brother of Justice John Marshall. He graduated from Yale University in 1845 and ten years later received a law degree from Lexington's Transylvania University. Little of this could have foreshadowed his future political life as a Democrat and a favorite of immigrants and the working class.

From 1845 to 1855, Harrison mostly lived the life of a Kentucky plantation owner. While a slaveholder, he attended an abolition convention, and though he disapproved of the slave labor system, he also believed that plantation owners should be fairly compensated if they gave up their enslaved people. His mixed views may have played a part in his leaving Kentucky after marrying Sophonisba Preston, selling his slaves, and eventually moving to Illinois, a free state.[8]

The Harrisons first visited Chicago in 1855, when it was still a frontier city of a little more than 80,000 residents. The opportunities presented by Chicago's rapid and sustained growth, especially in real estate, attracted Harrison. He purchased property on the southwest corner of Clark and Harrison Street, where he built a fashionable family hotel in which his wife gave birth to their first son, Carter H. Harrison IV.*[9]

Harrison quickly joined the entrepreneurial class, reaping the benefits of Chicago's economic and demographic expansion. He noted, "Men who five years ago invested their all, four or five thousand dollars, are now worth two or three hundred thousand. Where I now sit, ground is worth six hundred dollars a foot, and five years ago I suspect it could have been bought for forty or fifty dollars."[10]

In 1857, Harrison and his friend Henry H. Honoré, along with some other investors, bought up forty acres west of Ashland Avenue, a major street named after Henry Clay's estate. Honoré built a large

---

*Carter H. Harrison was the third Harrison to carry that name. His son would be Carter H. Harrison IV, but generally speaking, when historians refer to this political dynasty, they incorrectly refer to the first Mayor Harrison as Carter H. Harrison I and his Chicago-born son as Carter H. Harrison II or Harrison Jr.

home there that Harrison would later purchase. The onset of the Civil War in 1861 pulled Harrison in various directions, but he stayed out of the political limelight.

That changed after the Great Fire of 1871. When Joseph Medill ran for mayor at the top of a nonpartisan union ticket, the new party also nominated Harrison for Cook County commissioner. He joined the Cook County Board that December and served a three-year term. He served on the committees dealing with finance, towns, accounts, and education, as well as on the one supervising relief funds.

Harrison ran unsuccessfully for US Congress in 1872 but won a close race in 1874 by a scant eight votes. That campaign introduced Adolph Kraus, a Bohemian Jew, to Harrison's circle. Kraus, fluent in Czech, German, and English, had arrived in Chicago shortly after the Great Fire and in 1874 worked for Harrison's rival, Jasper D. Ward. But after a dispute, Kraus turned on Ward and convinced many of his fellow Bohemians to vote for Harrison, launching an influential alliance. Two years later, Harrison was reelected despite having to leave for Germany, where his wife, on an extended trip with their children, had just died. Harrison later declined to run for a third term, and instead, in 1879, turned his eyes toward City Hall.[11]

The Republicans seemed confident as the 1879 mayoral election approached. They believed that Mayor Monroe Heath's administration had been successful and that the Democrats stood in total disarray. But Chicago, once a Republican stronghold, had changed significantly through industrial and demographic growth. The fire had increased class conflict as the poor felt they had been betrayed by the city's Republican leadership. Anti-Catholic and anti-Irish hysteria after the conflagration only increased social fragmentation. The Great Railroad Strike of 1877 further accentuated the class divide as police shot workers in the streets. Indeed, across the country, unbridled capitalism, as well as a feeling that the nation had somehow gone astray, influenced politics. The Greenback movement, Populism, socialism, and anarchism began to have local impacts. This was especially true in big cities transformed by immigration.

On March 8, 1879, the Greenback-Labor Party nominated Harrison for the mayoralty. He neither accepted nor declined the nomination, but instead waited for the Democratic Party of Cook County to hold its convention. The next day, the *Chicago Tribune* warned of an alliance of Democrats, Greenbackers, and Communists to elect Harrison. When the Democrats met in Uhlich's Hall on March 15, saloonkeeper J. K. Miller nominated Harrison. After multiple votes, Harrison won the nomination.

The Republicans met at Farwell Hall two weeks later. "Long John" Wentworth, a legendary figure in Chicago politics who began his career as a Democrat, attacked Harrison and waved the "bloody red shirt" of the Civil War, claiming that Democrats had been and still were traitors and implying that the same could be said of Harrison, a born southerner. He called for his party to put an end to "these Rebel obstructionists" and further called Harrison an "ambitious politician with no taste for the office of mayor."

During the campaign, the Republican press, led by the *Chicago Tribune*, attacked Harrison as a "calamity" and the Democratic Party as the embodiment of ignorance, vice, and crime. They warned that the city would be turned over to the rabble should the Democrats prevail. Joseph Medill, who had run alongside Harrison in 1871, wrote a scathing editorial calling the Democrats "The Party of Revolution and Robbery." Despite these attacks, Harrison won the general election by a substantial plurality and took office on April 28, 1879.[12]

Adolph Kraus had become an important supporter, a longtime friend, and later the co-owner with Harrison of the *Chicago Times*. In June 1881, Harrison nominated Kraus to the Board of Education, beginning his career as a public servant. Their relationship proved to be crucial in developing Harrison's approach to politics in a quickly changing and challenging city. Kraus introduced Harrison to the city's many ethnic groups. After passing the bar in 1887, Kraus was the only Chicago lawyer who could speak Czech. His language skills and connections linked him also to the Germans and Poles. While Kraus brought along central and eastern European immigrant voters, various Irish aldermen and saloon politicians also rallied the working-class Irish around Harrison and the Democrats.[13]

Harrison originally hated making speeches, but he developed into quite an orator. He became known as "the Eagle," the result of a "spread eagle" or boastful speech he gave in Congress. The term, originally applied in ridicule, soon became his symbol. He used the eagle image on posters, and it became a stock part of his campaigns. In 1879, a bandwagon had a live eagle parading through the city's streets with a sign that announced, "Our Carter's Eagle and Victory." Crowds cheered the spectacle. Over the years his more familiar sobriquet became "Our Carter," as many Chicagoans embraced him.

Improvements in the efficiency and economy of the city marked Harrison's first term, but his relationship with the saloon and gambling underworld of the city riled his Protestant and upper-middle-class opposition. Republicans constantly called for reform and his ouster, while Harrison's "live and let live" attitude toward the so-called victimless crimes of gambling and prostitution spoke volumes to the city's old Yankee Protestant elite. The newspapers in general, and the *Chicago Tribune* in particular, claimed that vice and crime openly walked the streets of the city. Nevertheless, Harrison won a second term in 1881, defeating the Republican John Clark by a nearly twelve-point margin.[14]

The newspapers claimed that Harrison and the police let the saloon bosses—one in particular—rule the Democratic Party. Michael Cassius McDonald, known as "King Mike," owned a gambling house and saloon called "The Store" on Clark Street downtown. McDonald not only controlled all the gambling houses in the "wide open" city; he also ran the First Ward Democratic Party Organization. That ward included the notoriously crime-ridden Levee area as well as the central business district. He controlled the police there, and the police in turn largely protected the gambling establishments. McDonald delivered large numbers of votes for Democratic city, county, and state candidates. Harrison responded to charges that the gambling dens operated openly with a decree to restrict their operations: no dinner service or free lunches, no sales or service of liquor, and 7:00 p.m. closing times on Saturdays. The gamblers ignored the order.[15]

Michael McDonald was an early ally of Carter Harrison. He had arrived in Chicago during the early years of the Civil War along with other Mississippi riverboat gamblers who hoped to avoid conscription into the Confederate Army. To his opponents, McDonald symbolized everything that was wrong with Chicago in the years after the Civil War. Immigrants, many of them Catholic and Jewish, filled the poorer wards. Many streets, merely dirt roads with wooden sidewalks, routinely witnessed livestock parades to the packinghouses. With no zoning laws, factories and other business establishments appeared haphazardly across the cityscape. Saloons, gambling dens, and houses of prostitution abounded. While the largely Republican and nativist newspapers condemned the violence and sin of the city, the Democratic *Chicago Times* took a different angle. Wilbur Fisk Storey, its notoriously provocative publisher, liked to point out that Chicago's hypocritical men of wealth and standing owned and collected rent from many of the buildings occupied by "dens of iniquity." Many of these same men also frequented the very places they condemned. Simply put, sin was a trait common to humans.

The saloon sat at the intersection of Chicago's economic, social, and political life. Chicago's saloons developed out of grocery and bulk sales, unlike the early taverns and inns that spawned saloons in the east. By the 1850s, most retail liquor sales in Chicago occurred in general stores and groceries. Wholesalers opened "sample rooms" for customers. By 1860, the word "saloon" began to appear in city directories as retail establishments for the sale of liquor. More bars operated in Chicago in 1885 than in all fifteen southern states combined. In addition, the city did not restrict the number of liquor licenses. Most saloons were rather small, but some expanded wildly, such as the one started as a grocery by Gardner Spring Chapin and James Jefferson Gore in 1865. By the 1880s, the Chapin & Gore sample room evolved into a chain of five retail outlets. Their competitors, two immigrant Scotsmen, Alexander Donnan Hannah and David Hogg, bought an interest in a saloon named The Thistle in 1873, and over the next fifteen years grew it into eight saloons. All these enterprises developed into huge businesses with political power. Chicago's liquor interests often played both sides of the political street: Hannah became a prominent Democrat while Hogg became a Republican.

"Blind Pigs," or unlicensed saloons, created another problematic dynamic in Chicago before the Civil War. And by the late 1870s and 1880s, a new type of Blind Pig had emerged: the so-called bum boats.

Passengers boarded bum boats at the government pier and then set out beyond the jurisdiction of city police. In the 1870s, a colorful gambler, "Black Jack" Yattaw, owned a floating barroom and restaurant with a dance platform on its roof. Though Yattaw was arrested several times, his powerful friends, especially Mike McDonald, influenced the mayor to get him released from jail. Yattaw's clout always worked. By the 1890s, he had become such a well-known and popular hero as to have his boat mentioned as a tourist attraction in World's Columbian Exposition guidebooks.[16]

Harrison did not believe these vices could ever be eliminated, and he believed they could be somewhat contained to the downtown and Levee districts. He paid lip service to reformers, but like many Chicagoans he smiled and ignored those who bent or broke the laws regarding Sunday saloon closings, late hours, gambling, and even prostitution. Both those who profited from his attitude and those who took part in these vices campaigned and voted for "Our Carter."[17]

In May 1882, Harrison addressed the National Conference of Brewers, Distillers, and Liquor Dealers at the North Side Turner Hall. The meeting focused on ways to deal with the widening prohibition movement. Harrison praised the industry and said that God provided alcohol to mankind for "some wise purpose." He then went on to attack Theodore Gestefeldt, the city editor of the *Illinois Staats-Zeitung*, which had condemned him the day before for planning to speak to the Brewers' meeting. Gestefeldt said Harrison gave reputable German saloonkeepers a bad name by also licensing "brothels, gaming-hells, assignation houses, and low-down places." The paper further editorialized that Harrison had made the gamblers and concert hall proprietors a political powerhouse. It was not the paper's first attack on him.[18] Several days later, the city's Baptist ministers also attacked Harrison for addressing the Brewers' conference. The Rev. Mr. Burbee referred to the mayor as the "worst man in the city." In turn, the Rev. Dr. Kennard called him "derelict in his duty and lacking in self-respect."

During the election campaign the following year, ministers from across Chicago, including the Swedenborgians, referred to Harrison and Herod as the two greatest demagogues in history. The mayor responded by calling up the example of Catholic priests. He asked a crowd at one rally, "You go to the church hard by (Holy Family Church) or over to the Cathedral of the Holy Name, or St. Jarlath's did you ever hear the priests talk politics? (cries of 'never')." Harrison said the ministers should stick to the gospel.[19]

Harrison's efforts to build a relationship with the German community were fraught, especially in the early mayoral years. In addition to his battles with the *Illinois Staats-Zeitung* and other German Republican-leaning newspapers, Harrison created a deep rift with the community over his dismissal of Fire Marshall Matt Benner in favor of an Irishman. The Chicago Turners, a German social and athletic club, called Benner's firing an insult to the German community. Two years later, as Harrison campaigned for a second term, the German-language newspaper *Der Westen* recalled the uproar. The mayor also reduced the number of Germans on the school board from four to three and appointed two enemies of the Germans to it. In December 1879, the new board reduced appropriations for German-language classes. This was part of a long-drawn-out attack on German instruction that eventually pitted new, growing immigrant groups, such as the Poles and Czechs, against Chicago's German community.[20]

Despite these obvious conflicts, Harrison remained a favorite of a large part of the German population, particularly Catholics. In 1879, the German Sharpshooter Society hosted Harrison at their annual celebration. That same year, much to the chagrin of the *Illinois Staats-Zeitung*, attendees of the Chicago Turngemeinde Annual Old Settler's Festival voted Harrison the best Chicago mayor ever, besting Monroe Heath by eighty votes. He often spoke at German gatherings, including the 1880 Swabian Cannstadter People's Festival at Ogden Grove.[21]

Harrison actively courted other segments of the growing immigrant-ethnic population. In 1883, the Czech (Bohemian) newspaper *Svornost* reported that the general political meeting of all the Czech communities unanimously called for the renomination of Harrison for mayor, calling him an "intrepid and capable magistrate." Adolph Kraus, the main speaker, declared that all Czechs should vote for Harrison.[22] This ethnic support marked Harrison's career. His campaigns attracted Scandinavians, Germans, Irish, Czechs, Jews, Poles, and others as he won the office of mayor five times. Working-class voters especially rallied behind him because he supported labor unions and the eight-hour day.

Harrison's courtship of the Irish vote illustrates his political skill. In 1882 he gave a speech in Dublin, Ireland that called for an end to British control of the country, a sure way to appeal to Irish Chicagoans. Later that year, at a union hall in Bridgeport before a crowd of about 500 people, Harrison referred to his Dublin speech and claimed some told him the British would arrest him. He said let them do it, and the crowd went wild. He went on to ask the crowd to vote straight Democratic, because when the United States had a Democratic president there would be no Irish Americans in British jails. Furthermore, he asserted that Republicans would prohibit liquor and try to control Irish family sizes, while "Democrats did not care how many children Katy or Biddy had." The crowd laughed and applauded. He concluded by saying, "Boys I almost feel like getting drunk with you." The crowd again burst into applause and cheers. Harrison always played the ethnic card whether addressing the Irish, the Germans, or the Poles. It was good politics.[23]

In 1883, the Republicans ran Eugene Cary against Harrison. All of Chicago's newspapers opposed Harrison, for the usual reasons. Harrison won the election by 10,263 votes. The next election would not be that easy, as scandals took their toll on the Democrats.[24]

In 1880, Mike McDonald appointed Joseph Chesterfield Mackin his personal secretary at an annual wage of $3,000 ($98,100 in 2023) as a reward for his extraordinary services in the election of 1879. The saloonkeeper politician, also known as "Oyster Joe" because in 1875 he served a free hot oyster with every beer in order to attract customers, is generally credited with the invention of the free lunch in the city's saloons. Mackin escorted various drunks, tramps, and other unregistered voters to the First Ward polls, establishing his value to the local political organization. He quickly became part of McDonald's inner circle of friends, advisors, and enforcers. McDonald seemed to be the real power behind the Democratic Party in Chicago and beyond. The mayor had been a good friend of McDonald's and a frequent customer at his saloon, The Store, often partaking in gambling. He accepted McDonald's advice and welcomed his political know-how, but Harrison often vied with McDonald over patronage and slate-making, and he occasionally struck at McDonald's gambling interests. Joe Mackin, whom Harrison despised, soon proved to be a wedge in the McDonald–Harrison alliance.

With McDonald's support, Mackin was elected Secretary of the Cook County Democratic Party in 1883. Mackin's saloon became the unofficial headquarters of the Cook County Democratic Committee. He directed the operation of the Levee vice district, drawing a percentage of the take from gambling and prostitution to finance his and other political careers. That year Mackin raised money for Harrison's campaign from the gambling interests, and he expected to be named Harrison's private secretary. The mayor appointed someone else, and a rift occurred. Mackin attacked the mayor in Democratic circles, and McDonald began to reconsider his support of Harrison. Rumors spread that McDonald planned to run against him in 1885. Also, McDonald wanted Mackin to join the City Council as the alderman of the First Ward. In spring 1884, Mackin and McDonald clashed with Harrison over Mackin's plans to run for the position. The mayor attempted to get Mackin to withdraw his candidacy, but he refused until Harrison threatened to close every gambling establishment in the First Ward. The affair angered McDonald even further.

With McDonald's support, Mackin wanted to teach Harrison a lesson. Mackin proved capable of attracting the 1884 Democratic National Convention to Chicago and the McDonald faction felt they would have control of the gathering. On the eve of the election, a divided Illinois Democratic Party met in Peoria to select their delegates. Harrison found himself in the minority, even while being touted for higher office. Mackin would have been happy to see Harrison leave Chicago for either Washington, DC, as a senator or to Springfield as governor. Harrison let it be known he would be willing to take either position. The Democrats slated Harrison for governor, but since Illinois had not elected a Democrat as governor in decades, it was no surprise when the Republican Richard J. Oglesby handily defeated him.

Mackin's alliance with McDonald against Harrison soon unraveled. In February 1885, a grand jury charged Mackin with stuffing the ballot box in favor of Rudolph Brand, a Chicago brewer who had run for the state senate in 1884. Later that year, Oyster Joe was indicted on voter fraud charges. His long-drawn-out trial, which eventually ended up at the US Supreme Court, resulted in a five-year imprisonment in the Joliet penitentiary. McDonald raised money for Mackin's defense but then refused to pay his legal bills. Significantly, McDonald's political control also seemed to be waning as his personal and business interests diverted his attention. Harrison won a fourth term, beating Sidney Smith—but by only 375 votes. This slim margin of victory made many believe that "Our Carter" and the Democrats stood on the verge of extinction, and that the city might soon revert to Republican control.[25]

Labor disputes and the rise of anarchism as a political force marked Harrison's fourth term. While hardly anti-business, he did support labor rights. He also did little to prevent radical speech. Harrison believed in the right of anyone to say whatever they liked. The city had been a hotbed of radical thought since before the Civil War. Chicago gave refuge to many who fled Europe after the defeat of the 1848 revolutions. The German community in particular included many who wanted a socialist, communist, or even anarchist revolution. Czechs, Poles, Italians, and the Irish all had radicals in their communities. Harrison walked a fine line between the conservative, Native-born, Protestant, White American community and the immigrant enclaves who suffered under uncontrolled capitalism in the years after the Great Fire. Working-class militias formed, and they drilled with rifles and bayonets. Speakers violently denounced capitalism, and many prophesized violence against elites. The *Arbeiter Zeitung*, a radical German-language newspaper, printed inflammatory editorials. Harrison ignored these agitations and even hired socialists to work in City Hall.

Labor troubles abounded in the city, which in 1885 was crippled by a transit strike. Unlike other elected officials across the country, Harrison often kept the police out of confrontations between labor and capital, but the monied interests put a good deal of pressure on him to act here. The conflict between the Chicago West Division Railway Company and its employees caused violence to erupt between strikers, strikebreakers, and the company. Police Captain John Bonfield, a well-known opponent of organized labor, took charge of protecting the horsedrawn cars driven by strikebreakers. He ordered the arrest of any man who called strikebreakers scabs. His men brutally beat picketers and their supporters. Harrison, trying to placate business interests, named Bonfield inspector after the strike. His decision would come back to haunt him.

The following year, Chicago witnessed one of its most famous labor conflicts. Organized unions declared a general strike on May 1, 1886, to demand the eight-hour working day. Harrison supported the movement. To everyone's surprise, the strike was peaceful and successful. After groups of laborers went from plant to plant calling out their fellow workers to support the walkout, the packinghouses almost immediately capitulated, as did other businesses. To celebrate, a huge parade of strikers marched down Michigan Avenue on May Day. Chicago remained peaceful.

A largely unrelated labor conflict, however, at the McCormick Reaper Works on Monday, May 3, ended with the police, under the command of Inspector Bonfield, firing into a crowd of workers who harassed strikebreakers, killing two and wounding others. Anarchists and other labor sympathizers called for a protest against the police the next evening at Haymarket Square on the West Side. On the night of May 4, Harrison ordered police to be on alert and concentrated a large contingent of police at the Desplaines Street Station near the Haymarket. Harrison planned to attend the rally himself on his horse. To let the workers know he was there, Harrison repeatedly lit his cigar, as he listened to speakers. Albert Parsons called for workers to arm themselves. Still Harrison felt that nothing required police action. The crowd remained calm and orderly. Harrison went to the police station and told Bonfield to dismiss the police reserves. Nevertheless, Bonfield decided to keep some of them, even as the mayor returned to the rally and then rode home. Shortly thereafter, Bonfield arrived at Haymarket with a contingent of police, and someone threw a bomb into their ranks. Shooting immediately broke out as the police fired into the crowd. Chaos quickly engulfed the streets as people fled. The riot bell brought more police from across the city and nearly one thousand police cleared the three-block area around the Haymarket. Seven policemen and an unknown number of citizens died in the conflict.[26]

By the spring of 1887, Harrison's political future looked grim, clouded by labor troubles and the Haymarket disaster. The press, including the Democratic *Times*, constantly attacked him, and his age seemed to also work against him. Harrison himself felt it was time to move on. Many of his supporters, however, insisted on nominating him. Harrison refused the nomination. This threw the convention into an uproar, and Harrison yielded. Others opposed to Harrison caused a further rift in the party, as even President Grover Cleveland came out against Harrison. At the same time, Harrison's second wife, Marguerite E. Stearns, lay ill. All of this led to the mayor to withdraw his candidacy. The party suffered such confusion that it did not field a candidate and the Republican John A. Roche won easily. On April 18, 1887, Carter Harrison left the mayor's office and public life. Twelve days later, Marguerite died. Shortly thereafter Harrison left to tour the world with his son Preston and a friend. They traveled to Asia and then on to Europe before returning to the United States fifteen months later. The trip resulted in the former mayor's travel book, *A Race with the Sun*.[27]

Harrison's departure from the public eye was short-lived. "Our Carter" remained intensely popular with many Chicagoans. Piqued by political ambitions again, Harrison decided to make another run for the mayoralty in 1891. After four years, the public seemed dissatisfied with both the Roche administration and that of DeWitt C. Cregier, the Democrat who had succeeded him. The city had begun to talk about hosting the World's Columbian Exposition, which appealed to Harrison. Several factions in the Democratic Party encouraged him to run. Harrison threw his hat into the ring despite Cregier's stated desire for a second term. The Democratic organization, controlled largely by Cregier, moved against Harrison. In turn, he made an independent run, but the Republican Hempstead Washburne won the election narrowly. Many felt that Harrison had been cheated by ballot box stuffing and police harassment of known Harrison voters. This, however, would not be Carter Harrison's last campaign.[28]

The Columbian Exposition, originally scheduled for 1892, had been postponed until May 1893. Harrison still had a chance to be a World's Fair mayor. Carter H. Harrison Associations, put together by supporters, popped up all over the city. The organization rivaled the Regular Democratic Party and probably surpassed it. Harrison purchased the *Chicago Times* in the autumn of 1891 and began to use it as a political instrument.

When Harrison began his campaign, he found out that his friend and former trusted lieutenant, Washington Hesing, now editor of the *Illinois Staats-Zeitung*, opposed his candidacy. The Democratic organization stood with Hesing, as did the other Democratic newspapers. At the convention, however, 531 out of 681 delegates voted for Harrison. But the party was in turmoil. The campaign proved bitter and acrimonious. The *Chicago Tribune* declared that the German community, particularly on the North Side, stood united against the former mayor. In fact, the newspaper proclaimed that all major newspapers as well as the business community and organized labor opposed his candidacy.

Yet Harrison's backing ran deep among the immigrant groups of the city. While Harrison spoke fluent German and French, he could also get by in Italian. He had a retentive memory that allowed him to use phrases in Dutch, Swedish, Danish, Norwegian, Polish, and Czech and deliver them with the proper accents. These attributes, decided positives for a political life in a rapidly ethnically diversifying city, won him wide support. In 1892, the year before the convention, he spoke to a crowd of some 5,000 at Bohemian National Cemetery for the unveiling of a monument to the Czech Civil War soldiers. He also attended a concert organized by the Hans Christian Andersen Monument Association at the Central Music Hall to raise money for a statue of the Danish children's writer. Harrison made sure he and

1.2 Funeral procession for Mayor Carter H. Harrison from Church of the Epiphany on Adams Street and Ashland Avenue, near Harrison's home, to Graceland Cemetery on November 1, 1893. Author's Collection.

Adolph Kraus attended the wedding of the Polish Democratic leader Piotr Kiołbassa's daughter. Later that July, he spoke at a Polish meeting commemorating the eighteenth-century Battle of Dubienka, against the Russians. By 1893 he had garnered the support of much of the Czech and Polish communities. Even the Scandinavian community, which traditionally voted Republican, largely supported Harrison. When the results came in, Harrison won by more than 21,000 votes. The Poles rejoiced and the *Dziennik Chicagoski* characterized it as a victory over the German community: "The Germans have received their just deserts," it reported, in an obvious reference to Hesing's betrayal.[29]

In the more than twenty years following the Great Fire, the seeds of the Chicago political machine had been planted in immigrant communalism rooted in the urban slums, especially in Bridgeport and other industrial neighborhoods. These communities provided a solid base for the Democratic Party, as Harrison's career demonstrated. A political machine based on ethnicity, class, and culture emerged. Favors, jobs, protection, and power were not merely abstractions, they were the reality of urban politics in the nineteenth and through most of the twentieth century. In the Chicago vernacular, they all meant "clout." For Chicago's immigrant neighborhoods, clout offered agency in the industrial city, a city that seemed to be violent, unfair, and controlled by those who had little regard for the working masses. When voters clamored for "Our Carter" they were expressing their bond with a politician who seemed to understand them. Unfortunately, no one knew how short Harrison's fifth term would be or that, ironically, an Irish immigrant would end his storied life. His work building a political machine rooted in immigrant and ethnic communities would find its full expression in the next century.

2
Bridgeport and De La Salle Institute

The Birth of the Machine

> It was a community that drank out of a beer pail and ate out of a lunch bucket.
>
> MIKE ROYKO,
> referring to Bridgeport[1]

Born on hardscrabble dirt streets lined by wooden sidewalks in the city's poorer neighborhoods, the legendary Chicago political machine grew up along the banks of a polluted, stinking river and in the smoke-filled back rooms of saloons. Nuns, religious brothers, and priests nurtured it in the halls of Catholic schools amid the smell of wax candles and incense. It wrestled power from an urban elite who met in fancy lace-curtain parlors and Protestant churches and built a city while making their own fortunes. Money, power, and security always defined the goals of Chicago's political machine. Above all, it meant protection and a future away from an impoverished immigrant past.

The machine also meant community, a reality that reformers and those parlor politicians never fully grasped. The rise of the Chicago system of clout resulted, in large part, from the reaction of people to the Industrial Revolution—not only in Chicago but across America. It was in neighborhood places like Bridgeport and De La Salle Institute that the sacred and the profane came into contact, sometimes working together and other times clashing. These neighborhoods and institutions offered responses to the new realities of life in the

American city, and at times pitted residents against those who held economic power. Often, when sociologists describe *gemeinschaft* giving way to *gesellschaft*, or communal societies giving way to modern individualistic society, they fail to understand those *gemeinschaft* communities that made Chicago neighborhoods such as West Town, South Chicago, Back of the Yards, or Bridgeport livable. To many, the political machine gave hope in the hardscrabble secular world, while the Catholic Church provided succor and aspiration to a better life in the next one.

BRIDGEPORT

Archer Avenue runs through the oldest section of Bridgeport, a legendary Chicago neighborhood. Lying south of the South Branch of the Chicago River, the early neighborhood was known as "Hardscrabble."[2] This name implied a place that repaid great effort with little or no improvement in living conditions or prospects. Bridgeport developed early as a poor, rough-and-tumble, working-class district. The river, and the industry the waterway attracted after the opening of the Illinois and Michigan Canal in 1848 and the subsequent extension and expansion of the railroads, dominated the area. While the Irish prevailed politically, Bridgeport, from its very beginning, included other ethnic groups that gathered to work along the busy South Branch.

Chicago's neighborhoods are often thought to have rigid and unchanging boundaries, but actually their borders are rather malleable. Bridgeport today "officially" includes the area south of the Chicago River and north of Pershing Road (39th Street) and from Canal Street west to the South Fork (Bubbly Creek) of the South Branch of the Chicago River. But these boundaries are debatable. In the nineteenth century, Bridgeport had a much smaller footprint, roughly a mile and a half long and a mile wide. The neighborhood spread out along Archer Avenue, also known as Archey Road, from Halsted Street on the west to the rolling mill on Ashland Avenue to the east; the Chicago River marked a permanent northern boundary while 31st Street marked the southern boundary. Legend has attributed the name to a low-lying bridge that crossed the canal at Ashland Avenue. "Archey Road" came to define the neighborhood, especially after the appearance of Finley Peter Dunne's "Mr. Dooley" columns, which both celebrated and mocked the Bridgeport Irish, in the *Chicago Evening Post* in the 1890s.[3]

Irish and other immigrants first arrived in Bridgeport in the mid-1830s to dig the depression-plagued Illinois and Michigan Canal, which finally opened in 1848. These workers and their families, some of whom had labored on the Erie Canal in upstate New York, settled along Archer Avenue, the service road for the canal, and erected meager wooden homes. They and their children eventually found employment in the railroads, factories, packinghouses, rendering plants, and steel mills that followed the construction of the canal. The Bridgeport Irish organized St. Bridget's Church in 1850, which anchored the small community. Archer Avenue quickly developed into a commercial strip with saloons, businesses, meeting halls, bakeries, and cheap eateries centering on its intersection with Throop Street. The Great Fire of 1871 spared the district; as Dunne's Mr. Dooley famously joked, "Out this way we didn't pay much attention to it."[4] Larger structures appeared in the 1880s and 1890s, some reaching five stories. Small wooden-frame working-class cottages and two-flats, some with storefronts, continued to dominate the side streets.[5]

THE RIVER AND THE BRIDGEPORT STENCH

The noxious smell of the river and the pollution from the industries that lined it added to Bridgeport's hardscrabble reputation. Even before the 1865 opening of the Union Stock Yard just to the south, Chicagoans complained about the "Bridgeport stench" from packinghouses, the gas works, and other industries. The *Chicago Tribune* cautioned readers to beware of the ice harvested from that part of the river, beset by "villainous stenches, stinks, and smells." By 1862, no fewer than seventeen packinghouses, all but two of which included slaughterhouses, lined the river. The larger ones each slaughtered 700 to 900 cattle — and in total probably more than

5,000 cattle, hogs, and sheep—each day, turning the water red with blood. Tanneries and distilleries added their effluents to the thick gruel of the river. In addition, some forty sewers emptied into the listless stream. The thick, murky waters also posed a health hazard, as the river flowed into Lake Michigan and polluted the city's drinking water. The odors wafting from Bridgeport, carried by the prevailing southwest winds, became more than a nuisance across the city. In addition, the citizens of Bridgeport suffered from the smell of dead animals left unburied in the neighborhood. In a very early example of the search for environmental justice, this working-class enclave petitioned the City Council to rid them of these nuisances.[6]

In 1872, Mayor Medill headed a committee to inspect the source of the horrid smell emanating from Bridgeport, especially the Healy Slough, the Ogden Slip, and the slaughterhouses that filled these places with "filthiness and corruption." One wet and dismal afternoon, the mayor and his entourage visited Bridgeport with their pants rolled up and investigated for three and a half hours. In their final meeting, the committee proposed filling in Healy Slough with a large sewer running through the middle of it. They also called for closing the Reid and Sherwin packing plant. The committee report should have come before the City Council, but it contained recommendations that seemed "quite antagonistic" to the interest of an unnamed someone and thus to those of several aldermen. Chicago politicians therefore "stowed away" the account in the City Council's "rubbish." The Bridgeport packers obviously had the ears of the city's leaders.[7]

But the larger health concern remained. The *Tribune* raged against the polluted river, demanding that the city employ pumps to clean it. Again, the newspaper indicted Bridgeport for the stream of blood that emptied eventually into the lake. Drains added mud, offal, and impure liquid compounds to the river. Old hats, boots, tin pans, decaying fish, discarded pipes, slime, and swill abounded in the sluggish tributary.[8] In 1871 the city engineer, Ellis Sylvester Chesbrough, deepened the canal in an attempt to reverse the river and ameliorate the flow of pollutants. Bridgeport's pumps sat idle in the face of these engineering improvements, and in 1873 the city sold them for $2,500.

But spring floods in 1877 forced water from the South Branch, causing large quantities of putrid animal matter to flow into the river and into Lake Michigan.[9]

The South Branch and the South Fork of the Chicago River posed other difficulties, especially a threat of flooding of riverfront neighborhoods. The February 1871 flood saw portions of Bridgeport under water and families driven from their homes. Residents could reach their homes only by wading through the filthy water or by floating on a plank. Over the next few days, the river receded and left behind a coating of black smelly mud.[10] The 1877 flood caused even more extensive destruction.[11]

Yet Bridgeport's reputation went beyond smells and filth. Its early image as a hardscrabble neighborhood morphed into that of a violent and dangerous lower-class district, first on the edge of the city and then as part of the burgeoning South Side.

RUM, RIOT, AND ROMANISM

From its earliest days, Bridgeport was rough. Fights broke out along the river and canal all the time. Much of this violence became associated with the immigrant Irish, who were typically accused by nativists of propagating "Rum, Riot and Romanism." Residents had a reputation for heavy drinking, fighting, crime, and murder, as well as a devotion to Catholicism and clannishness. Some even referred to Bridgeport as the equivalent of New York's notoriously violent Five Points neighborhood. Among their own, the Irish who lived on Chicago's West Side called the denizens of Archey Road "Pig Shit" or "Shanty" Irish. Working-class Bridgeport would remember these slights for a long time. Old World rivalries between different parts of Ireland often erupted into violence. A typical disturbance broke out in 1857 as two groups of Irish fought in a brickyard, using clubs, brickbats, and other weapons. The combatants appeared in Police Court with bruised faces and blackened eyes.

Indeed, murder and mayhem seemed to be an everyday occurrence in Bridgeport. In 1857, the Grand Jury in the Court of Common Pleas found against Michael Mack, who had stabbed Henry Eibler in a Bridgeport packinghouse and then disappeared. In 1858, Chicago police arrested Catherine Loveland, a ten-year-old girl in Bridgeport who had been sent to the city by her parents to beg and steal. In October, police arrested six Bridgeporters for beating Mike Lynch and Mike Fagin with brass knuckles, beer mugs, and ax handles. Ten years later, a *Tribune* reporter wrote that Bridgeport had long been "celebrated as a rendezvous of the hardest criminals by whom Chicago is cursed." The reporter recounted yet another murderous fray that had begun in Luke Lally's saloon near the Bridgeport canal docks.[12]

Poverty and alcohol often took their toll on the women and children of Bridgeport. During one week alone in 1858, five infants drowned in the South Branch. Domestic violence occurred frequently, as in the case of a young wife, Catherine Mullen, who died after being beaten by her husband, Patrick. In "A Glimpse of Social Life in Bridgeport," a *Tribune* reporter told a story of knife-fighting women. Bridgeport became well known for a culture of poverty that included alcoholism and all the psychological problems presented by the transition from a rural society to an urban industrial environment. Drunkenness often ended in death, sometimes in the river. The historian Lawrence McCaffrey called the Irish America's first group social problem. Dirty, dreary, and poor, largely Catholic Bridgeport spawned violent crime. This did not match up well with the middle-class, Anglo-Saxon, Protestant ideas of virtue espoused by the city's elites.[13]

Bridgeport residents did not accept their conditions as natural or permanent; they organized protests against both the industries that dominated the neighborhood and the forces of law and order that they recognized as tools of the corporations. The historian Richard Schneirov traced what he calls "mass" strikes in Bridgeport to 1875, when the coal heavers walked off their jobs and brickyard workers and lumber shovers joined them. Large neighborhood crowds turned out in support of the workers. This and subsequent strikes had much community support but little organization. In 1876, residents and workers rallied again, only to be met by police action. The next year, crowds from Bridgeport and Pilsen, across the Chicago

River, fought police in the so-called Battle of Halsted Street during the Great Railroad Strike. After this strike, an embryonic organization led Bridgeport's working class to a more organized and modern labor movement. The 1886 eight-hour strike and the Haymarket Affair saw a good deal of organizational development in Bridgeport, especially in the Hamburg section. Nativity of Our Lord Parish on West 37th Street provided a center for the discontent. Bridgeport workers played active roles first in nascent local unions and then in the national Knights of Labor. This fomented a very vigorous labor movement that called for strikes in the packinghouses and other industries between 1875 and 1922.[14] Pope Leo XIII's 1891 encyclical, *Rerum Novarum*, argued that workers had the right to organize for better pay and conditions. The encyclical sustained the development of Catholic social thought over the next seventy years.

In the strange mix of sacred and profane in Chicago's neighborhoods, various institutions coalesced around a communal frame to protect residents and to protest conditions. The Catholic Church with its local parishes, the saloon, labor groups, and of course the local Democratic Party, which pledged to protect immigrants and working people alike, created a communal response. At first this communal response was rather inward-looking, but it would eventually turn outward to ally the Irish with other groups living under similar conditions. The communal response would give the Bridgeport Irish a sense of agency. They formed a tightly knit community based on parish life and carried it into the world of politics.[15]

THE WORKING-CLASS RESPONSE

This communal response to conditions—social, economic, and political—that the Irish saw as just another way to combat oppressive Anglo-Saxon rule eventually brought them political power. Anti-Irish prejudice would fuel this communalism, but the taking of power, of clout, would propel it. Clout meant political influence, and influence meant power. This power, on a very basic plane, leveraged jobs and status.[16]

Nativism propelled the Irish to build a Catholic institutional structure that grew out of parish life. St. Bridget's Parish was the outpost of Irish Catholicism in Bridgeport. Founded in 1847 as a mission of St. Patrick's Church on the West Side, it provided both a spiritual home and a community center for the struggling working-class neighborhood, which was soon to be overwhelmed by the surge of "famine Irish" refugees. The impoverished community had a difficult time maintaining the parish. For a time priests held Mass in the homes of parishioners, until James McKenna donated Scanlon Hall in 1850. In 1862, parishioners finally constructed a permanent home. Shortly thereafter, the French (LaSallian) Christian Brothers opened a school for boys that eventually came to be named the Bridgeport Industrial Institute. In 1872, the Sisters of St. Joseph Carondolet arrived to serve the parochial school founded a year earlier by a laywoman, Ella Rodgers. The Sisters of Charity of the Blessed Virgin Mary took charge of the school in 1876 as the Carondolet order shifted to Nativity of Our Lord in the Hamburg section of the neighborhood, closer to the stockyards. The French Christian Brothers moved the Bridgeport Institute to the suburbs in 1883, but St. Bridget's opened a commercial high school in 1902. Parishioners celebrated the laying of the cornerstone of a new church in 1905. Ironically, by this time Archer Avenue's ethnic composition had begun to change. Poles and Lithuanians strolled down the street as often as did the Irish worshippers at St. Bridget's.[17]

Eventually ten Catholic parishes representing five ethnic groups called Bridgeport home. The non-Irish groups built large and impressive churches and, in a manner, challenged the two Irish parishes. They may not have been able to dominate politically, but they certainly cemented Bridgeport's Catholic character. In 1910, the Catholic parishes counted about 35,000 parishioners, out of a total population of just under 50,000. German and Swedish Protestants made up another large group.

The laity almost always took the initiative in creating Catholic parishes in Chicago, starting with the formation of a mutual aid society under the patronage of an especially revered saint and then petitioning the bishop for a priest who spoke their language. Across the city Catholic parishes of each nationality—except for the Irish, who dominated the Catholic hierarchy—came together in loosely feder-

2.1 St. Bridget Catholic Church, 1913. Parishioners erected the church on Archer Avenue in 1905 to serve Bridgeport's Irish Catholic community. By this time the ethnic composition of this part of Bridgeport had already begun to change. Percy H. Sloan Photographs, Newberry Library.

ated "leagues." Individual parishes established parochial elementary schools and some high schools. They organized a wide variety of social and charitable organizations and often jointly financed hospitals, orphanages, cemeteries, and even settlement houses and day nurseries.[18]

CHAPTER 2

In Bridgeport, a full set of communal social activities emerged. Church fairs and raffles, parochial and public school graduations, marriages, births, baptisms, and funerals ruled the calendar. School sporting events and youth clubs attracted large crowds. Football especially seemed to be an outlet, though it often bred violence. Mr. Dooley commented in 1896 that "Downtown it's football; out here it's the Irish killing each other."[19]

A host of institutions appeared in Bridgeport. Some, like St. Bridget's, were formal organizations tied directly to Catholic life. Others, such as the many saloons, provided secular places of communal solidarity. Fraternal organizations, such as the Knights of Columbus and the Ancient Order of Hibernia, offered another layer of institutional development. Combined with stores, bakeries, funeral parlors, and other businesses, they provided much of the communal web that would benefit the Irish and provide a model for later Catholic and Jewish immigrant groups. Add to this network less formal but powerful neighborhood institutions such as street gangs and later athletic clubs. In Bridgeport, as in other neighborhoods, all these institutions organized a communal response to life and labor in the industrial city.

THE BRIDGEPORT WAY

Early on, Bridgeport (then a suburb) developed a reputation for questionable political practices. As early as the 1850s, newspapers reported the threat of "imported" and fraudulent Bridgeport voters meant to sway a Chicago election. In 1858, in Chicago's nearby 4th Ward, more than the legal number of voters cast votes for alderman, with obvious support coming from suburban Irish Democratic haunts, including Bridgeport. The *Chicago Tribune* claimed that "the stream of Hibernians — never seen in the city before and never to be seen again, till the next charter election — was uninterrupted and exhaustless."[20]

When Bridgeport joined the city of Chicago in 1861, the city had just begun to enter the modern industrial era. The Irish saw Chicago as a political plum ripe for the picking, and they quickly joined Democrats in their struggle against the Protestant native-born and upper classes. In 1863, the voice of the Republican Party, the *Chicago Tribune*, warned against the Copperheads—their term for pro-Confederate Democrats—living south of the river. During the Civil War, many of Bridgeport's Democrats openly supported Copperhead proposals to end the conflict. When Democrat Francis Cornwall Sherman won the mayoralty in 1863, the *Tribune* complained that his majority came primarily from the recently annexed districts, "where whiskey ruled." It further claimed that at least 1,500 bogus votes had given the election to the Democrats. In the 6th Ward, the *Tribune* said that wagonloads of drunken rowdies arrived after voting in Bridgeport, resulting in some five hundred more votes than there were voters in the ward. Such claims would not soon disappear from either Bridgeport's or the city's reputation.[21]

Bridgeport's Irish had learned from the British that whoever held political power held the power of the purse in more ways than one.[22] In Ireland, they had seen the naked use of power by the British under the false name of democracy. The potato famine delivered an especially hard lesson in politics as well as market economics. Those who made their way across the Atlantic witnessed again the use and abuse of political power in the Anglo-Saxon world.

The Irish quickly identified Chicago's ruling elites with their traditional enemies in Ireland. Anglo-Saxon Protestants looked down on the Irish as drunken, superstitious Catholics, unworthy of charity. As in other American cities, a bitter cultural and political clash emerged. Many Protestant groups sought to convert Catholics to Protestantism and thus to Americanism. Irish Catholic leaders naturally resisted and erected metaphorical walls around their communities. The Catholic Church, finding itself in an alien culture, became militant in this communal defense. As most immigrants joined the working class, the Church began to embrace organized labor.[23]

Out of the Bridgeport hardscrabble and many other such places in Chicago would emerge a political machine obsessed with ethnicity, class, and political spoils. The Irish knew it was all about jobs and upward mobility. They taught these lessons to the hundreds of thousands of immigrants who joined them on Chicago's streets.[24] Bridgeport attracted both industry and ethnic groups as the city helped to define the Industrial Revolution. Soon, the Irish led the great ethnic coalition emerging on the shores of Lake Michigan, especially in the river wards along both the North and South Branches of the Chicago River.

In many ways, Bridgeport provided a microcosm of the larger city. The Germans came in large numbers to work in the Union Steel Company on the river at Ashland Avenue, as well as in the packing industry, often as skilled butchers. Germans came in three cultural flavors: Catholic, Protestant, and Jewish. They erected their own religious structures separate from the Irish and from each other. Both institutionally and culturally, German immigrants quickly became rivals of the Irish, erecting both Catholic and Lutheran churches and schools. Soon Bohemians (Czechs), Poles, Lithuanians, eastern European Jews, Croatians, and Italians would also make their homes in Bridgeport and neighboring communities, creating an ethnic brew that occasionally boiled over.

Politics provided one way to deal with internal problems as well as to exert influence on the rest of the city and gain clout within Chicago's political structure. To exercise that power, however, these communities had to organize—not just churches, but savings and loans, small businesses, fraternal groups, hospitals, and even cemeteries—to support their members throughout their lives and afterward. The saloon surfaced as a frequent meeting place and the barkeeper often emerged as a political power, rivaled only by the local priest. Of course, neither the priest nor the bartender found much respect among the city's elites. Yet the growing number of ethnic voters would eventually upend the political, cultural, and social order of the city. While the parish priest could not officially enter the political world, he would have tremendous influence within his neighborhood. Catholic institutions soon became closely aligned with the power structure of the nascent Democratic organization.

DE LA SALLE INSTITUTE: THE CRADLE OF CLOUT

In 1889, the French or LaSallian Christian Brothers opened De La Salle Institute on 35th Street just east of Bridgeport, their second high school in Chicago. It was intended to house a commercial and industrial as well as a general education school. It would have a tremendous impact on the neighborhood and the city. On May 19, a vast parade marched to the corner of 35th and Wabash Streets for the laying of the cornerstone. The music of twenty bands could be heard on Michigan Avenue, one of the South Side's most prestigious thoroughfares, as the parade made its way south. A detachment of city police quickly followed a squadron of gray-coated park police. Grand Marshal John F. Scanlon arrived at the head of a score of aides on horseback in bright-hued sashes and gray plumes. One hundred and fifty Hibernian Guards followed with bayoneted rifles gleaming in the sun. The Christian Brothers band appeared, trailed by the Clan-na-Gael Guards. The parade, which included some forty Catholic societies, lasted a full hour, passing roofs crowded with spectators and young boys atop lampposts. As it ended, a religious procession began, led by two acolytes accompanying Chicago's Archbishop Patrick Augustine Feehan. It made its way to the site of the cornerstone, and Father Thaddeus J. Butler's clear voice began the litany to the Blessed Virgin. Father Maurice J. Dorney, pastor of St. Gabriel's in nearby Canaryville, gave the oration and pointed out that "Life is the activity by which we move and perfect ourselves. It is seen in the acts of the will and intellect." He praised the Christian Brothers as great teachers and held up the life of their founder, John Baptist De La Salle, as an example of sacrifice and dedication. Father Dorney hailed the founding of De La Salle Institute as a great turning point and predicted that it "would make us a better and a greater people." He further envisioned the school as a training ground for leaders. Dorney presciently saw that De La Salle would be a hothouse of lay Catholic leadership, especially in the political sphere.[25]

Built of gray Bedford stone, the four-story structure originally held twenty-four classrooms and could accommodate six hundred boys. It was laid out according to plans favored by the Christian Brothers. The classrooms were to be well ventilated, with sufficient light and the rooms tidy and clean. The Brothers insisted that their buildings should be constructed "in a healthy locality, sufficiently remote from noisy, dangerous, or unsanitary neighborhoods." The

2.2 De La Salle Institute's original building, located on the northeast corner of 35th Street and Wabash Avenue. This structure cost $210,000 ($6,867,000 in 2023). Classes began in 1892 with 150 students in six classes—one scientific, two academic, and three commercial classes—with eleven Christian Brothers as members of the faculty (Rev. Msgr. Harry C. Koenig, S.T.D., ed., *Caritas Christi Urgent Nos: A History of the Offices, Agencies, and Institutions of the Archdiocese*, 2 vols. [Chicago: Archdiocese of Chicago, 1981], 1:437–39). Courtesy of De La Salle Institute.

new school stood in the prestigious Douglas neighborhood, but close enough to Bridgeport and the Town of Lake's large working-class Catholic populations. Guidelines called for windows with lower panels frosted to reduce distractions. The school included a library and a museum. The brothers fitted all classrooms with a desk and a platform for the teacher at the front. Large windows at the back and front of the classrooms allowed the headmaster to observe all classrooms. Instructors had to keep doors always open, as brothers had to be always in sight of one another. The Christian Brothers were very aware of human frailties and hoped to strictly control any possible breach of regulations.[26]

The Christian Brothers' handbook for teachers, published in 1905, clearly stated, "As the school is to be a nursery of good citizenship, moral teaching accompanies the intellectual, the conscience being formed in accordance with the precepts of religion." Christian Brothers schools desired to produce men with a clear conscience following the precepts of Catholic teaching. The Brothers believed that education allowed man to acquire perfection "suitable to his nature." In this way the student would come "to know God, to love and serve him in this world, and by this means to attain heaven." Teachers should encourage students "to act only through motives of reason and faith." This allowed the young man to "conduct himself in accordance with prescriptions of duty and the maxims of the Gospel." Again, the pedagogical guide reminded teachers that "the child is not born good" and has strong inclinations toward evil. Christian Brothers saw the supernatural destiny of the child as vitally important.[27]

John Baptist De La Salle, later made a saint by the Church, founded the order of teaching brothers in seventeenth-century France to serve poor boys. At the time, the various French charity schools were deemed total failures, and De La Salle feared that French children would be lost to the faith because they could not read Catholic texts. A petty nobleman and son of a merchant family in Rheims, De La Salle spent his fortune establishing a system of "poor" schools to reach impoverished children. He saw his initial problem as one of recruitment and training — of attracting young men and instructing them in the art of teaching. After he opened a free school for poor boys in Rheims, De La Salle created a series of boarding schools for secondary education and reformatory schools. His order began as a simple gathering of laymen who took no religious vows, but came together to teach. While De La Salle, an ordained priest, had a formal Greek and Latin education, he did not see that particular type of education as relevant for these schools. In fact, he forbade the teaching of classical languages. De La Salle insisted his order of Catholic brothers would focus not on forming future priests, but rather on giving the lower and middle classes a practical education. To do this, De La Salle instructed his teachers to use the "simultaneous method," instructing the whole group of students at once, not individually. Though he did not invent this pedagogical method, he popularized it. Indeed, the practice could be seen as another form of communalism.

Prayer remained central to the pedagogical method of the Christian Brothers. At the stroke of each hour, brothers led students in a short prayer. The Christian Brothers should not "leave a simple one in ignorance . . . at least of Christian principles." De La Salle taught that "Religion is not something speculative, but practical," and warned, "Man's life on this earth was something far higher than the vulgar pursuit of wealth and power." Students of the largely vocational schools would anxiously pursue such goals, but hopefully tempered by the virtues also taught to them.[28]

On the South Side, this teaching and moral philosophy would be tested by the Irish of the stockyard hardscrabble. De La Salle had warned that disorders among artisans and the poor resulted from bad upbringing. The children of workers and the poor usually had little instruction, and parents, working all day, did not have the time to instruct or discipline children properly. The Christian Brothers aimed to save the souls of these children by intervening early. Evil habits seemed almost impossible to repair once students reached adulthood.

In 1861, the Christian Brothers had taken over St. Patrick's Academy on the West Side, previously run by the Holy Cross Brothers. By 1879, over four hundred students attended St. Patrick's. While the emerging Irish elite often sent their sons, many of whom aspired to the clergy, to nearby St. Ignatius, run by the Jesuits, St. Patrick's held to its charism to teach the poor and middle class and not to teach future priests. The head of St. Patrick's since 1879, Brother Patrick J. Goslin, known as Brother Adjutor of Mary, led the Christian Brothers' efforts to open another school to serve the South Side. In 1890 he became the first Director Principal of De La Salle Institute.

Legends of Brother Adjutor's fundraising skills abound. One had him literally agreeing to hand wrestling or boxing various State Street saloonkeepers for an offering and always winning. Another story had him dressing as Jesse James when he approached possible benefactors. He would tell them that he did not want to hold them up, but

2.3 Brother Adjutor of Mary, founder of De La Salle Institute, ca. 1890. A colorful character, Brother Adjutor's leadership allowed the school to be both a financial and an academic success. Courtesy of De La Salle Institute.

he did expect a substantial donation. Brother Adjutor embodied an example of "clout in a cassock." These stories may reflect more the type of people the Christian Brothers came to serve than the actual historical facts. While the brothers constructed De La Salle Institute on the right side of the tracks—that is, east of the new elevated line and the New York Central and Rock Island Railroad tracks, in the so-called "Irish Gold Coast"—it drew students from both the upwardly mobile ethnic middle class and the stockyard working-class families. In addition to instilling the fear of God in its students, De La Salle Institute hoped to prepare boys for careers and lives beyond the packinghouses, steel mills, and factories.[29]

De La Salle received its charter of incorporation from the state of Illinois on June 1, 1889. Three years later, the first class of one hundred and fifty students entered under the tutelage of eleven Christian Brothers. The school struggled for years to find its place. It included a grade school until 1914, and between 1895 and 1905 it accepted boarders. De La Salle abandoned its collegiate program in 1900 when the motherhouse in Paris forbade teaching Latin in the American

CHAPTER 2

2.4 De La Salle Institute, graduating class of 1925. De La Salle attracted boys from across the South Side, including those from working-class and middle-class backgrounds. The Christian Brothers insisted on middle-class Catholic values and prepared students for business positions and lives of Christian service. Courtesy of Ellen Skerrett.

provinces. Many in the American branch disagreed, but the rule of obedience required them to go along with it. There is some evidence that in response a few Christian Brothers left and joined the Jesuit brotherhood. The teaching of Latin would not return to De La Salle Institute until 1924.[30]

By the time a teenage Richard J. Daley attended the school in 1916, only the three-year commercial courses survived. These did fit Daley and other South Side Irish well. The program included three years of catechism, spelling, composition, and history. Boys studied arithmetic, bookkeeping, typing, penmanship, rhetoric, commercial law, and physics for two years. They also studied shorthand in their final year. Classes began promptly with the ringing of the bell at 8:30 a.m. and ended at 2:30 in the afternoon. The day began and ended with prayer.[31]

The Christian Brothers intended to make unruly working-class boys into gentlemen, though the school also attracted the children of middle-class Catholic families. Despite the challenges of teaching boys from across the South Side, the rule of St. John Baptist De La Salle strictly prohibited corporal punishment. *The Common Rules* expected the teaching brothers to demonstrate "great moderation and self-possession." They were to never punish out of anger, strike pupils with their hand, foot, or pointer, nor rebuff them rudely. In practice, the Christian Brothers often ignored these instructions and administered physical punishment when necessary.

The Christian Brothers sought to instill middle-class Catholic virtues of orderliness, hygiene, punctuality, and prayer in their students. An 1893 teachers' manual insisted on "well-kept copy books" as a way of encouraging proper concepts of order and method, which in turn would increase students' good character and future success. Order and punctuality in prayer was also part of daily conduct, as this description indicates: "The pupils shall enter the class-room [sic] in silence, one after another; each taking the holy water, making the Sign of the Cross, and saluting the Crucifix, the picture of the Virgin Mary and the teacher." At regular half-hour intervals, a pupil was expected to stand and say, "Let us remember that we are in the holy presence of God!" This orderly routine helped the teacher to refocus and the students to constantly think of God and their ultimate goal of joining Him in heaven.[32]

Christian Brothers designed the curriculum to form the conscience and thus shape the life of young men. They stressed the concepts of hierarchy as well as loyalty, charity, devotion, and community. In time, these Catholic virtues shaped much of the political outlook, both for good and bad, of many in the city. De La Salle encouraged Catholic attitudes toward fairness, duty, and sin, often in deep contrast to the rampant individualism and unbridled capitalism of post–Civil War America in general and its most capitalist of cities, Chicago. Nevertheless, De La Salle hardly promoted accepting one's place in society. Building on Catholic folk traditions, especially the popular idea of patron saints, the Christian brothers introduced their students to spiritual patrons upon whom they could rely for guidance and support in the face of sin in a fallen world. From there, it was only a short way to secular patronage: "everybody needs a friend, a patron." De La Salle provided an intellectual basis for generations of politicians, businessmen, and those who worked for both the city and the private sector. It provided a cradle for the Democratic machine as it developed in the twentieth century.

COMMUNAL CATHOLICISM AND CLOUT

Traditional Catholic culture emphasized communal loyalty. The individual, while important, remained a member of a larger body, whether the Church, the neighborhood, the city, or the nation. In this worldview, the group demanded loyalty and committed action from the individual, and in return the group took care of the individual. This conception proved central to gaining agency in a democratic urban environment and shaped much of urban politics, particularly in Chicago.

Chicago's immigrant communities experienced mobility, or lack of it, as a collective. They tended to live in neighborhoods integrated by ethnicity (spatial integration) but segregated by ethnic cultures and class (social segregation). As a result, many immigrant communities embraced the realization that "we are all in this together." Despite their differences, Catholicism, Orthodox Christianity, and eastern European Orthodox Judaism created cultures that implied social responsibility for the group. Although individuals might break or wander from this ideal, the overwhelming urban immigrant cultures of the nineteenth and twentieth centuries encouraged, even expected, unity within a community. Those who lived and worked in these communities saw such mutual connectedness as a means of survival, often against outsiders. For Catholics in particular, the parish church and the parochial school provided the center of community, with other communal institutions radiating out from them. While the first goal of the parish and the school remained the salvation of souls and the preservation of the Catholic Church, the increasingly dominant Irish model also created a sense of turf to be defended.[33]

After the German sociologist Ferdinand Tönnies published his seminal work, *Gemeinschaft und Gesellschaft*, in 1887, sociologists and others have written extensively about these two types of social relationships: of community and of society. Modernization theory pointed to the eventual movement away from community to the larger society. As the American sociologist Charles H. Cooley pointed out, *gemeinschaft* implied face-to-face association. These permanent relationships, made up of a rather small number of persons, implied a relative intimacy. These *gemeinschaft* communities were thus small and familiar in nature. They implied a certain sense of exclusion of other communities. In contrast, *gesellschaft* societies are rooted in advancing the instrumental aims of individual members. These concepts capture the nineteenth- and twentieth-century clash between traditional Catholic society and the emerging modern culture of individualism and capitalism. Bridgeport, and other working-class immigrant communities, developed as communal in nature, or *gemeinschaft*. In these neighborhoods, the relationship between the individual and the larger group was not a demanding one, but a giving one.[34]

The communal values of *gemeinschaft* endured on the streets of immigrant Chicago and in the classrooms of De La Salle Institute and other Catholic schools. Neighborhood people had obligations to each other, a communal relationship drawn from various European experiences—be they Jewish *landsmen*, Polish *rodacy*, Italian *paisani*, or others. Once in the United States, this concept proved a powerful force in the new industrial milieu. Roman Catholic theologians might claim that God in the form of the Holy Spirit finds expression in a network of mutual interpersonal relationships of concern and assistance, but the average Bridgeport resident didn't think in these theological or philosophical terms and did not have to. They simply lived a life of close personal relationships with their neighbors.

Catholic parishes provided a sense of belonging, a sense of family, and a sense of obligation in the industrial city. As representative of a structured faith, the Church presented a sense of order in what could seem to be a very chaotic and individualistic world. The demands of group preservation emphasized an internal communalism and a collective identity. Catholicism's emphasis on hierarchy and obedience presented a model to the community that proved essential in understanding the organization of the political machine as it developed in

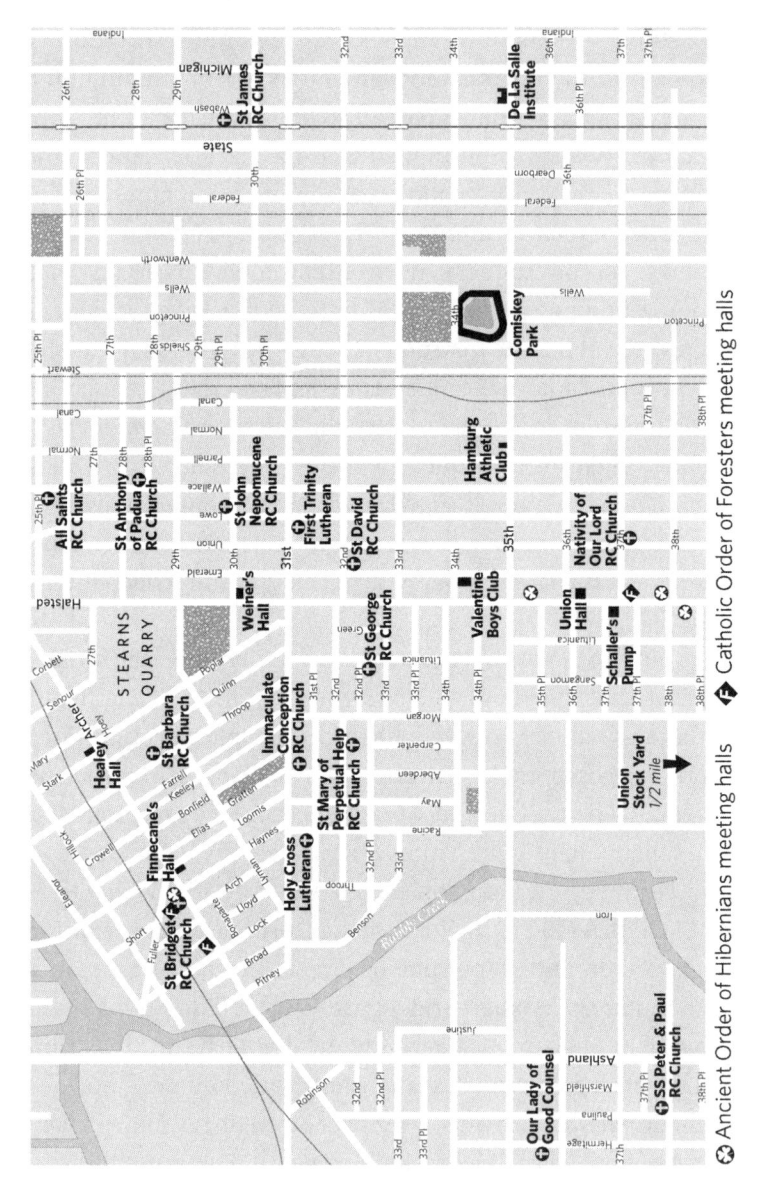

2.5　Communal Bridgeport. This map shows the ten Catholic parishes in Bridgeport, two German Lutheran parishes, and two Catholic parishes in neighboring McKinley Park to the west in the 1920s. These parishes were part of a group of more than thirty Catholic parishes that surrounded the Union Stock Yard, located just to the south of Bridgeport. It also marks major meeting halls over time and the Hamburg Athletic Club headquarters, then on 35th Street. This institutional communal web played an important role in establishing the neighborhood's political clout. Courtesy of Chicago CartoGraphics, with Parker Otto.

the late nineteenth and twentieth century. The local parish's support for the labor movement united neighborhoods like Bridgeport—despite the Church's opposition to socialism and communism. A language of obligation and interdependence marked Catholicism's public stance.

In Europe, communalism meant local control and the preservation of local traditions. Sacraments such as baptism, confession, and communion, as well as devotions of lesser significance like processions and the praying of the rosary, provided popular religious practices that proved central to Catholicism. In the surrounding neighborhoods, more than thirty-five Catholic churches could be counted within three miles of the stockyards by the early twentieth century. Most represented different ethnic groups and emphasized different rituals. Of course, this could cause conflict in Chicago and across urban America. The rise of Cahenslyism in German American communities, which called for a German ethnic bishop, as well as the creation of the Polish Independent Church movement and eventually the schism that saw the creation of the Polish National Catholic Church, resulted from this long tradition of communal control over parishes.[35]

The inward-looking nature of communal Catholicism and communal Judaism created a powerful defensive force. Neighborhoods rooted in this communalism were seen as places to defend. This often resulted in the formation of youth gangs. Some of these, such as Bridgeport's Hamburg Athletic Association, developed into powerful political organizations.* Bridgeport could be an ethnically diverse neighborhood if no one threatened the discrete ethnic communities within it. Chicago attracted wave after wave of European Catholic, Protestant, and Jewish immigrants who might live in the same geographic space but maintained separate cultural institutions. Chicagoans of each ethnic group wanted to be baptized, married, and buried by someone who understood their culture, who was one of their people. Bridgeport tolerated diversity within the European tradition. Race, as we will see, was another matter.[36]

The parochial school stood out among the most important com-

---

*For the Hamburg Athletic Association, see chapter 8.

munal institutions. The first mission of a parochial school, whether Catholic, Lutheran, or Jewish, was of course the preservation of the faith. Catholics feared their children would lose their faith if they attended a public school in the dominant Anglo-Saxon Protestant culture. By the mid-nineteenth century, despite the nominal separation of church and state, public schools in the United States were decidedly Protestant in culture. Conversely, Protestant leaders argued that Catholic schools and other institutions were un-American. In the mid-nineteenth century the Know-Nothing political movement further challenged Catholic institutions. Newspapers often warned about "popish" plots to subvert American democracy.[37]

Ethnic parochial schools not only insured that ethnic culture would be transmitted to future generations, but defended against the dominant culture. These schools remained essential for those with parishes defined by immigrant/ethnic backgrounds. The ethnic parochial school allowed for the preservation of their ethnic language, culture, and heritage and furthered the idea of community. Children would learn their ethnic languages and histories, as well as religious and cultural traditions, and yet they would still be Americans.[38]

PATRON SAINTS AND PATRONAGE

The Catholic cult of the saints expressed an especially widespread popular devotion among immigrants. The Catholic Church confers the designation of saint on those who lived exceptionally holy lives. The path to sainthood, called canonization, involves rigorous investigation, and often takes centuries to complete. Canonization dates to the early years of the Church in Mediterranean countries, and today the Church recognizes roughly 10,000 such saints. A saint may be designated as a patron of various causes, professions, or locales, and as such they are highly respected and venerated. St. Joseph is the patron of workers and St. John Baptist De La Salle is the patron of teachers. St. Jude is the patron of lost causes. Central to the cult of the saints is the idea that saints could intercede on behalf of a petitioner. Especially powerful saints such as the Blessed Virgin, St. Joseph, and St. Jude are revered by the Catholic faithful. Many Catholic parishes are named after them, and they hold a special place in popular Catholicism. In many cases, the cult takes on a meaning beyond official theological formulations. They are seen as part of folk religion. Parents give their children the name of saints at baptism, and that saint becomes their patron who will pray for them and be their spiritual guide throughout their lives. The cult joined heaven and earth together, as heavenly saints could intercede for the living and protect them. Wherever Catholicism spread, it brought saints and their relics. The Church became a type of kinship group extending beyond families, regions, ethnicity, and even death. The need for intimacy with this heavenly yet human champion is a hallmark of the cult of the saints, which remained a powerful force in Catholic culture.[39]

Accordingly, a patron saint could convince God that a mortal who had died should be allowed into heaven. Catholic folklore had the Virgin Mary often intervening with her son on behalf of those who said the rosary and took part in various Marian devotions. These stories allowed pre–Vatican II Catholics with little or no theological training beyond the Baltimore Catechism to take part in devotional life. Even the not-so-churched could ask for heavenly aid in their daily pursuits and believed that the saints interceded on their behalf at the time of their death. These holy dead became both patrons and friends of those on earth who prayed that they might intercede on their behalf. In a way, it made the concept of heaven a rather democratic one. Much like in everyday life, knowing someone could benefit you on earth and in the afterlife.[40]

The Bridgeport Irish understood that having a connection provided an advantage. Not all patrons were saints! A worldly patron, a benefactor who had clout or power, a patron in a derby hat and with a cigar, might help in a time of need with a job or a favor. This secular patron saint was a master of the political arts. And so perhaps it is no surprise that St. Joseph is portrayed on the side altar at Holy Family Church on 12th Street (Roosevelt Road) in a derby hat looking a little like a politician. The immigrant experience in Chicago, shaped by both hard realities and communal ideals and institutions, fostered a distinctive type of politics where the sacred could coexist with the profane, even if in a sometimes stressful way.

3

The Communal Web

> In places like the 35th Ward, voters don't worry much about international trade or environmentalism. In the bungalows and two-flats of Chicago's interior, politics means a chance for a job, a curb or sidewalk repair, or simply a helping hand to navigate the bureaucracy of a new country with an unfamiliar language.
>
> CHARLES LEROUX AND RON GROSSMAN[1]

In many ways Chicago is a collection of small communities or towns. Many White ethnic Chicagoans, like their ancestors, identified with their neighbors and built institutions that reflected those relationships. They created a sense of community that shaped their response to the industrial city. Well into the twentieth century, these mindsets helped to forge alliances that could make or break politicians and political organizations. Your neighborhood was an important marker in Chicago's social and economic world. It could even define what kind of life a person might lead, be it as a member of the working class, the middle class, or the upper class.

Looking at Chicago's neighborhoods as small towns reveals a structure that proved vital to political development. Residents often established a communal relationship centering on a religious institution. The local house of worship, whether Protestant, Catholic, or Jewish, laid down an institutional base for a community. This communalism protected various immigrant ethnic groups. Native White Anglo-Saxon communities were too much a part of the dominant culture to need such protection. Also, the dominant culture in a capitalist society most often promoted individualism rather than communalism.

Distinctive neighborhood economic engines created the symbolic identity of each neighborhood. For example, the steel mills of South Chicago, the stockyards and packinghouses of Back of the Yards, the sweatshops of the West Side, the tanneries of the Northwest Side, or the University of Chicago in Hyde Park shaped the social class, ethnic makeup, and physical nature of their respective neighborhoods. As industrialization rapidly changed the city, Chicago's West, South, and North Sides all contained such districts. They often seemed hostile to each other, especially early on, in what might be called the communal phase.

THE PRIEST, THE MINISTER, AND THE RABBI

The establishment of religious institutions distinguished the communal phase of neighborhood development in Chicago. The church provided a solid institutional base that fostered other neighborhood institutions, including parochial schools that preserved ethnic as well as religious traditions. The establishment of St. Patrick's Church, the first Catholic church west of the river, in 1846 marked the beginning of the phenomenal growth of Irish Catholic parishes throughout Chicago. The community first built a wooden-frame church on the corner of Desplaines and Randolph Streets. Later, after the Haymarket opened nearby, it moved to Adams and Desplaines. In 1856, the parish dedicated a new church built of cream-colored Milwaukee brick. This investment proved extremely important for the Irish community. The church immediately became a landmark on the West Side and stood as a symbol of permanence for the Irish and their ambitions. In order to raise funds for the new church and to continue to expand the parish's footprint, parish leaders divided the neighborhood into districts that resembled ward precincts. While some volunteers used their familiarity with business owners to solicit funds from saloons and other establishments, others went door to door asking residents for funds. This approach resonated with Irish immigrants who had given to "penny-a-week" collections for new chapels in Ireland. It also provided a possible model for the city's political structure. In October 1859, the parish held a four-day fair and concert at Metropolitan Hall in a campaign to complete the church. In fact, the congregation did not complete the church steeples until 1885. Thomas O'Shaughnessy's delicate Celtic-inspired stencils and windows were not completed until 1912. This long-term investment testified to the commitment of Chicago's Irish to the parish system and its importance for the sense of community.[2]

Months after the dedication of St. Patrick's Church, the expanding Irish community opened Holy Family Parish on 12th Street (Roosevelt Road). This new Jesuit parish joined the German Catholic parish of St. Francis of Assisi, which had opened in 1853. Czech, Italian, and French parishes followed shortly thereafter. The eastern European Jewish community established synagogues in the neighborhood, too. A few, like the Romanian synagogue at 14th and Union Streets, had originally been Christian churches. Others were large, beautiful synagogues, like Anshe Kanesses Israel on Clinton and Judd Streets and Ohave Sholom Mariampol (later Anshe Sholom), located at first at Canal and Liberty Streets and then at Ashland Avenue and Polk Street.[3]

For Catholics, priests—and especially parish pastors—played essential roles in the communal ethnic neighborhood. Often the most educated members of the community, they generally spoke the native language of the immigrants they served. Priests acted as a cultural resource maintaining the connection of the immigrants to the homeland and preserving their linguistic, cultural, and religious traditions. After all, just because one had immigrated to America did not mean that the past had been washed away. Pastors played essential roles in defining the communal response of these groups to their new industrial milieu. The roles of Father Arnold Damen on the West Side, Father Vincent Barzyński on the Northwest Side, Father Joseph Molitor in the West Side Czech community, and Father Wojtalewicz in South Chicago cannot be overemphasized. In Back of the Yards,

3.1 St. Patrick's Church, 1963. St. Patrick's, located at 700 West Adams, provided an early anchor for the West Side Irish community. Having survived the Great Chicago Fire, it is the oldest public building in the city. Library of Congress, Prints & Photographs Division, HABS, Reproduction number HABS ILL,16-CHIG,35-.

Fathers Louis Grudzinski and Francis Karabasz played significant roles in the labor movement, an essential pillar of communalism. The legendary priest Father Maurice Dorney established Irish parishes in both Canaryville and Back of the Yards. Dorney also intervened in several labor disputes in the packinghouses and the livestock market. Priests became natural leaders in these neighborhoods and remained so well into the twenty-first century. Eventually reformers discovered their importance too. In the 1930s, Father John Lange, pastor of St. Michael's Polish church, made it possible for the University of Chicago's juvenile reform effort, the Chicago Area Project, to get a foothold in South Chicago's Bush neighborhood.

In many ways, the parish itself became the neighborhood for Catholic Chicagoans. They organized two different kinds of parishes: the Irish dominated territorial English-speaking parishes, while other immigrant groups founded parishes defined by languages such as German, Czech, Polish, or Lithuanian. Catholic parishes humanized urban life and sacralized it for newcomers. Many parish churches were large and beautiful structures, landmarks amid the rows of two-flats, tenements, and cottages of working-class Chicago. For many, the buildings themselves provided a source of pride.[4]

The Church of Rome saw itself as universal in scope. All over the world priests celebrated the Catholic Mass in Latin. In the ethnic or national parishes, however, the sermon would be delivered in the language of its members. So would the sacrament of confession and other services such as Holy Hours and various devotions. The parish church offered a place to maintain the ethnic language of its congregation. It also served as a community center for social organizations. The laity took the initiative to establish these ethnic parishes. They raised money, and at times volunteered labor, to build the initial church building, rectory, school, and convent. These buildings became the property of the archdiocese, which often caused conflict between church leaders and local parishioners and reinforced the hierarchical relationship prevalent in the Roman Catholic Church.[5]

By 1903 the Catholic Church in Chicago had expanded, from a single parish in 1833 to 157 parishes, 80 percent of which maintained a parochial school. Twenty-seven years later, one hundred more city parishes would be organized. This network intensified the connection between church and neighborhood. The parish provided a sense of community, but also of power, demonstrating that residents had arrived and thrived. Above all, it gave the appearance of stability and therefore of permanence. The unprecedented scale of Catholic parish construction created a unity that evolved into political strength. While most parishioners did not put it in these terms, this Catholic critical mass resulted in political clout or agency for the neighborhoods. The sacred and the profane mixed amicably. This was central to the creation of a culture of clout and a Democratic political machine led largely by Catholics and representing a wide coalition of ethnic groups.[6]

Of course, other denominations also created parishes and community centers. Protestant churches could be found across the city, and often also reflected particular ethnicities. Unlike the hierarchical Catholic Church, Protestant groups were less centralized and, in some cases, very divided. By 1900, sixty-six separate Lutheran synods operated in the United States, distinguished by ethnicity, geographical location, and varying degrees of Americanization. The Methodist Episcopal Church organized separate conferences for Germans, Swedes, and a combined Danish-Norwegian community. In the 1920s, Chicago Baptists embraced congregations speaking thirteen languages. By 1923, Chicago's 860 Protestant congregations belonged to thirty-one separate denominations, about half of which were identifiably ethnic.[7]

Race and migration also proved important for Protestant congregations. The African American Protestant church followed a similar pattern of theological divisions, especially as the Great Migration expanded and transformed Chicago's African American community. The well-established Black churches, such as the African Methodist Episcopal (AME) Church and northern Black Baptist congregations, found themselves overwhelmed after 1915 by the tens of thousands of Blacks emigrating from the southern countryside. The city's Black population quadrupled from 1915 to 1930. These newcomers presented various challenges for established churchmen such as Bishop Archibald J. Carey of the AME Church. The new arrivals desired a more emotional and spontaneous religious experience than Chicago's traditional Black congregations provided. The AME Church had a centralized structure that demanded obedience, but some new Black congregants resisted this. Rural southern Blacks found the Chicago liturgy to be full of unfamiliar rituals. Migrants also found northern church music wanting. Carey disdained emotional displays of shouting, jumping, swaying, and dancing. His attitude guaranteed contention, and friction soon appeared between the AME Church and various South and West Side congregations, some of which split off from the main body.

Baptists adjusted better to the new situation because their churches had more independence and therefore responded more effectively to the needs of the new migrants. Baptists also had added familiarity with the traditional folk religion of the southerners. As a result, many Baptist churches expanded. Olivet Baptist Church saw rapid growth as it expounded a theology with a solid social gospel grounding. Pilgrim Baptist Church, which soon rivaled Olivet Baptist, became the home of a new form of liturgical song, created by Thomas A. Dorsey, known as gospel music.

The Great Migration brought many new faces and new religious institutions to Black Chicago. In their emphasis on worshipping a personal and somewhat frightening God, newcomers considered extensive ritual and elaborate ceremonies questionable and favored dramatic expressions in prayer and song. Black migrants created many congregations that ranged from storefront churches to larger and more powerful parishes. The sociologists St. Clair Drake and Horace R. Cayton found some 500 churches in Bronzeville around 1940. Migration from the South changed the face of Black Chicago as much as immigration from Europe shifted the experiences of White congregations.[8]

The Black Catholic community was comparatively small but growing. Its origins date to the 1880s, when the pastor of Old St. Mary's Church on Ninth Street and Wabash Avenue permitted African American Catholics to worship in the basement. By 1893, African Americans had raised enough funds to organize a parish of their own, St. Monica's, on the corner of Dearborn and 36th Streets. Many

3.2 Olivet Baptist Church. This church building originally served as the home of the First Baptist Church, a White congregation. In 1917, Olivet Baptist Church purchased the building, and it became home to the city's largest African American Baptist parish. Olivet played a crucial role in the expansion of the Black community during the Great Migration. From *The Negro in Chicago: A Study of Race Relations and a Race Riot* (Chicago: University of Chicago Press, 1922).

Blacks, Catholic and non-Catholic alike, resented having a "Blacks only" parish and viewed it as an example of segregation. Father Augustus Tolton, the first Black Catholic priest ordained in the United States, had been appointed to organize the small community in 1889, but after his sudden death from sunstroke in 1897, a White priest, Father Daniel J. Riordan, took over St. Monica's.

Unlike the rest of the city, Bronzeville was treated as a foreign missionary territory by the Catholic hierarchy. Cardinal Mundelein invited the Society of the Divine Word missionaries to take over St. Monica's in 1917. Father Joseph Eckert, a legendary White priest, became the pastor of the parish in 1921 with the goal of converting African Americans to the Catholic faith. His work proved so successful that the Black Catholic community outgrew the small parish church. In 1924, St. Monica's parish merged with nearby St. Elizabeth's parish. In 1932, the archdiocese gave Eckert control of St. Anselm parish as well. Other Catholic missionary orders soon joined the Divine Word missionaries in Bronzeville. These included the Franciscan friars, as well as the Sisters of the Blessed Sacrament for Indians and Colored People and the Sisters of St. Francis from Dubuque, Iowa. All these orders dedicated themselves to missionary work and the conversion of African Americans to Catholicism.[9] Many saw conversion as a sign of upward mobility and respectability in Black Chicago. Catholic identity also provided Black Chicagoans a means of getting ahead in the Democratic machine, particularly in the heavily politically influenced police department.

Black churches of all denominations shared a common history and experience of slavery, prejudice, and racial violence. Excluded by White Americans since the seventeenth century, African Americans created their own communities. Blacks developed an intricate web of families, churches, and other institutions such as fraternal organizations. These organizations forged a unity that transcended theological disputes and southern regional differences, and in turn led to a robust communal response and eventually to political power.[10]

Another community with a long history of persecution was also growing in the city. By 1845, there were enough Jews in Chicago to create a *minyan*, a quorum of ten men over the age of thirteen, for traditional religious services on Yom Kippur. They held the first services in a room above a store at Wells and Lake Streets. The next minyan did not convene for a year. By November 1847, some twenty men organized a congregation, which became Kehilath Anshe Ma'ariv (Congregation of the Men of the West) or KAM. All members were from the same general area in Germany. They eventually built a small wooden-frame structure on the northeast corner of Clark and Quincy Streets, the first synagogue in Illinois, and dedicated it in 1851.

Like Christian immigrants, Jewish immigrants came in several waves and from different parts of Europe. Jews first arrived from Germany and other western European countries. By 1852, just over two hundred Jews lived in Chicago, but already the group had begun to splinter. Polish Jews, probably from the German partition of the old Polish-Lithuanian Commonwealth, did not feel at home in the largely German Jewish congregation of KAM. They formed their own more Orthodox synagogue assembly in 1852 and called it Kehilath B'nai Sholom (Congregation of the Children of Peace). Over the years, other breakaway groups formed.[11]

Chicago's Jewish community thus became very diverse from the outset. German Jews and east European Jews often clashed over religious issues and created parallel societies. Nevertheless, they all faced anti-Semitic prejudice and cultural difference with the city's Protestant majority. By the 1870s and 1880s, Polish, Russian, and Lithuanian Jews arrived in large numbers. These poor, Yiddish-speaking Jews gathered first in the downtown area and then the Near West Side along Maxwell Street. By 1910, east European Jews occupied the area south of Taylor Street to the 16th Street railroad yards, from Canal Street west to about Damen Avenue. Between 1880 and 1910, some 55,000 Jewish immigrants crowded into this area, where they attempted to recreate the eastern European *shtetl* or Jewish village. Synagogues anchored the neighborhood. These not only provided for the neighborhood's religious needs, but also offered other services such as Hebrew schools, health funds, charitable aid, and burial arrangements, as well as providing loans to the growing Jewish business community. On the Near West Side, Jews organized some forty synagogues. Founded by men from the same community in Europe,

3.3 Maxwell Street Market, ca. 1908. This market, which resembled similar markets in eastern Europe, drew immigrants and their families from across the city. It originally stood in the heart of the Near West Side Jewish neighborhood. From *Souvenir of Chicago in Colors* (Chicago: V. O. Hammon Publishing Company, 1908).

or by men from the same occupations, or organized along particular theological principles such as Hasidism, these Jewish religious institutions served the purpose of community. The West Side Jewish community also established an outdoor market familiar to eastern Europeans along Maxwell Street, a *cheder* (primary school for young boys), *mikvahs* (ritual baths), and other institutions.

In addition, Jews organized *landsmanshaften verein*, or fraternal groups. These organizations of Jews from a particular town or province in eastern Europe also fostered community. Some of these began originally as religious groups, others as family circles or cousins' clubs, literary societies, or social clubs. Through monthly meetings, picnics, celebrations, and other events they sought to maintain traditional values, dispel loneliness, and support members emotionally. Eventually landsmanshaften groups provided medical and burial benefits, affiliated with Jewish loan societies, and even organized their own cemeteries. The founders were steeped in Yiddishkeit, the age-old traditions and ideals of Yiddish culture. These landsmanshaften verein provided a sense of belonging for Jewish immigrants and their children as well as bridges to the American city.

In 1901, Jewish Chicagoans maintained thirty-nine charitable organizations, sixty lodges, eleven social clubs, thirteen loan associations, and four Zionist groups, along with many landsmanshaften organizations. Many Yiddish-language newspapers also appeared, along with Yiddish theaters. The eastern European West Side Jewish neighborhood soon became known as "the Ghetto," while the more prosperous and assimilated South Side German Jewish community was known as the "Golden Ghetto."[12]

Eastern European Jews quarreled with the earlier Jewish migrants from Germany, who often looked down upon them. Much of this tension derived from the evolution of Reformed Judaism. One eastern European immigrant said of his German Jewish co-religionists: "They parade around as Jews, and down deep in their hearts they are worse than *goyim*, they are *meshumeds* (apostates)." In his classic 1928 study of Chicago's Jewish community, Louis Wirth wrote that the more Orthodox ghetto members referred to the assimilated German Jews as *Deitchuk* because they affected German ways, were not so particular about kosher food, did not go to synagogue often, and seemed less Jewish. The disagreement resulted not only from theological issues, but also from their cultural backgrounds, language, dress, demeanor, and economic status. Like the Christian migration to Chicago, ethnic and theological differences divided the Jewish community.[13]

The older western European Jewish immigration, fearing that the eastern Europeans—with their different language, dress, and customs—would cause an outbreak of anti-Semitism in the city, tried to create various communal institutions. These included the Jewish Training School (1890), the Chicago Maternity Center (1895), and the Chicago Hebrew Institute (1903), as well as Michael Reese Hospital (1881). The organizers hoped to speed up the assimilation process. Over time, West Side Jews moved farther west to the North Lawndale community, which housed some sixty synagogues, the Jewish People's Institute, the Hebrew Theological College, and various Zionist institutions. The Jewish community grew to be very insti-

3.4 Michael Reese Hospital. The hospital opened in 1881. Reese, a real estate developer who died in 1878, left funds in his will to build a new hospital. The hospital provided charity care, medical research, and education. It closed in 2009. Postcard, Author's Collection.

tutionally rich, which provided a firm base for the growth of political activism, and thus gained political clout. This influence would eventually find expression in the political organizations of Adolph Sabath and Jacob Arvey. Jewish communal culture and a history of persecution generated a form of unity that helped shape Jews' identity and would, as it had with Black Protestants, allow them to claim agency and eventual political power.[14]

National origins fragmented both Protestantism and Judaism in the city. Both traditions emphasized the autonomy of the individual congregation. Thus, new congregations developed frequently. Continual immigration increased these divisions. Catholics, on the other hand, despite significant ethnic, linguistic, and cultural differences, found themselves more tightly bound together through their hierarchical Church. This unity proved essential for the development of Catholic agency and political power. The archbishop stood at the top of the local pyramid, with auxiliary bishops, monsignors, and pastors below him. In addition, Catholic congregations did not own the buildings and property of their parishes; rather, the diocese did. These features of Catholicism centered control in the office of archbishop. The main Catholic ritual, the Mass, was celebrated in Latin, even if other services were held in ethnic languages. This too provided for a unity unknown among other Christian denominations and had implications for the neighborhood.[15]

THE SALOON

In addition to religious organizations, secular institutions contributed to a sense of community and created an opportunity for the development of a public sphere where important issues could be discussed. These included fraternal organizations, clubs, societies, newspapers, and businesses such as grocery stores, funeral parlors, dried goods stores, and others. Yet it was the saloon that provided one of the most essential places for people to meet and discuss issues. Here working-class men and, depending on the ethnic group, women and even children would gather. The saloon was a sort of social club for the working class. Neighborhood residents often met in the back rooms of saloons to create churches, banks, savings and loans, labor unions, fraternal organizations, and political organizations. The working-class saloon also provided a space for neighborhood celebrations such as weddings, christenings, and funeral lunches. Wedding parties gathered to celebrate after the church service. A band played well into the night as couples whirled around the dance floor performing both traditional ethnic and more modern American dances. The saloon offered a public space to create community and to celebrate it.[16]

The saloon offered basic face-to-face communications. New arrivals sometimes only had the address of a saloon where they hoped to meet up with a relative or a friend. They could garner information there, like how to get downtown, contact a lawyer, get a job, or hear neighborhood gossip. The bartender knew the local ethnic and racial leadership. Residents, who moved frequently in these poor industrial neighborhoods, often used the saloon as a mailing address. Proprietors complained that unclaimed trunks and packages filled their

3.5 The South Shore Inn in the Hegewisch neighborhood, ca. 1942. Saloons afforded neighborhood spaces where people could gather and discuss local issues and form communal bonds. Courtesy of the Southeast Chicago Historical Society.

basements. The saloonkeeper interpreted the new industrial world for his patrons. He read letters for illiterate friends and often stocked newspapers in the native tongues of his customers. Eventually the tavern also made telephones available.

On the neighborhood level, information provided the cornerstone of political power. In Back of the Yards, a Czech real estate man commented that "the saloon is a very wholesome discussion center. Here men bring their ideas and compare them. It helps to get to the truth in a situation and fight manipulation by unscrupulous men." Barkeepers became important figures and rose in the political structure of the neighborhood and ward.[17]

Indeed, many a saloonkeeper also served as the local ward politician. Alderman John Powers owned two saloons with another alderman, Billy O'Brien. He also operated a gambling house. Michael C. McDonald owned a saloon and gambling den, as did Aldermen John Coughlin and Michael Kenna in the notorious 1st Ward. Big Jim O'Leary, the gambling boss of the stockyards, who played a crucial role in 29th Ward politics, owned an establishment across from the main entrance to the Union Stock Yard on Halsted Street. West Side politician Barney Grogan ran a place in the 18th Ward. Alderman Edward F. Cullerton also owned a saloon. The line between serving customers and gathering voters during elections often blurred.[18]

The priest, the saloonkeeper, and the ward politician played central roles in the creation of community and in setting the roots of Chicago's politics. All three understood the communal web of institutional development that neighborhood residents created. Again, the sacred and the profane mixed, as the priest and the politician might stop into the saloon to visit with their parishioners or constituents. The ward boss, or his representative, might buy the house a round of drinks or play a game of chance to show their solidarity with voters. Religious observances such as baptisms, weddings, and funerals took place in a church, but were commemorated in the back rooms of saloons.[19]

THE WARD BOSS

The ward boss played a central role in the development of the city's politics. The legendary alderman John Powers acted as a patron and sometimes a savior to his constituents in the West Side's 19th Ward, but also as a villain, thief, and grafter to reformers and those he fought in the City Council. In 1898, the reformer and journalist Ray Stannard Baker pointed out that Powers played a more than ordinarily successful role as ward boss. He used the words "cunning" and "wholly unscrupulous" to describe the alderman. Most importantly, Baker pointed out that Powers had the "gift" of good-fellowship or good-heartedness. He gave out turkeys by the thousands at Christmas. He also gave out jobs. Indeed, in the neighborhood, he played the role of feudal lord or patron saint.[20]

The 19th Ward had changed demographically during the years of Powers's reign. When Powers won his first election in 1888, it contained large numbers of Irish, German, Dutch, and Scandinavian residents. But Italians, eastern European Jews, and Slavs soon displaced them. Powers, especially astute about riding this wave of ethnic change, used methods that might seem corrupt to reformers, but made perfect political sense to him and his like. Ward politicians found jobs for their constituents, in both the public and the private sector. They performed favors for voters. They obtained franchises for companies and profited at the public's expense. Constituent services coexisted alongside public graft.

For Jane Addams and her fellow reformers at nearby Hull House, Powers's ways embodied evil and corruption. Addams attempted several times to marshal the power of reform and defeat Powers, but to no avail. Many neighborhood residents, particularly the poor, did not see what the problem was. Powers had pulled himself up out of poverty, something they also hoped to do, and now provided for those at the margins of the capitalist economy. Powers also did the bidding of powerful businessmen, who rewarded him handsomely. In fact, Powers gloried in the title "Prince of Boodlers." He worked not only to maintain that title, but to reap its monetary rewards.

At the height of his power, the 19th Ward alderman had a dominant role in the City Council. He served as chairman of the Finance Committee and member of the Judiciary Committee, as well as several other positions. Powers ruled the caucus that handed out chairmanships. After 1900, he became the chairman of the Cook County Democratic Party. He led the campaign in the City Council to authorize franchises for the following companies: North Chicago Railway, Union Elevated Railway, Chicago Economic Fuel Gas, Chicago and Jefferson Urban Transit, West Chicago Street Railway, Ogden Gas, Chicago General Electric, and Union Consolidated Elevated. Charles Tyson Yerkes, the leading financier of Chicago's mass transit systems, provided much of the economic power behind the Prince of Boodlers.[21]

Jane Addams did understand that Powers's Irishness shaped his politics. She explained that since Irish politicians came from a tradition of being exploited by the English, they saw influence over government as a rightful claim after years of oppression. She wrote: "Many a politician has come from Ireland, not only with the desire to feed at the public crib, but with a conviction that it is perfectly legitimate to do so, and it is the Irishmen who largely teach political

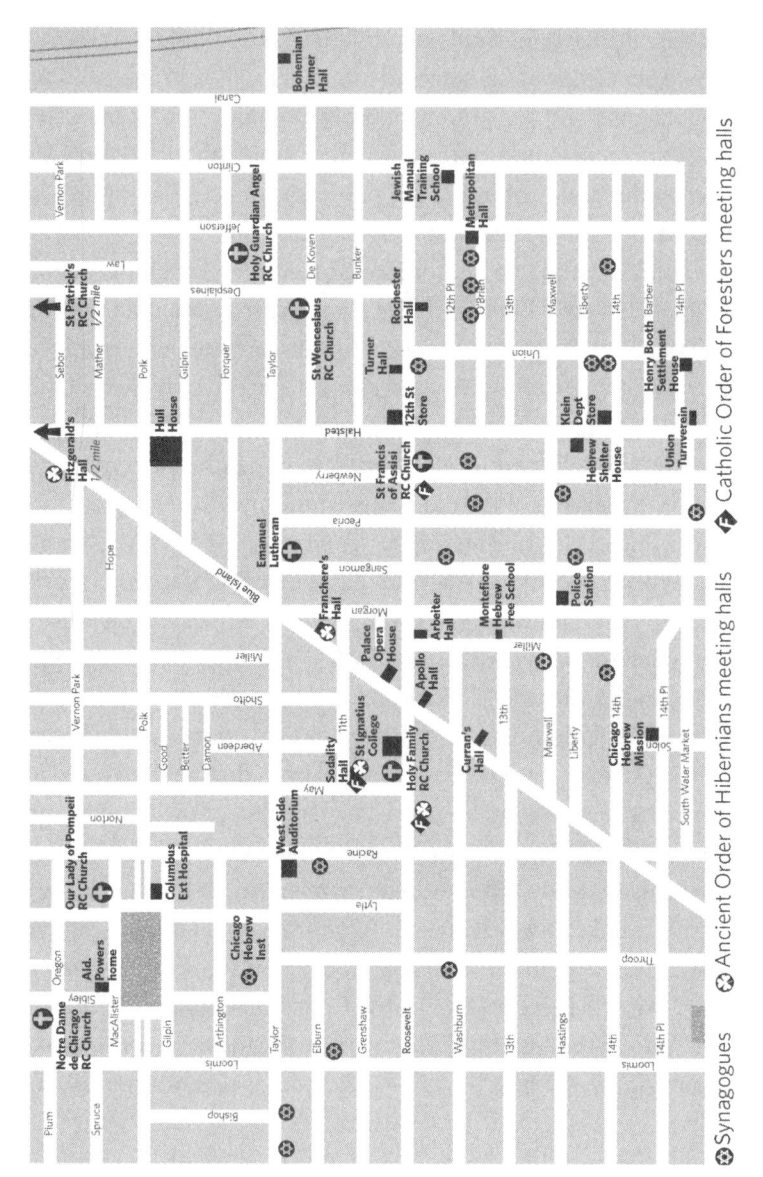

3.6 The Near West Side communal web. This map shows the vast amount of institutional development on the Near West Side, one of the city's poorest districts in the 1890s. Churches, synagogues, meeting halls, and saloons existed throughout the area. Many of the smaller synagogues do not appear on this map. Saloons were too numerous, and too often changed location, to be marked. Notice the home of Alderman John Powers on MacAlister Place (Lexington St.). Courtesy of Chicago CartoGraphics, with Parker Otto.

methods to the others living in their vicinity, and who dramatize for them the aims and objects of civic government."[22]

For many of his constituents, Powers was simply a helpful, powerful man to whom they could turn in time of need—unlike many a reformer. Powers provided coal for those who could not afford to heat their homes. He made a habit of attending wakes, gaining another of his nicknames—"The Mourner." He offered financial help to widows struggling to pay for their husbands' funerals. At times, he provided housing to those in need. During the Christmas season, he distributed turkeys and geese without questioning need. Compared to traditional charitable organizations, the alderman indeed looked like a kindly saint, handing out food and giving children small gifts without asking embarrassing questions.

Most of his constituents stood in awe of his wealth and his power. It would have been most impolite to ask where the money came from. He owned two saloons, but never took a drink himself. He maintained a gambling house, but never gambled. Powers gave generously to churches in his ward. He wore fine clothes and a diamond ring, something his constituents hoped one day to possess themselves.

Above all, Powers could grant someone a city job. He reported that the city employed 2,600 of his constituents because of his political clout. All he asked in return was loyalty at the ballot box, perhaps a small donation to his election fund, and for his precinct captains to make sure the vote got out. Of course, such power had a dark side. Should Powers feel that someone had been disloyal, they could quickly find themselves out of a job or their business closed because a city inspector had suddenly found a problem or City Hall had denied a license. At times, political violence and bombings occurred. The 1921 election proved to be especially violent in the 19th Ward. In the end, a mobilized Italian community did oust Powers, but not until after decades of his political dominance.[23]

At least in theory, the ward boss represented and helped his constituents. Of course, given the realities of the relationships the ward boss had with other ward bosses, this role had an impact on the entire city, and in many cases on both state and national politics. The type of elected position held by a ward boss mattered. If elected as a party committeeman or alderman, he played a largely local role. If elected either to the state legislature or the US Congress, he had a wider focus. In both cases, the core of the ward boss's power lay with constituents. If they saw the ward boss as their friend and protector, the boss would have their loyalty, much like a patron saint. Culturally, this made sense to vast numbers of immigrants.[24]

While some aspects of the ward boss's role changed over time, much of it remained the same throughout the nineteenth and twentieth centuries. However, by the last third of the twentieth century, both the national and the local political landscape had changed. Still, the role of the ward boss remained important and continued to rely on his or her relationship with constituents, now through an elaborate system of ward workers that fed information to the committeeman and alderman.[25]

A telling example of this evolving landscape can be seen in the role played by Dan Rostenkowski, who like his father, Joseph Rostenkowski, served as committeeman and boss of the 32nd Ward. His constituents also elected him to represent them in the Illinois House and then in the state senate. Afterwards he served in the US House of Representatives on behalf of Illinois's 8th District, until he was indicted in 1995 on several charges. In 1996 he pleaded guilty to two felony counts. Despite his fall from power, his life as the ward boss and major spokesman for his legislative district revealed how the politics of clout played out in the last half of the twentieth century.

A prolific letter writer, Rostenkowski answered calls for aid, debated with constituents, called on friends, and granted favors. He regularly sent letters of congratulations to his constituents when they received their citizenship papers. Often, he interceded with US officials on behalf of a constituent's relative or friend to obtain a visa to enter the United States. Rostenkowski consistently supported organized labor, reflecting the working-class character of his district and ward. While careful in dealing with patronage jobs, Rostenkowski interceded on occasion to help constituents with job applications, writing letters of support or making helpful phone calls. As a congressman he responded to a myriad of constituent concerns including the need for better inspection of meatpacking plants, worries about inflation, questions about why the minimum wage bill did not include laundry workers, and concerns about medical care for the aged, Great Society programs, the National Endowment for the Humanities, the right of labor to picket, and other such issues. This intense interaction with his constituents proved the statement by Speaker of the House Tip O'Neill that "all politics is local." It also spoke to the communal and hierarchical nature of the political machine.[26]

Rostenkowski, like his father, maintained strong ties with his Polish American constituents. Polish issues and Polish American concerns were often brought to him. He agitated for a postage stamp celebrating the millennium of Poland's founding as a state, as well as for other such commemorative stamps with Polish themes. Rostenkowski defended Poland's acquisition of the so-called lost territories from Germany after World War II. He championed the cause of Polish sailors who wanted to defect to the West from Communist Poland. Rostenkowski made several trips to Poland and supported US economic ties with the country. Polish American concerns included discrimination against Polish Americans in hiring practices, the preservation of Polish-language radio broadcasts, and ethnic cultural concerns, as well as what his constituents considered slander against their ethnic group by comedians on television.[27]

Rostenkowski recognized the importance of the Catholic Church in his ward. He maintained his family's connection to St. Stanislaus Kostka Parish and supported other Catholic institutions. He informed both DePaul and Loyola University presidents of financial aid opportunities and other matters. The congressman even helped on occasion with getting federal aid for students attending local public universities. He also made sure to stay in touch with both public and Catholic school principals throughout the 8th District, often welcoming them as they began their tenure or sending pamphlets and other information he thought they might find useful. Of course, he was not above asking for a favor in return. When President Kennedy and then President Johnson visited Chicago, he requested that students line the expressway as their caravans passed through the Northwest Side from O'Hare Airport to the Loop. Rostenkowski also did favors for other constituents or business associates. He secured tickets to sporting events for friends and supporters, either for free or by paying for them out of Democratic Party funds. Despite criticism from members of his own party, he called this "good politics."[28]

A colleague of Rostenkowski's, Roman C. Pucinski, also played the role of ward boss, of the Northwest Side's 41st Ward. He served as a congressman and then, in 1973, after losing an election to the US Senate, became a city alderman. His career also fit the pattern of communal leader.[29] Like other aldermen and committeemen, Pucinski held a Ward Night every week, for those who wished to court Pucinski's favor or get help for a problem such as a traffic ticket or a zoning change. Sometimes that included a constituent who needed work papers. Pucinski, who often had no control over such issues, usually knew someone who might be of help. At other times, the loss of an apartment lease, or dogs that terrorized the neighborhood, or even more private affairs such as a wayward husband came across his desk. Pucinski said that he felt like a father confessor during the Tuesday sessions, but it helped him to understand his constituency. Often the alderman helped his petitioners with the promise of a corner stop sign, advice on a zoning issue, or simply a call to a bothersome neighbor. City jobs, however, eventually became more and more scarce due to the Shakman decrees.[30]

Pucinski also involved himself in matters of ethnic and racial equity, complaining to the Equal Employment Opportunity Commission that 106 area corporations discriminated against Blacks, Latinos, and persons of Polish and Italian descent. He based his complaint on a study by the Institute for Urban Life at Loyola University Chicago, which showed that among nearly 3,000 directors at these corporations Polish, Italian, Black or Latino people made up only 3 percent. Although primarily concerned with Polish American representation in corporate boardrooms, he nevertheless did see it as a larger matter of equality and civil rights.[31]

Another mid-twentieth-century politician, Michael A. Bilandic, became the 11th Ward alderman in 1969. While not completely fitting the model of a ward boss, Bilandic, alderman of the Daley family's home ward, still sheds light on the day-to-day work of the role.

Bilandic's office interceded with Mercy Hospital to release a body being held because the doctor had forgotten to sign the death certificate. Complaints about a problematic tavern on Halsted Street and a request for a business license on 31st Street also landed on Bilandic's desk. In the latter case, Bilandic granted the favor despite a comment that the applicant did not have the best voting record. Some petitioners asked for support to secure a position with the city or to have their Park District job hours increased. Bilandic also lobbied the city to provide ping pong tables, card tables, and other equipment to the Chicago Housing Authority's Wentworth Gardens. He pointed out that these would serve some 500 children. Working-class people often depended on aldermen for these matters.[32]

Like the Catholic Church, ward organizations and the entire political machine were based on a hierarchical model. Much like the Church, the machine also maintained its own worldview and moral code, which stressed loyalty to both the leadership and the party. In the Catholic Church, the Pope was the head, with the bishops below him exercising broad authority, followed by parish priests as the foot soldiers. In ward organizations, the hierarchical structure was very similar, though perhaps more complex and layered. The ward boss, usually the ward committeeman, who also might hold another elected position such as alderman or congressman, played the role of a bishop. His word was law—in the ward. He, in turn, dealt with more powerful committeemen who played the role of cardinal. The mayor and the head of the Cook County Democratic or Republican parties acted as pope. In this analogy, the foot soldiers are the precinct captains.[33]

Each ward was subdivided into numerous precincts, each of which contained approximately 300 to 500 voters, and each local precinct captain served as the eyes and ears of the ward boss. These captains listened to their constituents' problems and concerns and passed them up the ladder to the ward boss. The roughly 3,000 precinct captains citywide often held patronage jobs as well, and members of the community looked to them as people with clout. These machine foot soldiers might also make recommendations for (or against) patronage jobs. Precinct captains paid close attention to the political life of

CHAPTER 3

3.7 Flyer distributed to precinct captains citywide, 1955. Chairman Richard J. Daley of the Regular Democratic Organization of Cook County distributed this flyer, which included a copy of a *Sun-Times* editorial cartoon celebrating precinct captains. Richard J. Daley Collection [MSRJD04], box SIIss1B24, folder 9, Special Collections & University Archives, University of Illinois Chicago.

their constituents. Did they vote? Did they vote the right way? Did they display a campaign poster in their window? Did they speak on behalf of a favored candidate?

At times, even though the constituent could apply directly for a city service such as getting an abandoned car towed, a streetlight fixed, or a welfare application reviewed, they did not understand the bureaucratic structure and hesitated to communicate with city government offices. The precinct captain, however, could deal with the problem and take credit for aiding a constituent. A precinct captain might give his constituent a card of introduction to carry to the welfare office. He might make a telephone call. While this more often than not made no difference to those who ran the welfare office, most people felt grateful for any help and the political machine received considerable advantage for the effort. Both before and after the Great Depression, Chicagoans took it for granted that they received welfare checks because of the machine. The precinct captain provided a vital link between the neighborhood and the larger world.

If precinct captains did not produce results on election day, they faced dismissal—or, in the language of the machine, they were "vised." They therefore maintained personal contact with those who lived in their precincts. The captains canvassed their constituents, bought votes if they had to, made donations to churches whose pastors would often support the party, and on occasion, especially in impoverished wards, threatened to cut off sources of public assistance. Many times, residents voted for a machine candidate not because of their worth or their party affiliation, but because they voted to support the precinct captain. The bond between precinct captains and voters could be powerful. Sometimes, when ward boundaries were redrawn, residents would ask to keep their old precinct captain. In this manner, the ward bosses relied on their foot soldiers to reach into every part of the ward and maintain control.[34]

THE GANGSTER

Not all of the neighborhood-level clout was exercised by the political machine. As in most large American cities, gangsters played a leading role in many Chicago neighborhoods. For many immigrants and their children organized crime sometimes provided a path for upward mobility, an alternative to politics, religious life, or small business. For the gangster the rise could be quick and even heroic. Gangsters often acted out of a sense of communal friendship and ethnic loyalty. Crime, politics, and the business world interacted within the neighborhood. The parish priest, rabbi, and minister knew the boys who had become gangsters and, even if they did not condone it, they understood their role. Gangsters gave freely to charities, neighborhood improvement projects, and ethnic clubs, and they ran legitimate businesses as well.

Various ethnic groups dominated different parts of the crime world. During the first thirty to forty years after arrival in the United States, immigrants found that crime provided wealth as well as extensive contacts in the political and business worlds. It offered valuable leverage both within and outside their communities. Criminals made up a small, but important, minority in these neighborhoods, especially the poorer ones. Early on, an intricate web of Irish politicians, gamblers, and police shared in the profits of gambling in Chicago. This system remained intact until about World War I, after which others began to join the underworld. By the 1920s, Black politicians and operators dominated the rackets in Bronzeville.

With the onset of Prohibition, many things changed. Jewish gamblers and Italian bootleggers emerged. Italians also dominated the prostitution business, while Poles and others shared in the bootlegging business. Organized crime provided employment in the immigrant and Black ghettos. Moonlighting police often served as truck drivers for Capone and other bootleggers. An intimate relationship between various levels of society emerged. Basically, organized crime seemed to be everywhere. Of course, customer demand for what the gangster provided, whether that was illegal alcohol, prostitution, drugs, or protection, played a role.

Many in the community depended in part on the money circulated by organized crime. Small businesses depended on customers who had some connection to the mob for the purchase of goods or services. Taxi drivers, bartenders, and bellboys shared information about where gambling or prostitution could be found. And organized crime often helped local politicians by providing campaign workers to get out the vote, or more likely the right voters.[35]

Back of the Yards residents considered Johnny Oberta, the Republican committeeman in this largely Polish neighborhood, a bit of a Robin Hood character. He dropped coins for children who followed him around, handed out toys and Christmas trees, and aided families in the neighborhood. Despite his rather sadistic tendencies and open brutality in the criminal world, many in the neighborhood viewed him as a hero. Oberta, under the influence of his mentor, Big Tim Murphy, joined Joe "the Polak" Saltis's gang. Saltis, a Slovak American despite his nickname, controlled much of the illegal beer trade in the neighborhood's so-called ice cream parlors, which actually operated as taverns during Prohibition. Oberta began as a beer truck driver and then became a gunman. He soon rose to the position of Saltis's chief lieutenant and enforcer. Murphy, a one-time Illinois legislator and labor racketeer, was murdered in 1928, and a few months later his widow, Florence, married Oberta, who was one of his pallbearers. Oberta is often given the dubious distinction of being the gangster who invented the one-way ride. Ironically, someone took him for a one-way ride and left him murdered in the southwest suburbs in March 1930.[36]

In the Jewish community, Davey Miller and his brothers, Hirschie, Max, Al, and Harry offered another example of the intricate relationship between the ethnic neighborhood, organized crime, and the larger society. Born in Cincinnati, Miller moved with his family to Chicago, and he grew up in the Maxwell Street area on the Near West Side. Miller began his career as a prizefighter, representing Chicago as a teenage heavyweight in the national amateur championship of 1914. Miller established a foothold in legitimate businesses by opening a restaurant in 1912, and by 1915 he opened his landmark restaurant in the expanding Jewish community in North Lawndale. The restaurant business also allowed him to get involved in gambling, and later in bootlegging. Alderman Manny Abrahams befriended him and provided protection from police harassment. Abrahams's successor, Morris Eller, reputedly sold him protection from police raids during the early years of Prohibition.

Above all, Davey Miller became known as a protector of his fellow Jews, who referred to him as the "Samson" or "Judah Maccabee" of the West Side. Miller spent much of his life showing up with his fellow gang members to defend Jews throughout the city, from the West Side to Uptown and as far away as South Chicago. Miller and his gang of *shtarkers* (Jewish toughs) fought with Polish Catholic gangs throughout the Douglas Park and Garfield Park areas. His reputation brought Miller and his family plenty of goodwill in the community. It also secured political clout that gave him cover for his gambling and bootlegging operations. Young people in the neighborhood regarded Miller as a hero. Eventually, the rise of Jacob Arvey and the Democrats put an end to Miller's local power.

In contrast, Julius "Lovin" Putty Anixter, a mostly behind-the-scenes gangster, rode out the political shifts. He safeguarded his place by working with the rising crime syndicate and ensured his political clout by backing Arvey and the Democrats. Known as the "high priest" of graft, Anixter acted as someone who could connect with ward bosses and gamblers. Others acted in much the same way. Politicians looked for support whether through organized crime, street gangs turned social athletic clubs, or other avenues as they built their organizations.[37]

That the priest, rabbi, minister, saloonkeeper, ward politician, precinct captain, and gangster were important members of their neighborhoods goes almost without saying. Still, it is important to note the essential roles they played in building a sense of community within their neighborhoods. They often worked together to protect their communities, even if they may have disagreed with each other's methods. They played the role of "good man," as Jane Addams explained. For the poor of Chicago's industrial neighborhoods, they became patrons that could protect and maintain immigrant culture and religion. They provided a place to gather in the church hall or the back room of saloons, and even provided aid in times of duress. These neighborhood leaders acted as essential links for community and thus helped build a citywide political machine based on a communal sense of obligation.

The dark side of this reciprocal communalism in the political sphere lay in the repercussions that could ensue if a voter did not return a favor. The political machine rewarded loyalty and punished disloyalty. Bernard Neistein, Committeeman of the West Side's 29th Ward, who served for twenty-seven years as a precinct captain, said: "In that era, everyone understood that a precinct captain's services were not freely given." One election, Neistein got every constituent's vote—save for three: a fellow he had gotten a city job for, along with his wife and mother-in-law. The morning after the election, Neistein had the traitor fired. "They lived in a two-flat," Neistein said, "which I bought and then had them thrown out on their ass. Later, I sold the building at a $500 loss. It was worth every penny."[38] The laws of communalism could be harsh and fiercely enforced.

4

The Machine's Growing Pains

> The rooms of the Democratic headquarters are in themselves a study. At any hour of the day the place is filled with anxious inquirers, workers, from wards and precincts, colored men, white men, laboring men, men of all nationalities, Germans, Hollanders, Bohemians, Polanders, Swedes, Norwegians, and Irishmen. The only class of people who are not represented there are the Chinamen.
>
> CHICAGO TRIBUNE[1]

After the assassination of Carter Harrison, the city mourned his death, but none mourned as deeply as his children, especially his two sons, Carter H. Harrison IV and William Preston Harrison. When their father purchased the *Chicago Times* in 1891, they both went to work for the newspaper, an institution that had long supported Democrats and even attacked Abraham Lincoln's policies during the Civil War. The Harrison boys quickly busied themselves in the paper's day-to-day operations. After their father's death, the brothers took control of both the editorial and the business side. They supported Populist policies such as free silver, free trade, an income tax, government control of the railroads, and the restriction of monopolies. During the Pullman strike, the Harrisons backed the workers but condemned all violence. They also carried out a prolonged attack against President Grover Cleveland and the "Gold" Democrats as they fought for control of their party's soul. The newspaper's liberal policy fueled readership as it appealed to populist interests across the West.

Nonetheless, the *Chicago Times* struggled financially. The Harrison sisters wanted to sell their shares in it, and the brothers did not have the resources to buy them out. Adolph Kraus, their father's old friend and political ally, owned a small number of shares, and he stepped forward to secure control. But he did not agree with the editorial ideas of the Harrison brothers, and they also sold their interests. Each of the siblings gained $7,500 ($245,250 in 2023) from the sale of the newspaper.[2]

Carter H. Harrison IV (also known as Harrison Jr.) was born on April 23, 1860, in a home built by his father two years earlier in the notorious 1st Ward. Although he did not grow up in the neighborhood, the fact of being a son of the 1st Ward helped him in his later political campaigns. As a youth, Harrison Jr. studied in Germany for three and a half years, becoming fluent in German. Harrison later claimed that he had become German to the core, admiring German customs, culture, and aspirations. Perhaps most importantly, he acquired a taste for beer, beer gardens, and song. German culture further infused him with liberal ideas—such as seeing no harm in drinking. These experiences and attitudes would eventually endear him to Chicago's vast immigrant population while earning him enemies among those who feared that alcohol and foreign traditions would endanger society.

Harrison returned to Chicago after his mother's death in 1876 and attended the Jesuit-operated St. Ignatius College (now Loyola University). At St. Ignatius, he made solid friendships with several up-and-coming Catholic boys from various ethnic backgrounds, which put him in good standing in the growing Catholic community. Furthermore, he married a Catholic and had two children raised Catholic. His years at St. Ignatius shaped much of his future relationship with the Catholic Church and the ethnic groups flooding into Chicago. Harrison claimed that the "rigid mental discipline, the close logical reasoning, and the analytical training" of his Jesuit education proved invaluable. He practiced law until 1889, when he joined his younger brother first in the real estate business and then at the *Chicago Times*.[3]

Politically, Republican George Swift replaced Harrison's father, and then Democrat John P. Hopkins won a special mayoral election in December 1893. Along with his friend, Roger C. Sullivan, Hopkins attempted to build a citywide Democratic machine. The new mayor, an Irish Catholic Democrat and friend of President Cleveland, left office in 1895. Hopkins did not, however, leave Democratic politics.

ROGER SULLIVAN AND JOHN HOPKINS

By the 1890s, Roger C. Sullivan and John P. Hopkins emerged as rivals to the Harrisons within the Democratic Party. They took control over much of the Party, but failed to create a viable citywide organization. Although Richard Allen Morton has argued that Sullivan founded Chicago's Democratic machine, Sullivan's organization did not control Democratic politics across the city.[4] Sullivan and Hopkins only laid the groundwork.

In the late 1870s, Sullivan arrived in Chicago at the age of seventeen from Belvidere, Illinois, where his family had settled after emigrating from Ireland. He contacted Bernard "Barney" McDevitt, a former neighbor from Belvidere who worked as a master car builder for the West Side Street Car Company. McDevitt helped get Sullivan a job and also supposedly introduced him to local politics. He asked him to work for the company's candidate for mayor, a Republican, in the 1881 primary. Despite being a Democrat, Sullivan agreed. This, however, brought him to the attention of Democratic organizers, who soon lured him back to their party, which cost him his job. These early stories about Sullivan are largely wrapped in legend, but they do highlight the personal relations that typified Chicago politics throughout much of the nineteenth and twentieth centuries. Personal relationships proved necessary for success in the political and the business sphere.

By 1884, Sullivan was working as a custodian at the Cook County Hospital, a position he received through his Democratic Party connections. There he renewed his friendship with John Patrick Hopkins. This lifelong relationship would shape both men's political futures.[5]

Sullivan and Hopkins entered Chicago politics at a time that veritably reeked of boodle or graft. Various politicians held sway over different wards like feudal lords. No central control existed. In 1881, several young Democrats had conceived of forming a Democratic Club. They launched the Iroquois Club at the Palmer House with support from the first Mayor Harrison, which proved an important initial step in building a centralized organization like Tammany Hall in New York City. They hoped the new association would compete with the Republican Union League Club. Many Chicagoans referred to the Iroquois Club as a "silk-stocking" club. To join required a $25.00 initiation fee (equivalent to $737 in 2023 dollars), with semi-annual dues of $20.00 ($590). This placed membership well beyond the reach of average working-class Democrats. Elite Democrats made up the membership and included Mayor Harrison, his sons, and Cyrus Hall McCormick Jr., who soon replaced his father as president of the McCormick Harvesting Machine Company. The preamble to the club's constitution proclaimed that every good citizen must take "not only a deep interest, but also an active part in the political affairs of the country." Furthermore, it stated that the principles of the Democratic Party should dominate both federal and local governments.

The organization met downtown at the newly built Haverly's Theater on Monroe Street, in a suite on the third floor. By 1886 the organization occupied all of the floors above the theater, which had been renamed the Columbia Theater. The rooms were open daily from 9:00 a.m. until midnight, and the club maintained a restaurant and bar. Apparently, the restaurant did not do well initially, but the sales at the bar more than made up for it.[6]

The Iroquois Club held its first banquet on March 15, 1882, at the Palmer House — a rather elegant affair attracting important local and national Democrats. The Club elicited the ire of the city's largely Republican press, which compared it and the Democratic Party to the Native American Iroquois Nation in terms most unflattering to both of them. The following year the *Chicago Tribune* reported

4.1 Iroquois Club banquet. The Democratic Iroquois Club held a banquet in honor of Republican President Theodore Roosevelt at the Auditorium Hotel on May 10, 1905. Over 600 attended the dinner to hear Roosevelt speak. The club presented him with the club badge and challenged him to wear it. Members suggested he change parties, to which Roosevelt replied with his trademark grin. Stereograph, Author's Collection.

again on the annual banquet and attacked a speech given by Carter Harrison.[7]

In 1883, the headquarters of the Cook County Democratic Club (CCDC) opened just a few doors down the street from the Iroquois Club. One member proposed that the space be outfitted with a bar that served "mixed drinks," a billiard room, a reading room, and other such accoutrements, as well as a restaurant. Another member objected that the membership included only "plain men who drank plain whiskey," and some members insisted that the "silk-stocking" Democrats should go to the Iroquois Club. The CCDC represented the interests of middle- and working-class members of the party as well as the downtown bar owners and gamblers. German and Irish immigrants dominated the membership. Both clubs agreed that the

CHAPTER 4

Iroquois Club supported civil service reform while the Cook County Democrats concerned themselves more with patronage—which was, of course, an essential ingredient of political clout. This proved to be a major fracture in the Democratic Party.[8]

Harrison and others hoped to use the clubs to create a unified Democratic Party in Chicago. Many such organizations existed across the city and the state, and they divided over various issues. Many of the ethnic clubs, both Democratic and Republican, mirrored the city's increasing diversity and embodied the problems of building a centralized machine. The party's social class, geographic, and ethnic diversity pulled Democrats in various directions. Chicago's Democrats tended to divide along the same lines as the national party—over issues like bimetallism. Gold Democrats aligned with the upper classes and Silver Democrats with lower-middle-class and working-class constituents. Democratic factions played a complicated game as individuals and their followers flowed back and forth ideologically in attempts to better their position and capture the local party.

While Roger Sullivan lived on the West Side, his friend John Hopkins made his life in the Township of Hyde Park, south of the city. Hopkins had known Grover Cleveland as a boy in Buffalo, New York, and proved to be a lifelong supporter. Like many upstate New Yorkers, he made his way west to Chicago. He worked first as a lumber shover and then as a machinist at the Pullman Palace Car Company. Hopkins quickly climbed the management ladder at the Pullman Works and followed Pullman into the Republican Party. The party elected him treasurer of the Town of Hyde Park in 1885. Pullman supported the young man's ambitions, but by 1888 they had a falling out, probably over Hopkins's support for Cleveland and the local annexation movement that would see Hyde Park, which included Pullman City, join Chicago the following year. Hopkins moved shortly thereafter to neighboring Kensington, where he operated a grocery store. Democrats selected him to serve on the Democratic Cook County Central Committee, and in 1890 he became Vice Chair of the County Executive Committee. That same year Hopkins became the Democratic campaign chair for the city and county and a potent new force in the party. He joined the Iroquois Club, but he and Sullivan developed their own organization called the Nectar Club. The group, made up largely of immigrants, lasted at least until 1898 and met at Hopkins's restaurant downtown.[9]

When an assassin's bullet cut down Mayor Carter H. Harrison in October 1893, chaos reigned in the City Council. The selection of an acting mayor led to a near riot. In the fight, Democratic Alderman Stanley Kunz from the Polish Northwest Side picked up former Councilman Jake Miller and threw him over a railing. Bathhouse John Coughlin grabbed a chair and swung it at his Republican opponents. The fracas finally ended when Republican George Bell Swift grasped the hand of Democratic alderman John McGillen in a show of unity and quieted the council floor. After a contested vote, Corporation Counsel Adolph Kraus and Alfred S. Trude, both Democrats, advised that Swift had been elected acting mayor.

A special election was scheduled for December 1893. The Republican Party nominated Swift, while Democrats more contentiously nominated Hopkins. The anti-Hopkins group ultimately failed in its efforts to use meeting rules to derail his nomination. Moreover, Hopkins's friendship with President Cleveland attracted support for his candidacy. During the campaign, Hopkins supported traditional Democratic principles and promised not to politicize the police. While his Catholic religion and Irish ethnicity became an issue for some, he defended immigrant rights and lauded their customs and traditions, like keeping saloons and beer gardens open on Sunday. He promised better and cheaper public transportation as well as the elevation of railroad tracks. Hopkins bemoaned high unemployment and spoke about creating jobs despite the economic depression. Chicago's largely Republican press, again led by the *Chicago Tribune*, attacked his candidacy, claiming that he was anti-union and that he knew little about governance and had abused his political clout in Hyde Park. Swift lost to the thirty-five-year-old Hopkins by a slim margin of 1,290 votes. It seemed that Hopkins, Sullivan, and their friends might now be able to create a lasting organization that could bring the city under centralized political control.[10]

Hopkins assumed office in a simple ceremony in the City Council chambers on the evening of December 27, 1893. Despite the recent assassination and lack of security, Hopkins walked to City Hall the next morning, shaking hands along the way. Some 600 visitors greeted the new mayor at his office. Hopkins welcomed them from 11:30 a.m. until the last handshake at 5:00 p.m. Many asked for jobs and favors. Business leaders (including Potter Palmer), clergy, judges, commissioners, aldermen, saloonkeepers, bankers, and workers mixed in the crowd. Hopkins seemed to know most of them personally and addressed many by their first names. One visitor, ten-year-old Willie Twyman, who lived near the Union Stock Yard, waited three hours to ask for the release of his dog, which had been seized by the dogcatcher the day after Christmas. A cheerful Hopkins happily granted his request. Over 200 letters of congratulations arrived, each opened and read by his secretary, Felix Senff. More than 100 of these included applications for patronage jobs.[11]

The Hopkins administration would not be an easy one for either the city or the mayor. In the spring and summer of 1894, workers at the Pullman Rail Car plant began to organize and agitate. The nationwide depression in 1894 had resulted in reduced wages for Pullman workers, but neither rents nor other expenses charged to those who lived in the wholly company-owned neighborhood were adjusted. By early May, some 35 percent of Pullman workers joined the American Railway Union. Negotiations between workers and management failed, and a strike began on May 11.

The union organized a Strike Relief Committee and Mayor Hopkins's store donated goods worth $1,500 to aid those on strike and $1,000 in cash (about $52,472 and $34,981 in 2023). Other Kensington merchants followed the mayor's lead. This increased public support for the workers and even the *Chicago Daily News* donated a store for use by the union. Hopkins also contributed the use of a seven-room apartment and issued a proclamation encouraging Chicagoans to provide money, food, and clothing to the strikers. He also allowed the police to raise funds for the strike committee.

The strike disrupted delivery of the US mail, rendering the conflict a federal affair. The situation escalated, with federal troops brought in over Hopkins's objections to protect Pullman's trains and, ultimately, end the strike. While Hopkins's reputation survived the

Pullman tragedy, the event, along with the national depression, hurt the Democratic Party.[12]

This made it all the harder for Hopkins to build a citywide machine. Clout played a central role in Sullivan and Hopkins's efforts, but immigrant communal culture further shaped them. Hopkins and Sullivan, both devout Irish Catholics, had grown up in a world that would be recognizable in the halls of De La Salle Institute and other Catholic educational institutions as well as on the streets of Bridgeport and the Near West Side. This world would also be familiar to Irish, Polish, German, and other Catholic immigrant groups.

Both Sullivan and Hopkins operated successful businesses, as many politicians of their generation did, but additional cultural factors powered their political ideas. Clout certainly meant financial gain, but it also meant protection for their community. If someone could create a citywide organization—a machine—to focus on issues and values that working-class and immigrant neighborhoods inherently felt to be important, such as a sense of community with the Catholic Church or the synagogue at the center and a flourishing ethnic culture, then a new kind of protective relational politics could emerge. For these newcomers to industrial capitalism and Anglo-Saxon democracy, political clout also meant a chance for advancement beyond being cheap labor in the city's factories, sweatshops, and slaughterhouses.

Sullivan, Hopkins, and other Chicago politicians walked a fine line between legality and illegality, between so-called "honest graft" and boodle. "Honest graft" meant profit that, while not overtly illegal, depended on political clout. The Ogden Gas Scandal, in which Sullivan and Hopkins were involved, captured the difficulties of negotiating this fine line. The scandal would be a black mark on the Hopkins administration and the city for years to come, fomenting political outrage toward public corruption. The affair rocked Chicago and shed light on the often fraught relationship between private companies and city government. It illustrates the growing pains of the Chicago machine.[13]

In the spring of 1895, the City Council voted on franchises for two companies: the Ogden Gas Company and the Cosmopolitan Electric

Company. Most observers felt that these two companies existed only to compel their purchase by local utility monopolies. The providers of gas and electricity were induced to pay the usual bribes to aldermen in order to obtain a vote that would give them the franchise. Sullivan emerged as the chief operating officer of both enterprises.

After blocking several other attempts to set up false franchises, Hopkins had gained a reputation as a modest reformer, while the aldermen retained their reputation as boodlers. Everyone expected the mayor to lead the fight against these attempts at creating phony franchises. In mid-February 1895, Hopkins announced he would not run again for the mayoralty, citing his business interests and health problems. He said he also planned to travel.[14] Shortly thereafter, the City Council granted a franchise to the Ogden Gas Company, run by Sullivan and others, by a vote of 61–4. Mayor Hopkins immediately left for New Orleans with a small retinue and did not veto the granting of the franchises.[15]

The whole scheme seemed suspicious. Gas Trust officials said they did not even know who to deal with in regard to the Ogden Gas Company. One insider claimed that the mayor hated the Gas Trust and wanted to support his friends' franchise endeavors. The Gas Trust and the utility barons initially refused to bow to the scheme. After a few years, however, the Ogden Gas Company, with Roger Sullivan as its president, actually began to provide gas to the city. In February 1907, the Ogden Gas Company finally merged with the Peoples Gas, Light, and Coke Company. Sullivan made a considerable profit on the transaction.[16]

In early April, Mayor Hopkins made a sort of farewell tour of City Hall officials and employees. He walked through the building shaking hands with everyone from chief clerks to janitors and wishing them well. When he left, a crowd of about fifty men followed him. Hopkins spent the summer in Europe and never ran for public office again. He did remain very involved in Democratic politics, working with Sullivan to attempt to control the party, until he died in 1918, leaving behind a considerable fortune. Sullivan followed him less than two years later, also leaving a substantial fortune. Neither Sullivan nor Hopkins hesitated to use their political clout to gain wealth. Chicago politicians certainly benefited from what some called honest as well as dishonest graft.[17]

DEMOGRAPHIC AND TECHNOLOGICAL CHANGE

The twentieth century brought many changes to Chicago. Before the outbreak of World War I, the city remained a haven for European immigrants. In 1901, Germans still made up the largest immigrant group, but the eastern European Slavic and Jewish neighborhoods continued to grow. The Czechs began to arrive in large numbers before 1870 and acted as a kind of bridge for their fellow Slavs and a new wave from eastern and southern Europe. This demographic and cultural transformation affected the development of clout in outlying neighborhoods. Czechs and Poles proved especially adept at creating an institutional base that led to considerable political power. They became political allies in the immediate post–Civil War years, and their alliance continued to grow, especially during the World War I era.[18]

At the time of the First World War, Czech neighborhoods spread across the Southwest Side. Czechs originally settled to the south of what would be Lincoln Park, but they soon moved in large part to the Near West Side in a neighborhood known as Praha or Little Prague. Here, despite religious and ideological divisions as Catholics, Protestants, Jews, and Freethinkers, Czechs built various institutions. In the first half of the twentieth century, the Freethinker faction, a group of Czechs who had broken with the Catholic Church and thought that belief should be based on logic and reason rather than tradition, revelation, or dogma, made up the largest group in the community. The Czechs then moved to Pilsen and to what became known as Czech California (Little Village).[19]

The Great Migration, another important demographic change that began during World War I, drew African Americans from the South to northern industrial centers as the war cut off the supply of cheap European immigrant labor. This influx had a tremendous impact on the city's economic, cultural, and political structure. The African American population had been growing for some time, but after 1915 the Black population in Chicago increased enormously. From 1890 to 1915, it grew from about 15,000 to over 50,000. By 1920 the number doubled again. This brought increased racial hostility and fighting in the public schools and on the streets, and the racial segregation of neighborhoods grew as well. It also resulted in the 1919 Chicago race riot, which rocked the city and established housing patterns in the city for generations.

Like other ethnic groups, African Americans attempted to build their own city in the middle of Chicago. They created institutions, businesses, and fraternal groups in the area that they later christened Bronzeville, and began to develop power within the Republican Party. Black leaders saw the growing number of migrants as a source of voters, and therefore of clout. African Americans had been largely denied the vote in the South, but in Chicago they might give the Republican Party permanent dominance. In addition, because of racism, Black Chicagoans could not easily move out of the emerging ghetto; as a consequence, these voters did not disperse across the cityscape, which might have diffused their political power.[20]

Other changes were to things rather than people. The pace of technological transformation accelerated after 1900. While railroads and steam power symbolized the nineteenth century, the internal combustion engine, electricity, and advancements in communication shaped the new century. These made a centralized political machine more possible. Chicago's politics had long resisted centralized control as local politicians ran their own organizations and dominated their wards. But technological change enabled City Hall to exert more and more control. Stricter control of patronage proved important, especially as the workforce employed by the city expanded. The telephone made communications between City Hall and the wards faster and in some ways more ominous. Threats and rewards could be delivered quickly, and wards could be flooded at election time with political operatives if aldermen and committeemen did not cooperate. The automobile made the personal delivery of power even more potent.

Progressive reforms also transformed the political structure of the city, contributing—perhaps unintentionally—to politicians' efforts to build a machine. In 1909, the architects and pioneer city planners Daniel Burnham and Edward Bennett put forth a visionary Plan for the City of Chicago that they hoped would restructure the urban world in progressive ways. Most saw the public works encouraged by the 1909 plan as positive. At the same time, the plan provided substantial opportunity for politicians to dole out contracts, hire workers and control the flow of public monies. Chicago mayors embraced the urban plan as a way to extend their power base and create what they hoped would be a lasting political machine.[21]

YOUNG CARTER

The Democratic Party held its 1896 presidential convention in Chicago's Auditorium Theater. The split between Gold and Silver Democrats broke out early, creating a rift in the party. William Jennings Bryan's "Cross of Gold" speech in support of free silver electrified the convention and gained him the nomination. But Gold Democrats then left the party and held their own convention, nominating Senator John M. Palmer of Illinois for the presidency. During the ensuing campaign, Bryan went down in defeat to Republican nominee William McKinley.[22]

By early 1897, Carter H. Harrison IV, commonly known as "Young Carter," decided to run for mayor of Chicago. Democratic supporters pointed out that he inspired positive memories of his father. They called him the eldest son of Chicago's favorite citizen, whom they claimed he resembled in "stability, strength of character, and utter independence." Young Carter, while never previously a candidate, had long been active in Democratic politics. He worked in campaigns and had been a party organizer, a club man, and a delegate.

Various other Democrats vied for the mayoral nomination, including Judge John Barton Payne. Many doubted the wisdom of Payne's nomination given that he held membership in the anti-immigrant American Protective Association, opposed organized labor, and did not support silver as the basis of the economy. Alfred S. Trude, a shrewd lawyer and political operative, had reportedly turned down the nomination and supported Payne. Trude had long been an ally of

Mike McDonald, the influential gambling and political boss who had backed Harrison Sr. in the 1880s. Former Governor John Peter Altgeld, the head of the party, remained uncommitted. Over the next few weeks, the race took many twists and turns. The powerful and notorious West Side alderman John Powers quickly came out in support of Harrison, as did many other Democrats, including the infamous duo who had replaced McDonald as leaders of the 1st Ward, "Bathhouse" John Coughlin and Michael "Hinky Dink" Kenna.[23]

Judge Payne sought William Jennings Bryan's endorsement, but the William Jennings Bryan League soon voted to support Harrison. Many Democrats planned to wait until Party Chairman Thomas Gahan returned from Mexico to see whom he would back. These divisions in the Democratic Party's ranks might have spelled trouble for the general election, but the Republicans still seemed demoralized and divided. Some Democrats rebelled against the Harrison faction, claiming that he could not unite the Gold and Silver Democrats, leading to a Republican victory. In turn, the Populist Party, which supported free silver, planned to nominate Harrison and force the Democrats' hand. The Silver Democrats also planned to nominate the younger Harrison.[24]

Trude, Altgeld, Payne, and Harrison danced around one another. Gahan finally supported Trude and said Altgeld did, too. Altgeld promptly denied the claim. Trude decided to quit, but his backers convinced him to stay in until they could make a deal with Harrison. Trude's envoys made several demands of Harrison. They asked to control three posts in his administration: the Commissioner of Public Works, Chief of Police, and Corporation Counsel. Harrison promised fair treatment on ordinary patronage, but he insisted on control of his cabinet. Trude quit the race, and Payne's run also ended. The Municipal Voters League, an organization founded to elect honest aldermen in 1896, moved against Harrison with the same complaints that had haunted his father, plus some new ones.

On March 10, 1897, the Democrats met at the Tremont House for what the *Chicago Daily News* referred to as a "Love Fest." The next day, they nominated Harrison for mayor at the North Side Turner

Hall. Bathhouse John Coughlin, alderman of the 1st Ward, when called upon to make a nomination, gave way for the representative of the 32nd Ward. Trude stood to make the nominating speech. The crowd welcomed him with an ovation. After a long speech, in about a dozen words he nominated Harrison. Every ward committeeman then also endorsed Harrison. Coughlin and several other Democrats proposed that the nomination be made by acclamation.[25]

Harrison began his campaign by stating that if elected he "would not sanction a puritanical administration of affairs," an attack on one of his four opponents in the general election, Judge Nathanial C. Sears, a Republican. The *Chicago Inter Ocean* claimed that this signaled that he would allow unrestricted gambling and reimpose the "illegal tax" (bribes) on these establishments by politicians and the police. The *Chicago Chronicle* came to the judge's defense and accused unnamed former mayors of looking the other way after receiving "hush" money from gamblers, an obvious reference to Harrison's father.

As the campaign proceeded, a rather bizarre affair took place. Nineteenth Ward Alderman John Powers attended the James J. Corbett and Robert J. Fitzsimmons boxing match in Carson City, Nevada on St. Patrick's Day. Fitzsimmons knocked out Gentleman Jim in the fourteenth round. The winner won two eagles, one named Corbett, the other Fitzsimmons. In turn, Fitzsimmons gave the eagles to Alderman Powers to be presented to Harrison, whose father had been called "The Eagle."[26]

Like his father, Harrison played the ethnic card. Powers's very diverse 19th Ward enthusiastically supported him. The *Chronicle* made fun of the immigrants who populated the ward, but Chinese, Italian, Greek, Bohemian, Polish, Jewish, French, German, and Irish voters all rallied around Young Carter. At a rally, the candidate, like his father before him, addressed each group in their own language, even uttering a greeting in Gaelic for the Irish. He campaigned throughout the city. On April 6, 1897, voters elected Carter H. Harrison IV mayor by a plurality of 75,434 votes as the Democrats swept the election. He became the first Chicago-born mayor of the city.[27]

CHAPTER 4

Cyclist campaign poster in 1897.
"Not the Champion Cyclist but the Cyclists' Champion."

4.2 1897 Carter Harrison campaign poster. Unlike his father, who rode a horse over Chicago's streets, Harrison favored the bicycle. From Carter H. Harrison, *The Stormy Years: The Autobiography of Carter H. Harrison* (New York: Bobbs-Merrill Company, 1935).

Of the various issues Harrison faced during his first term, two would haunt him: civil service reform and the transit franchise issue. The first would see him caught between many of his supporters and municipal reformers. In fact, the civil service issue also saw him go to war with Adolph Kraus, his father's old ally and business partner. The other would pit him against Charles Tyson Yerkes and the boodle politicians. His political future hung in the balance. These issues would plague more than one mayor of Chicago.

PATRONAGE AND THE TRACTION ISSUE

Throughout the late nineteenth century, activists pursued civil service reform and the end of patronage. Many saw patronage as a corruption of the body politic. Of course, most politicians understood it as a "just reward" for their efforts, a resource to guarantee the loyalty of those they hired and their extended families. The ethnic groups that had rallied behind Harrison demanded their share of patronage as one part of their communal response to the industrial city. The great majority of citizens saw patronage as an opportunity and a right. "To the winner goes the spoils" had been practiced from time immemorial. Of course, it did have its downsides. In 1881, Charles Guiteau, a disappointed office seeker, assassinated President Garfield. Patrick Prendergast, also a disappointed office seeker, had done the same to Harrison's father. These assassinations gave impetus to the civil service reform movement, but patronage and clout remained the bone and sinew of the communal response and of the slowly emerging citywide political machine. Simply put, clout meant power.

Harrison supporters Bobbie Burke and John Powers claimed that the Civil Service Law, passed under the previous Republican mayor, unfairly hurt the Democrats. Per that law, on August 16, 1897, civil service-eligible persons would replace the 1,000 so-called sixty-day appointees of the Democrats. These Democrats worked for the city outside of the Civil Service regulations as "temporary" patronage workers. Rumor had it that the Harrison administration wanted to avoid the switchover. Harrison had appointed Adolph Kraus to the Civil Service Board of Commissioners, and board members elected him president. That Board might, at Harrison's urging, assert that the eligible list needed revision and in the meantime extend the time of service of the temporary appointees. This could delay the changeover until a challenge to the law could reach the Illinois Supreme Court, which Corporation Counsel Charles S. Thornton felt confident would find the law unconstitutional. Harrison himself favored the reformist law, but the interests of his party increasingly pushed him to oppose it. In many ways, Harrison found himself caught between the reformers he somewhat favored and the Regular Democrats who had powerful ward machines. Again, the sacred and the profane came into conflict.

Board President Kraus apparently wanted to resign but believed he had to see the matter through to its end. Alderman Powers threatened that the City Council might defund the commission. On August 10, Harrison claimed that he planned to treat the list of eligible candidates fairly. In fact, supporters and friends constantly besieged Harrison with requests for patronage jobs. Even William Jennings Bryan, although he claimed not to, petitioned Harrison to give a position to his wife's distant relative.[28]

During the previous administration, a large number of policemen, known as the Star League, had been removed for political purposes. Superintendent of Police Joseph Kipley, a Harrison appointee, now planned to replace about 500 to 600 police officers—likely Republicans—with Star League members who passed the civil service examination. But they had been rejected by medical examiners under the leadership of Dr. William Cuthbertson. The *Chicago Tribune* reported that Harrison had sent a letter to Kraus just before taking a trip to Lake Superior, asking that the commission replace Cuthbertson with Dr. J. M. Walsh. Kraus denied getting the letter and furthermore refused to remove Cuthbertson as long as he did a good job.

More than 900 members of the Star League revolted against the Harrison administration. During the last municipal election, the Star League had developed into the most powerful independent political organization in the city and had more than 1,000 members work every ward to secure Harrison's election. At that time, Kipley, a seventeen-year veteran of the police force, served as organizer and president of the club, as well as president of the 4th Ward Democratic Club. In these roles, he controlled roughly 180 votes at the Democratic nominating convention. The Star League conditioned their support for Harrison on Kipley becoming Superintendent of Police, as well as a promise that all those given positions under the previous Republican administration be dismissed and replaced by loyal Star League Democrats.

A virtual civil war broke out in City Hall not only over the Star League, which obviously expected to have influence in the Harrison administration, but among Democrats in general who depended on patronage to fuel campaigns. Several members of Harrison's cabinet threatened to resign if the mayor did not remove Kraus. If Kraus and his advocates left, then Harrison would be under pressure to appoint men that his City Hall supporters Burke and Powers would approve of, thus handing control of the commission over to them.

By the end of August 1897, the situation began to show signs of compromise. Apparently, Bobbie Burke had ordered his supporters to give up the struggle—probably in order to keep the Harrison coalition intact. To some it seemed as if the spoils system had been dealt a death blow. Many also predicted that this doomed Harrison politically because he could not deliver patronage for his party. Harrison's supporters contended that he had appointed enough Democrats to hold onto the organization. Harrison's enemies in the party continued to coalesce around the Gahan-Trude-Jones faction and the John P. Hopkins and Roger C. Sullivan Gold Democrats, who looked for any slip by the mayor as a reason to remove him. To say the least, former Mayor Hopkins and his ally Sullivan held a considerable amount of power in the Democratic organization. Alderman Coughlin, a proponent of the mayor's, led the City Council and hoped to knock the merit system out and save Harrison's political future.[29]

While Harrison was on vacation, the Civil Service Commission fired Henry Lutzenkirchen, Secretary of the Department of Public Works. A member of the Bobbie Burke machine and the Democratic Party organization, Lutzenkirchen, a German American, claimed that someone working for the commission had asked for a bribe. The commission summoned him to testify about his allegation, but he defied the order. The commission then ordered him discharged from his position and informed Public Works Commissioner Lawrence E. McGann that unless he obeyed the order, they would not approve the department payroll. Burke met with party officials in the mayor's office, and they determined to force the mayor to take their side and give up his neutrality concerning the Civil Service Commission. McGann refused to enforce the commission's demand to fire Lutzenkirchen. Harrison tried to be diplomatic, stating that the commission did not have jurisdiction over Lutzenkirchen's position. He was attempting to give all sides a way out of the conflict. This implied that Kraus and the others should back down, but that the commission would remain in their hands.

On September 9, 1897, the *Chicago Tribune* reported that a settlement had been reached. Harrison announced that he had to enforce the Civil Service Law whether or not he agreed with it. The mayor and the commissioners now agreed that Lutzenkirchen was not under the commission's jurisdiction. The mayor promised that if Lutzenkirchen, or any of his other appointees, interfered with the work of the Commission they would be disciplined. Harrison further stated that he believed in a reasonable interpretation of the Civil Service Law and that when a doubt on technical points emerged Democrats should be favored. On the surface, it seemed that the matter had been decided amicably, with Harrison showing support for Kraus and the other commissioners. Kraus, however, remained enraged and threatened to have Lutzenkirchen charged with contempt if he refused to appear before the commission. Harrison said he had no intention of firing Kraus, but that the commissioner might well be putting himself in a dangerous political and legal position. Lutzenkirchen remained in office until the following year, when McGann dismissed him for being absent from his duties while doing political work for the Democrats. Harrison liked Lutzenkirchen, who continued to play a role throughout the mayor's various campaigns and administrations, but the issue of patronage continued to haunt him.[30]

Adolph Kraus found his term as president of the Civil Service Commission to be one long agonizing trial. While the State Supreme Court upheld the Civil Service Law in December 1897, in February 1898 Kraus resigned, along with two more commissioners. They and others were then indicted by a grand jury for alleged violations of the Civil Service Law. (The charges stated that they had allowed the hiring of a policeman who stood at just under five feet eight inches, the minimum height requirement.) While they were found not guilty, the commission that had given Harrison so much trouble had been neutered. While the politicians had basically won, the issue remained contentious for the rest of the century.[31]

Another major conflict during Harrison's first administration involved the private companies that provisioned municipal public transportation, known as the "traction franchise." The new streetcar companies would have to lay tracks on Chicago's streets, for which they would need City Council to grant them a franchise.

The issue had deep roots. The first horsedrawn streetcars appeared on Chicago's streets in 1859. In 1866, the three companies serving the North, South, and West Sides of the city joined in asking the state legislature to extend the life of their franchises to ninety-nine years, instead of the previously granted twenty-five years. The legislature overrode a veto by Governor Richard Yates to enact the proposal, which had obviously been "greased" by money from the companies. However, under the Cities and Villages Act such franchises could only be legally granted by the city itself and then for only twenty years. Although the ninety-nine-year act did not expressly extend the rights of the streetcar lines to the city streets, their management would claim that it did. In 1883, Carter Harrison III approved extending the franchises of the three companies by twenty years. At the same time, it became increasingly obvious that horsecar lines could not satisfy Chicago's growing need for safe, reliable public transportation. Cable cars proved to be a temporary solution. On January 17, 1880, the City Council granted the Chicago City Railways permission to operate cable cars. The conversion began on State Street in August 1881.[32]

Charles Tyson Yerkes, the savvy financier from Philadelphia, arrived in Chicago that year and quickly became involved in the transit business. He secured majority control of the North and West Side companies and adopted the cable car system. Soon, the Transit King owned twelve traction companies, in addition to gas and electric interests with handsome privileges in the city's outlying regions. Yerkes sought to completely rule the city's streets, but he grew weary of the various hoops he had to jump through in the City Council to get block-by-block privileges.

CHAPTER 4

A few days before the 1897 mayoral election, Yerkes went to the state legislature armed with cash and had Senator John Humphrey introduce three bills to create a state commission empowered to give street franchises in all streets of the cities of Illinois. The bills basically robbed Chicago of home rule. Instead of taxes, the companies would pay the state 3 percent of their gross earnings, a benefit of millions of dollars for Yerkes. The passage of the Humphrey bills immediately caused consternation in Chicago. Good-government reformers cried robbery, while the aldermen saw a boodle bonanza vanishing. Forming an odd alliance, they joined forces to fight the legislation. Harrison led the fight against Yerkes—bringing along both Bathhouse John Coughlin and Hinky Dink Kenna as reformers! Bathhouse John had long harbored a grudge against Yerkes, and he saw a chance to shine as a reformer while settling old scores against both Yerkes and his aldermanic point man, John Powers.

While the furor ended with the Humphrey bills' defeat, Yerkes soon had his supporters introduce the Allen bill into the state legislature. This legislation recognized the right of Chicago's aldermen to sell the rights to the city's streets. It empowered them to issue franchises of fifty years instead of twenty and eliminated any compensation for the city. That amounted to a loss for the city of $150,000,000 (some $5.4 billion in 2023 dollars) in revenue. The Gray Wolves didn't say no; but the extravagant bribe they demanded shocked even Yerkes. He suddenly departed for Europe to let the aldermen ponder their options.

In the spring of 1898, voters elected new supporters of Yerkes to the City Council, and his ally Powers again controlled the body. Powers placed choice men on various committees where they could smooth efforts to pass pro-Yerkes legislation. In June, the Cook County Republican Convention called for repeal of the Allen Law. By July 1898, rumors spread that Yerkes hoped to act and pass the legislation quickly. Yerkes company stocks soared in anticipation. Aldermen demanded payments of up to $75,000 ($2,718,434) apiece. Yerkes refused, and when the council met the topic did not come up. The next day, Yerkes's stock crashed. Nevertheless, Yerkes then purchased the *Chicago Inter Ocean* newspaper and used it to attack his enemies.

On December 5, 1898, Alderman W. H. Lyman, a Yerkes supporter, introduced an ordinance granting a fifty-year extension to the Transit King's franchises. Yerkes attempted to buy off Aldermen Coughlin and Kenna, sending emissaries to both of their Loop saloons. His allies offered money and jobs, but the two aldermen did not concede. Harrison took the fight to the neighborhoods, making speeches in wards across the city, including a rally in the Central Music Hall in the heart of the Loop. Angry citizens filled the council chambers on December 12 and yelled insults at the Yerkes aldermen. In the end, the franchise extension ordinance failed. Thirty-eight aldermen had backed the mayor, and the council could not override a mayoral veto. The anti-Yerkes people cheered. Coughlin received much of the congratulations. Powers, however, did not give up. The Yerkes forces led by Edward Cullerton moved that the Lyman bill be sent to the Committee on Railways, which was controlled by pro-Yerkes aldermen.

Powers bragged that the bill would come out of committee and easily pass. Hinky Dink Kenna, however, sat on the Committee on Railways, and the usually silent 1st Ward alderman tied up the committee sessions with a series of questions and speeches. Powers called a sudden meeting of the Joint Committee on Streets and Alleys, where pro-Yerkes aldermen drew up a substitute bill. The new bill seemed to satisfy the opponents of Yerkes by extending the franchise for twenty-five years instead of fifty and providing the city with considerable revenue. It seemed that Harrison had won on the substance, but the mayor still insisted on a twenty-year franchise. He also said that no legislation should be passed until the Illinois state legislature had a chance to meet in January. He seemed determined to drive Yerkes out of town.

When the City Council met on December 19, 1898, a series of legal maneuvers sent both the original Lyman bill and its substitute to the Committee on City Hall, an obscure committee to which Powers had banished leading Harrison supporters. This move placed the two measures under the control of the Harrison forces. The motion

CHAPTER 4

HARRISON HAS THE GRIP.

Courtesy *Chicago Herald and Examiner* (*Times-Herald*).

Cartoon by Charles Lederer.

4.3 Editorial cartoon. Harrison is portrayed as taking care of both Yerkes and the boodle aldermen who supported him in his struggle with the mayor over the transit issue. From Carter H. Harrison, *The Stormy Years: The Autobiography of Carter H. Harrison* (New York: Bobbs-Merrill Company, 1935).

passed by one vote. Three weeks later the state legislature killed the Allen Law, which had been the basis of Yerkes's efforts to control transit in Chicago. Bathhouse John and Hinky Dink had gained Harrison's friendship, and in turn he gained their support—for the time being.[33]

Yerkes left town in 1900 and eventually settled in England, where he began construction of the London "Tube" or subway. Still, Yerkes's departure did not resolve the city's transit issues. The major transit franchises would expire in 1903, and the companies expected to assert their ninety-nine-year rights under the 1865 law. Most reform organizations favored a swift settlement of the issue. Harrison stubbornly refused, citing five essential conditions for a settlement: a marked improvement in speed, comfort, and safety; adequate compensation to the city for using the public byways; the relinquishing of any claims to a ninety-nine-year franchise; a provision for eventual municipal ownership; and a referendum on the final settlement. The struggle dragged on, and the public grew tired of what they saw as Harrison's delays. Many demanded immediate municipal ownership of transit, especially after the passing of the 1903 Mueller Law, which allowed any city in Illinois to own and operate street railways. In 1907, the Illinois Supreme Court vindicated Harrison's approach and overruled the ninety-nine-year franchise act. The 1907 City Council ordinances embodied many of Harrison's ideas.

The historian Edward R. Kantowicz has called Carter Harrison IV a progressive reformer because of his support of many of the goals of civic betterment. However, while Young Carter championed some reform goals, he ignored others. A better characterization might be to call Harrison a type of reform political boss, much like his father. For example, Young Carter relied on the support of politicians like Bathhouse John Coughlin and Hinky Dink Kenna, who could hardly be called reformers. Harrison relied on machine methods to win elections but also pursued reform goals that he saw as benefiting urban society. Such reforms included the extension of city services to keep up with growth, track elevation that cut down on railroad accidents and the deaths of many children, and the insistence that private contractors provide honest and efficient service. The latter included stricter control over franchises. He called for honest government and sometimes worked with the Municipal Voters League to ensure an honest City Council, and he opposed the efforts of the Hopkins–Sullivan faction of the Democratic Party because they hoped for permanent dominance over the Party. In many ways, Young Carter had the same goals his father had. While the second Harrison, an avid bicyclist, did not ride around the city on a chestnut-colored horse as his father did, he did take a particular interest in the streets and alleys of Chicago. He too was a hands-on mayor, a quality his successors would emulate.[34]

CHAPTER 4

Both Harrisons considered drinking, gambling, and prostitution to be long-standing social evils. And yet neither saw the pleasures of the beer garden and the brasserie as sinful. They understood that Chicago's large immigrant populations, for the most part, opposed the prohibition of liquor. Harrison put himself on the side of those who later would be called "Wets" in the long struggle over Prohibition. This endeared him to many of the city's immigrant and ethnic groups, who saw the prohibiting of alcohol as part of a larger anti-immigrant and anti-Catholic program. Harrison's stand and those of other Democratic politicians helped to bring these immigrant and ethnic groups into the Democratic Party.[35]

Both Harrisons' travels and other life experiences exposed them to Roman Catholic sensibilities and culture. Young Carter attended a Jesuit school, had many Catholic friends, married a Catholic wife, and raised his children in the faith. In 1900, he even considered putting a Catholic priest on the Chicago School Board, but Archbishop Patrick Feehan would not allow it. Young Carter appointed a Catholic woman, Mrs. Meeder, to the office of Superintendent of Public Welfare, and the Archdiocesan Vicar-General personally thanked him. This understanding of and interaction with Catholic culture gave Harrison Jr. a means for connecting with the growing Catholic ethnic communities.[36]

Harrison won four consecutive terms, but like his father, he failed to create a citywide political machine that could guarantee Democratic Party ascendancy. In 1905 he decided to retire, and the Democratic nomination went to Edward F. Dunne, an Irish Catholic, who went on to beat Republican John Maynard Harlan. In 1911 Harrison returned to the mayoral scene. Like his father, he won a fifth term. Unlike his father, he would serve his out. During that term, Harrison moved against the Levee; closed the Everleigh Club, a fashionable house of prostitution; and became more of a moral reformer than his father. The breakup of the Levee as a segregated vice district meant that prostitution and gambling spread throughout the city.

This led to a break with Coughlin and Kenna and contributed to Harrison's defeat in the 1915 Democratic primary by Robert Sweitzer. Harrison maintained that Sweitzer had used Harrison's membership in the Masonic Lodge against him in Catholic neighborhoods, and had used his wife and children's Catholicism against him in Protestant neighborhoods. Harrison himself maintained no religious affiliation. He also asserted that Sweitzer used his German ethnicity as a weapon even though, unlike Harrison, he did not speak German. In June 1914, at the unveiling of the Goethe Monument in Lincoln Park, Harrison praised Chicago's Germans and lauded the community's virtues—steadiness, energy, perseverance, and ambition. Harrison spoke of their work ethic, their love of liberty, and their thriftiness. Nevertheless, when a German American candidate opposed him, especially during a time of war, the community voted against their erstwhile friend. Furthermore, Sweitzer had somehow been elected to the Ancient Order of Hibernians, and this caused many of Chicago's Irish to favor him.

The Woodrow Wilson administration had already begun to show hostility to Germany as war raged in Europe. Harrison failed to win a sixth term and had been unable to gain control of the entire Democratic Party in Chicago. Like his father he had played the ethnic and religious cards successfully throughout much of his public career, but in the end Chicago's changing ethnic and religious demographics and changing economy meant his defeat.[37]

In the general election, Republican William Hale Thompson defeated Sweitzer and eventually won three non-consecutive terms as mayor, almost creating a viable citywide Republican political machine based largely on native-born White Protestant voters and African Americans. Harrison remained a notable figure in the Democratic Party, but his power waned quickly. Harrison's balancing act between the sacred and the profane, between reform and clout, could carry him only so far.

5
A Republican Protestant Proto-Machine

> I have been maligned. I have been misunderstood. I hope in the ensuing four years to be understood. I want to make Chicago a great city, the summer resort of the United States. I want to build her a lakefront, to finish widening the streets and building bridges. I love this city.
>
> **WILLIAM HALE THOMPSON**
> on winning his second term in 1919[1]

William Hale Thompson took the oath of office as mayor of Chicago on April 26, 1915, and ushered in almost two decades of political transformation. Changes rooted in the ethnic and racial makeup of Chicago, as well as in technology, culture, and even international politics, shifted political allegiances. This upheaval saw the political life of the city permanently altered and reshaped in a way that few understood at first, but whose seeds had been first planted after the Great Fire. The two Harrisons and their Democratic rivals, Roger C. Sullivan and John P. Hopkins, had aimed to create a centralized, city-wide Democratic political machine but failed. Thompson and Chicago's Republicans now also attempted to build such an organization, in the wake of the chaos and ethnic tensions unleashed by the First World War.

CHAPTER 5

WILLIAM HALE THOMPSON

In 1881, as a fourteen-year-old, William Hale Thompson Jr. led a group of companions on horseback across the State Street bridge in pursuit of an imaginary Indian war party. The bridge attendants did not appreciate the boys' game. A scuffle ensued, and police arrested Thompson and his friends. The elder William Hale Thompson intervened with Mayor Harrison and secured the younger's release. A year later, the younger Thompson left Chicago, made his way to Cheyenne, Wyoming, working as an assistant brakeman on a railroad, and then got a job on a nearby ranch. Over the next six years he attended a business school in Chicago during the winter and lived in the West the rest of the year. In 1888, his father purchased a 3,800-acre ranch in Nebraska and named him the manager, where for three years he enjoyed the life of a rancher.[2]

In 1892, after his father's death, the twenty-five-year-old Thompson returned to Chicago to manage the considerable estate. The elder Thompson had dealt in Chicago real estate, including the Thompson Block on West Madison Street. In 1877 and 1878 he had represented his district in the state legislature as a Republican. His family had a long history of public service and of investing in real estate. His maternal grandfather, Stephen F. Gale, helped to draw up the city's 1837 charter.

Embracing his family's status, William Hale Thompson Jr. played the part of an upper-class Chicagoan. He captained the champion Chicago Athletic Association football team, served as the club's athletic director, and was elected vice president of the organization.[3] Thompson's athletic physique and abilities earned him the moniker "Big Bill."

Thompson took up residence at the Hotel Metropole on 23rd Street and Michigan Avenue in the city's 2nd Ward. At that time, two aldermen represented each ward. In 1900, his friend and roommate, 2nd Ward Alderman Gene Pike, encouraged Thompson to run as a Republican for the other seat. At first Thompson refused, but he later decided to run and won the election. He embraced progressive reforms including civil service reform and municipal ownership of public transit.[4]

The young alderman quickly made a major political mistake. Democrats Michael "Hinky Dink" Kenna and "Bathhouse" John Coughlin had helped Thompson win the 2nd Ward by denying William F. Gunther, a fellow Democrat, the "flop house" vote. After Mayor Harrison moved to break up the original Levee and vice moved south of the Loop, where it again began to thrive, Gunther had refused to cooperate with the 1st Ward leaders in their efforts to control the expanding vice district. Once Thompson was elected, they convinced him that the new Levee should be brought into their ward and therefore under their control. Despite being outmaneuvered by Coughlin and Kenna, Thompson made good use of his two-year term. He sponsored the city's first municipal playground in a predominantly African American section of his ward. He used this to his political advantage with the burgeoning Black community. The following year found Thompson and his new wife living in the expanded 1st Ward. Some thought he might take on "Bathhouse" John Coughlin for alderman, but fortunately for the young politician, he did not.[5]

THE BLOND BOSS

William Lorimer, known as "the Blond Boss," an English immigrant with considerable power in the Republican Party, convinced Thompson to run not against Coughlin but for Cook County commissioner. Lorimer, who faced a challenge from downstate Republicans, received sound counsel from one of his followers, Fred Lundin. Lundin, who had been a patent medicine seller, advised Lorimer to "get a tent": forget the issues and put on a show. Lorimer's tent shows traveled throughout Cook County, delighting crowds with circus-like entertainments. William Hale Thompson quickly learned the tricks of political oratory from people like Lorimer and won the 1902 election for Cook County commissioner.[6]

As Lorimer's power grew, he sought election to the US Senate, which was at the time handled by the state assembly. Surprisingly, he drew a good deal of Democratic support and was elected. Almost a year later, Democratic State Representative Charles A. White confessed that Lorimer had bribed him. Soon various other representatives also admitted to taking bribes from what turned out to be a $100,000 slush fund. Thompson organized the Blaine Club to raise money for Lorimer's defense. Late in 1911, Lorimer and his followers drew up a slate for the 1912 election, including Thompson for the Cook County Board of Review. The Lorimerites went down, soundly defeated. Moreover, in July 1912 the US Senate ousted Lorimer. When the despondent Lorimer returned to Illinois, Thompson organized a celebratory parade through Loop streets and a vast gathering of supporters at Orchestra Hall. Lorimer, however, lost control of his organization and Lundin took over. Thompson's loyalty and campaign abilities impressed Lundin, and Big Bill's star continued to rise within the Republican Party.[7]

MAYOR THOMPSON

In 1915, Thompson ran for the mayoralty. The remnants of the Lorimer machine supported him, but a large progressive faction did not. These Republicans saw Thompson as a tool of Lorimer and Lundin. Their candidate, Chief Justice Harry Olson of Chicago's Municipal Court, faced him in the primary. The judge also filed petitions for the Progressive Party nomination, as did Congressman Charles M. Thomson, who announced that should Olson gain the Republican nomination he would withdraw as the Progressive primary candidate. With the opposition in place, Thompson's campaign kicked into high gear.

Republican women organized the William Hale Thompson Women's Club, taking advantage of their new enfranchisement for municipal elections. They began a series of "soap box" speeches led by Mrs. Kathryn Rutherford. On the night of January 31, Mrs. Rutherford took part in an automobile procession led by a band and an African American quartet singing campaign songs.[8]

Thompson and Olson charged each other with cronyism. Olson implied that Thompson would be a tool of Lorimer and Lundin, who had indeed handpicked Thompson. Thompson called Olson a "Jekyll and Hyde" character who handed down judicial decisions by day and made alliances with political machines and cliques at night. He claimed that Olson had a suspect pact with Anton J. Cermak, a rising Democratic star. More positively, Thompson celebrated the "I Will" spirit of Chicago (which implied Chicagoans could accomplish anything they set their mind to) and his long family connection with the city. He won by 2,500 votes in the primary. The *Chicago Daily News* credited the growing number of Black voters in the 2nd Ward for his victory.[9]

In the general election, many Progressives quickly fell in line for Thompson. He attracted a good deal of support from those largely Protestant immigrant groups from northern and western Europe. The Dovre Club, a Norwegian American good-government club, endorsed Thompson. The Progressive (Bull Moose) Party agreed to support, or at least not oppose, Thompson if he adhered to their principles. The Republican Cook County Committee formally endorsed Thompson in the race against Robert M. Sweitzer, who had defeated Carter Harrison IV in the Democratic primary.[10]

In the first election for mayor in which Chicago women could vote, they overwhelmingly voted for Thompson.[11] Thompson also won the majority of votes from various ethnic groups, including African American, Bohemian, German, Jewish, and Swedish voters, as well as 41 percent of the Italian vote and 45 percent of the Polish vote. Not surprisingly, the White Anglo-Saxon Protestants and the middle-class wards voted heavily for him. Thompson also benefited from Black voters' preference for the party of Lincoln. This coalition was formidable in 1915 and would remain so through much of the 1920s, a decade that proved to be a very Republican one in Chicago and across the nation.[12]

Throughout the campaign, both parties deployed ethnic and religious attacks. Thompson used the anti-Catholic card against both Olson and Sweitzer. Olson had a Catholic wife and Sweitzer held a high rank in the Catholic fraternal organization Knights of Columbus. A new organization called the Guardians of Liberty spread stories about Sweitzer in largely Protestant neighborhoods, claiming that if the German Democrat won the Pope would rule Chicago. Democrats spread the word in Catholic neighborhoods that every Masonic Lodge Hall functioned as a political headquarters for Thompson's campaign. Thompson denied that he had brought up the religious issue and blamed the Democrats.

Sweitzer's campaign emphasized his German ethnicity. Democrats passed out fliers in German neighborhoods with photographs of Kaiser Wilhelm and Emperor Franz Joseph claiming that a vote for Sweitzer would aid the German war cause. Republicans reprinted the fliers and distributed them in Polish and Czech districts, decrying Sweitzer. German and Polish gangs clashed across the city. Violence even erupted in the Loop. Both candidates held daily rallies in theaters next to each other, and there was conflict between Thompson supporters and Sweitzer supporters. Mayor Harrison sent police in, but many police also had political affiliations and found it impossible to quell the rioting.[13]

When Thompson took office on April 26, 1915, he ushered in an era of Republican dominance that he and his supporters hoped would lead to a permanent centralized organization and perhaps even the presidency. Because African Americans were an important part of that coalition, as his first act in office the new mayor signed an ordinance presented by African American Alderman Oscar De Priest to make August 23 a city holiday commemorating the end of slavery. Thompson also listened to Black demands and blocked city screenings of D. W. Griffith's racist movie, *The Birth of a Nation*. In September, Thompson addressed 22,000 Blacks attending the Lincoln Jubilee Exposition. He spoke of racism and how he had been condemned by many for reaching out to the Black community.[14]

Thompson's administration faced a terrible disaster on July 24. The *Eastland*, docked on the main branch of the Chicago River, had been chartered to take employees of the Western Electric Company's Hawthorne Works in Cicero, Illinois, to a picnic in Michigan City, Indiana. Many Czech and Polish Americans who lived on the Southwest Side of the city and in the industrial suburbs of Cicero and Berwyn worked at Western Electric. After the boat capsized, rescuers recovered the bodies of 884 passengers and four crew members—

5.1 *Eastland* disaster. Pictured here is the SS *Eastland* after it capsized in the Chicago River on July 24, 1915. Nearly 900 passengers died after the ship tipped over due to overcrowding. Western Electric Company employees had boarded the ship to attend a company picnic in Michigan City, Indiana. Postcard, Author's Collection.

far more fatalities than there had been in the Great Fire. Mourners took part in funeral processions throughout the city, especially in the neighborhoods of Pilsen and Czech California. Czech and Polish fraternal organizations as well as prominent ethnic businessmen and leaders rallied to help their compatriots. Thompson had been attending the Panama-Pacific Exposition in San Francisco but returned to the city to deal with the catastrophe.[15]

Yet even as the city mourned, that fall Thompson insulted the very communities that had suffered the most from the *Eastland* disaster. In October, breaking with a long-standing tradition, he moved to support the Illinois Blue Law, closing saloons on Sunday. The Protestant middle class responded enthusiastically. Charles E. Coleman, chairman of the Dry Chicago Federation, declared, "Mayor Thompson . . . can have anything he wants from the dry federation." Bishop Charles P. Anderson said most Chicagoans supported the mayor's decision. The Rev. Philip Yarrow organized a huge "Dry Parade" for Saturday, October 9, predicting 30,000 participants. Protestant min-

CHAPTER 5

isters called for prayers for General Superintendent of Police Charles C. Healey in enforcing the mayor's order. The Swedish newspaper, *Svenska Kuriren*, backed Thompson's actions.[16]

While Thompson's initiative risked European ethnic support, he was backed by African Americans. Black saloon owners said they would obey the order and continue to support Thompson. African American newspapers also supported the move and claimed that most Black Chicagoans did as well. Cass Harris, manager of the Elite Bar, said that even though the order would hurt his business, he supported Thompson because the mayor was "O.K. on the race question." Black pastors congratulated the mayor on the move. When Thompson returned to San Francisco to again attend the Panama-Pacific Exposition after his proclamation, he brought Alderman Oscar De Priest with him. And during a stop in Portland, Oregon, the mayor's party met with a delegation of African Americans who presented Thompson with a banner that called him the "Man of the Hour."[17]

Among those who did not support Thompson's decision, a storm erupted. Peter Badovinac, in Pilsen, vented, "There's only one day in the week for us, and that is Sunday. I think Thompson should be ashamed of himself." Michael Foy in Washington Park warned, "We're going out of business after the first of the month." One saloon patron in Woodlawn took out his revolver and shot Thompson's picture.[18]

The Czech newspaper, *Denní Hlasatel*, pointed out that many German and Czech saloonkeepers had supported Thompson's election and now felt betrayed. A saloonkeeper and alderman of the 24th Ward, John Haderlein, had warned his fellow Germans, pointing out that Thompson had preached prohibition in the neighborhoods of Lake View, Hyde Park, and Austin. The paper warned that the Sunday closing law would hurt about 85 percent of the city's saloons. The United Societies for Local Self-Government, led by Anton Cermak, released a letter from Thompson's campaign months earlier that had promised to oppose all blue laws and keep the saloons open on Sunday. The organization protested loudly against the closing order as an unjustified attack on personal liberty.[19]

At the end of October, police found seventy-five saloons in violation of the Sunday closing order, including thirteen owned by Czechs. The United Societies for Local Self-Government increased their pressure on Thompson. Their president, George Landau, and Cermak invited the mayor and his cabinet to attend a protest on Sunday, November 7. The United Societies planned to erect a reviewing stand on Washington Street directly across from City Hall—a clear effort to antagonize Thompson.

That day, numerous floats and marchers—many of them Germans, Italians, Poles, and Czechs—carried signs condemning the Sunday closings and extolling personal liberty. Czech organizations, both Catholics and Freethinkers, were there. Cermak, John Cervenka (Červenka—a politician who also headed the Pilsen Brewery), Congressman Adolph J. Sabath, and all of the Czech aldermen also participated. Between 69,000 and 75,000 Chicagoans took part in the demonstration, and it is said that 800,000 spectators watched.[20]

Enforcement of the blue laws was uneven at best, with some proprietors seeming to receive preferential treatment. Some saloons seemed to be ignored, while others saw their licenses quietly restored. Political pressure from Republican allies such as Albert A. Michaelson (Thompson's aldermanic floor leader), William Burkhardt (Thompson's brother-in-law and Deputy Commissioner of Public Works), and Oscar De Priest soon allowed politically connected bar owners to reopen. More ominously, Chicago's underworld quickly renewed their Levee operations. Big Jim Colosimo resumed operations at his Wabash Avenue resort, known for prostitution, with a minimum of police interference. Obviously, these men had considerable clout.[21]

In 1916, as Thompson entered his second year as mayor, a scandal further damaged his reputation. Dr. Theodore J. Sachs, a Jewish immigrant, had been named head of the Municipal Tuberculosis Sanitarium in 1913. Thompson and Health Commissioner John Dill Robertson charged the doctor with various irregularities and planned to fire him when his term expired on July 1, 1916. However, various establishment organizations, including the Visiting Nurses' Association and United Charities, claimed that would be a calamity for public health. Thompson responded to this pressure by reappointing Sachs before the expiration of his term, but later claimed it was his worst decision. In the spring of 1916 Sachs resigned, criticizing what he viewed as the political management of medical facilities. He pointed to Robertson's use of patronage. Robertson then charged that Sachs had established a "Sachs Machine" at the sanitarium and connived to destroy the Thompson mayoralty. Other doctors also accused Robertson of being a political appointee and a hack.

Thompson himself claimed Sachs practiced the spoils system more boldly than anyone. On Saturday, April 1, he attacked Sachs in a speech at the Forum Hall at 43rd Street and Calumet Avenue. That evening Sachs committed suicide in the private sanitarium he had established in Naperville. He left a note expressing his love for the Municipal Sanitarium and its patients while condemning politicians. Ending in tragedy, the Sachs scandal illustrated the efforts of Thompson and his allies to manipulate the system of political spoils.[22]

Thompson's mayoralty coincided with the increased violence of the First World War. Chicago's diverse population represented all the nations at war, leading to conflicts within the city, particularly between Slavs and Germans. The two leading Slavic communities, the Czechs and the Poles, attacked both Thompson and the German community, which had largely backed him. The Poles and Czechs also protested the Germanic names of streets and public schools. They accused Thompson of being pro-German.[23]

These attacks on Thompson increased as the United States drifted toward war with Germany and its allies. The Czech community, which had feuded with Thompson since the Sunday saloon-closing controversy, continued to enthusiastically criticize the mayor. After Congress declared war, French and British delegations sought to visit Chicago. Thompson refused to extend an official invitation to French General Joseph Joffre, stating that he could not understand why Joffre would want to visit a city with so large a German population. The Czech National Alliance immediately protested and announced that their community would welcome the French and British emissaries. Defiant aldermen and prominent citizens arranged a reception for the French general. A *Denní Hlasatel* editorial claimed that Thompson had a "German spleen" below his five-gallon hat.[24]

This would not be the first (or the last) time Thompson's patriotism would be doubted. In May 1917, the time had come for the mayor to make recommendations for membership on the school board. The Czechs demanded that one of their own be nominated, as had been the tradition. Thompson ignored the request. The *Denní Hlasatel* editorialized that this did not surprise them, as the mayor had never been a sincere American, Chicagoan, or Republican. One school board member, Anton Czarnecki, a Pole, took up the cause and created problems for the Thompson appointees. Czechs and Poles had complained as early as 1915 about a textbook used in the public schools that included a pro–Kaiser Wilhelm II chapter. They campaigned against the book for years, and finally thousands of Slavic students simply tore out the offending pages. Also, a school in a largely Polish neighborhood carried the name of Otto Von Bismarck, the Iron Chancellor, who had promoted German unification and unleashed the anti-Catholic and anti-Polish *Kulturkampf* in German-occupied western Poland. The Czechs also resented Bismarck, as his armies had invaded Bohemia in 1866. In August 1917, Czarnecki proposed and passed a resolution that ended more than a half-century of German-language instruction in the public schools. Czarnecki then led the campaign to remove Bismarck's name from the school and to get the pro-Kaiser chapter taken out of the textbook. The school board, controlled by Thompson, did not want to offend the German American bloc. Nevertheless, in March 1918, it renamed the Bismarck School after General Frederick Funston, an American army hero. The next month, Czarnecki fought off a revenge-fueled attempt by board member Albert H. Severinghaus to change the name of the Kosciuszko School—Thaddeus Kosciuszko being a hero of both the American Revolution and the struggle for Polish independence. Thompson and his supporters hardly made friends among the growing Polish and Czech communities, as the ethnic tensions around the world war spilled into the politics of public education.[25]

Thompson's actions during the war caused yet more friction. In late 1917, after America's entry into the war, Thompson allowed a socialist anti-war group, the People's Council of America for Democracy and Terms of Peace, to meet in Chicago. Organizers called for a $50,000 ($1,175,156 in 2023) peace fund. Governor Frank Lowden banned the meeting, but on September 1 Thompson defied the order, and the group met that day at the West Side Auditorium on Racine Avenue. Lowden ordered the police to end it, which they did. Thompson reacted angrily and threatened to ask the courts whether Lowden had acted lawfully. At another pacifist meeting the next day, Lowden sent in the state militia. Thompson threatened to use city police to counter them, but the gathering ended before any confrontation. On October 15 the City Council voted overwhelmingly, 44–8, to commend Lowden for his actions, and directed that no further assemblies by pacifists be allowed in Chicago. The mayor quickly vetoed the resolution. That night the Society of the Veterans of Foreign Wars hung Thompson in effigy on the lakefront while thousands cheered and chanted "Hang Big Bill! Hang the Kaiser!" In November, the People's Council held another meeting in the Loop. State authorities did not intervene, but they informed the Chicago police that they would be held responsible for dispersing the meeting if anything treasonable took place.

Big Bill soon shifted his public attitude. While still claiming to defend free speech, he began to show more support for the troops. He started a relief fund for soldiers' wives and children. The mayor undoubtedly tried to burnish his public image as he was considering running for the US Senate. Thompson already had the support of pacifists, socialists, anti-war Republicans, anti-Wilson Democrats, and pro-Germans. Now was the time to sound patriotic. But Thompson could not shed his anti-war reputation as American soldiers fought on the Western Front, and he lost the Republican nomination for the Senate to J. Medill McCormick.[26]

In 1919, Judge Olson again opposed Thompson in the Republican primary for mayor. Democrats again nominated Sweitzer, and there were several other candidates. The crowded field produced an ugly campaign that emphasized race, ethnicity, and Americanism. Patronage also played a big role. Thompson had appointed over

30,000 "temporary" employees, including over half of the staff at the Municipal Tuberculosis Sanitarium, and those appointees were expected to vote for him.[27]

The *Abendpost*, a German American newspaper, supported Thompson and accused many Chicagoans of waving a "bloody red shirt" against the city's Germans. The *Deutsch-Amerikanischer Buergerbund* also endorsed Thompson, pointing out that he had protected the rights of the German community. The group lauded the mayor for his protection of free speech and allowing the People's Council to meet in the city. A Dutch American journal, *Onze Toekomst*, supported the Republican ticket in the general election. The Italian American gazette, *L'Italia*, praised the Republican Party and urged all Italians to vote for Thompson. Lundin decided that Thompson should concentrate on energizing the Black vote, as well as German and Irish voters. In order to capture the Irish, Thompson took a stand for home rule for Ireland and "the dissolution of the British Yoke of oppression."

Thompson won a second term by about 21,000 votes over Sweitzer, who nevertheless won the Polish, Lithuanian, Italian, and much of the German vote. Thompson captured enough of the Swedish, Jewish, and WASP vote, along with the middle-class wards, largely dominated by Protestants, to secure his victory. The terrific growth of the African American population also boosted his candidacy. In 1915, Blacks made up about 15 percent of the 2nd Ward's population. By 1919, they made up 70 percent. The 2nd Ward alone provided 11,000 votes for the mayor. The pro-Thompson *Abendpost* proclaimed it a victory for a "liberal, progressive, strong, peaceful, genuinely democratic, American Chicago." In many ways this election set the table for Chicago politics to follow easily discernible ethnic, racial, religious, and class lines for the rest of the century. Democrats had to face the possibility that a Republican Tammany Hall in Chicago might be possible.[28]

Thompson's second term saw the city explode with a race riot in the summer of 1919. The riot broke out in part over competition between Black Chicagoans and northern and western European White ethnics for jobs, housing, and political power. The clash fractured Thompson's machine. The so-called new immigrants from eastern and southern Europe largely stayed out of the fray, except for the West Side Italian community. Thompson also mishandled the situation, as he refused to ask Governor Lowden, with whom he continued to feud, to send in the state militia.[29]

Nevertheless, by 1920 the Lundin–Thompson political machine seemed unbeatable. The Republicans held their national convention in Chicago, and in the November election the Chicago Republican machine swept statewide elections just as the national party swept the Democrats out of the White House. What shattered the machine was not racial tension or elections; it was Prohibition.

When Prohibition came into effect in January 1920, Chicago's hoodlums saw a vast opportunity to profit from selling illegal alcohol. Gangsters soon controlled the liquor and beer trade. Thompson's police seemed helpless to control it. The mayor appointed a new police chief, Charles C. Fitzmorris, a former journalist who knew the criminal world. He quickly cracked down on gamblers and booze runners.[30]

Yet at this juncture, the powerful Lundin–Thompson machine began to crack. Lundin had been content to let Thompson take credit for their success, but now the mayor began to make decisions on his own. Lundin had not been consulted about Fitzmorris's appointment, and the relationship between the two politicians began to come apart. Other scandals stressed the machine. Governor Len Small, a Thompson ally, was indicted for mishandling funds when he had been state treasurer. This seemed to weaken Thompson's hold on the city.

Worse, Fitzmorris's gains proved temporary. Crime again proliferated as truck hijackings increased, vice flourished, and, during the aldermanic elections of 1921, several bombings took place principally in John Powers's 19th Ward. Powers's opponent, Anthony d'Andrea, was threatened by a secret organization known as the Black Hand. The police told him to ignore the threats, but d'Andrea was assassinated, and the police never found the culprit. When state's attorney Robert Crowe attacked Fitzmorris, Thompson came to his defense.

Scandals proliferated. Crowe indicted several school board members for real estate manipulation. Importantly, the Polish-born Democratic reformer Edmund K. Jarecki defeated Thompson's candidate for Cook County Judge. 1922 was a bad year for the Republicans, as other Democrats also won elections. In early 1923, Fred Lundin himself was indicted over the school board scandals. By that time, Thompson had decided not to run for reelection.[31]

A DEMOCRATIC REFORMER

William E. Dever was born in Woburn, Massachusetts, in 1862. His Catholic family owned a tannery, and he went to work there after the ninth grade. At the age of twenty he left Woburn and worked in various tanneries across the country. He married Kate Conway and headed to Chicago, where he heard tanners earned twenty-four dollars a week. In 1887 the couple settled in West Town near the many tanneries along the North Branch of the Chicago River. Dever attended night classes at the Chicago College of Law, where he earned a degree in 1890 and entered the profession. He joined the political discussion group run by Graham Taylor at the Chicago Commons, a local settlement house. This eventually led him to run for alderman as a reform candidate; after losing his first race, Dever was elected alderman of the 17th Ward in 1902. At that time he attracted the attention of Mayor Carter H. Harrison IV, and became an influential member of the City Council's reform group. When the reformer Edward Dunne captured the mayoralty in 1905, Dever became his floor leader. Five years later, voters elected Dever judge of the Cook County Circuit Court.

George Brennan, a protégé of Roger Sullivan, attempted to unite the Democratic Party and create a formidable political organization that could deliver victory consistently. In 1923, he turned to Dever as a possible unifier of the often warring factions of the Party. While a member of the Dunne faction, Dever nevertheless maintained good relations with both the Harrison and Sullivan Democrats. He became the Democratic candidate for mayor, running against the Republican businessman Arthur Lueder in the 1923 general election. Anti-Catholicism tarnished the rather dull campaign between the

CHAPTER 5

two reformers, as pamphlets appeared in Protestant neighborhoods warning of a Vatican plot to take over the city and the public schools. In the end, Dever easily won, and the Democrats took control of City Hall in April 1923.

Dever proved to be a welcome change from Thompson. He built public works, supported municipal ownership of transit, reformed the public school system, and cut waste. Despite his personal opposition to Prohibition, he moved against the illegal liquor interests and gamblers, maintaining that all laws had to be enforced. This may have been a crucial political mistake for the reformer, as he alienated not only the bootleggers but also some complicit ward politicians. In the end, despite an exemplary record, Dever lost popular support and faced a difficult rematch with Thompson in 1927.[32]

Thompson and various Republican politicians had been busy making, unmaking, and remaking alliances within the party. Thompson and Lundin stopped speaking to each other. Thompson's side won most internal conflicts, and he again became a force in the party. Always willing to put on a show, Thompson held a rally at the Cort Theater in downtown Chicago in support of other Republicans. He brought two caged stockyard rats along to represent Lundin and Dr. John Dill Robertson, both his former allies. He placed them on a table at center stage as the crowd gasped and howled. Thompson said: "Some of my friends have advised me against doing this. They tell me it is a political blunder. But I don't think so. Do you?" They responded by loudly yelling "No! No! Go on! Go on Bill!" He then reminded the two rats that he had been their best friend and had saved the rat "Fred" from the penitentiary and stood by the rat "Doc" in the struggle to control the Municipal Tuberculosis Sanitarium. The rat show became the talk of the town. While newspapers like the *Chicago Daily News* assailed Thompson, as did the Swedish Club of Chicago, voters loved the show.

On October 13, 1926, five thousand Thompson supporters gathered at the Medinah Temple. As Thompson walked onto the stage, an organ played, steamboat whistles shrilled, and ship bells clanged. A curtain dropped behind him that carried the message "Big Bill, Chicago Needs You!" Then the audience broke out in a new song

A Republican Protestant Proto-Machine

5.2 Music and lyrics, "America First, Last and Always." Big Bill Thompson supporters often sang this song. The America First movement turned into a pro-Fascist organization in the 1930s. Author's Collection.

written by Richard Wolfe and Milton Weil called "America First, Last and Always." Thompson spoke briefly and promised to run for mayor if enough people wanted him to. Organizers distributed pledge cards to the audience, and each audience member agreed to get twenty of the cards signed. Thompson's campaign to return to the mayor's office had begun.[33]

On December 10, several thousand people assembled in the ballroom of the Sherman Hotel, where Major Hamlet C. Ridgeway, a former Prohibition agent, collected 433,000 pledge cards. Every voter on a Republican payroll had been told to attend, and they did, with the exception of those who received their marching orders from Thompson's rivals. Ridgeway then asked Thompson to announce his candidacy. Ridgeway took Thompson's signature cowboy hat and literally threw it into a ring that contained the cards. Thompson said, "I accept with grateful thanks."[34]

THE RETURN OF BIG BILL

The primary campaign quickly sank into personal attacks on all sides. Other challengers were nominated: Dr. John Dill Robertson and the "Bridgeport Boy," Edward R. Litsinger. Both blamed Chicago's high murder count and gangland wars on Thompson and implied that he was in league with mobsters. Litsinger also accused Thompson's ally and supporter, state's attorney Robert Crowe, saying that on his watch murders had increased in the city and throughout Cook County. Litsinger promised to drive every crooked policeman off the force and make the streets safe. Thompson evoked Prohibition and claimed Robertson was so dry he never took a bath. He called Robertson "Dill Pickle" and Litsinger "The Liar."

Thompson based his 1927 campaign primarily on promoting the idea of "America First," railing against the World Court and, again, King George V of Great Britain. He embraced an American flag and proclaimed "This is the issue of the campaign! What was good enough for George Washington is good enough for Bill Thompson!" Thompson used the America First platform to attack School Superintendent William McAndrew, a Dever appointee, whom he charged with purchasing books for the schools that debased American heroes and praised the British.[35]

Thompson played to the crowds, while Crowe and his allies did the hard work of organizing the wards. Daniel M. Jackson, a powerful leader of the Black underworld, moved to collect funds and votes in Bronzeville. He told his constituents that Thompson would reopen hundreds of policy wheel stations (where bets could be placed on the numbers drawn that day) closed by Dever's police. In the suburbs, Crowe's people forced saloon owners to kick in money for Thompson's campaign as the boundaries between city and suburbs blurred. Al Capone supported such efforts and kept a daily tally of funds secured for the Thompson campaign. He even had a huge photograph of Thompson on his wall, alongside portraits of Lincoln and Washington. Violence and an appeal to prejudice, fear, and ignorance worked. Robertson withdrew from the race, and on February 22, 1927, Big Bill won the Republican primary by 180,039 votes over Litsinger.[36]

As intense and dirty as the Republican primary campaign had been, it would pale in comparison to the general election. That year, Dever's police chief, Morgan A. Collins, continued Prohibition raids in the Levee and in Bronzeville, including just prior to the general election. Thompson and Alderman R. R. Jackson bitterly assailed the police department and the administration, claiming they sought to intimidate Thompson voters. At a rally at the Masonic Hall on 51st Street and Michigan Avenue, Thompson called Dever a "Cossack mayor" and the biggest liar and crook who ever took the oath of office. He praised the Black population for its patience and good judgment and condemned the police raids. In response to Thompson's accusations, the Dever team claimed that Crowe enlisted "gangsters, gunmen, hoodlums, and disreputable characters" in the Thompson campaign.[37]

Thompson relied heavily on the South Side Black vote. In a *Chicago Tribune* poll 81 percent of Black voters said they would vote for Big Bill. This meant some 50,000 votes for the former mayor. The pollsters spoke with 8,029 people, at four intersections in White neighborhoods, five intersections in African American neighborhoods on the South Side, and several other miscellaneous locations. They concluded that Black voters preferred Thompson while upperclass Republicans wanted Dever to win.[38]

The racial insinuations of the campaign almost tore the city apart. At a meeting Thompson leaned over to hug a Black child, the nephew of supporter Oscar De Priest. Immediately, Brennan arranged to have cartoons drawn of Thompson kissing Black children and had them distributed in White neighborhoods under the heading, "Do You Want Negroes or White Men to Run Chicago? Bye, Bye, Blackbirds!" Examples of the cartoon even appeared in the *Chicago Daily News*, with Thompson kissing a Black child while kicking away a White child and City Hall portrayed as Uncle Thompson's Cabin. Thompson carried copies and showed them to voters, saying "Dever and Brennan are the scum of the earth."

After all the mudslinging, Chicagoans elected William Hale Thompson on April 5 by 83,072 votes. The three predominantly African American wards voted overwhelmingly for Big Bill, contributing 59,215 votes. While Thompson emphasized America First and the like, it was Prohibition that defeated Dever. His administration had been outstanding in many ways, but Chicagoans wanted beer and fewer police raids. Indeed, Thompson cut heavily into the German and Polish wards and held his strength among the Scandinavians. Dever attracted the Czechs and Italians, but not in enough numbers. The Crowe–Thompson organization now dominated the Chicago Republican Party.[39]

In his Metropole Hotel headquarters, Al Capone must have been well pleased. It was rumored that he had donated roughly $150,000 ($2,593,448 in 2023) to the Thompson campaign, although the Chicago Crime Commission estimated his contribution went as high as $260,000. Other gangsters apparently also donated to the cause. Vincent "The Schemer" Drucci, a Capone man, sent thugs to raid the offices of Alderman Dorsey R. Crowe (no relation to Robert Crowe), chastising the staff for anti-Thompson activities. They overturned file cabinets, terrorized a secretary, and kicked out a window.[40]

THOMPSON'S LAST HURRAH! 1927–1931

Thompson's last mayoral term began with the type of political appointment that marked Republican machine-building efforts. He appointed Daniel A. Serritella, the Republican Committeeman of the 1st Ward and a Capone man, as City Sealer. The position called for Serritella to ensure that Chicagoans received honest weights from butchers, grocers, and ice and coal dealers. Unofficially, Capone wanted Serritella to keep an eye on Thompson, to carry messages to politicians, and to get favors for the mob. Over the years, Serritella showed up when Capone's interests seemed threatened. He and First Assistant Corporation Counsel James Breen acted as the mayor's liaisons to Capone and controlled police activity in the Loop and outlying areas. Serritella also helped in union negotiations, such as when Capone and *Chicago Tribune* officials settled a pending strike by the newspaper drivers' union. As a result, the newspaper laid off Capone and, to a degree, Thompson.

Thompson nevertheless struggled to control the 1928 Republican primary, which featured contests for Cook County state's attorney, governor, and US Senate. The campaigns were marked by violence, underscored the close involvement of organized crime, and pitted Thompson against his rival, Senator Charles Deneen. The cycle of violence began with the March assassination of Joseph "Diamond Joe" Esposito, the Republican committeeman for the 25th Ward and a staunch supporter of Deneen. The morning after the Esposito funeral, two bombings occurred just twenty-eight minutes apart at the homes of Deneen and Judge John A. Swanson, the Deneen candidate for state's attorney. Both Thompson and Crowe maintained that Deneen supporters threw the bombs themselves to gain sympathy for Swanson. Then just after the polls closed, assailants murdered African American lawyer Octavius Granady, the Deneen candidate for committeeman in the 20th Ward and the first Black to run for office in the racially changing district. Speculation abounded about the role of gangsters in all this political violence. Five county commissioners, including four Crowe supporters, hampered the investigation by refusing to provide funds for a grand jury. Private donors raised the funds, and the grand jury returned a large number of indictments. The profane definitely outmatched the sacred in the Thompson years.[41]

The April 1928 Republican primary proved to be a political disaster for Thompson and Crowe. Judge Swanson beat the incumbent Crowe in the state's attorney race and Deneen's candidates won the governor's race and the US Senate race. Thompson even lost the election for committeeman in his own ward. The year, which had begun with a good deal of optimism on Thompson's and Crowe's part, now seemed to descend into pessimism and defeat.

Thompson faced yet more political, legal, and financial challenges later that year when Circuit Court Judge Hugo Friend handed down his decision in the *Chicago Tribune*'s expert fees case. The newspaper charged Thompson with paying outlandish fees to friends and allies who had been hired as experts, and said these fees included kickbacks to the Thompson organization. The judge ruled that Thompson, and his co-defendants, owed the city a whopping $2,245,604 ($39,506,872 in 2023). Thompson panicked, but George Harding, his city comptroller during his first term, used his and Thompson's real estate holdings as collateral and arranged for a $3,000,000 bond while his lawyers filed an appeal. The next two years would not be any easier for Thompson, who eventually suffered a nervous breakdown. Friends took him to a secluded estate in northern Wisconsin, where he slowly recovered. Upon his return to City Hall, it seemed he had lost much of his dynamism. In February 1929, the St. Valentine's Day Massacre occurred on the North Side, but Thompson showed little interest. By the end of the year Wall Street had crashed, and by 1930 Chicago was caught up in the Great Depression. Thompson seemed listless and unable to take command. Demands for his resignation mounted.[42]

Despite these challenges, Thompson ran for mayor again in 1931. His campaign attacked Democrat Anton Cermak in ways that angered working-class Catholics and Jews. He referred to Cermak as "Pushcart Tony" and made fun of his Czech name. Thompson often referred to Cermak as "that Bohunk." For his part, Cermak ran a dignified campaign and won the mayoralty by 191,916 votes. He carried forty-five of the city's fifty wards. Big Bill exited City Hall as the last Republican mayor of Chicago, leaving the city's reputation in tatters, marked by graft, crime, and corruption. The Republican attempt to create a citywide political machine had failed miserably.[43]

6

Bohemian Rhapsody

A New Ethnic Alignment

> Of course, we could not all come on the Mayflower—or maybe the boat would have sunk. But I came here as soon as I could, and I never wanted to go back, because to me it is a great privilege to be an American citizen.
>
> ANTON CERMAK[1]

As late as 1910, Chicago remained generally a German city with huge numbers of German immigrants (Protestant, Catholic, and Jewish) and their offspring. Much of the rest of the population came from Ireland, Great Britain, Scandinavia, and the Lowlands. Mostly Protestant, except for the Irish and the German Catholics and Jews, they easily fit into traditional ethnic hierarchies in the city and nation. Those from the British Isles, of course, had the added benefit of speaking English, even if with a brogue.

After 1890, immigrants from eastern and southern Europe soon outnumbered immigrants arriving from northern and western Europe. And they seemed very different. Slavs, Jews, Italians, Greeks, Hungarians, Lithuanians, and others found it more difficult to assimilate. Their unpronounceable names and strange languages, along with peculiar cultural customs, stood in stark contrast to Protestant Anglo-Saxon America as they gathered along the dirty crowded streets of Chicago. Moreover, most of the newer immigrants were not Protestant, but Catholics, Jews, or Orthodox Christians. Fears of popery and conspiracies abounded. By 1900 conservatives and progressives alike feared these new masses and their imagined potential for violence and revolution. Nevertheless, within two generations, Chicago became a largely Catholic and Jewish city with a substantial Orthodox Christian population.

As World War I cut off immigration from Europe, African Americans came to Chicago from the South in large numbers. Most settled on the city's South Side. Due to increased residential segregation, often enforced by White street gangs, they created a large community along State Street, Federal Street, and other nearby thoroughfares. Bringing greater racial diversity to Chicago did not come without conflict. White Chicagoans often greeted them with racial prejudice, hatred, and violence. Although the Black southern migration was largely Protestant and tended to vote Republican, they, like the immigrants from the "Other Europe," were viewed as unassimilable outsiders.

The 1920s witnessed various reactions against all of these newer groups. Congressional fiat basically stopped foreign immigration after the war by passing the Immigration Act of 1924, also known as the Johnson–Reed Act, a federal law that established a quota system to limit the number of immigrants allowed into the United States. It was especially prejudicial to immigration from eastern and southern Europe. The 1919 race riot and the resulting use of racial covenants by real estate firms and property owners resulted in the ghettoization of Chicago's Black community. The decade also saw the growth of the city's Mexican community, another group many Americans saw as not assimilable. Together, these demographic shifts changed the politics of Clout City for the rest of the twentieth century. Suddenly politicians in both of the major parties faced a quickly changing electorate, but one that also wanted a share of the pie. Clout remained a transformative word for these newcomers, and each strove to obtain it in a city formed by it and its practitioners.

BOHEMIA IN CHICAGO

Czech immigrants from Bohemia in central Europe came in waves after the failed revolutions of 1848 and the Prussian invasion of the

Austro-Hungarian Empire in 1866. They included a large number of anti-Catholic Rationalists who, by embracing the European Enlightenment and democratic thought, fit more easily into Anglo-Saxon American culture. This group, often referred to as Freethinkers (*Svobodomyslných*), provided the core of the Czech American middle and intellectual classes and much of the leadership in Czech Chicago. This first wave of Czech migration often gravitated toward the already well-established German immigrant colonies, some populated by German Forty-Eighters. Many Czech refugees spoke German fluently as a result of Austrian rule of their homeland.[2]

Along with the Freethinkers, a large Czech Catholic contingent and smaller Bohemian Protestant and Jewish cohorts arrived in the United States. The Catholics quickly rose to the intellectual and institutional challenge of the Freethinkers. A Bohemian Catholic school system emerged along with a Catholic intelligentsia and press. The result was a very intricate institutional base, as well as an energetic Czech American social, political, religious, and economic life.

Chicago's Czech community dated to 1852, when the first Bohemian settlers arrived from New York. They settled at North Avenue and Dearborn Street near the North Side German community. Within three years, the Czechs resettled along LaSalle Street near Van Buren in the southern portion of downtown. Commercial and business office developments eventually dominated this district, along with a growing Chinese community. As a result, another Czech settlement appeared on the West Side on Beach Street. This too proved to be a temporary location due to railroad and warehouse expansion. A fourth and more permanent settlement occurred along Canal Street south from Van Buren. Czechs settled in large numbers along Taylor, DeKoven, Bunker (Grenshaw Street), and 12th Street (Roosevelt Road). This neighborhood took the name "Praha" after the capital of Bohemia. In 1870, approximately 10,000 residents called it home, and Czech social life flourished.[3]

Chicago became the leading center for Czech organizations and culture in America, with Praha serving as the "mother" colony. The first Czech Catholic parish in the city, St. Wenceslaus, opened in Praha in 1866. After the Great Chicago Fire in 1871, Czechs began to move south along Halsted Street to 18th Street and the neighborhood that became known as Pilsen, after the Pilsen Inn, owned by Matthew Skudera. The neighborhood soon succeeded Praha and became the home of major Czech fraternal organizations, newspapers, and Sokol gymnastic groups, as well as Freethinker and Catholic schools and Protestant congregations. Czech stores lined the major thoroughfares, and the Bohemians and other eastern Europeans erected buildings that reminded them of their homelands.[4]

As the Czech community continued to grow, the Bohemian population moved southwest to the neighborhood in South Lawndale that soon took on the name Czech California (now Little Village). Some of the most successful Chicago Czechs lived there as they built single-family brick homes across the neighborhood. Many Czech institutions followed. The Pilsen Brewery Company and adjacent Pilsen Park opened at 26th Street and Albany and quickly developed into an important meeting place for Czechs and their politicians.[5]

The Czech community acted as a bridge between the newcomers from eastern Europe and the older ethnic groups, in particular the Germans and Irish. The Poles early on allied with the Czech community. In the 1860s, Chicagoans often mistook Poles and Czechs for each other, lumping them together simply as Slavs. The close connection continued as both attempted to flex their economic and political muscles. As the Polish population grew and became more institutionally developed, it followed the path set by the Bohemians. Czechs and Poles took active part in politics and had representatives across the political spectrum. The Polish newspaper, *Dziennik Związkowy*, often encouraged the community to vote for Bohemian candidates.[6]

From early on, Czech Jews played an important role in the community. The Czech lawyer and political leader Adolph Kraus held key roles in the various campaigns and administrations of both Carter Harrisons. Czech California shared a ward with what developed by World War I into a heavily Jewish district in North Lawndale. Here Czech Jews, such as William Loeffler and Adolph J. Sabath, forged links between the Czech and Jewish communities. Each spoke Czech well, and this proved to be an important factor in their political rise.

Like Kraus, both Loeffler and Sabath supported the goals of the Democratic faction of Carter Harrison IV. These groups provided a base for various ethnic politicians. In particular, they would be crucial to the rise of Anton Cermak.[7]

ANTON CERMAK: THE EARLY YEARS

Poor immigrants, many of whom worked in the lumberyards of Pilsen or the McCormick Reaper Works on Blue Island Avenue, made up the largest part of the Czech community. Many also worked in packinghouses just to the south. In 1876, Czech and Polish lumber shovers went on strike. The following year, they participated in the 1877 railroad strike. Both groups took part in packinghouse strikes as well. These experiences gave Czech politicians and those of other immigrant groups a distinctly working-class edge.[8]

Other Czech immigrants came from coal-mining communities. In 1874 Antonin and Kateřina (Franková) Čermak (Cermak), along with their year-old son, Antonín Josef, left the Bohemian town of Kladno, where Antonin worked as a coal miner, and sailed for the United States. At first they settled in Pilsen, where Antonin found construction work. Soon, however, they moved to Braidwood, another coal town some sixty-one miles southwest of the city. Antonin Josef Cermak's story is one of struggle in Braidwood's coal mines, where he joined his father at an early age. The family always maintained connections to Pilsen and at times moved there, only to return again to Braidwood.

The young coal miner grew up in a very ethnic environment. He attended school irregularly and joined gangs. Early on Cermak gained a reputation as a hard drinker and brawler. The young man spent more than one night in jail. His biographer said Cermak led "a lusty, brawling, drinking, pugnacious undisciplined youth." Nevertheless, he quickly developed leadership skills, and a driving ambition that would serve him well politically. In 1889, at the age of sixteen, he left his family and settled in Pilsen, living with his aunt. He found employment as a brakeman on the Elgin, Joliet, and Eastern Railroad; later, he worked for the street railway company and rode a horse that helped pull horsecars up a steep incline on Blue Island Avenue. He eventually started his own business selling kindling. Well known in Pilsen's saloons, Cermak joined a Czech street gang, in which he formed relationships he maintained throughout his life. As his business prospered, he moved to Czech California on 25th and Washtenaw Avenue. In 1894 he married a neighbor, another Czech immigrant, Mary Horejs, a Roman Catholic. Cermak, who had Freethinker leanings, learned how to build bridges across religious and social divides. This experience would shape his later approach to politics, as did his experience as a young entrepreneur. As the historian Alex Gottfried has pointed out, Chicago's Czech community reflected a cultural predisposition toward solid middle-class values. When Czechs opposed their Austrian oppressors they did so as cautious middle-class burghers rather than as romantic revolutionaries. The writings of Karel Havlíček Borovský, who exemplified this attitude and believed that a politician should act much like a businessman, greatly impacted Czech culture. Cermak embraced this approach.[9]

In 1902, after ten years of arduous work for the local Democratic organization, Cermak decided to run for the Illinois General Assembly. He won the nomination by one vote thanks to the support of the Zoldaks, a Czech social club. The state cumulative voting law aided Cermak. Each voter in the district had three votes and could cast all three votes for one candidate or divide them between three candidates. Cermak won as one of two Democrats elected from the district. Significantly, he won without the help of either the Harrison or the Sullivan factions of the party. His support came largely from his own ethnic community, a fact Cermak would never forget. The communal response gave him a solid voting base and thus clout.

Having grown up in a tough mining town and along the immigrant working-class streets of Chicago, Cermak felt self-conscious and out of place when he assumed his position among the many college-educated fellow representatives in the statehouse. At first, Cermak generally followed the party line set down by the Sullivan Democrats. In Chicago politics, however, he often supported the Harrison faction. While his first term was hardly spectacular, Cermak rose to lead the Democratic Party Steering Committee and take on the role of floor leader.

Cermak won reelection in 1904 as the only Democrat from his district. He served on several influential committees, including the Chicago Charter Committee, where he defended the people's right to drink alcohol. This led to his involvement in a group that would help him build a strong voting constituency not only in Czech California, but across the city's immigrant neighborhoods.[10]

THE UNITED SOCIETIES FOR LOCAL SELF-GOVERNMENT

An important component of Anton Cermak's emerging political organization developed in response to the rising number of attacks on immigrants and their cultures, which included the Prohibition movement. In 1905, the Anti-Saloon and Law and Order leagues demanded that the City Council more vigorously enforce oft-ignored state regulations concerning places that served liquor, especially the 1:00 a.m. closing time restriction and the Sunday closing law. In response, aldermen raised the fees on saloon licenses. Then, under further pressure, both the City Council and the mayor sought to restrict special permits for clubs and dance halls seeking to serve liquor after 1:00 a.m.

On March 25, 1905, an estimated 30,000 to 40,000 Chicagoans protested the new restrictions. The ordinances hurt ethnic fraternal organizations, clubs, and social groups, which had long used late-night dances to raise funds. Speakers brought up the idea of a new city charter that would allow Chicago to enjoy home rule and thus circumvent state laws. As a result of the demonstration, the City Council agreed to continue issuing the special permits. Obviously, the anger of tens of thousands of Chicagoans and the various ethnic groups they represented frightened the politically savvy aldermen. It also provided a sense of agency to ethnic and immigrant communities, especially to those from central and eastern Europe.

The new higher license fees, however, were not rolled back and took effect on May 1, 1906. Priced out, more than 1,300 saloons in poorer neighborhoods closed. A short time later, Alderman Daniel

Harken introduced an ordinance freezing the number of licenses until the population grew to a ratio of 500 to each permit, with the aim of further eroding the number of saloons in Chicago. The proposal passed the City Council easily. The new law gave those that already held a license preference for renewal and did not dramatically reduce the number of saloons, as similar laws did in Boston. Moreover, before the freeze law went into effect on July 31, entrepreneurs purchased nearly 2,000 new licenses and the number of saloons actually increased to slightly over 8,000—or one for every 239 men, women, and children—thus neutralizing the reform.[11]

On March 25, 1906, nearly 350 ethnic and social groups with over 60,000 members sent representatives to a meeting called by several of Chicago's German leaders and the German newspapers who supported the idea of home rule for Chicago. They agreed to organize as the United Societies for Local Self-Government. Germans largely made up the executive committee, but it included representation from the Czechs and others. The German newspaper *Abendpost* declared that obsolete laws should be improved or abandoned. The organization held its first meeting at the Sherman House on June 5. The United Societies grew quickly, and the Germans and Czechs made a deal that led to the election of Cermak as permanent secretary, a position he held throughout the lifetime of the organization. This provided the group with an important representative in Springfield. The appointment also expanded the political base of the ambitious politician.

The United Societies opposed blue laws that curtailed the use of alcoholic beverages, Sunday baseball, and other outdoor sports. Representatives of the United Societies attended a City Council meeting on May 27, 1906, to oppose the passage of a new dance hall ordinance. By May 31, thirty-one aldermen were reported to endorse the stand taken by the United Societies. The organization claimed to already have 432 member societies and to control 60,000 votes. The United Societies proposed an ordinance of its own that would allow drinking and dancing at the venues of "respectable societies." With this move, the battle lines between the United Societies and the Anti-Saloon League escalated.[12]

Opponents branded the United Societies as a stalking horse for the liquor interests. In reality, it had deeper roots, and the industry never controlled it. Those roots spoke to a deep-seated fear that traditional immigrant cultures would disappear with assimilation. For many ethnic groups, especially those from central and eastern Europe, alcohol was essential to their cultural traditions and sense of freedom.

The *Illinois Staats-Zeitung* claimed that the English-language press showed the United Societies in a false light, creating the impression that its members all worked for the brewing industry. The *Abendpost* decried the fact that various ministers attacked the United Societies, comparing "wets" to anarchists or claiming that the police and the saloonkeepers conspired to break the law. "Dry" ministers tended to be native White Protestants, but some Catholics like Father P. O. Callaghan also supported the abstinence movement.

The Irish in general did not rally to the protest movement. Rather, sharp tensions emerged between the Irish and Czechs, Poles, and eastern European communities. The Irish had no interest in sharing power with these new groups, nor with the more established Germans, and feared any new multiethnic organization. Nevertheless, two Irish Americans held important posts in the United Societies: Charles C. Gilbert, a lawyer, served as president, and Edward T. Noonan acted as general counsel.[13]

The United Societies emerged within the changing landscape of Chicago's immigrant communities. Nothing captured the full extent of the roiling politics of the day better than the fight around a new city charter, which engaged the old establishment, downstate politicians, progressive reformers, home rule advocates, labor groups, Prohibition stalwarts, and ethnic communities. Alliances in support of a new charter fell victim to fundamental cultural misunderstandings and political suspicions. Progressive reformers sought home rule to free the city from downstate control and provide efficiencies to city government. Chicago's ethnic communities saw home rule as a means of recognizing their autonomy, protecting their cultural interactions and public life. The reformers preferred to ignore the saloon issue as well as immigrant and working-class demands for more democratic reform. The United Societies played a central role in the vast ethnocultural struggle that ensued.

Back in 1902, when the first convention in support of charter reform took place, the Chicago Federation of Labor and most ethnic groups supported home rule. However, as the process unfolded, they began to lose faith in the undertaking, which seemed to be dominated by upper-class business-oriented reformers, many of them native White Protestants. Between November 1906 and March 1907, mainstream reformers drafted a new city charter that promoted their idea of the public interest. The United Societies, in turn, demanded that the city control liquor laws and not Springfield, where rural Protestant and conservative legislators prevailed. The United Societies formally raised this "unwelcome issue" at the Chicago Charter Convention on December 6, 1906. They demanded a provision to vest in the Chicago City Council the power to regulate the legal observance of the Sunday sale of liquors.[14] In response, the anti-saloon faction declared that it would oppose home rule if it included the liquor issue.

In 1907, Chicago voters elected Republican Fred Busse as the first German American mayor and the first to enjoy a four-year term. Initially, the United Societies supported Busse, until he used his political muscle to secure a huge Republican plurality through gerrymandering wards. The Illinois House Charter Committee, which had strong ties to Busse, trimmed the proposed charter to meet his political needs. The committee gutted the electoral reform and anti-corruption features of the document. It also, importantly, left out the liquor issue. The United Societies openly opposed the revised charter proposal.

On September 7, 1907, just ten days before the final vote on the proposed charter, the United Societies held a gathering for ethnic families from across the city at Riverview Park. A week later, it organized a huge anti-charter rally in Grant Park, attended by more than 30,000 people. Roughly 15,000 gathered at various points near downtown and paraded to the park with banners, flags, and marching bands.

On the day before the rally, Busse's election board reversed an earlier decision, and announced that the charter referendum was a special election and therefore employers did not have to give workers (unpaid) time off to vote. The United Societies quickly protested this brazen attempt to deny workers the vote, but the board upheld its decision. Busse's gamble badly misfired. On September 17, voters rejected the new charter by a vote of 121,935 to 59,786. Chicagoans also made Busse a one-term mayor, reelecting Carter Harrison IV in 1911.[15]

The United Societies, together with organized labor, women's organizations, settlement houses, and the Democratic Party, celebrated the defeat of the charter. However, they pointed out that they were not against reform in general. Even as supporters of the charter movement decried the vote as a result of partisan politics, the Chicago Federation of Labor, the Independence League, and the United Societies for Local Self-Government called it a victory for Chicago and independent politics. William O'Connell, Democratic Cook County Central Committee Chairman, declared that Chicagoans would never accept a charter written by special interests.[16]

During these years, the United Societies experienced phenomenal growth and came to exercise considerable influence. In 1908, the United Societies claimed that 131 new associations had joined the organization, and that German, Czech, Polish, Italian, and other ethnic organizations and associations sent 944 delegates to the annual convention. It claimed a total membership of 183,000, of which 155,000 had the right to vote. Four years later, at its annual meeting at the North Side Turner Hall, officers reported that while five organizations had quit the group, twenty-eight new ones had joined, bringing the total to 754 clubs and associations. The United Societies supported fifty-seven candidates in the November elections and elected forty-seven. In the municipal elections in April 1913, twenty-six of the group's twenty-nine aldermanic candidates won their races. Five years later, the United Societies claimed 1,105 societies and corporations as members with a total membership of 266,528. Mobilization around the liquor issue provided real clout.[17]

John Cervenka chaired a Czech branch of the United Societies whose membership included most of the Czech politicians and lead-

CHAPTER 6

ers, including Alderman John Toman, Judge J. Z. Uhlir, and Anton Cermak. By 1918, a large number of Czech organizations, including the Bohemian Saloonkeepers Association, had joined the United Societies. In May, at the United Societies' thirteenth annual convention, Czech groups formed the largest contingent of organizations.[18] The United Societies provided Cermak with a large, multiethnic and predominantly working-class base. It was a perfect example of an extra-communal response that crossed ethnic lines to provide agency to its supporters.

Cermak knew how to reach across what seemed like impossible social barriers. He learned to bridge the differences between Catholics, Freethinkers, Protestants, and Jews in the Czech community, and mastered the art of compromise. Cermak also understood the political ways of a frequently divided Cook County Democratic Party, effectively managing his relationships with the different factions controlled by Harrison, Sullivan, and Dunne. He eventually joined the Sullivan/Brennan circle, after that group seemed to have emerged victorious in the early 1920s. An immigrant himself, he spoke to the many Chicagoans of immigrant stock, especially recent arrivals. Notwithstanding his own successes as a businessman, Cermak reached out to working-class communities. Cermak's experience with the United Societies proved crucial to building his political base and rallying working-class communal support.

THE GROWTH OF A COMMUNAL POLITICAL MACHINE

In 1909, Cermak decided to run for alderman of the 12th Ward, a position that offered a higher salary and more patronage power. The *Chicago Tribune* and even the Municipal Voters League endorsed him, despite the misgivings of many members. Surprisingly, when he won the election, Cermak decided to also stay in the state legislature, which caused a great deal of controversy. Cermak finally did resign his office as state representative in April 1910. In addition, in 1908, Cermak had won election as the Democratic ward committeeman, a position he would hold until his death in 1933. One of the most important positions in Chicago's political structure, it gave the holder

6.1 Anton Cermak and family, ca. 1925. Cermak is pictured here at a campaign rally with his wife and two of his three children. Author's Collection.

a great deal of political clout. Committeemen served as members of the judicial circuit convention, which nominated twenty circuit court and twenty-eight superior court judges. Cermak also served on the Democratic Party's Central Committee, which selected delegates to the state convention and nominated Illinois Supreme Court Justices, as well as trustees of the University of Illinois and delegates at large to the national convention. All told, Cermak was accumulating considerable power, influence, and control over patronage.

After Cermak left the Illinois legislature, he found himself temporarily less attached to the Sullivan bloc. The Harrison faction, in turn, continued to lose ground across the city. As he faced reelection as alderman, he had to balance his position politically. The alderman's standing in both the Harrison and Sullivan alliances allowed him to broker a rapprochement. And being a leader of the United Societies helped him to secure their cooperation. Because of his skillful manipulations, Cermak got to choose a candidate for a prominent position on the slate, clerk of the probate court, which he awarded to his ally from the United Societies, John Cervenka. This allowed Cermak to pay off a political debt to an important member of the Czech community. While these political manipulations might seem archaic and even byzantine, they proved vital for the extension of Cermak's powerbase.[19]

In Chicago, power or clout depended on many different relationships. Alliances changed constantly. Republican aldermen and mayors often made alliances with Democrats. Power, patronage, and graft fueled the system. Also defending one's neighborhood and ethnic group proved to be imperative. While some might bemoan this system as tribalism, in the American city in the first half of the twentieth century, they were major factors in winning elections and even creating a sense of agency for long-ignored groups. Cermak, a child of this system, knew how to play the game. The question for the ambitious ward politician was how to extend his powerbase beyond the Czechs of Pilsen and Lawndale.

The Czech community remained loyal to the boss of the 12th Ward. All Czech factions generally came to see Cermak as a leader with citywide possibilities. Cermak remained the 12th Ward alderman and paid back his loyal constituency with a large celebration at Cervenka's Pilsen Park on the evening of June 2, 1911, to celebrate that April's victory, which gave Democrats not only the mayoralty but also control of the City Council. Roughly five hundred people packed the Pilsen Park Pavilion. Congressman Adolph J. Sabath, Cervenka, and other political notables spoke.

By September, it seemed as if Cermak and eight other Czech politicians had joined the Harrison faction, as 250 Democratic leaders attempted to wrest control of the Democratic State Central Committee from Roger Sullivan. These included Alderman Felix B. Janovsky, Congressman Sabath, and Alderman Frank Klaus of the 10th Ward. The Czechs began to feel a considerable amount of political power and organized the Česká Demokracie v Okresu Cook (Czech Democratic Organization of Cook County). Again Cermak, Cervenka, and Sabath played key roles in the new organization.[20]

In 1912, Cermak ran for bailiff of the Municipal Court, his first run for citywide office, as part of the Harrison slate. Always careful to have a fallback, Cermak also ran for his fourth term as alderman, though he ceded the office after he won. Naturally, the Czech newspaper *Denní Hlasatel* supported him, as did the United Societies. By this time, Cermak ruled over one of the most Democratic wards in the city, and his city-wide election as bailiff showed that he could reach beyond his ethnic constituency. To continue to do so, though, the rough ward politician would have to become more polished in his presentations, while still maintaining his image as an ordinary Chicagoan who represented the "little guys."[21]

As war clouds gathered over Europe, Cermak's star continued to rise. During Carter Harrison's last run for the mayoralty in 1915, Cermak threw his support to the Sullivan faction and the nomination of Sweitzer. As a result, Sullivan and his clique won a near total victory in the party. Still, Cermak delivered his ward for Harrison, the only one to vote for "Young Carter" in the primary. There is some evidence that Cermak worked against Sweitzer in the general election, but not openly enough to offend Sullivan. These intricate maneuvers illustrated Cermak's growing skill as an urban politician.

When Big Bill Thompson moved against the saloons, Cermak led the United Societies against him. By October 1915, the lines of contention were firmly drawn as Thompson moved to have the municipal judges remove Cermak as bailiff of the Municipal Court. Chief Justice Olson maintained that Cermak remained a duly elected official and only the legislature could remove him. The other judges agreed. The struggle against Thompson further enhanced Cermak's reputation in the Democratic Party.

When Cermak ran for sheriff of Cook County in 1918, the anti-saloon forces as well as the German American community organized against him. The prohibitionist organ *Patriotic Flag* portrayed Cermak as a tool of the liquor interests and appealed to anti-immigrant fears. It threw aspersions on Cermak by writing, "Let the voters draw their own conclusions about the really genuine Americanism of Cermak." But Cermak and the Czech community hardly supported pro-German organizations during World War I. Chicago Czechs rallied against the Hapsburgs at Pilsen Park at the start of the war and refused to return to Europe to serve in the Austro-Hungarian armed forces. The Czechs and Poles led the city's eastern European ethnic groups in attacking German American interests during the war. The *Denní Hlasatel* made a very ethnic and nationalist appeal in the November 1918 election, claiming that a vote for Cermak proved loyalty not only to Czech Chicago but to President Woodrow Wilson. Furthermore, the Czech newspaper complained that the city's German community campaigned to defeat Cermak and Cervenka because they had shown anti-German feelings during the war.[22] Cermak lost the sheriff's race by 3,083 votes, and it seems likely that his anti-German attitude did hurt him.

In fact, Cermak had thrown himself into war work. He spoke out in favor of Czech independence, and once the United States had entered the fighting in 1917, he wholeheartedly proclaimed his and the Chicago Czechs' love of the United States. He became the chairman of Czech war activities in the United States, chaired the Liberty Loan Committee of the 12th Ward, served as president of the National Army Aid Association, and spoke at rallies across the city. On Sunday, December 2, 1917, a large parade made its way through Czech California to the Sokol Havlicek-Tyrs auditorium on West 26th Street for a rally in support of Chicago Czechs who had enlisted in the US Army. As the war raged on, the new term, Czechoslovakia, was ever on Cermak's lips, and he frequently referred to Germans as Huns. Hardly surprising then, that Cermak's campaigns for bailiff and sheriff expressed patriotic, anti-German speech.[23]

Despite the outcome of the sheriff's election, Cermak continued to build his political career. He decided in 1919 to once again run for 12th Ward alderman, to replace his longtime friend Otto Kerner, who had served from 1913 to 1919. Cermak easily beat his primary opponent. In the general election, Cermak received the endorsement of the Chicago Federation of Labor and, once again surprisingly, the Municipal Voters League. In a hard-fought campaign, Cermak won a fourth term, and he won again in 1921. During these years, Cermak made alliances with various aldermen, including Jacob "Jake" Arvey of the West Side and James "Big Jim" McDonough of Bridgeport. These two relationships would serve him well. Arvey, the other 12th

Ward alderman, proved to be a master wheeler-dealer and bridge builder. He manipulated patronage, controlled committees, and did not hesitate to war with those who might oppose him. A force of nature, he walked up and down the council aisles lining up votes, and most often the council did his bidding. His supporters included Czechs, Poles, and others.

Thompson also won reelection as mayor, and although the Democrats won the majority in the City Council, Cermak had to work with his nemesis. Within the Democratic Party, the Sullivan–Brennan machine expanded its control, while the Harrison faction continued to fade. Arvey emerged as a powerful boss within the Brennan organization. Later, in 1922, as a reward for Cermak's support, Brennan nominated him for president of the Cook County Board. This would be a major victory for the ambitious Bohemian. He also became chairman of the Sullivan–Brennan Cook County Democratic Committee and a member of the Managing Committee.[24]

In the wake of Prohibition in 1919, Cermak and the United Societies initially seemed confused and ambivalent. The United Societies eventually challenged the Volstead Act, the enabling legislation of Prohibition, to allow the manufacture of light wines and beers. In 1921, Cermak pushed a similar resolution through the City Council. He corralled his colleagues to oppose any expenditure of city funds to enforce Prohibition. Cermak took the position that the federal government and not Chicago should enforce the new law. In 1922, he led the City Council in opposition to a plan to set up a special branch of the Municipal Court to try violations of the Prohibition law. Cermak demanded that the City Council "wholesome beers and light wines" resolution be distributed to all city councils in cities of more than 25,000 inhabitants with a request that they follow Chicago's lead. This led to a brawl in which Alderman John H. Lyle, known as the champion boxer of the council, threw a left hook at Alderman John Toman, a longtime Cermak Czech ally, who during the debate had repeatedly used an epithet to which Lyle objected. As Toman backed out of the way, Lyle's fist missed his nose; Lyle fell onto Toman's desk, his glasses flying into the Czech alderman's face. Toman went on talking and Lyle took his seat as the sergeant at arms and several aldermen rushed in to stop the fight. The City Council once again voted to defeat the few dry aldermen led by Lyle. Cermak and Lyle debated Prohibition at the City Club on January 6, 1922. They later took their argument out to the neighborhoods, debating at the Pilsen Park Pavilion in early March. A mass protest against Prohibition and all blue laws, also at the pavilion, followed two weeks later.

Besides debating with Lyle and other prohibitionist aldermen, Cermak carried his anti-Prohibition campaign across the city. Cermak attacked Mayor Thompson for establishing a law enforcement commissioner's office to administer federal and state prohibition laws. He played an essential role in the organization of the Anti-Prohibition League of Illinois. The league held a huge rally in Chicago at which many national leaders spoke, including Al Smith, the New York progressive. Cermak continued to build his political base across the city and even had influence across the nation as the Wet Movement gained momentum.[25]

Defense of personal freedom, embraced by anti-Prohibition forces, was a major political force in the city and the county, and spurred on Cermak's political career. On the evening of October 4, 1922, all of the largest Czech neighborhoods participated in an automobile parade in conjunction with a huge Czechoslovak rally in support of personal rights at Pilsen Park. Bohemians from Pilsen, Czech California, the Back of the Yards, and Cicero took part. Organizers held another mass meeting the following Friday afternoon at Pilsen Park. These rallies also continued to raise support for Cermak in his bid for the presidency of the Cook County Board, a campaign that had the full support of the Chicago Czech press. The *Denní Hlasatel* called for newly registered Czech voters to remember Cermak and pleaded for a campaign to register yet more Czech voters.[26]

The Anti-Saloon League attacked Cermak. It rallied behind Charles S. Peterson, the Republican opponent, and sent out anti-Cermak "Citizens Enrollment" pledge cards. Protestant churches rallied to the Republican banner. Yet Cermak, with his ethnic support, a growing alliance with some of the Irish faction, and a growing patronage army, looked invincible. Just days before the election, Prohibition agents raided saloons in Cermak's ward, and several newspapers reported that Cermak's saloon had not been targeted. The outraged candidate protested that he had never owned a saloon and that his political opponents had orchestrated the raids and the rumors. In the end, Cermak won by a relatively narrow margin of 20,000 votes out of over 700,000 cast.[27]

The newly elected president of the Cook County Board began his term in an unfavorable position. Republicans held a one-seat majority on the board and could block any of his proposals. Again Cermak demonstrated his political skill, bringing Republicans into his coalition. He knew how to use the rules of the political game and did not hesitate to play it well. His biographer called him pitiless as he changed the governing structure of the board and consolidated his control. Such actions would not go unnoticed among a younger, rising group of Democratic politicians that included Richard J. Daley, a member of the Bridgeport political organization of Cermak's ally, Alderman Joseph McDonough.[28]

Cermak, a Czech, remained in many ways an outlier of the Regular Democratic Organization, which was still under Irish control. Cermak was unprepared for a fight with Brennan to control the party. His relationship with newly elected Mayor Dever also proved distant. Despite Dever's attempts to enforce Prohibition and strike against organized crime, Cermak did not openly attack him. By 1927, Cermak helped broker an understanding between the Thompson–Crowe Republicans and the Brennan Democrats. In this way, Cermak was instrumental in helping to defeat the opposition forces in both parties during the primaries. The byzantine politics of Cook County and Chicago persisted.

In 1926 Cermak won reelection as president of the Cook County Board, but now he faced a board overwhelmingly controlled by the Republicans. Brennan may have been involved in a deal with the GOP to weaken Cermak so that he wouldn't run for mayor in 1927. By 1928, the wily North Side Irish leader had outmaneuvered Cermak as he sought the party's nomination for governor. Brennan's forces handed the nomination to Judge Floyd E. Thompson and nominated Cermak for the US Senate, a position he did not want. Cermak then went down in defeat in the very Republican year of 1928, which saw

CHAPTER 6

Herbert C. Hoover defeat Cermak's friend and fellow wet advocate, Al Smith, for the presidency.[29]

CERMAK RISING

Nevertheless, Cermak's star continued to rise in Democratic circles. In late July 1928, George Brennan had a tooth extracted; an infection rapidly spread, and Brennan died on August 8. The Democratic Party of Cook County stood leaderless, and the usual political maneuvering unfolded. The Irish hoped to hold on to the reins of power, but the party itself seemed to be in a quandary.[30] Reportedly, Brennan had on his deathbed crowned Michael J. Igoe as his heir. Many questioned that claim. The very management of the local party was at stake, including the national committeeman appointment. County Chair Martin J. O'Brien led a committee of ten to work on the issue. Four members threw their support to Igoe, while five others supported Cermak. Then George F. Getz, a millionaire coal dealer, emerged, and Igoe withdrew his name from consideration. But Getz responded that he had no intention of taking the national committeeman position for the local Democrats, as he had been a Republican all his life. The bizarre dance for control of the party continued unresolved.[31]

The local party dispute exploded after the November 1928 election as Cermak moved to consolidate control. Cermak had held office for a long time and enjoyed basically good public relations. Most Chicagoans knew of him because of his leadership of the United Societies. His tenure as president of the Cook County Board gave him a reputation as an able public official, and none of his opponents, except possibly Alderman John S. Clark, could match his stature or reputation. Importantly, he controlled more patronage jobs than any of his opponents. Several of the Irish, who might have joined the opposition, actually owed their offices to him. In addition, Cermak had a very important Czech core and the support of other immigrant groups, especially the Poles and the West Side Jews. The Irish had dominated the top party leadership since 1915, and in 1926 they held at least thirty-three of the fifty ward committeemen positions.

The 1926 Brennan slate for office consisted of twenty-five Irish out of forty-two candidates. Nevertheless, a number of Irish politicians had bristled under Brennan's rule, especially the "Pig Shit" Irish of Bridgeport.

Cermak found support among the Brennan-hating Irish, the old Harrison faction, Poles, Germans, and Jews. Importantly, a wealthy and powerful West Side Irishman, Patrick Nash, joined the Cermak coalition. Nash gave cover to the Irish who worried about retribution from those opposed to Cermak. This multiethnic coalition took control and Cermak took over the party. His final victory became apparent when he proclaimed himself a candidate for mayor in December 1930.[32]

Cermak's victory came on the heels of the vast demographic change in the city, which brought about a political realignment that would soon favor the Democrats. Cermak saw an opportunity to create a powerful force that might sweep him and the Democrats into office across the city, perhaps permanently, especially if he could win over the growing Black Republican base. The coming economic collapse and the ensuing Great Depression gave him and the Democrats that very opportunity. Cermak had long had his sights set on the mayor's office. More importantly, he thought he might be able to create the powerful citywide organization that had long been the goal of both Democratic and Republican politicians—a Chicago Tammany Hall. In reality, Cermak built a powerful machine that would outlast and, in many ways, outperform the legendary New York City Democratic organization.

MAYOR CERMAK

By 1931, many in both the Democratic and Republican parties knew that Thompson had run his course as mayor. After the primaries, Big Bill made several blunders that enabled Cermak to rally his forces, especially the vast ethnic coalition. The 1930 census counted the Poles as the largest ethnic group in the city, and they remained allied with the Czechs and Cermak. Jake Arvey and the Jews, another large voting bloc, also favored the Democratic leader. Other eastern and southern European ethnic groups looked on Cermak's candidacy with favor, as did many Germans.[33]

Thompson called Cermak "Bozo" and "Bohunk," trying to rally anti-immigrant prejudice once again. But by this time the foreign-born and their children made up 64.3 percent of the population. Thompson attempted to divide Cermak's voters, attacking them as ignorant immigrants, while evoking ethnic, racial, and economic prejudices, but to no avail. The Democrat won overwhelmingly, collecting over 58 percent of the total vote, 671,189 votes to Thompson's 476,922. He carried forty-five of the fifty wards. In the largest voter turnout in Chicago up to that time, 82 percent of registered voters voted, and women made up over 40 percent of voters. Cermak became Chicago's thirty-eighth mayor and the first (and so far, only) immigrant to hold that office.[34]

Cermak had finally captured what he saw as the ultimate prize. However, as the Great Depression spread, it placed the city under extreme economic duress. The Depression, of course, had played an important role in Cermak's victory. Many saw the need to change the administration, not only in Chicago, but nationally. Cermak realized the enormity of the task he faced. In September 1931, only 51 of the city's 228 banks remained open. A year later 750,000 Chicagoans did not have jobs, and of the 800,000 still working, many were only part-time. Evictions skyrocketed and rents plummeted. Riots broke out across the city as many lost their apartments or houses.

The city's inability to pay its workers, especially public school teachers, symbolized the catastrophe. By the summer of 1931, the school board offered to pay teachers in scrip, an emergency substitute for government currency. The board owed over $15 million in salaries and unpaid bills. Firemen, police, and other city employees often also went unpaid. Cermak approached both Springfield and Washington, DC, for aid, warning of thousands of hungry and desperate men in the city's streets. He said that the federal government could send Chicago either money or troops.[35]

Cermak naturally found himself enmeshed in statewide as well as national Democratic Party politics. In Illinois, he hoped to create a powerful statewide machine. In the lead-up to the next gubernatorial election, Cermak leveraged his power. The Irish Brennan faction of the Democratic Party wanted to nominate Michael L. Igoe, but Cermak turned to his Jewish base and supported a German Jew, Judge Henry Horner. Horner had played an important role in Cermak's campaign for mayor. With a solid reputation for integrity, Horner proved a good choice. Of course, Jews had not held many important elective offices up to that point. With this nomination, Cermak made an extremely bold move to recognize ethnic groups often ignored by the old Irish party bosses. Then, to balance the Cook County slate and unite the party, Cermak supported several Irish candidates as well. Above all, Cermak insisted on wet candidates who opposed Prohibition. His strategy worked: Cermak candidates dominated the Democratic primary. He applied this same approach nationally.

Cermak's interest in national politics revolved around the liquor issue. He wanted a candidate for the White House who would do away with Prohibition. Cermak favored his old friend Al Smith, while also supporting Illinois Senator James H. Lewis, a very dark horse candidate. This remained his public stance until the 1932 convention. The nomination of New York Governor Franklin Delano Roosevelt posed a problem for Cermak because it seemed he would be on the outside of any possible Roosevelt administration. Local Democrats feared this would hurt their chances to get federal patronage and would put Cermak in a difficult position locally.[36]

After Roosevelt's and the Democrats' overwhelming victory in the 1932 national elections, Cermak faced the question of how best to establish a working relationship with the new administration. Cermak reluctantly went to meet with FDR, who was recuperating in Florida from the long and demanding campaign. He wanted not only federal patronage but federal aid for his financially stressed city. On February 15, 1933, supporters held a huge reception for FDR at Bayfront Park in Miami. Cermak sat in the reviewing stand while FDR rode in an open car, waving to his supporters. He beckoned Cermak to approach, but the mayor waited until FDR finished a short speech. Then Cermak and others approached Roosevelt and exchanged a few words. As the presidential car prepared to leave, shots rang out, hitting Cermak and several others. All hell broke loose. The car moved away, and the police extracted the shooter, Giuseppe Zangara, from the crowd. With the help of two companions, Cermak walked to the car, and it sped to the hospital with FDR cradling Cermak in his arms. Over the next nineteen days the mayor struggled for his life, but he finally died on March 6.[37]

Cermak left a vital legacy: a well-organized administration, ethnic inclusiveness, and full party rule. Even when he had named Nash as his replacement in the Democratic Party structure, he retained control. Cermak dominated the City Council and could be ruthless in using his power to manage aldermen. He worked to expand his coalition, and therefore his power, by reaching out to the growing number of African American voters. Importantly, he kept his home in South Lawndale. By staying in Czech California, he showed his loyalty to his base. Unfortunately, Cermak's unexpected death meant that he had not groomed a successor. Democrats scrambled to find a replacement for their martyred mayor.[38]

7
Bridgeport's Victory

> I didn't even know I was a candidate for mayor—and I shall need the aid of all my colleagues to bring order out chaos.
> FRANK J. CORR,
> Acting Mayor of the City of Chicago, March 14, 1933[1]

Chicago found itself leaderless as a result of an assassination for the second time in just under forty years. Again, the City Council divided over how to proceed. The fact that Cermak lingered for weeks should have given leaders a chance to put together an agreement, but the vagueness of the law and the lack of enabling legislation hampered them, as did factionalism in the Democratic Party and a still strong Republican opposition. The closed-door negotiations further unsettled the situation. This would not be the first time, nor the last, that the death of a mayor would throw the City Council into a frenzy of torturous political maneuvering.

Several politicians began to organize to capture the mayor's office. Many Irish Democrats, who chafed under Cermak's rule, hoped to replace the martyred mayor. These included John S. Clark from the affluent West Side 3rd Ward, John Duffy from the prosperous 19th Ward (which included the Beverly neighborhood), and Dan Ryan, son of the late County Commissioner of the same name. Another possible candidate, Jacob Arvey, a West Side Jewish politician and alderman of the 24th Ward, realized that Illinois already had a Jewish governor, and decided to step back. Speculation revolved around Patrick Nash, Cermak's ally. While Nash did not want the office, he nonetheless eventually played a winning hand. Nash decided to stay in the background as the elder statesman of the party. Known as "the great harmonizer," he worked to settle intraparty disputes, which made him popular with the ethnic groups in the grand coalition Cermak bequeathed to the Democrats.[2]

FRANK J. CORR: A DE LA SALLE GRADUATE

On March 8, 1933, two days after Cermak's funeral, the Democrats met at the Morrison Hotel and affirmed Nash as party leader. But soon they maneuvered to identify an acting mayor. Alderman Clark, from the West Side, a fifteen-year veteran of the council and for a decade the chair of the Finance Committee, emerged as the leading candidate. Nash, however, opposed his candidacy. Six days later, a bruising contest unfolded between the Nash organization and a group of Republicans and Democrats allied behind Clark. The day began with a special meeting of the City Council as Corporation Counsel William H. Sexton gave the opinion that the aldermen had no legal power to elect an acting mayor. Immediately, the Democratic Organization went into session at the Morrison Hotel and decided that an acting mayor should be elected in order to give the appearance of continuity, even if he did not have the full powers of the mayoralty. Despite Sexton's legal opinion, Nash and his supporters decided to elect their choice, Frank J. Corr.

Less than an hour later, the fight went to the council chamber. Immediately the question arose of who would chair the special meeting. Legendary Alderman Bathhouse John Coughlin rose and named Nash's choice, Alderman James Quinn. The opposition nominated Alderman Bowler. After an emotional debate, Quinn won easily. Next came an argument over whether the ballot should be secret. Clark's supporters insisted it should, as it had been after the assassination of Carter Harrison in 1893. The Nash people clamored that the public deserved to know how each alderman voted. The open ballot passed easily when Clark's supporters refused to vote on the question. The City Council soon picked Frank J. Corr, alderman of the 17th Ward and the choice of the Regular Democratic Organization, as acting mayor.

Corr lived with his wife, Mary Burke, at 507 West Englewood Avenue in his longtime ward. Born in Brooklyn in 1877, he arrived with his parents in Chicago in 1889. Corr graduated from De La Salle Institute in 1895. After receiving a degree from the Kent College of Law in 1899, he entered the office of the city's corporation counsel. Englewood voters elected him to the City Council in 1931 and reelected him in 1933. As head of the 17th Ward Regular Democratic Organization, the alderman had aligned himself politically with Coroner Frank J. Walsh and County Commissioner Daniel J. Ryan, another De La Salle Institute graduate. He also served as treasurer of the Forest Preserve District under Cermak and later as special counsel to the district. When asked about his views on Prohibition, he responded, "I am wetter than Cermak ever was."[3]

No one, least of all the sickly fifty-six-year-old Corr, expected him to fill Cermak's shoes permanently. On his first day in office, Corr presided over a stormy City Council meeting to consider a proposal by Alderman Toman that 22nd Street be renamed after the martyred mayor. Toman explained that the heavily Czech suburbs of Cicero, Berwyn, and North Riverside also planned to change the name of the street, which ran through them.[4]

The day that Corr had been tapped as acting mayor, Illinois Senate Minority Leader Benjamin Adamowski, a Democrat, introduced an amendment in Springfield allowing the City Council to choose a new mayor from either within or outside its ranks. Previously, the law stipulated that aldermen had to choose a mayor only from among themselves. Nash supported the amendment, and Democrats in both houses of the Illinois legislature, who now feared him, voted for the change by an overwhelming margin. This allowed Nash to handpick the next mayor.[5]

CHAPTER 7

MAYOR EDWARD KELLY: A SOUTH SIDE IRISH CATHOLIC MAYOR

In 1865, fifteen-year-old Stephen Kelly arrived in Chicago from Galway, Ireland, and settled in Bridgeport. He married a German woman named Helen Lang in 1873 and joined the fire department the next year. The first of their nine children, Edward Joseph Kelly, was born on May 1, 1876. The family lived for a while in Bridgeport and then moved to nearby Brighton Park. Edward worked from a young age, first as a newsboy and later as a cash boy at the elegant Marshall Field's department store downtown. He dropped out of school after the fifth grade and continued to work at various jobs, including carrying growler cans of beer to men at the Armour cannery. By the age of eighteen, Ed Kelly worked for the Chicago Sanitary District, where he would stay for nearly forty years.

Kelly began as an axman there, clearing trees along the canal. He took engineering classes at night at the Chicago Atheneum. He also opened a funeral parlor with his friend, Jim Doran, at 2500 West 38th Street in Brighton Park. At the time, the neighborhood had a growing Irish population centering on the parish of St. Agnes. Many of these Irish migrated from Bridgeport as large numbers of eastern and southern Europeans, especially Czechs, Poles, and Lithuanians, arrived in the original settlement along Archer Avenue. Ambitious and energetic, Kelly also became involved in Democratic politics through the Brighton Park Athletic Club. These political connections often threatened Kelly's job at the Sanitary District, especially when Republicans had control. He became involved in a fight with a Republican supervisor and was called before Robert R. McCormick, the president of the Sanitary District and publisher of the *Chicago Tribune*. Kelly expected to be fired, but he impressed the Republican, who became his lifelong supporter. McCormick gave Kelly a very substantial raise of fifty dollars a month. By 1920, Kelly served as the chief engineer of the Sanitary District despite little or no formal training. Kelly's relationship with McCormick, as well as his important Democratic Party associations, ensured that he would have a bright political future. Most important, during his years as chief engineer, Kelly developed both a business relationship and a personal friendship with Patrick Nash.[6]

In 1933, Ed Kelly planned to meet Cermak in Havana, Cuba, after the mayor's meeting with Roosevelt in Florida. Giuseppe Zangara put an end to those plans. Kelly then rushed to Cermak's side. On Thursday, April 13, Nash chose Kelly to fill out Cermak's mayoral term, scheduled to end in April 1935. Thirty-seven Democratic aldermen voted unanimously to elect Kelly. The new mayor pledged to carry on Cermak's policies. He resigned as chief engineer of the Sanitary District but kept his position as head of the South Park Board.[7]

Kelly's first months in office were both difficult and celebratory. He officiated over the 1933 Century of Progress World's Fair held in the South Park district, over which he maintained control. At the same time, Chicago's finances struggled. Many public employees remained unpaid, tax assessments seemed muddled, tax resisters abounded, and need haunted the city. Kelly had a solid reputation as an administrator. He had cut the expenditures of the South Park Board by 37 percent in 1932, yet the South Park System had more visitors than ever, more than fifteen million people. McCormick's *Chicago Tribune* remained optimistic about Kelly's chances as mayor.[8]

Just two days into Kelly's term, public school teachers and students held a huge demonstration demanding back pay for the faculty and staff. Kelly prepared to go to Washington, DC, to renew the city's plea for a loan to meet the school payrolls. He asked citizens to invest in Chicago's 6 percent tax warrants. He called it both the duty and the privilege of Chicagoans to invest in the city. While he realized that many could not pay their taxes, Kelly urged those who could to step up. Kelly urged Chicagoans "to snap out of it." Referring to his pugilistic childhood near the stockyards, he promoted his personal motto, "stick and slug." He said, "The idea was stay in the fight and pound away. This is what Chicago must do."[9]

In Mayor Ed Kelly, the "Pig Shit" Irish of the stockyards finally had their revenge. Kelly transferred power from the West and North Sides to the South Side, and particularly to Bridgeport, where it would stay for generations to come. Bridgeport emerged as a polit-

7.1 Century of Progress World's Fair postcard, 1933. This view of the General Exhibits Group of the World's Fair shows the modernist style favored by the fair's designers. Unlike the 1893 Columbian Exposition, the 1933 fair looked not back to classical European architecture but forward to a futuristic design. Postcard, Author's Collection.

ical powerhouse. It did not matter that Kelly no longer lived in the neighborhood—Bridgeport's Irish Democrats happily supported the Kelly–Nash machine. More importantly, thanks to Cermak and the Roosevelt landslide, the new machine would be a citywide organization. Both Kelly and Nash understood that the once-in-a-lifetime chance this afforded must not be squandered.

Kelly quickly moved to solidify the Cermak coalition. He reached out to organized labor, including the Chicago Federation of Labor and the Teamsters Union, and promised a crackdown on labor racketeers. Kelly then reached out to business leaders announcing "Let's Go Chicago Week," a citywide undertaking to garner support for President Roosevelt's attempt to tackle the economic crisis. Kelly also made sure to reach out to the diverse ethnic and racial populations. The Century of Progress Fair gave the new mayor a grand stage, which he used to ingratiate himself with ethnic groups. Even as South Park commissioner he had courted various nationalities, including the Germans and the Irish. In 1930 Kelly had accepted a monument to the German dramatist Gotthold Ephraim Lessing in the Washington Park Rose Garden. As mayor, Kelly spoke at the August 1933 German Day at the fair, declaring that Chicagoans of German descent could claim, more than any others, to have done exceptional work in Chicago's growth. His remark that the Germans made up the best group of taxpayers in the city brought forth applause. In September, upon the urging of important German American leaders, Kelly nominated Arthur R. Seyferlich as Fire Commissioner. Throughout the next few years he would continue to court the still large German American vote.[10]

Kelly maintained his close relationship with the Irish. He chaired the committee that organized Irish Day at the fair on August 2. He greeted a group of Irish amateur boxers on Irish Night in Jackson Park and attended Mass with them at Our Lady of Sorrows Church on the West Side. Kelly thanked the Lord Mayor of Dublin, Alfred Byrne, for sending a letter along with the boxers and presenting him with a blackthorn cane.

Of course, Kelly continued to woo other important groups in the Cermak organization. He reached out to the Poles, many of whom remained disappointed that the party had not chosen M. S. Szymczak, the head of the Polish American Democratic Organization, as mayor. But Roosevelt did appoint Szymczak to the Board of Governors of the Federal Reserve, then the highest federal position obtained by a Polish American. This elevation also effectively removed a possible rival of Kelly's from Chicago.

The Polish community also gained various symbolic victories, such as mayoral participation in Polish Constitution Day celebrations. When Polish General Roman Gorecki visited the city, he met with the mayor and toured the Century of Progress Fair. Both Polish American veterans and veterans of the Polish Blue Army, organized in the United States, participated in the huge Memorial Day Parade down Michigan Avenue. Kelly also supported the movement to rename Crawford Avenue after Count Casimir Pulaski, the Polish hero of the American Revolution. Kelly greeted the Chicago Polonia during the Polish Week of Hospitality and Polish Day at the fair.

CHAPTER 7

Both Kelly and Governor Horner sponsored the Polish concert at the Auditorium Building during that week. In October, Kelly made sure to speak in the rotunda of the United States Court Building in the Loop during a ceremony honoring Pulaski.[11]

Kelly, notably, wanted to attract African Americans to the Democratic Party. Cermak had made substantial inroads, and the election of Roosevelt, as well as the onset of the New Deal, made the party more attractive to Black Chicagoans. The election of Governor Horner also helped. At his inauguration, Horner pledged a Fair Deal for Blacks and invited Robert S. Abbott, the editor and publisher of the *Chicago Defender*, to visit the governor's mansion. In April 1933, Kelly, as president of the South Park Commission, named three Blacks to the South Park Police Force to serve at the World's Fair site. The *Defender* had campaigned for ten years for African Americans to be appointed to that department. African Americans took part in the World's Fair, dispelling rumors that they would be excluded. On May 27, they proudly marched in the opening day parade as Spencer C. Dickerson, commanding officer of the famous Eight Infantry, and two of his staff officers joined Kelly on the reviewing stand. The *Chicago Defender* claimed that Blacks accounted for roughly three out of every ten persons attending the opening of the fair. In May, Kelly appointed Abbott to the mayor's committee on business restoration. By September, Kelly appointed Nathan K. McGill, legal advisor to the *Defender*, to the legislative committee of his Chicago Recovery initiative. Abbott's newspaper praised the mayor for living "beyond the hampering influences of petty prejudices and racial bigotry." Kelly began to win the hearts and minds of the African American community, as well as others, as he worked to maintain and expand the evolving Democratic coalition in the city. Many of these actions might be seen as purely symbolic overtures. But for both Polish Americans and African Americans, these actions proved to be meaningful, giving them standing in a society that had simply ignored or disdained them.[12]

In October 1934 the mayor met with a grievance committee of Black parents to discuss the de facto segregation of Morgan Park High School on the far South Side. Black parents told Kelly that the two branch schools set up near Morgan Park High, purportedly to relieve overcrowded conditions, actually resulted in segregation. Kelly rescinded the Board of Education's edict establishing the branch campuses and ordered that Black students be reassigned to the main high school. In response, over two thousand White students walked out of Morgan Park High in protest. Some two hundred White protestors arrived at Kelly's office on Thursday, October 11, where Kelly told them that he opposed any movement to "deny the right of any citizen of Chicago the privilege of attendance at any public institution of learning regardless of race, color, or creed." The following year, at the dedication of the all-African American New Wendell Phillips High School, Kelly said that he looked forward to integrated public schools. The mayor articulated the kinds of issues that Chicago's Black population wanted to hear, and he gave visibility to Black Chicagoans. For example, Kelly singled out for praise the Black firefighters who battled the massive Union Stock Yard Fire in May 1934. Kelly named boxer Joe Louis "mayor" for ten minutes in October 1935. These kinds of things paid off when over 80 percent of the voters in the three major Black wards threw their support behind Kelly in his 1935 campaign for the mayor's office.[13]

KELLY, THE POLICY WHEEL, AND THE GROWTH OF THE DEMOCRATIC MACHINE

Like many Chicago politicians before him, Kelly openly consorted with gamblers. From the days of Mike McDonald, gamblers and other underworld figures had figured prominently in Chicago politics. Now, as the Democratic Party courted Chicago's traditionally Republican-leaning Black community, gambling interests played an important role.

When Anton Cermak sought to woo the Black vote soon after taking office in 1931, he unfortunately used a rather blunt instrument, targeting the "policy wheel," an illegal lottery-style numbers racket long popular in African American communities that employed thousands of Black Chicagoans. Announcing an attack on gambling, prostitution, and other illegal activities in the Black Belt, Cermak told

Police Captain John Stege to "raise all the hell you can with the policy gang." Stege had some 200 persons arrested daily, tripling Black arrests. Apparently Cermak let it be known that the pressure would end if Black voters supported the Democratic Party. At the same time, Cermak hardly felt the need to wipe out gambling in neighborhoods where White gamblers operated openly.[14]

In response, numbers racket leaders then formed a "Policy Syndicate" to defend their enterprise. Fifteen men, twelve African Americans and three Whites, controlled the syndicate, and they used it as a neighborhood organization to provide jobs to the Black community. In 1938 the syndicate employed over 5,000 people with a weekly payroll of $25,000 ($494,802 in 2023) and an annual gross profit of at least $18,000,000 ($356,257,895). It provided financial aid to hard-pressed employees and maintained a team of lawyers and bondsmen. The syndicate handled relationships with downtown political authorities, in part through the strategic use of bribes. In 1938 at least $7,500 ($148,440) a week in bribes flowed from the syndicate, although some estimates went as high as $40,000 a week.

Politicians and police generally ignored the policy racket as long as they received payoffs. Like all corruption, this mixed the idea of the sacred (that is, the neighborhood) with the profane (or moneyed interests), but it was also a means of survival in a community that not only suffered from racism, but especially felt the impact of the Great Depression. Policy bosses situated policy stations, where a bet could be placed, throughout Bronzeville. Legitimate businesses—cigar stores, restaurants, laundries, and other small enterprises—fronted roughly half of the stations during the Depression. Lines of customers gathered outside the establishments with slips of paper on which they had listed numbers between one and seventy-eight. Runners distributed the winning numbers three times a day.

Black Chicagoans viewed Policy Kings as kindhearted people who looked after their neighbors and provided important social and economic supports. In this manner, they took on the same public image in their community as ward politicians like John Powers. Particularly when the Depression weakened legitimate businesses in Bronzeville, the Policy Kings emerged as race leaders. They exercised considerable economic control over community institutions, by giving or withholding funds and employment. They supported churches and charities, winning the loyalty of many in the community. African Americans often considered the attack on gambling in the Black Belt an attack on the race. The Policy Kings knew how to exploit this feeling, and they became folk heroes. A loyal church member stated that while he personally did not like the game, "If it takes policy to keep some people eating, that's all there is to it."

Other members of the community openly celebrated their success. When the Jones brothers, the most powerful Policy Kings, opened a legitimate store in 1937 on 47th Street in the heart of Bronzeville, a strip dominated by White-owned businesses, it became a source of community pride. The opening celebration included appearances by famed boxer Joe Louis and the well-known dancer Bill "Bojangles" Robinson, who entertained the crowd of several thousand. Prominent politicians, lawyers, and others, both Black and White, addressed the throng and lauded the Jones brothers. A Chicago Police lieutenant praised the crowd's behavior. Several prominent clergy prayed for the success of the undertaking. Others called it a credit to the race.

The popularity of the policy wheel ran deep in the Bronzeville community. Unlike his predecessor, Mayor Kelly adopted more of a hands-off attitude toward it. Kelly's tolerance of this local institution helped to grow his popularity among Black Chicagoans. It also amplified the power of those who played an extraordinary political game in Bronzeville and slowly turned the Black community away from the Republican Party, furthering the effort to solidify the Democratic machine.[15]

DAWSON, CLOUT, COMMUNITY, AND THE EMERGING BLACK DEMOCRATIC MAJORITY

The Kelly–Nash machine searched for a way to create and control a Black Democratic sub-machine that would not only bring African Americans into the Democratic Party but also discipline and control them as voters. They decided to partner with the Policy Kings.

Policy Kings gave ample funds to politicians and provided critical manpower for the Democrats, sending their employees out to gather votes. The Jones brothers even signed up as precinct captains. Kelly responded by protecting policy wheels and granting more patronage to Black wards than even Big Bill Thompson. The Democrat also improved the quality of city patronage jobs for Bronzeville and appointed African American leaders to prestigious committees. In addition, he broke down many of the barriers that blocked Black policemen from rising in the ranks. The Democratic machine, however, still needed a loyal supporter who could lead the new Black sub-machine. That leader would be William L. Dawson.[16]

In 1933, voters had elected the then Republican Dawson as alderman of the 2nd Ward. A World War I veteran and lawyer, Dawson started his career as a state committeeman. Both Dawson and 3rd Ward Republican Alderman Robert R. Jackson felt comfortable with Kelly's posture toward African Americans and the Bronzeville community. Kelly, who had previously supported Arthur Mitchell in his successful congressional campaign against Oscar De Priest as a way to undermine the Republican hold on African American communities, nonetheless supported the Republican Dawson's reelection as alderman. Afterward, Dawson again professed his support for Kelly. On March 31, 1935, Kelly appeared at the Eighth Regiment Armory in the 2nd Ward, where Dawson and other Black Republicans joined him. Pastors and other leaders also threw their support behind Kelly, including Rev. H. M. Carroll of the South Park AME Church and A. L. Jackson, president of the Board of Trustees of Provident Hospital. Many on the South Side believed that Kelly planned to take over the Republican Party in Bronzeville. Indeed, among the important Black Republicans, only De Priest did not get behind the mayor.[17]

Dawson played the traditional role of an alderman: getting traffic lights installed, supporting youth groups including the Dawson Boosters Basketball Team, a softball team, and organizing celebrations such as the 2nd Ward picnic. In addition, he also called for Blacks to be hired by street railway companies and argued that the Cook County Nurses Home should open its dormitory doors to African American students. William E. King, 2nd Ward Republican committeeman, feared Dawson's political ambitions and worked to impede the alderman's ability to hand out favors and distribute patronage. As the years passed, the two became intense rivals. In 1938, the break between the two men sharpened after Dawson won the Republican primary to oppose Arthur Mitchell, the Democrat incumbent congressman. While Dawson had the nominal support of the Republican Party, King worked against him.

By the end of the 1930s, Dawson began to look to Democrats to fulfill his goals, especially once an opportunity presented itself in the Regular Democratic Organization of the 2nd Ward. Black Democrats in the ward staged a revolt against the White committeeman Joseph E. Tittinger, who favored the small White minority in the ward with patronage jobs and favors. Tittinger vowed to continue as a committeeman as long as even a single White voter lived in the ward. Dawson advised the rebel Democrats to approach the mayor. The 2nd Ward had delivered more than 20,000 votes for Kelly's election that year. In June 1939, fifty-three precinct captains petitioned Kelly to remove Tittinger. After Tittinger fired all of the precinct captains, they banded together as an independent organization. Fearing a split in the Black Democratic ranks, Kelly decided to remove Tittinger. At this point, Dawson threw his support to Earl Dickerson, a Democrat, against his rival William King, who had beaten Dawson for the Republican nomination for alderman. Dickerson won and Dawson let Kelly know that he might change parties. After consulting with Dickerson, Kelly supported Dawson to become the Democratic ward committeeman. Pat Nash worried about the appointment, as he did not trust politicians who changed parties for personal gain, but Kelly prevailed, and Dawson found a new home in the Democratic Party.[18]

As Dawson sought to consolidate his power in the 2nd Ward, he faced another rival in Dickerson. The break between the two men happened quickly. Kelly chose both of them to lead fundraising in the 2nd Ward for the Mayor's Annual Christmas Fund, which provided clothing for poor children. They pledged to raise $5,000. After they did, Dawson felt that Dickerson took credit for what Dawson's team had achieved. The two argued, and Dawson moved to isolate Dick-

7.2 Bronzeville's communal web. This map shows several of the major African American congregations in the area under Dawson's control. It also marks several meeting halls, policy wheel stations, schools, etcetera. The great number of policy wheel stations, numbering in the thousands, and the many storefront churches added to this communal web but would be impossible to situate here. Courtesy of Chicago CartoGraphics, with Parker Otto.

erson from the 2nd Ward Democratic Organization. Over the next few years, the rivalry would draw the Kelly–Nash machine into the fray, with Dawson winning the machine's support and emerging as a powerhouse on the South Side.

In 1940 Dickerson decided he wanted to replace Mitchell in Congress. Dawson backed Mitchell's reelection knowing full well that the Kelly–Nash machine valued loyalty and would support the incumbent. Increasingly isolated from the mayor's orbit, Dickerson joined Alderman Paul Douglas and others in criticizing Kelly. In 1942, when Mitchell decided not to run for another term, Dickerson found himself cut off from the Kelly–Nash organization. Instead, Dawson became the candidate to replace Mitchell, easily defeating Dickerson, who ran as an independent in the primary. Dawson went on to win the congressional election against his old nemesis, the Republican William E. King. The 2nd Ward committeeman soon consolidated his power. In 1943, his candidate, William H. Harvey, defeated Dickerson for alderman in the 2nd Ward. In addition, his ally, Christopher Wimbish, became committeeman of the 3rd Ward. Eventually Dawson would control five South Side wards, and some 250,000 votes. By every measure Dawson had real clout.[19]

The policy game provided a financial base for Dawson's political, civic, and church work. He accepted contributions from the Policy Kings, who controlled the largest available pool of money in the Black community. The Policy Syndicate, while a viable institution in the African American community, required protection from both City Hall and the local Democratic organization. Dawson defended the policy racket, seeing it as no different from legal suburban racetracks and Catholic parishes' bingo games. Dawson also consistently protected the Policy Kings from outside White gangsters who sought to take over Policy.[20]

The African American community in Chicago was internally divided by religion, ideology, party loyalty, and social class, but the scourge of racism proved to be a uniting factor. Dawson did not have the advantage that widespread Catholic ethnic support gave so many White politicians. His clout came from the reality of race relations in Chicago. Ironically, the hostility of the White community allowed

CHAPTER 7

Dawson to unite a divided people and create political clout. It was a different kind of communalism.

LABOR, ETHNIC, CLASS CONFLICT AND THE KELLY-NASH MACHINE

Kelly and the nation confronted overwhelming issues during the 1930s. At the forefront was the economic collapse. As unemployment mushroomed to unprecedented levels, organized labor came back to life after languishing during the conservative 1920s. Racial, ethnic, and class tensions fomented unrest in big northern cities. Questions about the role of government fueled many debates. The growing appeal of radical organizations caused worry too. These included not only the Communist Party on the left but also right-wing nationalist groups connected with Father Charles E. Coughlin, the radio priest who spewed anti-Semitic rhetoric; Huey Long, the Democratic populist; and the pro-Nazi German American Bund. These coalescing challenges tested traditional institutions such as churches, fraternal groups, and other communal organizations. The crises of the 1930s changed American attitudes for several generations and had a lasting impact on the entire nation.

During the early years of the economic collapse, Chicagoans relied heavily on private charities, but these soon proved to be insufficient. Immigrant working-class and Black communities suffered the most. Bank failures occurred all over the city, but they hit Bronzeville especially hard. Chicago's Blacks comprised only 8 percent of the population in 1933 but accounted for 22 percent of the unemployed and 34 percent of those on relief.

Naturally, Kelly looked to Washington for aid. On August 6, 1934, Chairman Jesse H. Jones of the Reconstruction Finance Corporation informed President Roosevelt of a loan of $22.5 million (over $502 million in 2023) to Chicago to cover 15,000 teachers' back pay. Jones noted that Kelly had proposed the plan and the Chicago School Board put up school property as collateral. He also praised M. S. Szymczak, a member of the Federal Reserve Board and longtime leader in Chicago's Polish American community, whose appointment to the Federal Reserve Board had been in part orchestrated by Kelly. Chicago's business community, especially bankers, lavishly praised the deal, as did representatives of the teachers. Importantly, the loan underscored the role of the federal government in fighting the Great Depression and in society.[21]

The impact of Roosevelt's New Deal on the city and on its politics cannot be overestimated. Through various programs, it funded projects that called for a maximum of labor and a minimum of equipment, such as street repair, park improvements, and sewer construction. The unprecedented federal largesse resulted in the expansion of Municipal Airport (Midway Airport), lakefront improvements, an expanded Lake Shore Drive (now DuSable Lake Shore Drive), and creation of the State Street subway. Kelly's good relationship with Roosevelt and with New Deal administrators both in Washington, DC, and Chicago facilitated these investments. Kelly claimed credit for these programs and the resulting jobs. This skillful management of the relationship between federal and city governments would become the model for future mayors, particularly Richard J. Daley.[22]

Kelly quickly emerged as the most powerful Democrat in Illinois. In the first few months of his administration, he had several important triumphs. He met the municipal payroll, wiped out a significant portion of the city's debt, established good relations with the state legislature, and importantly kept the public schools open. Initially, he also enjoyed a good understanding with his fellow Democrat, Governor Horner, and had a good working relationship with the Roosevelt administration.

Of course, scandal also hurt Kelly. In August 1933, newspapers revealed that Kelly, as well as other local politicians, had filed fraudulent tax returns. Kelly avoided prosecution by settling with the Internal Revenue Service for $106,390 ($2,462,028 in 2023). It remained on the front page of Chicago newspapers as the IRS charged other Chicago politicians, including Nash, with tax evasion. The Hearst papers argued that the Kelly–Nash machine jeopardized Chicago's ability to attract federal funds under the New Deal. Kelly, however, kept quiet and the newspapers soon turned their attention to other events, such as the spectacular success of the Century of Progress Fair and the end of Prohibition.[23]

Kelly fully understood the intersection of Chicago's economic fortunes and his own political staying power. The magnitude of the Great Depression meant that the federal government became an even bigger influence on urban finances. Chicago's politicians wanted their share of both the money spent on projects and the gratitude of the newly employed workers. Clout became central to the execution of the federal-municipal relationship. Who would control the distribution of all the new jobs required to construct and maintain new buildings, roads, sidewalks, and other infrastructure? This became a crucial question for the Kelly–Nash machine. It would also be a crucial question for committeemen, aldermen, and others who hoped to maintain their political position in a communal world of mutual obligations.

The New Deal programs obviously presented an opportunity for the nascent citywide Democratic machine. Kelly and the Chicago Democrats received considerable credit for the impact of New Deal programs in the city, including those over which they actually had little control. The machine fostered the idea that relief checks as well as jobs with the Works Progress Administration (WPA) and Public Works Administration (PWA) resulted from Democratic control of City Hall. This deceit did not go unnoticed. Dwight H. Green, Kelly's Republican opponent in 1939, claimed that the machine forced people in the ranks of the WPA and PWA to vote Democratic. In reality, people voted Democratic not because of intimidation, but out of gratitude.[24]

Conflicts between workers and private firms, however, brought labor issues to the forefront. Organized labor had reawakened and felt its time had come. Under the leadership of John L. Lewis, the Congress of Industrial Organizations (CIO) emerged from under control of the American Federation of Labor (AFL). The CIO saw itself as bringing new energy and radicalism to the labor movement. For Kelly and Chicago Democrats, the CIO presented a challenge. The Democratic machine had been organizing working-class communities in industrial neighborhoods and had been pro-union. But the CIO seemed more radical to Kelly, and he had a difficult time figuring out how to respond to its growing influence.

Many CIO organizers took more radical stances than those who represented the traditional AFL skilled craft unions, and they engaged in much broader recruitment. The CIO welcomed African Americans, women, and immigrants. Many of the organizers had communist leanings. John L. Lewis, who was personally fairly conservative, proclaimed that he did not care as long as they built up the union movement. Industrial unionism, long associated with the Industrial Workers of the World, found itself now increasingly in the mainstream. In the 1930s and 1940s, the CIO radically changed the face of organized labor in Chicago's mass production industries, particularly steel and meatpacking. The new unions also interacted effectively with newly emerging neighborhood groups during this period. In turn, both labor and neighborhood organizations influenced the Democratic political machine.

While finishing out Cermak's term, Kelly maintained a friendly approach to the labor movement, especially with the AFL. After being elected in his own right in 1935, with nearly 76 percent of the vote, the mayor clashed with the CIO. Ward leaders feared that the organization's active involvement with neighborhood families might pose a threat to their power. This was especially relevant in traditional industrial neighborhoods, such as Back of the Yards and South Chicago, dominated by huge industrial concerns and sustained by long-established ethnic and religious communal institutions. The CIO also made headway in the West Side's garment industry, which again reflected the communal institutions of the Jewish and Catholic immigrant and ethnic working class.

Kelly approached the challenge of bringing organized labor into his coalition through a practice the Democratic machine had refined in ethnic communities. Cermak, Sullivan, and other architects of the party organization had themselves come into power by first being sub-bosses. In Bronzeville, Dawson had emerged as a powerful sub-boss for the Black community. This role would now be deployed to manage organized labor. The process took time but seemed well aligned with both the CIO and the emerging grassroots neighborhood organizations. As labor and neighborhood groups partnered and maximized their influence, Kelly and the Democrats moved to co-opt these organizations into the Democratic fold.[25]

Two major unions, the Steel Workers Organizing Committee (SWOC) and the Packinghouse Workers Organizing Committee (PWOC), both part of the CIO, presented particular challenges. SWOC organized the massive steel mills of the Southeast Side, while PWOC aimed to connect with packinghouse workers, particularly those in Back of the Yards and nearby Bronzeville.[26] These neighborhoods had long been among the poorest of the city. They suffered from not only substandard housing conditions and poverty, but also incredible industrial pollution. The "Stockyard Stench" had long troubled the city, as did the almost hellish atmosphere of South Chicago, where the emissions from the steel mills made it almost impossible to breathe. Nevertheless, ethnic groups in these industrial areas had established communal institutions that offered a valuable entry point to labor organizers.[27]

When the SWOC signed a contract with United States Steel on March 2, 1937, the steelworkers' union membership exploded and became a major force on the Southeast Side. That spring, SWOC organized other mills. On May 27, it launched a strike against both Republic Steel and Youngstown Sheet and Tube. In Chicago alone, 25,000 workers walked off the job. SWOC held a mass meeting on Memorial Day at Sam's Cafe, the SWOC command headquarters for Republic Steel. Some 2,000 union members and their supporters marched to the gates of the mill, where about fifty off-duty Chicago police met them. Soon police fired into the crowd, and panic ensued. Ten strikers died and another eighty-four demonstrators lay wounded. The Memorial Day Massacre quickly shifted the power dynamic in Chicago.

The union began a citywide campaign attacking Kelly and his police force. On June 8, SWOC held a rally at the Civic Opera House; another rally followed nine days later at Chicago Stadium. A motor parade of strikers made the long trip from the Southeast Side to the stadium on Madison Street. In his address to the roughly 12,000 strikers and supporters in attendance, SWOC leader Van A. Bittner decried "damnable beastly police" and "crazy hoodlum policemen."[28]

A Senate investigation of the Memorial Day Massacre held the police accountable. At first Kelly seemed indifferent, but he quickly appreciated that he might lose vital working-class support. The mayor also understood that the CIO had connections in the White House, and Kelly did not want to lose President Roosevelt's backing. Kelly and the Chicago Democrats began to curry favor with the CIO. Although the strike against the steel companies had failed, organized labor gained power in Chicago's political machine, a power it would hold for generations. As a result, the Chicago police subsequently protected labor organizers and strikers in the stockyards.[29]

WARTIME MAYOR

In addition to national and local challenges, the Kelly–Nash machine confronted a global crisis. Events in Europe and Asia quickly began to affect Chicago. When Adolf Hitler's Nazi Party rose to power in Germany and sought to assert its role in Europe, many in Chicago's German community felt nationalist pride. The most pro-Nazi among them joined the German American Bund. Ethnic tensions emerged as war clouds gathered over Europe and Asia.[30]

The outbreak of war had vast implications for Chicago's economy, people, and politics. Kelly rose to the task and organized Chicagoans. Even before Pearl Harbor, the mayor had warned of the eventual involvement of the United States in the conflict. While isolationism remained a strong force in America, it had little place in Chicago's ethnic communities. Czechs and Slovaks had seen their recently established country taken over by the Nazi regime. Polish Chicagoans witnessed their homeland ravaged by German and Soviet forces. Chinese Chicagoans watched in horror as China suffered a massive Japanese invasion. Ethnic Chicagoans began immediately to mobilize their communities.

The mayor's office positioned itself to take the lead on the home front should American forces get involved. On December 20, 1940,

CHAPTER 7

In war and peace Mayor Kelly's Leadership has kept Chicago marching forward

ISSUED BY CHICAGO CITIZENS—COL. A. A. SPRAGUE, Chairman

7.3 Kelly campaign brochure, 1943. Ed Kelly's campaign printed this brochure for his last campaign for mayor in 1943. It pointed out his leadership during both the Great Depression and World War II, including redeeming the city from near bankruptcy, the expansion of the Municipal Airport (Midway Airport), wartime mobilization of Chicago's economy, and the construction of the city's first subway. Author's Collection.

the City Council established the Chicago Commission on National Defense with the mayor as chairman. Seventy-one business leaders sat on the commission, which worked to prepare the vast industrial base for war. It also organized a recycling program, which in its first two days alone collected eighty thousand pounds of aluminum. The commission established a servicemen's center and created a register of possible volunteers.

In May 1941, Roosevelt appointed Mayor Fiorello La Guardia of

New York as the director of the US Office of Civilian Defense. La Guardia then appointed Kelly as administrative coordinator of the Chicago region. Kelly's domain included not only Chicago but the suburbs, an area that included half of Illinois's population. Kelly created a multilayered civilian defense hierarchy, superimposed over the Cook County Democratic Party organization. As the historians Perry Duis and Scott La France have pointed out, the Democratic machine and the local war effort became parallel organizations designed to unite a diverse and divided city. Even though the wartime economy eroded the party's control over patronage as jobs became plentiful in the aftermath of the Great Depression, the civilian defense program ensured that Kelly and the Democrats would retain influence and control.[31]

Even after Pearl Harbor ethnic Chicagoans continued to worry about the war in their respective homelands. Many agonized over the eventual alliance between the Soviet Union and the United States. Polish Chicagoans, for example, worried about what would happen as the Red Army pushed German forces back across Poland. Greek Chicagoans blamed Josef Stalin for the civil war in Greece and warned about the establishment of communist dictatorships in the Balkans. The Mexican community, which had seen its numbers fall during the Great Depression as a result of forced repatriation, formed the Comite Contra El Eje, or Anti-Axis Committee.

Groups supported their new country's war efforts, too. The Lithuanian, Croatian, Italian, and Chinese communities purchased substantial amounts of Liberty Bonds. Polish American media personality Lydia Pucinska, mother of the future congressman and alderman Roman Pucinski, raised funds for the construction of a B-29 Bomber christened "Chicago Polonia." The Jewish community organized rescue efforts for Jews in Europe and worked tirelessly to change American immigration policy to allow refugees entry. Over 45,000 Jewish Chicagoans served in the armed forces, with casualties including nearly 1,000 dead and 1,400 wounded.[32]

Racial conflict raised its ugly head again during the war. In the aftermath of Pearl Harbor, Kelly shut down the city's twenty-five Japanese lunchrooms and catering services. Various anti-Japanese incidents were reported, but unlike in West Coast cities, in Chicago these attacks proved small and isolated. Chicago became the new home of many relocated Japanese Americans, and soon it hosted the largest Japanese American community in the United States. By the end of the war, two Japanese neighborhoods emerged, one on the North Side centered at the intersection of Clark and Division Streets, the other on the South Side in the Kenwood and Oakland community areas. These neighborhoods functioned as buffer zones between Black and White communities as those racial tensions continued to grow.

Black migration had slowed to a trickle during the Great Depression, but Chicago's booming wartime economy set in motion the second phase of the Great Migration. During the war years roughly 65,000 rural Black southerners arrived in the city. In 1940, African Americans made up only 2.8 percent of workers in Cook and DuPage counties. By 1945, they comprised nearly 14 percent of the workforce. The number of Black women working in the stockyards soared. Racial tensions escalated, especially as Blacks crowded into ghettoes on the South and West Sides. Kelly created the Mayor's Committee on Race Relations, composed of six White and five Black civic leaders; they called for calm and tried to quell vicious rumors that could cause conflicts. Kelly named Robert C. Weaver, an African American Harvard-educated economist, executive director of the committee. Weaver convinced police officials to formulate a plan to prevent petty clashes from evolving into riots. Chicago did avoid major violence, but the situation remained tense.[33]

The Kelly administration embraced a complex mixture of traditional machine politics and more liberal New Deal attitudes. While Kelly cultivated the image of a self-made man from the Stock Yard District with his rough talk and straightforward political style, he also exhibited notable liberal traits. These included a concern for the underprivileged, a belief in the New Deal and its philosophical foundation, and a surprising commitment to African American hopes in an often hostile city. While these attributes appeared early in his administration, they took some time to fully develop as Kelly found himself tackling a wide range of serious issues during the

Great Depression and World War II. Kelly and Pat Nash would lead a chronically divided Democratic Party and Chicago through some of its most difficult history.[34]

Maintaining a successful citywide machine demanded political skill. Kelly and Nash needed allies who could deliver votes in huge quantities. The creation of sub-machines in neighborhoods, through ethnic or racial affiliations and labor unions, helped Kelly to attract new groups and solidify the party's position. Kelly understood the need to bring in important institutional players such as Catholic parishes, labor unions, and policy bosses, which guaranteed the loyalty of their constituents and brought in much-needed funds. They represented the communal web that brought large numbers of people together. Of course, the policies of Franklin Roosevelt also drew these groups into the coalition. Together, national and local forces helped to create a viable, successful, and permanent political organization that would rule the city for decades. Demographic changes, however, were setting the stage for decades of racial turmoil in Chicago.

8
Clout and Communalism Triumphant

De La Salle Men, De La Salle Men,
will crash right through that line!
Up and at 'em, we will get 'em,
we'll conquer every time!
Rah! Rah!
Win the battle, show your mettle.
We're Loyal to You Old Pal.
For the man whose name you bear,
through him we have no fear.
So Fight for De La Salle!
  TRADITIONAL FIGHT SONG OF DE LA SALLE INSTITUTE[1]

The Democratic Party is the party that opened its arms. We opened them to every nationality, every creed. We opened them to the immigrants. The Democratic Party is the party of the people.
  RICHARD J. DALEY[2]

The postwar years challenged the Democrats on both the national and the local stage. Republicans hoped to gain support by attacking Franklin Roosevelt's New Deal programs and the Yalta Conference agreements, which effectively ceded much of eastern Europe to Soviet influence. Many believed Roosevelt had been played by Stalin at Yalta. In particular, Chicago's Polish community leaders felt that

CHAPTER 8

they had been betrayed. While some Polish Americans did turn away from the Democrats and the local Republican Party supported various Polish candidates, most Polish Chicagoans remained loyal. Much of this loyalty was based on the idea of communalism and a belief that the federal, state, and local governments should support that sense of community and collective obligation.

Nevertheless, the Democratic hold was weakening. Suddenly the electorate, which had rallied behind Kelly and the Democrats during the war, seemed restless and in search of change. Housing shortages, especially acute among returning GIs hoping to start families, contributed to voter frustration. Kelly, who had championed African American rights, stated that Chicagoans should be able to live wherever they pleased. His public housing director, Elizabeth Wood, attempted to integrate public housing, threatening the racial divide that had been more or less enforced since the 1919 race riot. Ethnic voters, Chicago aldermen, and many committeemen began to question their support for Kelly.

Jacob "Jake" Arvey, one of the most powerful leaders in Kelly's political machine, had taken control of the party by becoming chairman of the Cook County Democratic Party in 1946 upon his return from service during the war. He soon realized that Democrats had to drop Kelly. Arvey searched for a "clean" candidate who could win the mayoral election and keep the Democrats in control. Arvey considered reform candidates such as Paul Douglas and Adlai Stevenson but claimed that Kelly recommended Martin H. Kennelly, a wealthy businessman and philanthropist who seemed to epitomize the American Dream as he had risen from working-class roots. Kennelly headed the Red Cross in Chicago during the war and played a prominent role in civic affairs. Active in Irish and Catholic circles, though a Democrat, he maintained a nonpartisan image with an unblemished reputation.[3]

KENNELLY: A BRIDGEPORT REFORMER

Jake Arvey and the Democrats did not bargain on how clean Martin H. Kennelly would really be once elected. Like his predecessor,

Kennelly grew up in Bridgeport and had become successful in the business world. Like Kelly, he also left the neighborhood, living with his sister in the stately Edgewater Beach Apartments on the far North Side lakefront. Unlike Kelly, however, he attended De La Salle Institute (class of 1905). A confirmed bachelor, he had been active only on the periphery of Democratic politics. He told the Democratic City Central Committee that even though he supported the campaigns of Democratic reformers such as the late Governor Horner, he had no real connection with the Democratic political organization and often opposed its policies. Kennelly told the committeemen that "we must get away from the idea that government belongs to a party and realize it belongs to the people. It is not for the benefit of the few but for the many." Despite these declarations that seemed to fly in the face of communal and machine politics, party leaders believed they could control him.[4]

Former mayor Carter Harrison IV served as Kennelly's campaign chair. This added to Kennelly's reform credentials. He waged a vigorous campaign for the mayor's office, beginning with a rally at the Lithuanian Auditorium on 31st and Halsted, not far from where he lived as a boy. The 11th Ward Democratic Organization, led by Alderman Hugh "Babe" Connelly, and the Old Timers of Bridgeport Association organized the event. A rising star in Democratic politics, Richard J. Daley, served as its chairman. The gathering showcased Kennelly's Bridgeport roots. Two teachers from his elementary school participated, as did twenty members of his Holden Public grammar school graduation class. Forty-two members of the De La Salle class of 1905 also joined the rally, though, like Kennelly, most had moved to relatively upper-middle-class neighborhoods or had left the city.

Kennelly intended the Bridgeport rally to not only launch his campaign but also remind voters of his stockyard roots. Perhaps Alderman Connelly and Daley also hoped it would remind Kennelly whence he came and what that meant to his political future. The 11th Ward Democratic Organization, a crucial component of the machine, had been part of Cermak's original coalition. While Kennelly ran unopposed in the Democratic primary, he needed to solidify his

CHAPTER 8

8.1 The 11th Ward Picnic, 1949. Bridgeport Democrats held their annual picnic in Pilsen Park in Czech California. Pictured here is Mayor Martin Kennelly on the merry-go-round with Richard J. Daley. At this point Daley supported Kennelly in his first term as mayor. Photo: Chicago Lawn Photos, Richard J. Daley Collection [MSRJD04], RJD_04_01_0002_0010_021, Special Collections & University Archives, University of Illinois Chicago.

position with all fifty committeemen, at least some of whom may not have been enthusiastic about a reform candidate. At the same time, others, including Daley, also had their eyes on the mayoralty.[5]

In his first radio address in January 1947, Kennelly promoted himself as a reformer, emphasizing his opposition to corruption, promising not to waste taxpayers' money, and committing to honest communication. Kennelly told listeners his life story: his Bridgeport roots, his first job at Marshall Field's, his attendance at the "poor boy's college," De La Salle Institute, his work as a clerk in Englewood, his service in the army during World War I, and finally his opening a storage and moving business with his brother. He declared what would become a constant refrain: "I am not going to have a different appeal from day to day just because I happen to be in a different part of town. I am not going to talk about things that have nothing to do with the office of mayor." Finally, in an obvious rebuke of the Regular Democratic Organization, he said he would not engage in ethnic and class-based politics.[6]

Kennelly gained widespread support as the party machinery went to work. Labor leaders rallied to his cause. Other reformers endorsed Kennelly, including Paul Douglas. The Polish Roman Catholic Union threw its support behind him.[7] His New Deal orientation generated further support. Kennelly wanted to mobilize both public and private sectors to provide more infrastructure, especially housing for veterans. He planned to eliminate slums. He promised to keep politics out of the public schools. Kennelly called for neighborhood participation in the planning process and the reawakening of Chicago's neighborhood spirit. In another radio address he said he would not get involved in aldermanic elections but would let the people choose. Kennelly denied that the machine controlled him and promised to be above party politics. The candidate stated that city employees would no longer be treated as "political pawns." Kennelly appeared to be against patronage, the lifeblood of the communal political machine. Regular Democratic politicians must have been confused and frustrated.[8]

Nonetheless, the organization delivered for Kennelly. Thousands of patronage workers, precinct captains, and Regular Democratic politicians held rallies for him across crucial wards. On election day, 1,500,000 Chicagoans, 75 percent of eligible voters, went to the polls, delivering a big win for Arvey, the Democrats, and Kennelly. The Democratic mayoral candidate received 919,593 votes, or 58.7 percent of the total. Reformers rejoiced as the Democratic machine seemed transformed.[9]

Kennelly's first inaugural address reminded the City Council of their duties to the city as a whole: "Let us always remember that we represent all sections of Chicago—all creeds and all races. Each Alderman, of course, is the spokesman for the people in his own ward, but he also represents, together with his colleagues, all the people of Chicago."[10] Kennelly spoke of his job as mayor as being similar to running a major corporation. This approach appealed to good-government reformers, independents, and even Republicans. His strict interpretation of the city charter, however, which called for a strong City Council and a rather limited mayoralty, meant that real power shifted back to the aldermen, after years of strong mayors such as Thompson, Cermak, and Kelly. Kennelly felt that the people's will should be expressed through the City Council, and in fact wanted aldermen to act as local mayors in their wards. In a speech in New York shortly after his election, Kennelly again attacked patronage, stating: "You know the system: Somebody is elected and then immediately everyone who is in office or who was employed by the defeated candidate is dropped and a new crowd, or may I say, crew, is brought in." Kennelly's decentralized and democratic tendencies threatened the foundation of Chicago's Democratic Party. If the mayor was against clout and the patronage associated with it, then what good was the machine?[11]

Kennelly's first term seemed to be largely a success. While he had promised not to implement massive political firings, he did make some changes, especially where workers proved to be inefficient, lazy, or incompetent. He also replaced the city's corporation counsel with Benjamin Adamowski, then known as an anti-machine Democrat and reformer. Kennelly attempted to rid the public schools and the police force of political influence. He laid out a vast infrastructure plan for the city, encouraged tourism, and commemorated the hundredth anniversary of the first railroad in Chicago with the highly successful Railroad Fair on the lakefront. Kennelly's administration took the first steps toward the creation of a convention center and explored the possibility of an annual industrial exposition.[12]

Kennelly ran successfully for a second term in 1951 with the continued support of the Regular Democratic Party. In his second inaugural address, Kennelly claimed that a "pattern of sound moral values in government" had been established. He lauded his administration's fight against gambling, but he spoke of the new organized crime business of narcotics as something that required hiring 500 to 600 more police.[13]

Kennelly's attack on gambling interests included the policy wheels in African American neighborhoods. The policy bosses anchored the organizational structure of the community, so Kennelly's policies caused unrest in both the traditional communal and the reform wing of the Democratic Party. The pressure on the policy wheels angered William Dawson, who would be among the leaders of the party who moved to drop Kennelly in 1955. Reformers too began to rebel against Kennelly and his hands-off approach to government. In particular, they reacted negatively as more and more evidence of police corruption emerged, while the mayor continued to defend the police.[14]

Kennelly, however, continued to see himself as a viable candidate and chose to run for a third term despite losing the support of party stalwarts. He faced two primary opponents: Richard J. Daley, as the candidate of the Regular Democratic Party; and Benjamin Adamowski. Kennelly mounted a vigorous campaign, with frequent telecasts on WGN-TV There, he drove home the argument that the contest for City Hall revolved around whether the government should be run for all the people or for Democratic Party leaders like those who had originally brought him to power.[15] He campaigned across the city and even dared to enter Dawson's domain, addressing a rally and "indignation meeting" in the heart of Bronzeville. Kennelly picked up support from various anti-machine forces in the city and even some Republicans. Several American Federation of Labor (AFL) unions also supported Kennelly, as did the progressive education expert Dr. John A. Lapp.[16]

Both Kennelly and Daley had graduated from De La Salle High School, which created a potential conflict over claiming its support. The Kennelly campaign seized the initiative, sending out 9,500 letters picturing Kennelly and his classmates in a De La Salle classroom with a Christian Brother encouraging the Class of 1905 to stand for "honesty and Christian principals." Alumni and friends of De La Salle and St. Mel's (another all-boys' Christian Brothers school) received the mailing, which included a message from Kennelly on the back: "My only desire is to live up to the principles which I was taught by the Christian Brothers. No greater humility characterizes any man, nor any more exalted ambition." Of course, the flyer made no mention that Richard J. Daley had sat in those very same classrooms.[17]

8.2 Kennelly campaign handbill, 1955. The Kennelly campaign circulated this handbill to emphasize the candidate's Catholic and De La Salle Institute roots. Martin H. Kennelly Papers [MSKenn77], box 28, folder 507, Special Collections & University Archives, University of Illinois Chicago.

In order to promote his agenda, the Kennelly forces attempted to elect aldermen in thirty-seven wards, including his own—a shift from his earlier vow to stay out of aldermanic elections. They ran a candidate against the infamous Mathias "Paddy" Bauler in the 43rd Ward. Just a few years earlier, Bauler had defended himself against charges by the Chicago Crime Commission with an unabashed and somewhat incoherent defense of the politics of patronage. Bauler celebrated the communalism of his brand of politics and was a firm believer in the use of clout to promote it. Independents and Republicans joined Kennelly's forces. In some wards, Kennelly and the Republican mayoral candidate, Robert Merriam, backed the same aldermanic candidate.[18]

Kennelly hoped for a turnout of 900,000 or more Democratic voters. He had a difficult time running in African American wards, where he had largely lost the support that Anton Cermak and Ed Kelly had earned. Many African Americans accused him of racism and blamed him for the recent race riots in the Trumbull Park Homes, a public housing project on the Southeast Side. They also accused him of racism because of his attacks on Dawson and the policy wheels. Indeed, raids on gambling and on the policy racket increased substantially during Kennelly's administration. Every year starting in 1951, the police raided dozens of policy headquarters and made hundreds of raids on policy wheels, ultimately making thousands of arrests of policy runners. Dawson resented the forays into his ward and the pressure on Black gamblers. At the same time, residents also disliked that Kennelly seemed to see only that side of their community. One Black housewife said, "Kennelly talks as if all our residents play policy and gamble. I think all the decent people here resent that slur."[19]

Kennelly faced extreme odds. Despite having the support of all the Chicago newspapers, many independents, and some labor unions, he confronted a well-oiled political machine that could turn out thousands of precinct workers on election day. Precinct workers in the 1st Ward alone numbered several hundred, if not a thousand. The power of communalism and clout confronted Kennelly, who believed in neither. On February 22, 1955, Richard J. Daley overwhelmed Kennelly and Adamowski in the Democratic primary. The final vote saw Daley garner 364,839 votes, Kennelly 264,775, and Adamowski 112,072. Kennelly remained neutral in the mayoral election, in which Daley beat Robert Merriam handily.[20]

In 1947 the Regular Democratic Party Organization of Cook County had turned to Kennelly and other reformers to refurbish its image. By 1955, however, party leaders had tired of Kennelly's sanctimony and anti-corruption reforms. That was when Richard J. Daley made his moves. This other Christian Brothers' boy had learned much from his mentors, Joe McDonough, Anton Cermak, Ed Kelly, and Jake Arvey. Unlike Kennelly, he respected the organization they had built, and better yet, understood it. No one would play the game better than the De La Salle graduate who returned to and stayed in Bridgeport. He understood loyalty to neighborhood, friends, church, and party. He recognized the needs of his constituents, even if they ran against the grain of "good" politics. As Daley said, "Good government is good politics and politics is good government."[21]

A TRUE BRIDGEPORT MAYOR

Although Richard J. Daley (1902–1976) was born in Bridgeport, his family left just before the United States entered into World War I. Michael J. Daley and Lillian Daley moved, along with their teenage son, to Michael Daley's mother's brick two-flat in St. Leo's parish. The Daleys would remain in the Auburn-Gresham neighborhood until their son married and they all moved back to Bridgeport with his new wife, Eleanor, in 1936. During his nearly two decades away from Bridgeport, he remained attached to the neighborhood and fell under the political tutelage of Joseph McDonough, alderman of the 5th Ward. The political relationship between the McDonough and Daley families spanned three generations. After graduating from De La Salle Institute, Richard worked in the office of the Dolan & Ludeman Livestock Commission Company in the Union Stock Yard, keeping him close to working-class Bridgeport and his old friends. He joined the Hamburg Athletic Association, a club sponsored by McDonough. The young politician quickly climbed the ranks of both the club and the 5th Ward political organization. By 1924, he was president of the club and the alderman's personal secretary. Daley served both as a precinct captain and a City Council clerk. When Cermak became mayor, with McDonough's support, Daley's star rose along with the alderman's. Close to the sources of power, he learned the ins and outs of Chicago politics from the precinct level to City Hall.[22]

The Hamburg Athletic Association played a valuable role in the social and political life of Bridgeport. It provided the military arm of the neighborhood and of the 5th Ward Democratic Party. The club's political clout showed itself in the election of one of its members, Tommy Doyle, as 5th Ward Alderman in 1914. Doyle went on to the state legislature and a different Hamburg member, McDonough, became alderman. While Ragen's Colts, another athletic club-street gang and political powerhouse sponsored by Cook County Commissioner Frank Ragen, led much of the racial fighting during the 1919 race riot, the Hamburg club also attacked Black Chicagoans. Many, if not most, Hamburg members served as precinct captains and election workers. They viewed this political service as a pathway to a patronage job, and a way to avoid work on the kill floors, hide rooms, and soap factories of Packingtown.[23]

Daley's world was marked by intense personal relationships. He remained a lifelong Catholic, a loyal supporter of De La Salle Insti-

8.3 Daley inauguration, 1955. Daley is pictured here speaking at his first inauguration. At the right is a large floral commemoration with the initials HAA—Hamburg Athletic Association. Daley maintained his connection with the club throughout his life. Richard J. Daley Collection [MSRJD04], RJD_04_01_0047_0006_014, Special Collections & University Archives, University of Illinois Chicago.

tute, and an active member of the Hamburg Athletic Association. Daley remained president of the Hamburg club until 1939, and many of its members rose with him in politics. In Bridgeport, he built a bungalow on the very street where he had been born, just a short walk from Nativity of Our Lord Church. But this constituted more than a simple homecoming: Bridgeport would anchor Daley's political base.[24]

Daley's membership in the Hamburg Athletic Association led him to his most personal, intimate, and long-lasting relationship, with Eleanor Guilfoyle, his wife. She was the eighth of eleven children in an Irish Roman Catholic family that dutifully worshipped at nearby St. Bridget's church. Known to family and friends as "Sis," Eleanor met her future husband during a softball game at Mark White Square (McGuane Park) at Halsted and 29th Street. Daley, a friend of her brother Lloyd, managed Hamburg's baseball team. He took her to a dance at St. Bridget's Hall that evening. Eleanor had attended St. Mary's High School on the West Side and St. Bridget's Commercial School, and worked at the nearby Martin Senour Company paint plant as a secretary. The couple dated for six years and married on June 23, 1936, in St. Bridget's Church. Everything about them spoke of loyalty and stability. Their identities revolved around their neighborhood, family, the Catholic Church, and the Democratic Party.[25]

Daley's everyday work was also grounded in personal relationships, particularly with Joe McDonough. Initially, McDonough bristled under the leadership of the North and West Side Irish. He eventually broke with Roger Sullivan's "Lace Curtain" Irish heirs and joined the emerging political organization of Anton Cermak. Bridgeport's "Shanty" Irish soon found themselves close to the center of power in the Democratic Party. Daley rose with McDonough, who became county treasurer. McDonough had little interest in the everyday business of the treasurer's office, and Daley became the master of the counting house, using the bookkeeping skills he had learned at De La Salle. During this period, Daley learned the basic financial parameters of Chicago politics.[26]

Daley's own earliest elective offices had been at the state level, in the Illinois House and Senate, where he served for about a decade. He became the 11th Ward committeeman, and in 1953 became chairman of the Central Committee of the Cook County Democratic Party, launching his tenure as the head of the party machine. In both the primary battle and the general election mayoral contest of 1955, Daley campaigned as the defender of the patronage system, touting the reciprocal loyalty and communalism at the center of it.[27] Daley easily defeated Republican Robert E. Merriam by ten percentage points, with the African American vote proving vital. The coalition put together by Cermak and Kelly continued to guarantee victory for the Democratic Party.[28]

Daley maintained strong ties to major Irish American organizations. He joined the Irish Fellowship Club of Chicago and the Harp and Shamrock Club, among others, and he served as director of the Irish Fellowship Club.[29] In 1956 he brought the St. Patrick's Day Parade back to the Loop after a more than fifty-year hiatus. West Side and South Side Irish had maintained their own parades, but now they all flocked to the Loop to celebrate, despite a massive snowstorm. (Daley ordered city workers to clear streets and sidewalks.) In 1962, Daley inaugurated the tradition of dyeing the Chicago River green.[30]

Patronage was central to Daley's administration. As both mayor and Chairman of the Democratic Party of Cook County—positions he held simultaneously—he controlled tens of thousands of jobs. Daley could use them to help his friends and supporters, or to punish political enemies or those whom he felt betrayed him or the party. Requests for employment came from many sources, including clergy, political supporters, neighbors, friends, and acquaintances. Jobs in both public and private sectors provided the oil that allowed the wheels of the machine to work smoothly and deliver on election day.[31]

Many favors showed the citywide contacts that the mayor's office handled. In 1965, Pilgrim Missionary Baptist Church in South Chicago asked the mayor for help in upgrading its property. Daley put Commissioner Lewis Hill of the Department of Development and Planning on the case. The next year Ray Spaeth, vice president and treasurer of the Illinois Institute of Technology, contacted Daley about the new bank he was helping to establish. Some years earlier when Spaeth had been president of the Beverly Bank, Daley deposited $200,000 ($2,032,702 in 2023) of the city's money there. For the Lakeside Bank, Spaeth approached Daley for a similar deposit.[32]

A Christian Brother asked for aid in getting an apartment in the Prairie Shores Housing complex near De La Salle, and the mayor wrote developer Ferdinand Kramer to help him get on the waiting list. Some requests came from applicants for apartments in Chicago Housing Authority projects. One rather surprising letter, again from a Christian Brother, asked for aid in getting a passport so that he could attend the general chapter meeting in Rome. Daley often intervened on more personal or familial matters: trying to get a friend's son into dental school or helping a friend's son-in-law secure a job or deal with a traffic ticket in Wisconsin.[33]

All of these diverse and often highly individual or particular requests demonstrate the nature of the machine and of Daley personally as a benefactor. Although he often surrounded himself with Irish Americans, De La Salle graduates, and Bridgeport neighbors, his reach went well beyond them. The citywide machine needed citywide clout, and it even built power beyond Chicago's boundaries. Appeals came from Democrats across the state and even from the Democratic National Committee.[34] Daley played the role of Chicago's patron saint of patronage and clout.

As Daley aggressively extended the reach of patronage, he overturned a major reform of the Kennelly years. Political influence again came to the board of the Chicago Public Schools. In the 1950s, Frank Whiston served as school board president; Daley sometimes suggested individual promotions to him. In 1966 he supported assigning a particular principal for the Thorp Elementary School in South Shore. At other times, he proposed that certain people be hired or transferred. Sometimes applicants for jobs traded on personal connections, even tenuous ones, with the mayor. One applicant for administrator at the Washburne Trade School made sure to note that his brother had attended Nativity of Our Lord grammar school with the mayor.[35]

Political patronage extended to the private sector. Politicians routinely placed people in positions with private businesses, a practice that went back to the nineteenth century. Daley's well-established ties with private firms enabled him to expand the practice and thus enlarge his sphere of control. Old friends like Morgan Murphy Sr., chairman of Commonwealth Edison's executive committee and head of Mayor Daley's Summer Jobs for Youth Committee in the late 1960s, could be counted on to help the mayor's supporters get jobs with Commonwealth Edison. Other companies did the same.[36]

Daley's understanding of the value of job patronage derived, at least in part, from the lessons he learned about industrialism and out-of-control capitalism in the neighborhoods that surrounded the

Union Stock Yard. His father had served as the business agent for the Sheet Metal Workers Union, while his mother had been an effective community activist and suffragette.[37] From them he learned firsthand about community organizing. The future mayor witnessed the union drive during World War I and the meatpacking strike of 1921–1922. He also understood the communal response of ethnic groups in the Stock Yard District and came to value the complex layering of their social structures. First, they created a parish and parochial school, and then other neighborhood institutions such as taverns, fraternals, and even street gangs out of which rose more formal organizations such as the Hamburg Athletic Association. Finally, they reached across ethnic and even neighborhood lines to form unions and political machines. The Irish involvement in Chicago politics fit well into this communal and extra-communal pattern, where faith, community, labor, and politics melded.[38]

The intersection of politics and the labor movement informed Daley's political life. Unions supplied votes and even election workers. In the Steel District, which comprised most of the 10th Ward, the United Steel Workers of America provided powerful support for Democratic candidates. In turn, they expected favors and aid from the machine. In 1954, the CIO had revolted against Martin Kennelly, laying out seven major areas where his administration had failed in their eyes: housing, transportation, industrial relations, education, juvenile delinquency, public safety, and human relations.[39]

During Daley's years as mayor, by contrast, labor unions always found a friend in City Hall. Joe Germano, a long-time machine supporter and union leader, held particular influence on the fifth floor. In 1958, Local 65, the big US Steel local in South Chicago, sought aid in getting a permit for its new building at 85th and South Chicago Avenue. The local had purchased the lots in 1956 but construction had been stymied, apparently, by city bureaucracy. Peter Tomczak, president of Local 65, made a direct appeal to Daley, reminding him that he represented some 12,000 steelworkers and always supported the Democrats. The mayor responded that he would do whatever he could, and he mentioned that he had already spoken directly with Germano, director of District 31 of the United Steelworkers of

America. After that, construction soon began. Daley kept a file of union leaders, the offices they held, and their contact information. He embraced his role as Chicago's primary labor mediator and often helped prevent strikes that might have crippled the city. Many of the union leaders had been his boyhood friends, and they seemed to have a mutual understanding. Management also respected and trusted him. Some feared him. Few industries did not need help from City Hall.[40]

During the Daley years the flurry of construction in the downtown area as well as on expressways and housing projects meant thousands of jobs for both skilled and unskilled workers. Union leaders received representation on various city commissions. Daley also made sure that the City Council did not pass anti-labor legislation. Union leaders informed Daley about prevailing wages and helped him to establish municipal pay scales. He guaranteed that city workers received top wages as well as benefits that often surpassed those in private businesses. In this manner, Daley kept most city workers out of unions, but also kept unions happy.[41]

Beyond labor unions, the mayor ruled over a carefully organized network that fed him useful information. Although Daley had honed this process before his election to the mayor's office, it reached its peak efficiency during his years as both chairman of the party and mayor. The hierarchy reached from Daley to the committeemen to officeholders and to those party workers he referred to as "minutemen": the precinct captains and their helpers. In early 1954, as party chairman, he invited precinct workers to a rally at the Civic Opera House, emphasizing teamwork and their role as a "good neighbor." Ward committeemen also regularly thanked precinct workers and urged their continue efforts for the party. One of the party's mailings reprinted an old column by famed *Chicago Daily News* columnist Edwin A. Lahey, calling precinct captains the "salt of this democratic (with a small D) earth."[42]

The Democratic machine under Daley handed out pocket-sized canvas booklets to each precinct captain to be used in gauging voter support and getting out the vote. These notebooks contained invaluable information about residents and their voting habits. They

Clout and Communalism Triumphant

"Meet Our DADDY"

Elect Richard J. Daley Mayor
CHICAGO NEEDS DALEY

8.4 Daley campaign advertisement, 1955. This appeared in the St. Angela Church bulletin, *The Angelus*, February 20, 1955, among other places. It emphasized Daley as a family man with deep neighborhood roots. Richard J. Daley Collection [MSRJD04], box SIIss1B24, folder 1, Special Collections & University Archives, University of Illinois Chicago.

recorded addresses, names, voter registration status, party affiliation, and how they promised to vote in the general election, along with a place for remarks. Daley cautioned precinct captains about confidentiality and advised them to hand in the notebooks to their ward committeeman. On the last page of the book, captains compiled how many votes they expected for each candidate. In addition, wards kept detailed lists of voters who had moved and where they moved since the last election. In this manner, ward committeemen could tell Chairman Daley what to expect on election day.

In some cases, when vote numbers dropped, precinct captains felt pressure to explain why. One wrote directly to Daley in 1959, stating that in his primarily German precinct, many could not forgive the United States for intervening in the two world wars and thus would not vote Democratic. Another precinct captain reported that despite the lower-than-expected voter turnout, Daley won his precinct by a ratio of four to one. At times residents complained to Daley's office that they did not have or did not know their precinct captain and hoped he would correct the problem. This tight, top-down yet hyper-local organization provided regular victories for the Democratic Party in election after election.[43]

THE CHURCH TRIUMPHANT

Catholic theologians and teachers use the term "Church Triumphant" to describe the Catholic Church in heaven. That is in the kingdom of God, where all would reach the fullness of salvation in Christ. They define the Church in the earthly world as the "Church Militant." Theological definitions aside, the Catholic Church in Chicago appeared to be very triumphant in the years after World War II. Its parishes, schools, and other institutions had large physical presences in the city and suburbs. Its charitable institutions provided valuable support services across the city. Its institutions of learning were growing in importance. And the various European Catholic ethnic groups gained more and more prominence in the social, cultural, economic, and political life of the city. The Chicago cardinal's limousine sported the Illinois license plate number "1," a mark of the Church Triumphant in the state. In particular, Irish Catholics seemed to have reached the pinnacle of power, controlling Chicago's City Hall and the Democratic Party. De La Salle Institute benefited from this success, and in turn proved its loyalty to the city and the ethnic group that had nourished it. While ostensibly a French order, the LaSallian Christian Brothers in the United States were mostly Irish

Americans. De La Salle Institute would see its greatest growth in the twenty years after the war.[44]

While Richard J. Daley learned politics at the feet of Joe McDonough, Anton Cermak, and Ed Kelly, he learned his moral and religious principles from the nuns at Nativity of Our Lord Parochial School and the Christian Brothers at De La Salle Institute. These included an emphasis on communal responses to social problems, something that would attract him to Franklin Roosevelt's New Deal and indeed to liberal Democratic politics more generally. The ideas of Pope Leo XIII's famous encyclical *Rerum Novarum,* supporting the rights of labor and the poor and condemning unfettered capitalism, constituted part of this point of view. Catholic principles of hierarchy and of obligation to the larger society also formed much of his worldview. Furthermore, a sense of loyalty, not only to the Catholic Church but also to the neighborhood, to the city, and to the Democratic Party were honed at De La Salle Institute. Daley represented a blend of the sacred and the profane if only in a tenuous balance of the two. During 1953, Daley served as the De La Salle Alumni Association president. The annual alumni dinners often drew over 1,800 "Brothers' Boys," including Daley.[45]

In the early 1950s, Daley chaired De La Salle's fundraising campaign to expand its campus. The plan included the demolition of some thirty residential structures, expanding the original campus to six acres encompassing the entire block from 34th to 35th Street and from Wabash Avenue to Michigan Avenue. It included a much-needed enlargement of the Christian Brothers' living quarters as well as a new classroom addition. The entire project would cost roughly $500,000 ($5,591,821 in 2023). Attendees at the groundbreaking ceremony on March 17, 1954, included Mayor Kennelly '05, Cook County Commissioner Dan Ryan '12, and Daley '19.[46] In 1961, Daley again lent his name to a De La Salle Building Fund campaign, this time as associate chairman. Ryan and Kennelly again took roles, as did other influential political figures who were dedicated alumni.[47]

Daley's loyalty to the Catholic Church and its institutions went beyond De La Salle. One of his daughters, Patricia, became a postulant of the Sisters of Mercy, a legendary Irish order of nuns that operated both St. Xavier College (now university) and Mercy Hospital (now closed) on the South Side. In the early 1950s, the Mercy nuns decided to move their college to the far Southwest Side on 103rd Street and Central Park Avenue. In 1955, St. Xavier further broke ground at 99th Street and Lawndale Avenue for an associated school, Mother McCauley Liberal Arts High School, which would accommodate 1,000 girls. That May, Daley attended a luncheon where more than 200 labor leaders pledged fundraising support for the educational complex. These unionists, of course, also supported Daley and the Democratic machine. Longtime Daley friend and fellow De La Salle alum Morgan Murphy chaired the drive. In October 1955, Daley took part in ceremonies that laid the cornerstones of both the new high school and the new college building.[48]

In 1960, Daley received the first honorary doctorate bestowed by the women's college. Sister Josetta Butler, new president of the college, acknowledged Daley's support in a personal letter. The connection between the Daley family and St. Xavier grew over time. Patricia eventually graduated from St. Xavier and, even though she left the Sisters of Mercy and married, later worked at the college as the director of development. In 1960, the mayor donated seven stained glass windows, celebrating each of the seven liberal arts, to St. Xavier's new library as a memorial to his father. The overall design is of a huge bird in flight, signifying the Holy Spirit.[49]

Daley's loyalty to the Sisters of Mercy manifested again as the order attempted to build a new Mercy Hospital on the South Side. By this time, Daley, busy with running the city and other concerns, could not put a great deal of personal effort into the fundraising campaign, but his name alone, as honorary chairman, activated his network. This meant galvanizing not only donors but also city assistance. Before construction could begin, the land for the new hospital had to be cleared. Here Daley's name meant success. Sister M. Huberta McCarthy contacted John G. Duba, Daley's commissioner of the Urban Renewal Department, asking for a tentative timetable for land clearance. Duba assured the Sisters of Mercy that much of the property had been acquired and that the city would soon acquire other necessary parcels.[50]

Daley, of course, remained loyal to his parish, Nativity of Our Lord on West 37th Street. He attended Mass every morning, either there or at a downtown church. His children attended the same parochial school he had. In the late 1950s and early 1960s the parish organized a fund to build a new school. The fundraising effort showed Daley's genius as an organizer.[51] He was aided in cultivating his vast system of donors by Morgan F. Murphy, who had worked for the Chicago Rapid Transit Company, the Public Service Company of Northern Illinois (which provided electricity to the suburbs), and Commonwealth Edison. Murphy aided Daley in his efforts to raise funds for Catholic institutions. A life trustee of St. Xavier College, Murphy also served as a member of the lay board of advisers to Mercy Hospital and of the provincial board of regents for the Sisters of Mercy. In 1957, Pope Pius XII named him a Knight of St. Gregory, in recognition of his service to the Church. Murphy's son would serve in the US House of Representatives, naturally as a Democrat.[52]

An impressive list of donors to the Nativity School Building fund included companies such as theater owners Balaban & Katz, the Gleneagles Country Club in Lemont, Illinois, and the Malan Construction Company of New York—hardly everyday donors to neighborhood Catholic parishes in Chicago. Politicians such as Marshal Korshak and Dan Rostenkowski also made contributions. Unions donated, including the Teamsters, Building Service Employees, Chicago Janitors Union, and the Chicago Journeymen Plumbers Union. Judge James J. McDermott of the Superior Court of Cook County sent checks garnered from several donors. In a letter to Nativity's pastor, Father Michael J. Conway, McDermott praised Daley's organizational skills and his loyalty to the Catholic Church. The personal connections the mayor made throughout his life and the clout he now held served various institutions, but especially the Catholic Church.[53]

The influence of Daley, Morgan Murphy, and other Irish Catholic leaders in Chicago extended into the national political realm, again bringing the sacred and the profane together. The Church Triumphant saw its greatest victory with the election of John F. Kennedy as president. Daley called the Democratic nominee at 3 a.m. on November 9, 1960, to deliver the news that Kennedy had carried Illinois with the help of a huge vote margin in Chicago and would be the next president. Chicago voters gave Kennedy an overwhelming margin over Richard Nixon of 456,312 votes, enabling a narrow statewide win of just 8,858 votes. As a result, Daley gained a reputation as "kingmaker." That election remains controversial to this day, with claims of voter fraud by both sides in Illinois. Nevertheless, with JFK in the White House, Chicago had an ally and Daley's power seemed undeniable. At the inaugural ball, Kennedy made it a point to walk over to Daley's table and invite the family to visit the White House the next day. When they arrived, they met the only person who had come before them, former president Harry S. Truman. The mayor and Truman shook hands, and the former president invited the Daley family to his library in Independence, Missouri. Not only did Daley rule Chicago, but now he seemed to have national clout.[54]

Daley relished his success and his new reputation. The cover of the March 15, 1963, *Time* magazine featured Daley with a background of his city and the headline, "Chicago: The New Facade, The Next Election." The article portrayed Daley as a Buddha with "a face unfathomable, hooded eyes, nose stubborn and strong," quoting him as saying, "If something is in the public interest, then it is in the party's interest." Daley, the article proclaimed, differed from his predecessors because he exercised his power for the purpose of "making Chicago a better place." *Time* called him a "Clouter with a Conscience." The mayor remarked, "the new objective of leadership is not what you can do for yourself, but what you can do for the people, We're the first of the new bosses—that is, the first of the new leaders."

Time claimed that Daley had gone a long way toward fulfilling his promise to rebuild the city, despite the fact that many of these projects had begun under the Kennelly administration. Still, Chicago seemed to have a new and exciting rhythm. New buildings appeared across the Loop. Bulldozers ran through slums. The Stateway Gardens housing project opened in 1958 in Bronzeville, providing apartments for roughly 3,000 residents just a block west of De La Salle

Institute. New schools appeared in neighborhoods. The city seemed to be on the move. Yet the *Time* article also pointed to the city's racial problems.

While generally laudatory, the *Time* article admonished the Catholic Church for opposing the Hyde Park–Kenwood Urban Renewal Project supported by Daley. The plan pushed poor African Americans out of the University of Chicago neighborhood and into White ethnic Catholic neighborhoods, causing conflict. These neighborhoods and parishes felt under pressure in Chicago's racial hothouse. The Catholic Church mounted campaigns against many of Daley's urban renewal projects, and for once he broke with the archdiocese. The Church Triumphant hit a wall manned by one of its most faithful sons. His alliance with Julian Levy of the University of Chicago advanced his urban renewal plans, but also proved to be a political liability. The sacred and the profane found themselves at odds with each other, and not for the last time.[55]

As the 1960s unfolded, Daley, like other big city mayors, faced long-lasting problems that their predecessors had ignored. Racial issues became aggravated and threatened the Democratic machine. The problem manifested itself not only on Chicago's streets, but in its segregated public schools. And the tensions raised by the Hyde Park–Kenwood Urban Renewal Project were harbingers of emerging social, ethnic, and political conflicts between the sacred and the profane.

A BATTLE BETWEEN THE SACRED AND PROFANE

While the sacred and profane often worked together in Chicago's Byzantine politics, they also clashed, as over the plan to build a four-year public university in Chicago. Connected with the University of Illinois at Urbana-Champaign, the campus was to be the first such public higher education institution in the city. It became a major goal of Daley's administration. A two-year branch of the university had opened in 1945 at Navy Pier, but many working-class and lower middle-class students could not or did not transfer to the downstate campus to complete four-year degrees. Daley, a graduate of DePaul

CHAPTER 8

University, a Catholic institution, realized that for many Chicagoans the Catholic university system was also not an attractive choice because of religion, cost, or both. Thus, he hoped to create a public university campus in the heart of the city to provide a local educational opportunity, a tremendous number of construction jobs, and a buttress against slums. As early as 1945, while serving in the state legislature, he had sponsored a bill to promote the cause.

Site selection for the new university presented various opportunities and problems, and Daley was a central player in the negotiations.[56] The final selection resulted from a complex series of events. A suburban location was proposed, but Daley blocked it, promising to make up any difference in the cost of land for a city location. At the same time, a city site posed difficult political choices, as it would inevitably involve various clout-heavy players in the public and private sectors. Railyards south of Roosevelt Road and the Loop soon emerged as the favored site. Importantly for Loop businesses, that site provided a physical buffer from the expanding South Side ghetto. The city also considered building the campus on Meigs Field or in the Garfield Park neighborhood. However, Loop businesses, represented by the Central Area Committee, wanted a site that would protect the Loop's economic base.[57]

Railroads, however, still used the yards and did not want to give them up. To change that, Daley pressed the various railroads to consolidate into a single Union Station, but they refused to bear the costs. At an impasse, the city then turned to a West Side site, which satisfied Loop businesses as it provided a barrier against a similarly expanding West Side ghetto. Unfortunately, this site presented a new problem: it encompassed a vibrant Italian, Greek, and Mexican community.[58]

Despite racial and ethnic changes, inhabitants of the Near West Side neighborhood known as The Valley had fought to keep their community alive. Much of the neighborhood was old and run-down, but residents rallied to reverse deterioration. The city had promised that urban renewal would stabilize The Valley and that new moderate-income housing would be erected. The announcement that the neighborhood would be largely razed for the new campus shocked the community. They had always been loyal to the machine. This was, after all, the ward that had sent John Powers to the City Council. Angered by the obvious disloyalty and disregard, residents soon rallied together in opposition.[59]

Father Italo Scola, the pastor of Holy Guardian Angel parish, challenged the plan. The church had already been razed for the construction of the Dan Ryan Expressway and rebuilt along with a new parochial school. But it now was to be razed for the new campus. He called a meeting on February 13, 1961, to protest the decision, where he was joined by Reverends Raymond Bianchi and Joseph Gallego of St. Francis of Assisi, a nearby largely Mexican parish. Neighborhood women flocked to the meeting, and several of them asked Florence Scala, a young, college-educated housewife from the neighborhood, to chair it. Scala, the daughter of Italian immigrants, had been involved in the Near West Side Planning Board and with the Hull House Settlement. She quickly emerged as the neighborhood spokesperson and led a protest to City Hall the next day.[60]

The sacred (that is, the communal neighborhood) and the profane (represented by downtown interests) went head to head. Scala led fifty women from Holy Guardian Angel Church to City Hall, and others soon joined the demonstration. Nevertheless, on May 10, the City Council overwhelmingly approved the site for the new University of Illinois campus in a raucous two-and-a-half-hour meeting held before 400 noisy spectators who packed the chamber's gallery. Neighborhood residents loudly booed those who spoke in favor of the site. Mayor Daley halted speakers six times to warn that he would clear the audience. The neighborhood group led by Scala protested afterward outside the council chamber.[61]

Florence Scala and neighborhood residents did not give up the fight. They appealed to the courts. They challenged the labeling of The Valley as a slum and blighted area—an essential precondition for urban renewal projects—declaring that strong and vital communities lived in the area and wanted to stay. The long appeal process delayed construction, but in 1963 the US Supreme Court upheld the city's power to condemn the land. The University of Illinois at Chicago Circle (now University of Illinois at Chicago) opened in 1965.

CHAPTER 8

The new campus uprooted some 8,000 residents and 630 businesses. Several thousand other residents also left preemptively, fearing that they too would have their homes knocked down for future expansions of the university. The neighborhood's housing stock fell from 6,850 units in 1960 to 3,400 units in 1970. The Chicago Circle campus immediately found itself in a rather tense relationship with a small contingent of Italian American residents and businesses that remained in the neighborhood, along Taylor Street, often referred to as Little Italy.[62]

Ultimately, this episode was not about whether the University of Illinois should have a Chicago area campus. It was about clout. A working-class neighborhood filled with ethnic groups lacked sufficient clout to survive. Garfield Park residents wanted the campus, but they also lacked clout and were overpowered by influential business interests. Mayor Daley had clout but also wanted support from others who did, too. In the long run, the campus had a positive impact on the city, especially its working-class residents, but the battle over site selection revealed the basic difference between the sacred and the profane. Frankly, the profane had more clout.

9

Fragmentation

Clout and Communalism in Decline

> I look forward to the day ... when we develop a new breed of political leader that will more represent the constituency of the impoverished and dispossessed people of this city.
> AL RABY,
> July 10, 1966[1]

In 1963 Richard J. Daley ran for his third term against his old rival, Benjamin Adamowski. The former Democrat and now Republican made inroads into Daley's base, using the issue of race in hoping to win support among White voters. Daley beat him by 138,000 votes, a much narrower margin than expected. Again, Daley counted on the solid Black vote across the South and West Sides. But the Democratic machine needed both the Black vote and the White ethnic vote. As the 1960s progressed, race became more and more of a contested issue. The decade would be one of increased conflict, although in 1963 few would have understood the magnitude of what would soon happen.[2]

That year brought other events that would shape the city's history. On November 22, Lee Harvey Oswald assassinated President John F. Kennedy in Dallas and Lyndon Baines Johnson became the 36th president of the United States. The man whom Daley had helped gain the White House was gone. What this meant for Chicago's relationship with Washington, DC, was initially unclear, but it would prove to be perhaps even stronger than it had been. Both Daley and Johnson came from poor backgrounds, and they seemed to understand each other in an almost visceral sense. Johnson's legislative initiatives and foreign policy blunders would both affect Chicago and Daley.

The demographics of the city continued to shift as well. By the 1960s, more African Americans lived in Chicago than in Mississippi. In 1963, Blacks made up roughly 26 percent of the population and lived mostly in large, segregated neighborhoods in expanding swaths of the South and West Sides. The African American portion of the public school population swelled to 48 percent in elementary schools and 34 percent in high schools. The Black population was becoming a defining demographic and political force. And it was restive. For the growing Black middle class, social change took place too slowly. Conservative Black leaders cautioned against militancy, but Black youth began to struggle for something more than what a city mired in racial animosity was willing to offer.[3]

THE RACIAL DIVIDE: THE SACRED AND PROFANE IN CONFLICT

The modern Black civil rights movement exploded in the national consciousness the same year Chicagoans elected Daley mayor. In 1955, Rosa Parks refused to give up her seat on a segregated Montgomery, Alabama, bus and the resulting boycott launched the public career of Dr. Martin Luther King Jr. Many saw the ongoing struggle for civil rights as a "southern" problem, but as northern ghettoes festered, civil rights quickly became an issue in cities like Chicago. Of course, the city had a long history of racial conflict going back to the 1919 race riot. In the years after World War II, many neighborhoods witnessed race-fueled riots, most notably the Trumbull Park riots, the Airport Homes riots, and the Peoria Street riots in Englewood. The city and some of the media attempted to keep these out of the headlines in the hope of not inciting more racial violence and White flight.[4]

The relationship between the civil rights movement and Democratic Party politics in Chicago proved complicated. William Dawson and the Black Democratic sub-machine welcomed a calm approach to Black issues. They saw progress as coming through the tightly controlled political order. Indeed, by the end of the 1950s substantial economic progress had been made by Black Chicagoans, who enjoyed a median income close to $5,000 ($51,690 in 2023), far above the national median Black income. One NAACP member claimed Chicago seemed near heaven. Others disagreed.[5]

The local branch of the NAACP had been conservative in its approach to civil rights, but the ascension in the 1950s of Willoughby Abner as the branch's executive secretary and then president ushered in a more combative style. Abner, shaped by a militant labor union tradition, called for direct confrontation with the forces of racism. He represented the aspirations of middle-class Blacks who felt frustrated by the slow response of Dawson, who did not want to shake up political relationships he had worked for years to nurture. As a result, Abner clashed with Dawson. The Chicago NAACP now advocated boycotts and picketing along with negotiations, letter-writing, and publicity. Membership increased, energized by the murder of Chicagoan Emmett Till in Mississippi and his funeral in Chicago. Till's murder epitomized the savage racism of the Jim Crow South. The historian Adam Green has pointed out that the murder and the funeral provided Blacks an opportunity to sum up their past and think about their future in a racially divided America and Chicago. Till's mother, Mamie Bradley, insisted on an open coffin at the visitation so that the world could see what had been done to her boy. The *Chicago Defender* took photos of the casket, although not the body, and the African American magazine *Jet* took the first close-ups of the mangled corpse. These images shocked Blacks throughout the city and the country. Racial disturbances in Trumbull Park, tensions between the Black community and the police, and the civil rights movement increased Black militancy and membership in the Chicago NAACP. Abner's activism met the moment, and under his leadership membership peaked in 1956 and 1957. But by that time both Daley and Dawson, along with Black moderates, especially Rev. Archibald J. Carey Jr., moved against Abner, maneuvering to oust him from the NAACP.[6]

Abner's defeat, however, did not mean the end of Black militancy in Chicago. Others stepped up. Longtime activist Timuel Black and

CHAPTER 9

others connected with the Negro American Labor Council educated young African Americans for roles in the movement. In 1960, a series of riots and "wade-ins" took place at Rainbow Beach on the South Side. Because of widespread racial change, many South Side Whites saw Rainbow Beach as their last lakefront oasis. The wade-ins raised the temperature between White and Black Chicagoans.[7]

The next year, on June 27, a fire at the Douglas Hotel in Bronzeville displaced roughly 100 Blacks. They took refuge in nearby Holy Cross Lutheran Church in all-White Bridgeport, the mayor's neighborhood. A mob of about 1,000 residents threatened to destroy the church. The Red Cross moved the fire victims to another church, in a Black neighborhood. Daley condemned the near riot and claimed that mostly teenagers made up the hostile crowd. Community leader, real estate man, and former president of the Chicago NAACP Dempsey Travis stated, "democracy in Chicago is going to have to start in the mayor's own backyard." Travis and others pointed out that the police had done nothing to disperse the White mob. Word of the incident made the national news. Ironically, Senator Olin D. Johnston of South Carolina quickly condemned the incident, claiming that any church, Black or White, in his state would have welcomed the fire victims.[8]

Increased racial protest and conflict in Chicago's public spaces, especially beaches, parks, and streets, marked the 1960s. On July 4, 1963, Daley marched with members of the NAACP in an Emancipation Parade through the Loop and then attended a freedom rally of about 20,000 people in Grant Park. Originally not scheduled to speak, Daley was asked to make welcoming remarks. As he began, a group of between 100 and 200 Blacks and Whites carrying anti-Daley placards marched through the crowd chanting, "Tokenism Must Go!" and "Down with Ghettoes." One sign asked, "Mayor Daley, No Negroes Live in Your Ward—Why?" Daley attempted to speak, accusing the protestors of being disruptive Republicans. Chairman Bishop Stephen G. Spotswood of the NAACP national board of directors seemed to quiet the demonstrators, but when Daley resumed speaking even more shouting arose from them. Daley left the stage. When Reverend Dr. Joseph H. Jackson, president of the National Baptist Convention and pastor of Chicago's Olivet Baptist Church, attempted to speak, the jeering became even louder. Now the great majority of the mostly Black crowd became angered and cried out "Uncle Tom must go!" Jackson had previously taken a stand against Black protest demonstrations, including the freedom rides and sit-ins. It would not be the last time Daley and his allies would feel the wrath of Black Chicagoans.[9]

The issue of segregation in Chicago's public schools was a long-festering one, but animus toward Superintendent Benjamin Willis was especially deep. The so-called Willis Wagons—mobile classrooms set up outside Black schools to reduce crowding—hid a deeper problem. Since Chicago was among the most residentially segregated cities in the country, setting school boundaries by neighborhood resulted in de facto school segregation. In the fall of 1961, the Chicago Urban League submitted a resolution to the school board concerning the unequal education provided by the city's public schools. The president of the school board informally agreed with the premise that all American children are entitled to equal educational opportunities. Differences emerged as to how to achieve that equality. The Urban League believed that only a full-scale attack could eliminate the problem. It called for student transfers from overcrowded schools in Black neighborhoods to those with underused classrooms, often in White neighborhoods. It also wanted equality among teachers. As it was, the system frequently assigned teachers who were inexperienced, non-certified, or substitutes to African American schools, diminishing the educational opportunities of Black children. The Urban League charged that the school board had not met its responsibilities to desegregate the schools and school staffs.[10]

In December 1961, Harold Baron of the Urban League's Research Department submitted an analysis to Executive Director Edwin C. Berry concerning two reports and various recommendations by School Superintendent Willis. Willis, Baron found, had seriously underreported the number of available classrooms, which were located predominantly in White schools. This had the effect of making those rooms unavailable to accommodate the overcrowding in Black schools. Furthermore, Baron suggested that Willis's policy recommendations would also perpetuate overcrowding in Black schools.[11]

Berry wrote Daley on January 6, 1962, pointing out the great inequalities in Chicago schools just as the City Council received the new school budget. The letter included testimony from the December 19 Board of Education meeting showing that in 1961 the budgeted expenditures for predominantly African American schools were 20 percent lower than those for White schools. It further claimed that integrated schools, in areas with populations that might be anywhere from 40 percent to 95 percent White, experienced a funding shortfall of almost 14 percent. This suggested that cutbacks in school funding in integrated areas promoted White flight and resegregation.[12]

In 1961, the Chicago Public Schools had fired Doris Baker, a Black teacher, for taking part in a protest against discriminatory school policies. Al Raby, a teacher at a nearly all-Black high school on the West Side, responded by helping to found Teachers for Integrated Schools. In 1963, the organization nominated him as a delegate to the newly formed Coordinating Council of Community Organizations (CCCO); the following year, Raby became that organization's convenor. The CCCO constituted a broad-based interracial coalition. Through his work there, Raby emerged as a prominent civil rights leader. In 1965, he went to work full-time for the organization. The CCCO had a middle-class flavor to it, but it played an important role in the creation of what became known as the Chicago Freedom Movement.

The school problem galvanized organizing among Chicago's African Americans. Superintendent of Schools Willis became a target for those who hoped to create a more equal school system. In the 1950s, Willis, once one of the most admired men in America, received an honorary degree from Harvard University as a defender of neighborhood public schools. In the 1960s, however, he became a symbol of northern apartheid. The Chicago NAACP likened him to the notoriously racist Governor George Wallace of Alabama.[13]

In July 1963, a movement for a student boycott of the schools emerged in the African American community. The Congress of Racial Equality (CORE), founded in Chicago in the 1940s, held ten days of sit-ins and picketing of the school board offices. Meanwhile, parents, upset that the public schools had begun erecting eighteen mobile classrooms at 73rd and Lowe Avenue, picketed the site and planned a boycott. The parent group, in a twenty-five-minute meeting with Mayor Daley, presented a petition signed by 1,300 residents. They asked Daley to discharge Willis, which the mayor refused to do. Protest at the mobile classroom site continued.[14]

Conflict between the Black community and the school board lasted throughout the fall of 1963. Black parents and civil rights groups staged demonstrations at six public schools, while about 100 parents and children took the protest to Board of Education offices on September 4. A partially successful boycott of classes, as well as a sit-in at the principal's office in the Beale School at 60th and Peoria Streets, resulted in thirteen arrests. The 71st and Stewart Committee maintained that 40 percent of approximately 600 students boycotted classes, though observers claimed lower numbers. At the Wentworth School, roughly twenty persons manned a picket line. Less than a week later, White parents at Bogan High School on the Southwest Side protested the admission to the high school of gifted, presumably Black students from outside the district. Willis decided not to send transfers to Bogan and more than twenty other predominantly White high schools. This further exacerbated the situation. Willis then argued with the school board over his policies and resigned. The board refused to accept his resignation, however, and he returned to his job by mid-October. This caused even further conflict with the Black community, which had hoped that Chicago had been rid of the controversial superintendent.[15]

The African American community organized a massive boycott of the public schools for Tuesday, October 22. On what the organizers called Freedom Day, they planned to target seventy schools where they predicted almost 100 percent of pupils would not attend classes. Roberta Galler, secretary of the Chicago Area Friends of the Student Nonviolent Coordinating Committee (Chicago-SNCC), said that at least eighteen churches had arranged programs to take in grammar-school children of working parents. The group organized civil rights exercises and activities for students, including the singing of freedom songs. The Chicago Federation of Settlements and Neighborhood Centers urged its members to provide adult supervision and special programs for children who boycotted the schools. In addition, organizers planned a demonstration outside City Hall and then a march to Board of Education headquarters.[16]

The boycott proved spectacularly successful. Lawrence Landry, chairman of the boycott committee, claimed all social classes in the Black community embraced the movement. Nearly 225,000 students stayed away from classes. A second boycott took place in 1964 when roughly 175,000 students stayed home on February 25. Despite being smaller than the first boycott, it underscored the potential for grassroots support for civil rights activities in Chicago.[17]

That summer the Democratic Party, still reeling from the assassination of President Kennedy in November 1963, met in Atlantic City to nominate Lyndon Johnson as its presidential candidate. Meanwhile, the Mississippi Freedom Democratic Party (MFDP) formed as an integrated and progressive alternative to the all-White Regular Mississippi Democratic Organization. The new party resulted from years of systematic exclusion of African Americans from the political process across the South. Leaders planned to challenge the seating of the Mississippi Delegation at the national convention.[18]

Al Raby and other Chicago civil rights leaders organized what they called Freedom Clubs of Illinois to support the MFDP. They took out a full-page ad in the *Chicago Defender* on August 17 calling on Chicagoans to write or call Cook County delegates to the Democratic Convention in support of seating the MFDP. They also appealed to all 114 delegates from Illinois to stop the seating of the all-White Mississippi delegation. Members of the clubs passed out handbills in front of City Hall on August 19 asking people to contact their delegates.[19] Letters inundated Daley's office calling for support for the MFDP. Daley agreed to meet with supporters of the MFDP in his offices on August 20, including Charles Hayes of the United Packinghouse Workers of America, Timuel Black, Al Raby, and civil rights activist Phil Moore.[20]

At the end of July, Illinois Senator Paul Douglas had proposed creating a hybrid delegation of both Mississippi factions, but the

MFDP rejected the idea. Later that August, Daley stated that the Illinois delegation planned to take up the matter at the convention. But in his usual manner, when confronted with a difficult situation, Daley refused to entirely commit. He had met with Democratic leaders in Washington, DC, to discuss the situation. President Johnson, worried about party unity, moved to not seat the MFDP despite widespread support for the organization among Northern Democrats. When it came down to it, the Illinois delegation, including Dawson and other Black delegates, sidestepped the issue by voting that "no delegate who is not pledged [shall] be seated at the convention." This amounted to ignoring the issue.

In the end, Daley supported LBJ in his attempt to keep the South in the convention. Daley's attitude reflected both practical politics and recognition of hierarchy. Johnson, the president and head of the party, thought it best to quell a White southern revolt, and Daley fell in line. The *Chicago Defender* condemned the Illinois delegation, although they praised Daley for his loyalty to Johnson. The newspaper understood that Goldwater hardly provided a viable alternative for Blacks. Although the MFDP initially rejected the plan, Democrats worked out a compromise and two members of the MFDP were permitted to join the convention (after which much of the regular Mississippi delegation walked out anyway). William L. Coleman, Chairman of the Ohio Democratic Executive Committee, thanked Daley for helping to work out the compromise.[21]

Neither the MFDP nor the Freedom Clubs disappeared from the scene. On a weekend that October, the clubs launched a founding convention in affiliation with the MFDP at the La Salle Hotel in the Loop. Well-known activists such as Fannie Lou Hamer, Robert Moses, and Dr. Aaron Henry spoke to the group. In December, Henry spoke at other meetings in both the city and the suburbs.[22] On December 10, Al Raby asked Mayor Daley for a meeting to discuss the role the Illinois congressmen would play in the Freedom Party's challenge to the seating of congressmen elected from Mississippi. After the December 23 meeting, the congressmen voted to support the MFDP challenge. Daley's support included a resolution from the City Council to make the city aware of the struggle in Mississippi.

Although the MFDP failed to unseat the Mississippi congressmen, the effort made an important point about the biased southern electoral systems. This would bear fruit later in 1965 with the passage of the Voting Rights Act. In Chicago, as Daley navigated this fraught issue, he recognized the practical dilemma he faced. He needed the support of the African American community to maintain the Democratic hold on the city. He also required the support of White ethnic communities. Daley walked a razor-thin line in maintaining both groups' loyalty.[23]

Another area of tension between the Daley administration and the Black community involved issues of police violence, corruption, and prejudice. In 1960, Daley hired Orlando W. Wilson, Dean of the School of Criminology at the University of California, Berkeley, as superintendent to reform the department. During his first year in office, Wilson changed the nature of police patrols to make them more efficient, created better ways of reporting crime, and added 500 police cars to the motorized fleet. Wilson's reforms, while not popular with the rank and file, brought the department into the twentieth century. Daley insulated Wilson from aldermen, who resented his reforms. In the second year, Wilson reformed police districts, reducing them from thirty-eight to twenty-two in order to prevent powerful politicians from influencing local commanders. Fearing his patrolmen had too much opportunity for misconduct and abuse, Wilson issued a multitude of orders and training bulletins. He narrowed the limits of police discretion in the hope of reducing and eventually eliminating misconduct. While his many reforms proved laudable, the race issue continued to trouble Chicago and the police force.[24]

RACIAL CLASHES

By 1964 Chicago seemed to be a powder keg ready to explode. In January, a brawl broke out in the Calumet High School gymnasium in Auburn-Gresham during a basketball game between the predominantly White school and Oliver Westcott Vocational School, a largely Black school. A strong undercurrent of racial tension prevailed in

Auburn-Gresham as racial change came to the area. Police arrested seven Black and White students.

Two nights earlier, Assistant Superintendent of Schools James A. Smith addressed a White group, the South Deering Improvement Association, in the Irondale community, which was not far from Calumet High School. He told the group, which had been associated with the riots against a Black family moving into the Trumbull Park Homes, a Chicago Housing Authority project, that Superintendent Willis thought highly of them. Smith declared that Chicagoans like them paid the taxes that built new schools. He thus implied that the anti-Black riots were justified. He defended Willis's neighborhood school policy and lashed out against pro-integrationist reform proposals. The atmosphere fostered by Smith's remarks may have helped fuel the student clash at Calumet High two nights later.[25]

On the night of August 15, a race riot broke out in Dixmoor, a suburb just southwest of the city. A liquor store owner accused a Black woman of trying to steal a bottle of gin. She claimed he then beat her. The next evening, thirty-seven people were injured as rioting continued. Sherriff Richard B. Ogilvie told his deputies to announce that the police would return fire if fired upon. Dixmoor and Harvey police called for help from other suburbs and from the city. Skirmishes continued on August 17, as a crowd tried to burn down the liquor store. By August 19, quiet had returned, but it would prove to be temporary.[26]

The next year, 1965, rioting arrived in the city proper. In July a civil rights organization, Austin Coming Together (ACT), began picketing a fire department station at Wilcox and Pulaski Avenue, just a few blocks south of the busy Madison and Pulaski shopping district. ACT demanded that the Chicago Fire Department hire more African Americans. The crowd swelled when several hundred Black teenagers joined the demonstration and began to throw bricks and bottles at cars as they passed through the intersection. Then on August 12 violence broke out again in the North Lawndale community in the Fillmore Police District. For several days crowds looted stores, attacked policemen and motorists, and set fire to buildings. The genesis of this outbreak was the death of a Black woman when a fire truck swerved out of control, hitting a stop sign that then hit her. ACT held a rally near the fire station in the racially tense neighborhood, handing out circulars denouncing White firemen for the accident. Later, a band of teenagers smashed store windows. The group attacked an off-duty policeman as he drove to the station. More police quickly arrived. Rioters turned cars on their sides and set several on fire. Police arrested 169 persons over two nights. Al Raby rushed to the West Side to appeal to rioters to stop. The CCCO also called an emergency meeting to find a way to calm tensions. At the same time, a much larger confrontation took place in Los Angeles's Watts neighborhood. The *Chicago Defender* argued that the disturbances in both cities resulted from an accumulation of instances of police brutality against the African American community. The long hot summers of the 1960s had begun.[27]

Daley responded to the 1965 conflict by calling twenty organizations to his office. He claimed that the riot had nothing to do with civil rights but reflected lawlessness. His response seemed out of touch. The mayor did not talk about racism, poor living conditions, lack of employment opportunities (including city hiring practices, especially in the police and fire departments), or long-standing allegations of police brutality against the Black community. Instead, he implied that communists might be creating agitation.[28]

Daley's actions mirrored his lifelong attitude toward hierarchy. As mayor, he or his handpicked people would come up with some answers, and, in turn, he expected the West Side populace to behave and go along with the decisions made from above. This is how the Catholic Church dealt with problems, and Daley saw no reason why the political machine should operate any differently. Unfortunately for Daley, no one like the South Side's Dawson had yet emerged in the West Side ghetto to enforce such a structure. With the Black sub-machine helping to manage relations, the South Side ghetto did not explode; but the newer and poorer West Side ghetto, with fewer long-settled institutions, did. Its trajectory of development did not fit the communal model. Daley never seemed to understand the different historical experiences of Blacks and older immigrant groups.[29]

THE CHICAGO FREEDOM MOVEMENT

The Coordinating Council of Community Organizations and the burgeoning Black activist movement in Chicago caught the attention of Dr. Martin Luther King Jr. and the leadership of the Southern Christian Leadership Council (SCLC). By April 1965, King announced that the SCLC planned to take its movement beyond the South and carry nonviolent protests across the nation. On April 3, Reverend James T. Bevel, an aide to King, conducted workshops for about 170 religious and civil rights leaders in the First Congregational Church of Chicago on the Near West Side. The Rev. C. T. Vivian of Atlanta, another King ally, held a meeting on the South Side at Grace Methodist Church on April 5 to discuss the SCLC's Chicago plans. Rev. Vivian said the SCLC would refrain from coming to Chicago in the summer of 1965 if the Board of Education removed Superintendent Willis. Al Raby announced that a rally demanding Willis's firing would be held in two days at the United Packinghouse Workers Hall.[30]

On Good Friday, April 16, 1965, roughly 2,500 marchers gathered at Buckingham Fountain to protest Willis and the Board of Education. They then marched to City Hall, where they listened a series of speakers, including the fiery Hosea Williams. He stood on the hood of an automobile and told the crowd that Chicago had no more intention of freeing Negroes than had the power structure in Selma, Alabama. He pressed on: "The outcome we seek today is not getting rid of Willis. It's getting rid of Mayor Daley." The school issue provided King and the SCLC an opportunity to organize more broadly in Chicago. Increasingly the city became a major target of the Black civil rights movement.[31]

Demonstrations against Willis continued throughout the spring and into the summer of 1965. So did protests over the use of War on Poverty programs, which Daley was skillfully directing to expand patronage for the Democratic Party. The Woodlawn Organization (TWO) emerged as another major player in Chicago's civil rights struggles. TWO and CCCO fought to wrest control of the War on Poverty programs away from the mayor, and they continued protests against the leadership of the public schools. The activist comedian Dick Gregory announced daily demonstrations after a march downtown on June 11, when police clubbed demonstrators and arrested 250 protestors. By the end of July, the protests moved to Bridgeport and the mayor's block. Bridgeport residents came out in large numbers to heckle the protestors. They held mass-produced signs that read "We Love Our Mayor" and "Daley is for Democracy." Homemade signs expressed more threatening messages, celebrating the Ku Klux Klan or using racial epithets. Bridgeporters threw eggs, tomatoes, and stones at the marchers. Police detained few area residents and often joked with them as the marchers went by. On August 2, police arrested sixty-five demonstrators "for their own protection." The next day, in a pouring rain, Gregory led marchers from Buckingham Fountain in Grant Park to Bridgeport while hundreds of police officers contained a White mob. Finally, the demonstrations stopped, but Raby pointed out that the Bridgeport marches showed the need for Chicagoans to confront their own racism.[32]

The CCCO and other civil rights organizations planned another boycott of the schools. Circuit Court Judge Cornelius J. Harrington issued an injunction against it, and Federal District Court Judge Julius Hoffman refused to overturn the injunction on appeal. The CCCO petitioned the federal government to withhold funds for Chicago's schools on the basis that they had been deliberately segregated. On July 7, Dr. King announced that he would come to the city to join with local civil rights organizations in their fight for quality integrated education and better housing conditions. Four days later, Dr. King's brother, Rev. A. D. King, addressed some 200 demonstrators in Grant Park. During a march from the park to City Hall, police arrested Chairman Robert Lucas of the Chicago chapter of the Congress on Racial Equality (CORE) at the corner of Monroe and State Streets. This sparked a clash that led to the arrest of twenty-seven demonstrators.[33]

Dr. King arrived in Chicago on July 23 to lead a series of streetcorner rallies and learn about the problems faced by African Americans in Chicago. His itinerary included an address to a mass meeting and a march on City Hall. His three-day visit began with a stop at

El Bethel Baptist Church on the South Side. He then visited Black neighborhoods across the city. The next day he offered a sermon at Quinn AME Church and at Progressive Baptist Church and held five other street-corner meetings. The second day ended with a speech on the village green in Winnetka on the North Shore.[34]

The July 26 Buckingham Fountain rally created a sense of unity as all of Chicago's civil rights leaders appeared with King. He led the march to City Hall to again demand the ouster of Willis. Afterward King announced that "Chicago is on fire with a nonviolent movement." The SCLC established a presence in Chicago when a dozen or so members of King's staff moved into the West Side Christian Parish's Project House in the heart of the Near West Side. These workers came to Chicago to assist Rev. James Bevel, a leading SCLC activist who would soon be appointed director of the SCLC's Chicago Project. Al Raby believed that only a concerted effort by the SCLC could change conditions for Blacks in the city. He announced in December that King would return to Chicago the following January to begin a vigorous civil rights campaign. The SCLC along with the CCCO created the Chicago Freedom Movement (CFM).[35]

What happened over the next few months would shake the city and its political structure to its core. In January 1966, Dr. King moved into a decrepit apartment in North Lawndale to highlight his goal of ending slum housing not only in Chicago but across the nation. He announced the first significant freedom movement in the North and called for the mobilization of the city's Blacks. King planned demonstrations against specific targets, culminating in a massive action in May directed at both public and private institutions that he claimed created slum conditions. The Chicago Freedom Movement planned to hold informational meetings for ministers across the city and would make special efforts to reach the large Roman Catholic community.[36]

Some Chicago civil rights leaders disagreed with King's plans and called for a continued focus on the education issue rather than slum housing. SCLC and CCCO leaders expected the hostility of the Black Muslims, headquartered in Chicago, and the antagonism of radical African Americans, but conservative forces in the Black community presented the most formidable opposition. These leaders preferred a more gradual approach to social change and championed the local political process. Older members of the Black community, who had ties to the centers of power in the city, worried that further protests and marches would do more harm than good. Many ordinary Black Chicagoans simply did not commit themselves to the campaign, while some Black leaders publicly expressed their concerns. The Chicago NAACP refused to join King's movement. Reverend Joseph H. Jackson, pastor of Olivet Baptist Church and an ally of Richard J. Daley, criticized the movement. In general, the reaction of Chicago's established African American leadership revealed both a generational and a class rift within the community.[37]

Mayor Daley met several times with Dr. King and his aides to de-escalate the looming conflict. The first meeting took place on March 24, 1966, when King and forty religious leaders, including Cardinal John Cody and Rev. Jesse Jackson, met with the mayor to discuss problems in the Black community. King described the meeting as friendly and meaningful.[38] Nonetheless, in late May King announced plans for a major rally and march on City Hall, where he intended to present demands to the mayor. Hoping to attract 100,000 Chicagoans, the CFM held the rally on Sunday, July 10, at Soldier Field. John A. McDermott, executive director of the Catholic Interracial Council, called for all Catholics to attend.[39]

Although more than 30,000 people attended the rally in Soldier Field in the sweltering summer heat, White ethnic Catholics had not, for the most part, heeded McDermott's call. Whites made up roughly 10 percent of the crowd. After the rally, King led some 5,000 protestors to City Hall. He taped his demands concerning open housing and integrated schools to the door of City Hall, recalling his namesake's protest against the Papacy hundreds of years earlier. The next day, King, Raby, and their aides met with Daley in a cordial meeting, though apparently not as friendly as their first one had been.[40]

King encountered a savvy politician in Daley who had a decent if limited record on civil rights. The civil rights leader demanded bold action, but the mayor refused to promise anything. After the meeting, King decided to escalate the confrontation. The next day, July 12, however, a riot broke out on the West Side. Black youth had opened a fire hydrant to cool themselves in the ninety-degree heat, leading to a confrontation with the police. In no time, the neighborhood exploded. The next day, officials secured fire hydrants throughout the West Side, and riots broke out again in Lawndale and to a lesser extent in East and West Garfield Park. On Friday morning, Daley asked Governor Otto Kerner to mobilize the Illinois National Guard.

The mayor lashed out, charging that Rev. Bevel had been talking about violence for the last year and instructing people in how to conduct it. King went to Daley's office but could not get an appointment. He then staged a sit-in, joined by other religious leaders including Cardinal Cody. Daley finally met with King and seemed receptive to his demands. The mayor then tried to act as a peacemaker. He consented to attach sprinklers to fire hydrants and to construct more swimming pools, and he agreed to appoint a civilian committee to improve police relations with the community. Unfortunately, the rioting had both immediate and long-term consequences. Two people had been killed and over eighty injured. Police arrested 400, and much of the neighborhood lay in ruins. The riot proved a blow to the Chicago Freedom Movement. For the West Side communities of Garfield Park and Austin, the riots and, most importantly, neglect by the city impacted and increased racial change. These factors shattered the always tenuous interaction between the sacred and the profane in Chicago's neighborhoods.[41]

Marches continued that summer, as did meetings with realtors, businesspeople, and civic leaders, as well as Daley. King, determined to keep the pressure up, marched into White areas demanding open housing. Chicago had become a critical test case for the SCLC, as it feared losing ground in the African American community to the more radical and more aggressive Black Power movement. King sent teams of his supporters into White neighborhoods on the Northwest and Southwest Sides to challenge real estate firms to allow open housing. On August 5, a rock thrown from a crowd of hostile White counterdemonstrators felled King during an open housing march in Marquette Park. Afterwards, King expressed his shock and disappointment: "I have seen many demonstrations in the South, but

CHAPTER 9

I have never seen anything so hateful as I've seen here today." Later members of the American Nazi Party, headquartered in that neighborhood, picketed a meeting at a Black church on the South Side. Frustrated and worried, Daley and other leaders called for an end to all demonstrations.[42]

Daley, always the pragmatic politician, knew he needed both Black and White votes to retain power. He also understood that King needed a win. On August 26, King announced that all marches would stop as part of an agreement between the city and the Chicago Freedom Movement. Basically, Daley had agreed to an unenforceable pact that promised open housing and other reforms while King declared victory. Many were disappointed in the agreement, including Daley's constant critic, Alderman Leon Despres. Following this détente, King began to shift his focus to jobs. In a rally at Liberty Baptist Church, King called the lack of equal economic opportunities the major problem facing the African American community. A little more than a year later an assassin would kill Dr. King in Memphis. Chicago and other cities witnessed horrific riots in response to King's assassination. The West Side, pained and angry, again erupted in destructive violence. In many ways it has not yet recovered.[43]

The arrival of King and the Chicago Freedom Movement divided support for the machine. Increasingly, both Blacks and Whites became disenchanted with the Daley administration. Despite this fragmentation the Democratic Organization was able to hold on to power based on its ability to maintain loyalty in the neighborhoods and through the complex composition of the party, but more shocks soon appeared on the horizon.

At 4:45 a.m. on December 4, 1969, fourteen Chicago police under the aegis of Democratic Cook County State's Attorney Edward V. Hanrahan entered a West Side apartment. The resulting gun battle left two Black Panther Party leaders dead: State Chairman Fred Hampton and organizer Mark Clark. The police claimed that the Panthers had fired upon them first. Reporters visiting the flat took a tour led by Party Defense Minister Bobby Rush and Deputy Information Minister Chaka Walls, who pointed out evidence that police had been unprovoked and initiated the massacre. Hanrahan defended his men. Four separate investigations followed, including a federal grand jury, which on May 15, 1970, released a scathing report condemning the police. Nevertheless, the grand jury did not indict the policemen because the surviving Black Panthers refused to testify. In June, a special state grand jury led by Barnabas F. Sears, Daley's choice to head the investigation, began. The grand jury prepared an indictment against Hanrahan and thirteen police officers in April of the following year, but Judge Joseph Power, a neighbor and former law partner of the mayor, refused to sign the formal presentment. Finally, on August 24, 1971, the Illinois Supreme Court ordered the indictments to be delivered. The case dragged on and Judge Philip J. Romiti, another Democrat, acquitted Hanrahan in November 1972. Despite falling out of favor with the party leadership and failing to obtain the Democrats' endorsement, Hanrahan managed to win the primary. He went down to defeat in the general election to Republican Bernard Carey.[44]

These events and more made the relationship between the African American community and the Democratic Party increasingly tense. In fact, as the racial divide deepened over issues of equity in education, housing, policing, and jobs, the Democratic coalition threatened to come apart. Mayor Daley struggled politically to reconcile competing values and attitudes, as commitments to communalism encountered intractable racial prejudice. Cermak's "House for All Peoples" seemed a distant dream.

COMING APART: THE DEMOCRATIC CONVENTION

While race relations continued to embroil the nation, a foreign war also demanded attention. As the Vietnam War escalated, anti-war demonstrations broke out on college campuses and city streets. While Chicago's campuses hardly resembled those in Madison, Berkeley, or New York City, anti-war feeling ran high, and groups such as the Students for a Democratic Society organized local colleges and universities. By 1970, various campuses would be rocked by demonstrations as that long cruel war dragged on.

Many of Chicago's young men found themselves fighting in Viet-

CHAPTER 9

nam. Others would face the choice of being drafted, joining the armed forces voluntarily, resisting the draft and facing jail time, or fleeing the country. For Chicago's political machine, the Vietnam War and the anti-war movement presented challenges far beyond its power to cope. A national tragedy that reshaped the nation, the Vietnam War also fundamentally altered the political landscape in Chicago.

As the war dragged on and American casualties mounted, President Johnson announced in March 1968 that he would not run for reelection. Assassins killed Dr. King in April and then Robert F. Kennedy in June. As trauma after trauma piled up, the Democrats chose Chicago as the site of the 1968 nominating convention. The president believed that Daley would be able control the volatile situation and prevent demonstrations from getting out of hand. Daley's reputation as a strong mayor who exercised tight control over his city no doubt influenced the party's and LBJ's decision.

In the lead-up to the convention, Daley was urged to provide public spaces for demonstrations, with the hope of minimizing violent confrontations. Activists such as David Dellinger, Dr. Sidney Peck, and Rennie Davis requested a suitable march route to the convention site at the International Amphitheater on the South Side. The trio hoped to meet personally with Daley to work out a plan. Daley telegrammed Senators Eugene McCarthy and George McGovern, the leading candidates, complaining that while the press reported that the city planned to shut down public meetings of their supporters, he in fact wanted to have the views and positions of all candidates thoroughly expounded and presented to the nation. McGovern's campaign coordinator, Edward C. McDermott, thanked Daley, but said the campaign had no need at the present time to hold such gatherings.[45]

Daley seemed upset by the threat of massive civil disobedience. Especially after the riots that wracked the city following King's assassination, he saw the Democratic gathering as a chance to showcase his city as a safe and attractive place. On August 19, he wrote Governor Samuel Shapiro, his political ally, to request that the Illinois National Guard be deployed to the city for the convention. Chicago soon became an armed camp, even though fewer demonstrators than expected arrived in the city. In fact, more police and troops patrolling

> # The Daley News
>
> Section 15,288 — Tuesday, April 4, 1967 — Volume 4
>
> ## DEMOCRATS WIN BY A LANDSLIDE IN THE 34th PRECINCT!
>
> **DALEY - MARCIN - KORSHAK ... 256**
> **WANER - PRICE - SISLER 86**
>
> A "BIG" THANK YOU to each and every Voter who helped Re-elect Mayor Richard J. Daley to a 4th term in office, also for electing his capable running mates John C. Marcin, City Clerk and Marshall Korshak, City Treasurer.
>
> I'm sure that Chicago will become the Number One City in the in the World under the great leadership of Mayor Daley....
>
> Let's all wish him strength and continuing good health in the next four years, so he can go on with the gigantic job of running Chicago.
>
> Congratulations on your wise choice !
>
> *John L. Paukstis*
> Democratic Precinct Captain
>
> JOHN L. PAUKSTIS
> Democratic Precinct Captain
> 4400 SOUTH CALIFORNIA AVENUE
> CHICAGO, ILLINOIS 60632

9.1 The Daley News, April 4, 1967. In the 1960s, despite racial conflict and antiwar protests, the Democratic machine still maintained an army of precinct captains to get out the vote. One Brighton Park precinct captain, John L. Paukstis, printed and distributed this handout in 1967 thanking his 34th Precinct voters for continuing to support Mayor Daley in that year's election. Richard J. Daley Collection [MSRJD04], box SIIss1B80, folder 5, Special Collections & University Archives, University of Illinois Chicago.

Chicago outnumbered the so-called "outside agitators." Approximately 5,600 National Guardsmen augmented the 11,500-member Chicago police force, 1,000 federal agents, and 7,500 federal soldiers. The profoundly divided Democratic Convention ran from August 26 to August 29, 1968.[46]

The clash between police and demonstrators in Lincoln Park just before the convention and around the Hilton Hotel and in Grant Park during the convention highlighted the sense that Daley had lost control of the situation. Clashes made unflattering headlines across the country and the world. While the world watched, violence and mayhem enveloped Daley's convention and Chicago's streets. In public, Daley supported the police and his beleaguered superintendent, James B. Conlisk Jr. Privately he criticized their tactics, complaining that a lack of discipline and supervision resulted in clashes with the demonstrators. Afterwards, Daley's national reputation seemed tarnished and diminished.[47]

The US National Commission on the Causes and Prevention of Violence appointed Daniel J. Walker to head the team that investigated the incidents around the convention. The Walker Report, released on December 1, 1968, called the conflict a "police riot." The report launched Walker's political career. Earl Bush, the mayor's longtime press secretary, wanted Police Superintendent Conlisk to respond to the report, but Conlisk refused to make a public statement. After prodding by Bush and Frank Sullivan, the police department's press secretary, and Daley himself, Conlisk issued a written response, but he refused to address the media in person.[48]

Mainstream public opinion supported Daley and the Chicago police. Letters arrived from across the country that were sympathetic to the police and the mayor. Some even sent traditional Catholic spiritual enrollments. The turbulence of the 1960s and especially the visibility of radical movements and urban violence meant that in 1968 public opinion sided with the police on most issues. After the convention, calls for law and order predominated and helped propel the Nixon/Agnew Republican campaign to victory in November's election. The city no longer had an ally in the White House.[49]

DARK DAYS

Daley's and the Chicago Democrats' problems mushroomed, which buoyed the hopes of reformers who sought to dismantle the machine. In 1969, Michael L. Shakman, an unsuccessful independent candidate for the Illinois Constitutional Convention, and Paul M. Lurie, an attorney who had supported Shakman's run, filed a lawsuit arguing that political patronage was unconstitutional. At first, Federal District Court Judge Abraham L. Marovitz, a longtime friend of Daley's, dismissed the suit on the grounds that the plaintiffs had not been patronage employees and therefore had not been injured by the system. In October 1970, appeals court judges ruled by a vote of two to one that the lower court had left significant questions unanswered. Immediately, the American Civil Liberties Union (ACLU), the Better Government Association (BGA), the Committee for an Effective City Council (CECC), and the Independent Voters of Illinois (IVI) combined forces to establish the Joint Committee to End Patronage Abuse.

When the case was returned to Judge Marovitz, the ACLU requested his removal on grounds of his long connection to the Daley machine. Marovitz admitted being Daley's friend but said the mayor never influenced a case tried by him. Eventually, the lower court ruled that the city's patronage system indeed denied non-Democratic candidates and voters an equal voice in government. Finally, in April 1971, the Supreme Court of the United States denied an appeal by the Cook County Democratic Party to set aside that ruling.[50]

In July 1971, the party's regular organization adopted a resolution abandoning compulsory precinct work and contributions but allowing volunteer gifts and work in place. In September, when the IVI elected the twenty-eight-year-old Shakman as its state chairman, he promised increased efforts to enforce the patronage decision. The IVI and the Daley organization engaged in a series of meetings. A tentative pact called for an end to firing or demoting workers for not doing political work. It also forbade doing political work on government time. Despite obvious loopholes in the pact, most saw it as a good first step. Daley claimed the modest reforms would not destroy the party organization.

The settlement depended, however, on the Republican Party agreeing to also not use patronage as a political tool. In October, Judge Marovitz gave the Republicans until November 5 to agree to the proposal. DuPage County Republican leaders called the pact illegal and

CHAPTER 9

"hogwash." Republican James "Pate" Philip claimed that the Cook County Democrats would never abide by the agreement. The Republicans' counterproposal included other curbs on the patronage system, which threatened to derail the whole matter. Shakman's attorney, Robert Plotkin, called the counterproposal a rejection of the original plan. Nevertheless, by January 1972 both Democrats and Republicans signed the consent decree. It covered all Chicago and Cook County governmental employees and all state employees in the other eighteen counties of northern Illinois. David Goldberger, the legal director of the ACLU, promised that the subject of political hiring, which was not covered, would be settled in later court action.[51]

Local 505 of the American Federation of State, County, and Municipal Employees then sued the city and the Civil Service Commission to bar hiring of so-called temporary workers for political reasons. The union claimed that the extensive hiring of temporary workers rather than civil service workers limited chances for promotion. Indeed, the city had long used this ruse to get around civil service rules.

Democrats who did not agree with the consent decree also fought back. State's Attorney Hanrahan halted the formal signing of the Shakman agreement on April 20, 1972, because while twenty-seven elected officials and political organizations agreed to the order, suburban Republicans still refused to sign it. Shakman suggested that Hanrahan may have filed his objection to embarrass Mayor Daley and other top Democrats. Judge Marovitz overruled Hanrahan on May 5 and signed the settlement formalizing the Shakman agreement.[52]

More twists and turns ensued in the Shakman saga. At the end of July, Judge Marovitz found that some patronage firings were still legal despite the consent decree. When the Chicago Park District sought to have the entire Shakman settlement thrown out, Marovitz ruled that although it was illegal to force government employees to work for candidates as a condition of employment, it was not illegal to require party affiliation. This decision appeared to legalize patronage firings. A new administration, he determined, could fire all employees of a previous administration so long as retention was not conditioned on coerced political activity. Shakman called the ruling inconsistent with recent US Supreme Court rulings and promised to appeal it. The plaintiffs accused Marovitz of having secret talks with Daley. The judge denied the allegations, and ordered the case back to the chief justice for reassignment. In October 1972, city and county employees received notices detailing provisions of the Shakman understanding. Word reached employees that the traditional use of patronage could result in contempt-of-court penalties. Shakman promised to go to court if the IVI heard of any examples of "patronage-as-usual."

The first Shakman decree struck at the very heart of machine politics. It undermined the foundation of the communal response that formed the bedrock Chicago's political life. Subsequent Shakman decrees would further weaken the operations of the traditional political machine, which had been built upon the exchange of jobs and favors for loyalty. If not immediately, then eventually, precinct captains felt the impact of this consent decree on their ability to get out the vote. The 1972 election supposedly gave proof of the impact of the new ruling, as fewer Chicago voters went to the polls than in previous presidential election years.[53] After more than seventy years of reform efforts, Shakman and his supporters had put the first true nail in the communal machine's coffin. A decades-long struggle seemed close to finishing the mission of breaking apart the Democratic machine.

Other factors, however, including the national climate, may have had an even greater impact. The disastrous 1968 convention, continued conflict over the Vietnam War, and racial strife cast a long shadow over the Democratic Party. In the years following the 1968 convention, reformers led by Senator George S. McGovern, and later by Representative Donald M. Fraser, worked to change the rules by which state parties chose delegates. This intraparty fight contributed significantly to weakening the grip of the Chicago machine.

In June 1969, at a fundraising dinner for the New Trier Township Democratic Committee in the northern suburbs attended by various opponents of the Daley organization, McGovern declared that the previous year's convention had damaged the party and contributed to Hubert Humphrey's loss to Richard Nixon. The next day a tense exchange took place between Daley and McGovern during Daley's surprise participation as a witness before the Democratic Commission on Structure and Delegate Selection, commonly called the McGovern-Fraser Commission. Daley had decided to face his accusers. McGovern challenged Daley on how Democrats picked convention delegates in Illinois, claiming that a small group of leaders controlled the process. The mayor reacted strongly, countering that the process was open and fair. Commission members, of course, remembered the 1964 conflict over the Mississippi Freedom Democratic Party. Daley proposed a reform of the entire process, including of the Electoral College, arguing that there should be as much dialogue between candidates and delegates as possible.[54]

Daley remained a powerful force in the Democratic Party, nationally as well as locally, so even reformers sought to maintain contact with him. McGovern wrote to Daley to thank him for testifying at the commission and for a subsequent phone call. He also praised Daley's role in the Conference of Mayors and asked for his advice on urban problems. The senator saw no reason to provoke an attack.

Both McGovern and Angelo G. Geocaris, vice chairman of the Committee on Illinois Government, invited Daley to attend a rally at Adlai Stevenson's farm in Libertyville on September 7, 1969. The theme of the event, "There's Room for Everybody," expounded the idea of the Democratic Party as a "Big Tent."[55] Daley attended and gave a speech calling for reform. In a note to a supporter, the mayor wrote that "there must be room in the Democratic Party for divergent opinions." He went on to call for party unity. McGovern, Daley, and other party leaders sought to avoid a clash if possible.[56]

The McGovern-Fraser Commission established new rules for the selection of delegates and broke all traditional power structures within the party. In an effort to democratize the convention, the commission decided that delegates should be chosen by gender, ethnicity, race, and age criteria and not by the party leaders. As a result, the 1972 Democratic Convention did not resemble those that had preceded it, and certainly not those that Daley had participated in. Party bosses saw their power erode while younger people, African Americans, and women made up a much larger percentage of convention delegates.

In the March 1972 primary Chicago voters selected 59 of the 170 Illinois delegates. The winning Daley slate included nine Black men, three Black women, four White women, two Hispanic women, and five Whites under the age of thirty. Nevertheless, it fell short of the demographic mix called for by the McGovern–Fraser reforms. Daley's opponents, led by 43rd Ward independent Alderman William Singer and the civil rights leader Reverend Jesse Jackson, challenged the validity of the slate. Reformers held caucuses throughout the city to assemble an alternate slate of delegates. The Singer–Jackson coalition petitioned to be seated at the national convention, again recalling the MFDP.

The Regular Democrats repudiated the Singer–Jackson group and affirmed the legality of their slate, with Daley asserting that once the delegates got to the convention no one would dare throw them out. Daley's forces filed a lawsuit and Judge Daniel Covelli issued an injunction blocking the Singer–Jackson group from being seated at the convention. When the Singer–Jackson group took the case to federal court, the McGovern–Fraser Commission filed an amicus curiae brief defending them. After the US Supreme Court affirmed the party's right to determine its own selection process, the battle then moved to the Democratic Party's Credentials Committee. In a stunning move, the party chose to seat the Singer–Jackson group and disqualified the Regular Democrats. Daley's delegates hoped that a floor fight might overrule the Credentials Committee, and refused all compromise. Daley saw the struggle as threatening his very control over the Cook County Democratic Party. He lost the floor fight and his seat at the Convention—a shocking defeat. Nevertheless, the reformers could not sustain their victory. The reform group squabbled, while Daley's forces worked behind the scenes to navigate the setback. Later, after winning the nomination handily, McGovern's forces sought to mend their relationship with Daley.[57]

Initially, Daley ignored McGovern, but putting his loyalty to the Democratic Party first, he openly supported the presidential nominee even if his heart and that of the Chicago Democratic Organization was not fully in it. Others bristled on Daley's behalf and refused to openly support McGovern's candidacy. One letter to the mayor called him a "sucker" for supporting the party's nominee. Although McGovern overwhelmingly lost the national election, he did carry Chicago and Cook County, garnering 55 percent of the city's votes. Soon after McGovern's crushing loss the Democratic Party reconsidered the 1972 reforms, and Daley saw himself reinstated as a delegate four years later.[58]

Daley faced local threats as well. Dan Walker, the head of the Chicago investigation into the violence surrounding the 1968 convention, had quickly emerged as a critic of the machine and a leader of the progressive wing of the Democratic Party. In August 1970, David Green, a political operative, told Walker that he could win the governorship without the backing of Daley's organization. On November 19, Walker announced his candidacy for governor and his willingness to take on the Regular Democratic Organization. The *Chicago Tribune* called Walker reckless, as the Daley machine had just pulled off a sweep of the November elections. Even Senator Adlai Stevenson III, whom Walker had long supported, seemed bemused. He assured Daley that he would not support Walker.

After Illinois Secretary of State Paul Powell died on October 10, 1970, over $700,000 was found in a shoebox in his closet. In January 1971, Walker leveraged this scandal, charging that the machine had foisted itself on the people of Illinois; Powell should never have been elected. Shortly afterward, Walker named Victor De Grazia as his campaign manager. DeGrazia had previously worked for Judge Abner Mikva, as part of the independent Democratic movement. Walker also attracted many of the people who had run Stevenson's successful campaigns.

In July, Walker announced that he would start a walking campaign across Illinois to gather support. He made his way from the Kentucky-Illinois border to the northern border with Wisconsin, and then to Chicago. Wearing a red bandanna, Walker cultivated rural support, which would help offset Chicago's opposition. His journey attracted significant media attention and made Walker a household name across Illinois. Walker vowed to break Daley's influence outside of Chicago. He denounced machine-backed candidates, including Lt. Governor Paul Simon, saying that he did not believe they could maintain their independence. Walker boldly claimed that "a machine candidate has to have machine priorities and those priorities are set on the fifth floor of city hall." On December 6, 1971, the Democratic Organization of Cook County threw its support behind Simon for governor.[59]

Walker narrowly won the primary against Simon, and then defeated the Republican incumbent Ogilvie in the general election. Daley, always the good Democrat, did officially throw his support behind Walker, but the newly elected governor soon proved to be a formidable foe. Walker immediately threatened to block one of Daley's favored infrastructure proposals, the crosstown expressway. Daley refused to get into a public argument with the governor-elect. A factor in Daley's reluctance to fight may have been the waning popularity of the project in Chicago. Other politicians also opposed its construction, including Democrats on the Northwest and Southwest Sides of the city who refused to go against their constituents' wishes. By this time expressway construction—which Daley had long enthusiastically abetted—had proven more and more unpopular not only in Chicago, but across the nation's cities. Expressways such as the Dan Ryan, the Kennedy, and the Stevenson had cut across neighborhoods and caused all kinds of havoc in the wards Democrats represented.[60]

During Walker's four years in office, he and Daley maintained a tense if polite relationship. Still, Daley Democrats in Springfield worked against the governor. Meanwhile, voters elected Richard M. Daley, the mayor's oldest son, to the state senate. He emerged as the informal leader of the city's Democrats and led their opposition to Walker's program. Chicago mayors rarely got along with governors of their own party as they vied for control of the statewide party. The elder Daley referred to Walker as a "bad man." He promised to think about how to deal with him before the next gubernatorial election.[61]

Beyond Daley's lack of rapport with Governor Walker, a series of scandals hit Daley's administration in 1973 and 1974. Perhaps the most damaging involved Daley's decision to transfer the city's insurance business to an Evanston firm, Heil and Heil, which employed his son John, who handled the account. Additional charges of nepotism soon followed. Daley's two lawyer sons, Richard and Michael, benefited from lucrative court appointments made by Judge Daniel Covelli, a mayoral ally. When the story broke, Daley responded furiously, telling his machine colleagues, "if I can't help my sons then they can kiss my ass. I make no apologies to anyone." Leaning into the core values of the communal worldview, he went on: "If a man can't put his arms around his sons, then what kind of a world are we living in?"

Alderman Dick Simpson, a foe of the administration, introduced a resolution in the City Council requiring Daley to give an account of the "nepotism and conflict of interest" involving his sons. Alderman Claude Holman, who chaired the City Council in Daley's absence, refused to allow Simpson's resolution to be presented. Simpson stood in silent protest for five and a half hours, attempting to be recognized. In April 1973, he used a parliamentary maneuver to raise the issue again. In response, the mayor directed the police and the sergeant at arms to silence and seat the independent alderman. When that failed, Daley simply turned off Simpson's microphone. Using another parliamentary ploy, the City Council sent the resolution to the Rules Committee, which buried it. Simpson persisted, and when the council finally voted on the resolution it went down to defeat, thirty-five to seven. Only anti-machine aldermen supported Simpson's proposal.[62]

The nepotism affair hit at the very heart of the Daley organization. In fact, it went to the very center of machine politics. Neighborhood people understood Daley's position. His explanation resonated in the halls of De La Salle and in churches and synagogues across Cook County. The reformers seemed to want to take away the very relationships that created the sense of community that defined these immigrant and ethnic neighborhoods. To outsiders, favors and loyalty meant corruption, but to those raised in the culture of communalism they were part of the social contract. Both things could be true.

Other scandals rocked the Daley administration. Again, the police department came under public scrutiny. In 1973, a police traffic chief and eighteen vice detectives faced charges of extortion. In addition, a grand jury indicted thirty-seven other policemen on charges of shakedowns, bribery, and income tax evasion. Daley fired his police superintendent, James Conlisk, and replaced him with James Rochford. The new police superintendent tried to weed out unethical police, but the taint of corruption continued to haunt the department. Moreover, issues concerning a lack of minority hiring persisted.

Bad news continued to mount, even as Daley considered running for another term. Indictments for corruption came down against longtime Daley press secretary Earl Bush as well as Aldermen Paul Wigoda and Tom Keane. The indictment of Daley's neighbor and political ally Matthew Danaher, who had been with Daley since his first election, hit closest to Daley himself. In addition, Daley's own finances came under investigation by US Attorney James Thompson.[63]

As problems mounted, Daley suffered a mild stroke on May 6, 1974. The mayor celebrated his seventy-second birthday in the hospital as questions of a successor arose. Released from the hospital after ten days, he returned in the first week of June for follow-up surgery. He then left for his vacation home in Grand Beach, Michigan, to recuperate. As he convalesced, more bad news befell the beleaguered Chicago Democrats. Former Governor Otto Kerner, the son-in-law of Anton Cermak, went to prison after being found guilty of mail fraud, bribery, conspiracy, income tax evasion, and perjury. On September 3, after a three-month absence, Daley returned to City Hall and promptly faced questions about his own investments. James Thompson, who had successfully prosecuted Cook County Democrats, finally acknowledged that he had uncovered no indictable offenses by Daley.

While Daley was recovering, independent Alderman William Singer, who in 1972 had led the effort to unseat the Daley convention delegates, announced his candidacy for mayor. African American State Senator Richard Newhouse and former prosecutor Edward Hanrahan, whom Daley had earlier dumped, soon joined Singer in challenging Daley. Suddenly Daley faced stiff competition in the Democratic primary. Nevertheless, he won 58 percent of the vote. Even the African American wards supported the mayor, and it seemed the organization remained largely intact despite the recent string of events. Daley went on to win the 1975 general election by a record total. The machine wasn't gone yet.[64]

As Daley entered his sixth term, the world had changed dramatically. Many Catholic nuns and priests concerned about civil rights now opposed him. He clashed with Cardinal Cody. The old bonds that had held so much of his world together had been weakened. Friends and close colleagues had gone to jail. Even Matt Danaher, his longtime neighbor and aide, had died broken and under indictment. His trusted circle of advisors shrank to his four sons and his wife. State's Attorney Bernard Carey, another De La Salle Institute graduate but a Republican, emerged as an adversary.

The communal response seemed to dissolve. Many of Chicago's Irish had climbed the ladder of mobility with the help of the Democratic Party. However, their success often weakened their ties to their old neighborhoods and to the party. Other Catholic ethnic groups and Jews headed for the suburbs. The death of the machine would be slow, even as its legend would continue to inspire writers and journalist for years to come. Yet in 1975, Daley and the Democrats still held power and were looking forward to the 1976 elections. The paradox might well be that the machine reached its zenith under Mayor Richard J. Daley but also experienced its earliest signs of fatal trouble.

10

Changing Times

> If a man ever reflected a city, it was Richard J. Daley and Chicago. In some ways he was this town at its best—strong, hard driving, pushing, building.... In other ways he was the city at its worst—arrogant, crude, conniving, ruthless, suspicious, intolerant.
>
> MIKE ROYKO[1]

Although Daley secured the nomination in the 1975 Democratic primary, vote totals hinted at problems. Black wards did not come out in the numbers that they had previously, and only 48.5 percent of African Americans who voted cast their ballot for Daley. Daley became increasingly dependent on White ethnic neighborhoods, a vote that while dependable could be weaned away, as in 1963. Daley won handily in his own ward, where 81.6 percent of registered voters came to the polls, 87.1 percent of them for him. In the nearby 14th Ward, where Eddie Burke served as both alderman and committeeman, voters gave Daley 72.8 percent of the vote. But citywide only 54.1 percent of registered Chicagoans voted—a disappointment. Nevertheless, Daley won the general election by the greatest margin in his career. The organization could have been forgiven for thinking everything was under control.[2]

Daley and the Regular Democratic Organization looked to 1976 with optimism. For some time, Daley had viewed Governor Dan

Walker as weak and ineffective. When Walker vetoed a bill that would have aided Chicago's public schools, Daley vowed to get rid of him. In October 1975, at a special meeting of the Democratic Party of Cook County's Central Committee, many Democrats, including Lieutenant Governor Neil Hartigan, rose to denounce Walker. Daley successfully pressured Secretary of State Michael Howlett, a West Side Irishman, to challenge Walker in the primary, and in December the Regular Democratic Organization endorsed him. In the spring of 1976 Daley got his revenge: Howlett defeated Walker, though he did eventually lose the general election to James Thompson, who had prosecuted many of Daley's allies.[3]

That year brought other victories for Daley. Chicago voters again elected and certified him as a delegate to the Democratic National Convention. While unchallenged on the convention floor, he did not play a crucial role there. He delivered Chicago for the Democrats, but the numbers were eroding, and Republican President Gerald Ford won the state.[4]

On Monday, December 20, 1976, Mayor Richard J. Daley began his day with a breakfast held in his honor by city department heads in the Medill Room of the Bismarck Hotel. Colonel Jack Reilly, the mayor's director of special events, asked every department head to donate $100 toward the purchase of airline tickets to Ireland for the mayor and Mrs. Daley. After various meetings at City Hall, Daley viewed some ice sculptures in Civic Center Plaza (Daley Center Plaza) and then left for the Southeast Side to dedicate a new park gymnasium, where he proceeded to sink a basket while both Alderman Edward Vrdolyak and Park Commissioner Ed Kelly missed their shots. Earlier in the day, the mayor had experienced chest pains and decided to see his doctor that afternoon. Dr. Coogan recommended that Daley enter Northwestern Memorial Hospital. Daley agreed and Dr. Coogan went to make the arrangements. The mayor called his son Michael to tell him he was being admitted. When the doctor returned, he found Daley on the floor. Specialists from Northwestern's cardiac unit raced to the scene. In all, five doctors and two paramedics tried to save the mayor, but Coogan pronounced the mayor dead at 3:50 p.m.

As the news spread, crowds gathered in the bitter cold, and

police officers had a difficult time containing them. Family members and close personal friends soon appeared. The body was taken to McKeon's Funeral Home in Bridgeport. Meanwhile at City Hall, department heads, aldermen, and other public figures flooded into the mayor's fifth floor office, many in shock that the seemingly invincible Daley was gone.[5]

The next day, a long line of Chicagoans again stood in the bitter cold to pay their last respects. Visitation began at noon at Nativity of Our Lord Church in Bridgeport, where Daley had been baptized, received the sacraments, and attended parochial school. Funeral rites were held the next day at 9:30 a.m. Bells tolled from Catholic churches throughout the city to mark the beginning of the liturgy. Rev. Gilbert Graham, a friend of the late mayor, led the funeral Mass, assisted by John Cardinal Cody and other priests. The mourners included Vice President Nelson Rockefeller, President-elect Jimmy Carter, Senator Ted Kennedy, and Democratic National Committee Chairman Robert Strauss, along with many other dignitaries. An overflow crowd spilled into the streets of Bridgeport. Outgoing Governor Walker proclaimed a state of mourning and urged that flags on all public buildings be lowered to half-mast for thirty days. Friends and foes alike sent their condolences. Chicago had lost the only mayor it had known for a generational span of twenty-one years. An era had passed.[6]

LET THE CHAOS BEGIN!

The mayor's sudden death made it apparent he had no clear successor. Despite the funeral and the holiday, Democratic leaders gathered on Tuesday, December 28, to pick an interim mayor. Not since Anton Cermak's death in 1933 had such a situation occurred. A pecking order in the City Council soon emerged. Michael Bilandic, Edward Vrdolyak, Wilson Frost, and Edward Burke, all sitting aldermen, met with Daley's aides, seemingly contending for the position. The competition for power among Democrats revealed the fissures within the powerful machine. Frost, the African American alderman of the 34th Ward and president pro tempore of the City Council, claimed that he was acting mayor. The group agreed that Frost would preside over legislative matters until the next Tuesday. They also decided that Deputy Mayor Kenneth Sain should oversee the administration of city business. The quartet of aldermen met with party elders, while later most of the Black aldermen met in Frost's office. Alderman Roman Pucinski, whom most people believed would run in the special election, invited nine of the thirteen Polish American aldermen to discuss the issue. Other cliques discussed their next moves. Bilandic emerged as the council's leading choice for interim mayor. He hailed from Daley's 11th Ward, chaired the Finance Committee, and had served as the mayor's floor leader. Older party leaders hoped to assure the continuation of Daley's policies.

As aldermen scrambled, political intrigue also focused on who would replace Daley as chairman of the Cook County Democratic Party. Many Democratic committeemen strategized over next steps even as they paid their respects at Nativity of Our Lord Church, mixing the sacred and the profane. George Dunne, another De La Salle graduate and president of the Cook County Board of Commissioners, who often acted as chairman during Daley's absence, told reporters that the county Democrats would probably pick a new chairman in January. The negotiations would involve those party officials who controlled the most patronage. An alliance between Frost and Vrdolyak could provide an opportunity for the Southeast Side Croatian to secure the party chairmanship. Dunne also made it clear that the Central Committee would pick a candidate for mayor in the special election. He further hinted that he might attempt to replace Daley as both party chairman and mayor.[7]

Aldermen worked out a deal that named Frost as chair of the Finance Committee and Bilandic as interim mayor. Independent Aldermen Martin J. Oberman and Dick Simpson cast the only votes against yet another Bridgeport and De La Salle mayor. Bilandic announced that he planned to return to his private law practice after the special election decided Daley's ultimate replacement. Less than two hours later, Pucinski announced that he planned to run in the special election.

Meanwhile, members of the Polish and Black communities threatened rebellion. Rev. Jesse Jackson demanded Frost explain why he had agreed to put Bilandic in office. The opposition of most of the other aldermen as well as the offer to head the Finance Committee brought Frost into the coalition that gave Bilandic the mayoralty. Renault Robinson, co-founder of the Afro-American Patrolmen's League (African American Police League), Rev. Jackson, and other Black leaders urged supporters to attend a meeting at the Progressive Community Church to discuss running a candidate in the special election. Robinson threw down the gauntlet: "We are going to field a Black candidate for mayor. Unfortunately, Alderman Frost will not be that candidate."[8]

Bilandic promptly adopted a nonpolitical stance and promised to stay out of patronage decisions, leaving that up to the Cook County Democratic chairman—Dunne. Furthermore, he declared he would not get involved in the special election race. On his first day as acting mayor, Bilandic followed his mentor's habit of stopping at St. Peter's Church in the Loop. He then spent a more than ten-hour day meeting with politicians, department heads, friends, bankers, businesspeople, and labor leaders. Bilandic announced that he would meet with more than 100 business leaders on January 4 to assure them of continuity with the Daley administration's programs. The next day, the new mayor met with labor leaders and assured them that he intended to continue the relationship they had with the previous administration. He pledged that the city would continue to pay prevailing wages to trades employees. And then, little more than a week after taking office, Bilandic surprised the city by reneging on his promise not to run in the special election.[9]

This further opened fissures in the reeling party. Steeped in the traditional communal politics of Chicago, Roman Pucinski felt that the Party owed him support as the representative of a large and loyal ethnic group. Pucinski seemed a natural nominee: always a loyal member of the political organization and with well-developed national connections. Party leaders, however, felt little enthusiasm for his candidacy and began to line up behind Bilandic. Pucinski called the process a charade, claiming that Bilandic's candidacy eroded credibility in the slate-making process. The Polish American Political League endorsed Pucinski, as did the Chicago-based Alliance of Central East European Nations. Nevertheless, on January 26, 1977, party

CHAPTER 10

10.1 Mayor Bilandic, St. Patrick's Day Parade, ca. 1977. Like all Chicago mayors, Bilandic, a Croatian American, attended the annual St. Patrick's Day Parade in the Loop. Standing next to him on the right are Richard M. Daley and John Daley. Photo: László Kondor, László Kondor Photograph Collection [MSKond13], MSLASZ13_0004_0012_080, Special Collections & University Archives, University of Illinois Chicago.

slate-makers met in the Bismarck Hotel and selected Michael Bilandic as their candidate. The Bridgeport Democrats hoped to retain control over the party, and they supported Bilandic as a step in that direction. Many saw him holding office only long enough for Richard M. Daley, the late mayor's oldest son, to eventually become mayor.[10]

Despite the snub, Pucinski ran in the April 1977 special election primary against Bilandic, state senator Harold Washington, and several other candidates. This represented the first mayoral challenge from within the organization since Daley's rise to power in 1955. The ethnic and racial divisions in the party that Daley had long held in check now erupted into full view. Polish Americans and African Americans made up a large part of the Democratic base and could, if united, defeat a Bridgeport Democrat. Pucinski ran as a Polish American, as a vocal defender of White ethnic neighborhoods, and as an alternative to Bilandic from within the organization. Pucinski even

10.2 Pucinski mayoral campaign handout. The interior of this handout detailed Pucinski's accomplishments as a congressman and an alderman. Author's Collection.

received some African American support from a group of dissident Republican and Democratic Blacks called "The Bridge Builders."

Bilandic, however, had the Regular Democratic Organization behind him. Despite the Shakman decree, plenty of patronage workers and their families and supporters came out for Bilandic. Some 4,000 precinct workers from seven North Side wards and all those they could drag along cheered Bilandic on at an Aragon Ballroom rally just before the primary. Bilandic was accompanied by the Shannon Rovers. Daley's precinct organizations, despite all the shifts in the party and in society, remained intact.[11]

Yet Bilandic won the primary with a smaller proportion of the votes than at any time since 1955. He garnered 51 percent of the vote to Pucinski's 32 percent, with Washington a distant third. Bilandic took thirty-two wards, while Pucinski won seven and Washington five. Although the Northwest Side provided Pucinski's base, he failed to make inroads in the large Polish and eastern European communities throughout the rest of the city, as South and Southwest Side Polish Americans remained loyal to the Regular Democratic Organization of Cook County. Many also saw a Bilandic administration as simply a continuance of Daley's policies. As a result, Pucinski did not carry any wards south of the Loop. Both Pucinski and Washington faced a lack of unity from within their racial and ethnic bases. As Joseph Zikmund has pointed out, if Blacks, lakefront reformers, and many White ethnic voters, particularly Polish Americans, had united behind a consensus candidate, the Regular Democratic Organization would have been in real trouble. But they didn't, so to casual observers the outcome suggested that the Democratic machine still worked just fine.[12]

THE DEMOCRATIC CIVIL WAR BEGINS: BILANDIC, BYRNE, DALEY, AND WASHINGTON

Michael Anthony Bilandic was a quiet bachelor who, at the age of fifty-three, still lived with his mother in Bridgeport. In 1969 Daley had convinced him to run for the 11th Ward aldermanic position. An honest and untested politician, he rose in a City Council tainted by corruption and became chair of the Finance Committee as well as Daley's floor leader. As acting mayor, he seemed like a perfect caretaker. Yet Bilandic inherited a city wracked by racial strife, White flight, an economy that seemed to be in a downward spiral, and a decline in machine power.

There was always another election on the horizon. Bilandic soon began preparing for reelection in 1979. Jane Byrne announced her candidacy for mayor on April 23, 1978. Byrne had been a regular party member and a Daley favorite. He had named her co-chair of the Cook County Democratic Central Committee, but Democrats had ousted her from that role shortly after Daley's death. She was also head of the Consumer Affairs Department, but Bilandic fired her after she accused him of making a back-room deal to increase taxi fares. The Daley family, especially Daley's widow, Sis, never liked her. Initially, few people took Byrne's candidacy seriously. Simply put, she did not appear to be a formidable challenger.[13]

Bilandic, on the other hand, as the machine candidate, seemed an easy winner. But as 1978 gave way to 1979, nature threw Bilandic's campaign a curveball. Over two days in mid-January 1979, a blizzard dumped more than twenty inches of snow on top of a seven-to-ten-inch base from a New Year's Eve blizzard, setting a record for snow cover in Chicago. Temperatures plummeted to fifteen degrees below zero, making snow removal difficult. Many thoroughfares became impassable. Expressways closed, and public transportation could scarcely function. The mayor requested that businesses stagger work hours to ease pressure. He claimed that the city would be up and running in two days.

The storm made it seem that the machine could not deliver services well anymore, even to its main constituents. Some residents accused aldermen and committeemen of having their streets plowed while neglecting others.[14] The *Chicago Tribune* reported that both Bilandic's Bridgeport residential street and the street on which Daley's family lived had been thoroughly plowed![15] Then a new storm dumped another two inches of snow on the city. Public and parochial schools closed. At least seventeen deaths were blamed on the weather. City Hall seemed confused by the entire situation. Residents became more and more angry at what looked like the city's inability to deal with the catastrophe.[16]

The administration's handling of the storm gave political ammunition to its opponents, including Jane Byrne. Independent aldermen called for an investigation but were voted down. Newspapers soon reported a scandal involving Kenneth Sain, a former deputy mayor under both Daley and Bilandic. Sain, whose firm had won a contract with the city to devise an improved snow removal plan, admitted that the city chose his firm over others that were more qualified because of his long-standing association with both Daley and Bilandic. Sain's family had a longtime relationship with the Democratic Party, despite the fact he did not attend De La Salle. As deputy mayor, Sain had acted as the first line of defense for both Daley and Bilandic, and they rewarded him well. The Sain scandal shone another light on the use of clout in city politics. While Bilandic claimed he knew nothing about it, Streets and Sanitation Commissioner Francis Degnan said the mayor had directed him to give the contract to Sain. State's Attorney Bernard Carey launched an investigation. Jane Byrne insisted that the city stop payments to Sain's firm. She also demanded that Bilandic resign.[17]

The storm paralyzed the city and Bilandic seemed lost in the snow. While Chicagoans could not get to work or school, the mayor's public statements seemed to be out of touch with reality. City garbage trucks, which had been diverted to plow the streets, left tons of garbage in alleys across the city. The overwhelming snow accumulation stressed Chicago's many flat roof structures. By January 18, roughly 220 roofs had collapsed across the city, with fears of more to come.

The aldermanic elections and the mayoral primary were only four weeks away, and the danger to incumbents seemed clear. A *Chicago Tribune* pundit, Bob Wiedrich, pointed out that both Byrne and the Republican candidate, Wallace Johnson, might garner more support than expected given the snow-driven chaos. But close associates of the mayor predicted he would win by a margin of two to one. Most other analysts agreed Bilandic would beat Byrne handily.

Vernon Jarrett took a different angle in his *Chicago Tribune* column, arguing that Bilandic and the machine were continuing to take African Americans for granted. During the snow emergency, the CTA had closed nearly all the train stations on the South Side Dan Ryan line (now the Red Line) and on the Black West Side. A precinct captain said Bilandic and his cohort knew who to take care of first: the White people on the city's outskirts and suburbs who rode trains into the Loop. Alderman Tyrone Kenner accused the administration of racial prejudice, and Black Chicagoans fumed. While Jarrett worried that African Americans would forget being slighted by the time of the primary election, the Black vote would prove crucial as usual then.[18]

As election day arrived, the stakes could not have been higher. That day, Byrne visited US Steel's South Works on the Southeast Side to rally voters. She attended Mass before voting herself and then continued campaigning. Close aldermanic elections came under the scrutiny of State's Attorney Carey and the FBI, who feared cheating and even violence on February 27. Carey received over 2,000 complaints of election irregularities. The State Board of Elections reported a complaint from the 1st Ward that political operatives had threatened senior citizens with eviction from public housing if they did not vote for Bilandic. Don Rose, Byrne's campaign chief, heard of some supporters getting beat up in Uptown. He responded, "Get some thugs up there." Director of Volunteers Bob Lincoln said, "I got a great guy. This guy got out of dope and into politics. He wasted a guy once who raped his sister." Rose told him to get up to the 46th Ward. Chicago's reputation for political violence and corruption received yet more corroboration.[19]

Byrne edged out Bilandic in the primary. A woman had beaten the Democratic machine. Male politicians and commentators made nasty remarks, including that Byrne would be better off in the kitchen cooking breakfast for her new husband, Jay McMullen, than in the mayor's office. Did Byrne's victory mean that the city's politics had been reset? Byrne had broken her longtime bond with the regular organization, and she attributed her victory in part to liberal independent Democrats such as Martin Oberman, Bill Singer, and Dick Simpson as she captured the lakefront vote. When she defeated Republican Wallace Johnson in the general election with the largest majority in mayoral election history, 82 percent of the vote, independent Democrats and reformers rejoiced in her victory.

Byrne appointed Northwestern University Professor Louis Masotti to assemble a blue-ribbon panel to author a blueprint for reform. But she then treated Masotti with benign neglect. She did not return his phone calls and the report went unread. Instead, she looked to those she knew all too well. Byrne turned to the Regular

Democratic Organization and embraced those she had so recently condemned as an evil cabal, especially the two Eddies, Vrdolyak and Burke, as well as Fred Roti, the alderman of the notorious downtown 1st Ward. Byrne returned home to the only political house she knew, the Cook County Regular Democratic Organization.[20]

In February 1979, lakefront liberals, African Americans, and disgruntled White ethnic voters had brought about what no one thought possible: the defeat of the incumbent, machine-endorsed candidate for mayor in the Democratic primary. Then, the Chicago political universe returned to form. Byrne quickly shut out the reformers and turned toward the Regular Democrats, who still controlled the City Council. The liberal or reform faction hardly had the numbers Byrne needed to push through her agenda. She faced a city with myriad problems: White middle-class flight, deindustrialization, a growing Latino population that needed to be brought into the power structure, disgruntled Polish American and Black voters, and a growing public union sector. Facing these daunting issues, Byrne turned to those she knew and who, while she did not fully trust them, might see their prospects as aligned with hers. An early example of this pragmatic shifting of allegiances occurred in response to a lobbying effort by representatives of Richard M. Daley to push Byrne to slate Daley loyalists to key chairmanships in the City Council. This maneuvering angered her, and she turned to machine politicians Vrdolyak and Burke to appoint council committees and chairmen.[21]

Byrne administration soon found herself embroiled in various conflicts with labor that threw her administration's approach into sharp relief against Daley's more conciliatory stance. During the Daley years, the relationship between organized labor and the administration had been rooted in a tradition of communal rapport. Many Chicago labor leaders grew up in the working-class neighborhoods that Daley knew. Most were Irish and Roman Catholic. They understood each other and they understood Daley. The head of the Chicago Federation of Labor (CFL), William A. Lee, who became the organization's president in 1946, grew up in an Irish neighborhood on the West Side, graduated from St. Ignatius High School, and understood the Irish Catholic ethic based on mutual exchange and bargaining. Lee became close with Daley and aided him during a number of labor disputes. For example, Lee helped avoid a crippling transit strike in 1974, and intervened in a musician's dispute with the Chicago Symphony Orchestra as well as one with firefighters in the 1970s. Although Daley opposed unions for city workers, he gave them union-level benefits and wages. In turn, Lee and the CFL did not push the question of unionization among municipal workers. The bargain between Daley and organized labor had worked for more than twenty years, and the communal relationship remained unbroken.[22]

This détente endured with one exception late in the Daley administration. The Chicago Teachers Union (CTU) emerged as a potential disrupter of the arrangement, at a time when public union discontent mushroomed. As early as 1966, CTU flexed its muscles, demanding bargaining rights. This, coupled with racial strife in the schools, gave CTU bargaining leverage when it threatened to strike. Daley gave in to the union's demands and counted on the conservative leadership of the CTU to go along with the status quo. Nonetheless, this step toward recognizing a public union opened a door for other city workers.[23]

When Byrne became mayor, she broke with Lee and refused to renominate him for the seat on the Chicago Park District Board he had held for eleven years. Eventually, as labor problems exploded, she reconsidered; in 1982 Lee returned to his seat and also as an advisor to the mayor.[24] During her campaign, Byrne, like Roman Pucinski, had promised that the city would recognize public unions and give them bargaining rights. However, she reneged on the pledge, fearing public unions would be too powerful. Strikes followed in quick succession: a transit strike in 1979 and both a teachers' and a firefighters' strike in 1980. These threatened the traditional Cook County Democratic Party alliance with organized labor. They certainly shook the public's faith in the Byrne administration.

Another conflict soon riled racial relations in the city. In 1979 Byrne won praise for appointing a majority Black and minority school board, but in 1980, in a nod to the White aldermen and their White ethnic constituency, she replaced two Black board members with two White members who opposed the busing of schoolchildren. In addition, she appointed White members to the board of the Chicago Housing Authority (CHA), even though residents of CHA housing were overwhelmingly Black. The African American community felt betrayed once again. Don Rose, Byrne's former campaign manager, pointedly captured the cost: "It's absolutely amazing how she managed in such a short time to antagonize both the Blacks and Whites." He added, "there's just no way around the fact that the first two years have been a political disaster." Accordingly, the public came to see Byrne as vindictive, mean-spirited, and small-minded. The still largely misogynist media began to refer to her as "Calamity Jane" and "Attila the Hen." Some called her a "gutsy blond," others called her harsh and too emotional. Sexism followed Byrne, and the public increasingly reacted against her. Martin Oberman, one of the independent aldermen who had supported Byrne in 1979, said that he expected Daley to run and that he would find it hard to support Byrne.[25]

Byrne knew that many people saw Rich Daley as the rightful inheritor of his father's mantle. Bridgeport bristled under Byrne's rule as she maneuvered to oust longtime Daley allies from positions of power and destroy the Daley base. She could not have been more different from those streetwise politicians who worked their way up from precinct captain to committeeman or alderman, and who were steeped in the traditions of communal politics. Byrne grew up the daughter of a steel company vice president in the manicured, middle-class neighborhood of Sauganash on the far Northwest Side. She never worked as a precinct captain, never previously ran for office, and definitely never belonged to the working class. Sis Daley, the family matron, united the family against Byrne.[26]

The fault line between the Daley family and the Byrne administration was deep. Members of her administration started referring to Daley Plaza by its old name, the Civic Center Plaza, as if that could erase the Daley dominance in Chicago. As early as December 1981, a low-key operation to draft Rich Daley for mayor surfaced. All over town, window cards with Daley's photo announced, "Chicago Loves

You." Daley claimed he knew nothing about them. Other factions emerged as well.

Alderman Danny Davis of the 29th Ward urged Congressman Harold Washington to throw his hat in the ring for mayor. In October 1982, a *Chicago Sun-Times* poll found Daley leading both Byrne and Washington. The poll, however, did suggest that Washington would take more votes away from Daley than from Byrne. In reality, the mayor faced strong resistance from Black Chicagoans, as many felt disrespected by her actions and looked to Washington as a savior. On November 4, Richard M. Daley formally announced his candidacy, and Washington followed on November 10.[27] Black voter registration increased dramatically, and many Black committeemen and alderman threw their support to Washington. Significantly, when Washington declared his candidacy in front of a racially diverse gathering in Hyde Park, he offered a blistering assessment of the city: "Chicago is a city divided. Chicago is a city where citizens are treated unequally and unfairly. Chicago is a city in decline."[28]

A three-way race widened the cracks in the Democratic coalition, and especially within the machine. A letter, widely circulated in White neighborhoods, from former Republican Governor Richard Ogilvie, who had endorsed Byrne in January, argued that the race was really between Byrne and Washington, not Daley. The Democratic machine then circulated Ogilvie's letter as well as other thinly veiled political mailers on the Northwest and Southwest Sides, aiming to raise racial anxieties among Whites. Alderman Vrdolyak, a Byrne supporter, City Council leader, and chairman of the Democratic Central Committee of Cook County, warned precinct workers on the Northwest Side, "It's a racial thing. Don't kid yourself. I'm calling on you to save your city, to save your precinct. We're fighting to keep the city the way it is."[29]

In the February 22, 1983, primary, Daley and Byrne split the White vote while a coalition of Blacks, Latinos, and lakefront independent voters overwhelmingly supported Washington. The African American challenger won with 37 percent of the vote, versus 33 percent for Byrne and 30 percent for Daley. For the second straight primary, the choice of the Cook County Regular Democratic Party had gone down in defeat. The well-oiled political machine, built over decades, had stalled. The Democratic civil war became even more real.

Almost immediately, the party divided along racial lines. The old bonds of party loyalty faded away as race divisions drove a wedge through the city. Rumors spread like wildfire. Although Washington promised to reform patronage, the rumor mill promoted the idea that he would kick all Whites out of city government. Another rumor claimed that public housing would be erected across the mostly White Bungalow Belt of the Southwest, Southeast, and Northwest Sides. Predictions of a massive White flight that would turn the entire city into a Black ghetto fueled the flames of hatred.

The Republicans nominated Bernie Epton, a lakefront liberal Republican and former state representative whom few figured to have much of a chance in the heavily Democratic city. Of course, few had planned for a Washington primary victory. Despite his history as a liberal Republican, Epton appealed to voters who viewed Washington's nomination as a crisis, including many White Democrats. Pucinski, who knew that his constituents favored Epton over Washington, hesitated to make an endorsement. The slogan "Epton for Mayor, Before It's Too Late" and the distribution of bigoted literature throughout White neighborhoods shattered any illusions that race did not matter.

By early March, it seemed apparent that the party organization would not give its support to Washington. Many White committeemen decided to either sit out the election or endorse Epton. The Democratic Party seemed on the verge of disintegration. Byrne decided to run a write-in campaign but just as suddenly backed down. As Epton's momentum picked up, many Democratic committeemen decided to support him, including Pucinski. He and the others claimed that they were reflecting the wishes of their constituency. In the end, no more than six White committeemen supported Washington, while eight openly opposed him. Democratic precinct workers on the Southwest and Northwest Sides worked for Epton. Vrdolyak had been right—it was a "racial thing."[30]

Harold Washington won the polarized election on April 12, 1983, by a razor-thin margin and became Chicago's forty-second mayor on April 29. At an informal meeting the Friday after Washington's victory, Alderman Ed Vrdolyak, the chairman of the Cook County Democratic Party, broke with him. He took to the council floor and proclaimed that a war would continue between the Washington forces and the Regular Democrats—or at least the White ones. Sixteen Black aldermen supported Washington despite their past allegiances to the regular organization. Washington became enmeshed in a long struggle with the recalcitrant City Council, dominated by twenty-nine White aldermen, including Pucinski, Vrdolyak, and 14th Ward Alderman Ed Burke. The "Council Wars" resulted in near chaos, legislative deadlock, and continued racial infighting. Fundamentally, they revealed the deep frustrations of the weakened Regular Democratic machine.[31]

Privately, Washington had friendly relations with several of the aldermen in the opposition, but that did not break their solid stand against him in the City Council. When Pucinski's wife, Aurelia, died shortly after the election, Washington made a surprise visit to the chapel on April 18. Pucinski, obviously pleased, introduced him to everyone and took him into the adjoining parlor to visit another wake and introduced Washington to the family. Stunned expressions soon turned into smiles. Washington and Pucinski both supported the Polish Solidarity movement, and so someone pinned a Solidarity Labor Union button on the mayor's lapel. Along with columnist Mike Royko, they attended the Pulaski Day celebration at the White Eagle restaurant in suburban Niles in support of the Polish labor union. Yet Pucinski remained a staunch member of the "Vrdolyak 29."[32]

In 1986, the courts ordered the redistricting of seven Chicago wards, and a remap election on March 18 gave Washington three more votes in the City Council. Then, in the heavily Latino 26th Ward, Washington's candidate, Luis Gutiérrez, beat a Vrdolyak-backed nominee, Manuel Torres. With a now evenly divided City Council, Washington could break ties and move his agenda. In 1987, he won a second term, drawing close to 54 percent of the vote over both Vrdolyak, who ran on the Illinois Solidarity Party ticket, and Republican Donald Haider.[33]

CHAPTER 10

10.3 Harold Washington campaigning in 1987. Always the active campaigner, Washington grew up in the Democratic machine. He won his second term in 1987 but unfortunately died that November. Courtesy of Mark Dobrzycki, photographer.

Washington, who had increased his control over the City Council by picking up several additional seats, moved to reshape the leadership. Pucinski supported that move and retained his control over the Intergovernmental Relations Committee. Vrdolyak, recognizing he had been outmaneuvered, decided to finally give up the chairmanship of the Democratic Party and officially become a Republican. In November, Mayor Washington supported Aurelia Pucinski over Jane Byrne as the Democratic nominee for clerk of the Cook County Circuit Court, despite her father's consistent opposition to him. He also supported Rich Daley for state's attorney, hoping to widen his coalition. A few days later, on Wednesday, November 25, 1987, Harold Washington suffered a massive heart attack and died.[34]

Harold Washington's death came just as it seemed he had successfully put together a working coalition that could pass his agenda, focused largely on long-neglected neighborhoods and on righting many wrongs of the past. Many of his supporters had expected to reap the fruits of his victory. Washington's sudden demise left many in the Black and Brown communities stunned and pained. On Friday, November 27, 1987, Chicagoans gathered at Daley Plaza under a gray sky for an ecumenical prayer service. Blacks, Whites, Hispanics, old people, and young people gathered to pay their last respects. More than 4,000 people an hour walked by Washington's bronze-colored coffin in City Hall to say goodbye. The line stretched for blocks. After the funeral service on Monday at Christ Universal Temple at 11901 S. Ashland Avenue, the hearse carried Washington's body through several neighborhoods to its final resting place in Oak Woods Cemetery on the South Side.[35]

The second sudden death of a mayor in a little more than ten years shocked the city and the body politic. Chaos reigned once more. Whatever peace had been negotiated by Washington disappeared. David Orr, a 49th Ward alderman who also served as vice mayor, acted as mayor until the City Council could settle on a replacement for Washington.

Washington's coalition quickly assembled, including Alderman Jesús "Chuy" Garcia, who represented the Latino community, and lakefront liberal aldermen Orr and Larry Bloom. They hoped to keep the alliance together, but divisions among them had already emerged. Alderman Timothy Evans, who served as Washington's floor leader and chaired the powerful Finance Committee, sought to fill Washington's term. Several of Washington's top aides, reform aldermen, and some Black politicians supported Evans. But several

CHAPTER 10

Black aldermen had bristled under the Washington administration's tight grip over them, controlling their votes in the City Council and threatening to run candidates against them in primaries if they did not cooperate. These aldermen did not want Evans in control. The Black coalition began to unravel.

Opposition aldermen, mostly White, were hardly united either. Richard Mell, alderman of the North Side's 33rd Ward, tried to create an alliance with Latino aldermen to gain the office of mayor for himself. Other names that surfaced included Ed Burke and Terry Gabinski, a hard-liner opposed to the Washington platform. Most White aldermen soon recognized that the new mayor would have to be chosen from among their Black colleagues. Eugene Sawyer, 6th Ward alderman and the longest-serving Black alderman, emerged as a likely candidate. Sawyer, who had come up as part of the Regular Democratic Organization, appealed to them but seemed reluctant.[36]

On the evening of December 1, about 4,000 people gathered outside City Hall to protest the possible election of Sawyer as acting mayor. Some 900 protestors also gathered inside, chanting and shouting epithets at the City Council. Among them were champions of Tim Evans, who had been encouraged to come downtown. Roughly 100 protestors filled the council balcony as the meeting dragged into the morning. In the end, the aldermen voted 29 to 19 for Sawyer. Twenty-three White aldermen and six Black aldermen voted for him.[37]

The decade between the death of Richard J. Daley in 1976 and the death of Harold Washington in 1987 brought tumult to city politics and fragmentation to the Regular Democratic Organization. While reformers and regulars had long battled, the one-term Byrne administration offered a glimpse into the perils of switching sides. First running as a reformer and winning, then running as a machine candidate and losing, Byrne opened the door to a political space that looked very different from the communal politics of the mostly working-class, mostly immigrant, mostly Catholic Democratic machine. And as the Black "sub-machine" confronted the overt racism of machine politics, it pursued a more independent agenda. These political developments, churned by changing cultural winds, called into question the future of the Regular Democratic political machine.

THE CHURCH DISPIRITED

While the Democratic machine seemed to be spinning out of control, one of its main pillars also shifted under the shocks of the 1960s and 1970s. Both Catholicism and Judaism came under tremendous stress in the decades after the election of John F. Kennedy. The traditions that fostered communalism slowly disappeared as both Jewish and Catholic ethnics ventured beyond the old ethnic ghetto walls, joined the middle and upper middle classes, went to universities, and left the old neighborhoods. For Catholicism in particular, the transformation upended the grip of the hierarchy and lessened the Church's authority.

Both Jewish and Catholic groups climbed the ladder of upward mobility. The old West Side neighborhoods saw huge demographic shifts, as religious institutions followed their congregations elsewhere. In Jewish North Lawndale and Irish Austin, more recently arrived and poorer African Americans replaced them. Jewish congregations moved across the city and eventually into the suburbs, but Catholic parishes stayed. Yet inner-city working-class districts, such as the neighborhoods surrounding the stockyards that had once contained over thirty Catholic parishes, soon had fewer Catholics. This would eventually lead to the mass closing of parishes in the 1990s and beyond. While many factors account for this change, the dismantling of ethnic barriers in many walks of life loosened parishioners' ties to their institutions. Both Jewish and Catholic communalism declined dramatically as a result of intermarriage, assimilation, and secularization. No longer peasants or workers, these groups' political focus shifted as well. For Catholics, who still ruled the city into the beginning of the twenty-first century, this proved especially devastating.

Chicago Catholics made up a more than significant portion of the support for the Democratic machine. In the 1950s, the Catholic Church seemed triumphant in the city. Its school system, charitable organizations, and hundreds of parishes defined the lives of Catholics and non-Catholics alike. The Chicago Public Schools allowed Catholic students to leave class and take catechism lessons once a week at the local parish.[38]

The election of Cardinal Angelo Giuseppe Roncalli as Pope John XXIII in 1958 opened a new era of change and disruption in the Church. Pope John called the Second Vatican Council, often referred to as the Ecumenical Council, to reform the Church. And indeed, the council unleashed many reforms, starting (shockingly) with changing the liturgy.[39] The liturgical modifications jolted the average lay Catholic. But many members of the clergy supported the wider use of the vernacular and experimentation with the very form of the Mass. In 1963, the Vatican Council allowed the use of the vernacular in the sacraments, including baptism, confirmation, confession, and extreme unction (last rites). All but 100 of the approximately 2,200 bishops voting approved these changes. Soon the vernacular took over the Church.[40]

Catholics had long regarded their Church as standing outside of time. The shock of liturgical change showed that it did not. Traditionally, most Catholics viewed their Church as perfect, and therefore in no need of change. They believed the Mass was timeless and that priests celebrated it unchanged throughout the centuries. Catholic priests had long asserted that the Church of Rome perfectly reflected the original Christian community, while Protestants had erred in breaking with the model. The Vatican Council challenged that worldview.[41]

As Andrew Greeley and others have pointed out, American Catholics soon embraced the changes in the liturgy. On May 25, 1964, Protestant and Roman Catholic parishes, as well as other groups including the Catholic Adult Education Center of the Archdiocese of Chicago, sponsored a "demonstration" vernacular Mass in Rockefeller Chapel on the campus of the University of Chicago. Later in the summer, Rev. Frederick R. McManus, a professor of canon law, celebrated the first official English-language Mass in the United States in St. Louis. In October, the Joliet diocese began training laymen for active participation in the new Mass. Old St. Mary's Church, the first

Catholic parish established in the city, held its final Tridentine Latin Mass on February 28, 1965. More than 1,200 people jammed inside the 900-seat church to experience the ending of an era. Hundreds more worshippers stood outside, some attending a hastily arranged special Mass in the basement, others heading over to St. Mary's chapel at Wabash and Van Buren for a final Latin Mass.[42]

On Sunday, March 7, 1965, Catholics across the Chicago archdiocese and the world finally witnessed the new liturgy. Parishioners in many of the 450 Catholic parishes of Cook and Lake Counties saw a freestanding altar. Chicago priests referred to the reformed liturgy as the Rite of March 7, with a new emphasis not only on the Eucharist, but on scripture. Chicago's Cardinal Albert Gregory Meyer directed his priests to face the congregation and not turn their backs to them, as they had for so long. This profound liturgical transformation implied the inevitability of further modifications in Catholic practices.[43]

The Second Vatican Council had also called for the reform of religious sisterhoods and brotherhoods. While this call appeared moderate and constructive in Rome, it took on a life of its own in North America. The bishops suggested that nuns' habits should be simple, pleasant, modest, and appropriate. They explained that the habits should be "suited to the circumstances of time and place as well as to the services required by those who wear them."[44] These sisterhoods, especially in the United States, had lived under a cloister mentality since the 1920s. Both the American bishops and the Vatican had traditionally warned the orders to restrict their contact with the outside world. Now, the Church called upon nuns to reexamine their founders' visions and to commit to closely following them. This opened the possibility that some would reconsider teaching in parochial schools. This prospect panicked many American bishops, who feared that Catholic schools would lose their free workforce. Suddenly nuns took on a more public role in society.[45]

In October 1964, the Ecumenical Council put forth six proposals to bring religious orders into the twentieth century. These included encouraging monks and nuns to replace their religious habits with more modern dress. It also included reforms to get monks and nuns out of monasteries and cloisters and into the streets, where prelates felt they could accomplish more good in the community. They also said that nuns no longer had to live in convents.[46]

Once they were out in the streets, there was no turning back the clock, as Chicago's nuns took up the cause of social justice in the world at large. As early as the summer of 1963, seven Franciscan nuns had picketed the Illinois Club for Catholic Women because of racial restrictions on its facilities and membership. The nuns carried signs questioning the club's Catholicism. Despite the nuns' protests, the Illinois Club for Catholic Women refused to change its policy.[47]

Chicago priests and nuns took part in civil rights demonstrations during the 1960s. When some participated in the Selma protests, the Rev. Robert M. Kearns, assistant archdiocesan director of urban affairs, defended them. Kearns suggested that the Constitution of the Church adopted by the Ecumenical Council provided ample justification for the public activism of priests and nuns. At the same time, he acknowledged that many, including the bishops in Rome, did not fully understand what involvement in the world entailed.

It was one thing to see members of religious orders marching in the South, but quite another to see them involved in Chicago protests. In June 1965, Chicago police arrested nearly 200 demonstrators during a mass protest in the Loop opposing Chicago Public Schools Superintendent Benjamin Willis. Six sisters of the Daughters of Charity of St. Vincent DePaul, dressed in their habits, marched at the front of the protest along with the Rev. John H. Porter, pastor of Christ Methodist Church; all were arrested. A number of priests and ministers also took part in the sit-down demonstration at the corner of State and Madison. Not only did Catholic religious order members demonstrate against Mayor Daley's choice of superintendent; they did it in union with Protestants! The courts found the nuns guilty of obstructing traffic, and Judge Lester Jankowski fined them twenty-five dollars each. When the sisters pleaded that their vow of poverty precluded them paying, they were jailed. Two African American attorneys, Maurice Scott Jr. and Howard D. Getter, contributed money to obtain their release. Rev. Thomas Heaney and Rev. John J. Hill, Catholic priests, received fines of $125 for their conduct June 12 during another civil rights demonstration in Grant Park.[48] Members of Catholic religious orders also took part in protests against the Vietnam War and soon stood at the forefront of a broad progressive movement.[49]

Members of both men's and women's religious orders continued to challenge the old order. In 1966, a Roman Catholic nun from Michigan urged the Church to approve birth control, aligning with the feminist movement. Sister Mary A. Schaldenbrand, a professor at Nazareth College in Kalamazoo, declared, "any contraceptive device that respects the dignity of woman should be approved." Increasingly, nuns and priests left their orders in reaction against traditional restrictions on their personal autonomy. A Milwaukee priest and a former nun from Chicago chose to marry in a Lutheran ceremony. The priest understood that his marriage would result in his excommunication, and he expressed regret that he could not marry in the Catholic Church. In September 1968, nuns wearing short skirts protested the Vietnam War along with socialists and others on Michigan Avenue. One nun wearing a white wool sweater carried a sign that read "Pax Vobiscum" (Peace be with you). Women religious left their orders in record numbers.

The once unquestioned tradition of Catholic education in the United States came under attack. Nuns and brothers left classrooms and headed out into the world. Lay instructors in schools such as De La Salle taught more and more students. The American Catholic Church began to abandon unofficial "commandments" such as that Catholic children must attend Catholic schools. While those schools remained a viable alternative to what many saw as a failing public school system wracked by racial strife, Catholic parents increasingly sought out the suburbs and their public schools. Catholic schools soon presented more of a financial burden to parishes and parents.[50]

These developments naturally also had political effects. Andrew Greeley, the noted Catholic priest and University of Chicago professor, pointed out that political and religious commitment had seemed to go hand in hand in American parishes, strengthening and reinforcing each other. The inverse was now true: Catholic loyalty to the teachings of both the Church and the Democratic Party waned precipitously. Over the coming decades, the diminished role of communal loyalty and connectedness would indeed transform Chicago's political system. The Catholics and Jews whose urban worldviews had defined the base of the Democratic machine were gone. Individualism was triumphing over communalism.[51]

11

Not Your Father's Machine

> I think the Daleys are like the Kennedys. Don't you?
> ADELINE PIETRASZEK[1]

On December 6, 1988, Richard M. Daley announced his candidacy for the mayoralty of Chicago. He had planned the announcement for some time, but had not discussed it with his wife, Maggie. When she found out, she warned Daley and his advisors to avoid race-baiting. They agreed. Daley's campaign began with a media blitz emphasizing his non-confrontational approach. The Bridgeport native and De La Salle graduate called for an end to racial politics. He promoted himself simultaneously as a new, progressive Daley and as his father's heir. A photograph, taken by his friend Victor Skrebneski, the famous Chicago fashion photographer, portrayed him as a young and vital leader. It presented a new Daley, more open to the world beyond the city's boundaries, young, well-educated, if not particularly articulate.

Daley still hailed from Bridgeport, but he became—largely because of Maggie—more worldly. She would be an important part of his public image. His mother, Sis Daley, had presented a model of domesticity and of neighborhood loyalty. She kept the home fires burning for her husband and then their children. Maggie would be a symbol of a new Daley generation.[2]

The campaign began with a visit to Manny's Delicatessen on the

Near West Side. Rich and Maggie Daley feasted on corned beef sandwiches with "real people" as four camera crews and thirty journalists crowded the establishment. Daley then made eight campaign stops across the city, including one at a Hispanic senior center, Casa Central, in Humboldt Park. There Daley told the friendly crowd, "the race issue should go away." *Chicago Sun-Times* columnist Irv Kupcinet reported that Luis Gutiérrez, an early supporter of Harold Washington, had thrown his support behind Daley, hoping to swing Hispanic voters. At the same time, Vernon Jarrett also reported in the *Sun-Times* that the machine expected independents and Black voters to divide their support between Acting Mayor Sawyer and Tim Evans.[3]

Daley attempted to put a new coalition together that included at least some Blacks and lakefront liberals. In an attempt to prove that his campaign included more than just a bunch of "Bridgeport Irish guys" trying to reclaim power, Daley named as his press secretary Avis LaVelle, a young, Black City Hall reporter from Hyde Park. LaVelle's appointment demonstrated that Daley welcomed active participation from African Americans and women—indeed, from all Chicagoans. He hoped her appointment would send a message of racial harmony, something that many in Chicago wanted to hear. Various White candidates began to withdraw from the race, including Ed Kelly, the general superintendent of the Chicago Park District and 47th Ward Democratic committeeman, as well as Ed Burke, 14th Ward alderman and ward committeeman.

Ideologically, Daley's advisors, including the progressive David Axelrod, supported a liberal agenda. In his campaign announcement, Daley expressed his support for the gay rights ordinance under discussion in the City Council. Daley's campaign seemed to bring together various factions of the Washington coalition including Hispanics, lakefront liberals, White ethnics, and some African Americans. During a visit to a Black congregation in Englewood, at the Mount Sinai Missionary Baptist Church, Daley said that name-calling had to be replaced with sensible talk: "It is time we stop fighting each other and start working together." Daley invoked the memory of Harold Washington as a man who knew how to serve all the people, and he promised to do the same. He understood that the Washington legacy would haunt any Daley administration.[4]

While Daley attempted to identify with at least a part of Washington's program, Sawyer got the endorsement of the late mayor's brothers. Tim Evans's campaign seemed to sputter as he failed to distance himself from 3rd Ward African American Alderman Dorothy Tillman, who had called Sawyer an "Uncle Tom." Evans seemed upstaged by his prominent supporters: Tillman, Jackie Grimshaw, Alderman Helen Schiller (46th Ward), and Schiller's ally Slim Coleman. In mid-December, Alderman Danny Davis ended his campaign and called for Black unity. By the end of the month, Evans dropped out to run in the general election as an independent under the banner of the newly formed Harold Washington Party, thus giving Sawyer a clear shot at Daley for the Democratic nomination.[5]

RESTORATION?

The contest moved into high gear. Maggie Daley campaigned along with her spouse, and his mother also made appearances. Both gave the candidate advice. On February 1, 1989, the family dedicated the Richard J. Daley Library in Bridgeport. Mayor Sawyer attended the ceremony, and the Daley clan and their Bridgeport neighbors greeted him with a standing ovation. Sawyer told the crowd, "some people thought I wasn't coming, but I surprised you." The mayor and Sis Daley cut the ribbon together.

Already voter registration numbers did not look good for Sawyer, who would need a large turnout to win. Even more ominously, the highest in-precinct registrations were in House Speaker Michael Madigan's 13th Ward and Daley's own 11th Ward. Observers expected both wards to overwhelmingly support Daley. On February 7, the only scheduled debate between Sawyer, Daley, and long-shot candidate and 5th Ward Alderman Lawrence Bloom yielded no clear winner. After the debate, Chicago Bears coach Mike Ditka endorsed Daley and presented him and Maggie with team jerseys emblazoned with the number eighty-nine.[6]

In the days leading up to the primary, Bloom dropped out, while

CHAPTER 11

Sawyer and Daley again took their appeal to Black churches. Daley brought his campaign into the heart of his opposition by speaking before Rev. Jesse Jackson's congregation at the Fellowship Missionary Baptist Church. He cloaked his candidacy in the legacy of both late mayors, Washington and Daley. At Greater Progressive Baptist Church, he again cited the Washington legacy.[7]

On February 28, 1989, Richard M. Daley won the Democratic primary for mayor. Voter turnout, however, proved disappointing. Only the 11th Ward showed signs of the traditional Chicago political spirit, as precinct workers passed out literature outside polling places. On the other hand, Black wards showed little enthusiasm. The Washington coalition disappeared in the fighting between the Sawyer and Evans factions. Hispanic wards, except for Gutiérrez's 26th Ward, also saw little action. In the end, Sawyer won only African American wards.

Tim Evans had withheld support for Sawyer in the primary, angering many Black voters. He now looked to take on Daley in the general election as an independent. As payback to Evans, Sawyer now remained neutral. Meanwhile, Eddie Vrdolyak had won as a write-in candidate in the Republican primary. The stage was set for another three-way showdown.[8] When the voting ended, Daley defeated Evans and Vrdolyak to become the forty-fifth mayor of Chicago. Vrdolyak had almost no organization outside of his home ward and no real political or fundraising plan. Evans, like Sawyer, suffered from a low turnout in the Black wards. Daley won 1,671 of the city's 2,911 precincts, Evans carried 1,237, and Vrdolyak only 2.

The restoration of a Bridgeport-anchored Democratic machine had been accomplished, but Chicago and the world had changed significantly since Daley's father's death and the subsequent defeat of Michael Bilandic. Newspapers made the obligatory comparison between Daley the father and Daley the son, while acknowledging that the Shakman decrees had destroyed much of the patronage infrastructure that once powered the machine. Reporters also pointed out that the first Daley benefited from federal largesse that no longer seemed to exist, after a string of Republican presidents and congresses.[9]

The new Daley era opened on April 24, with a ninety-minute swearing-in ceremony at Orchestra Hall. The stage featured a backdrop of banners showcasing all of Chicago's community areas. Over 2,300 Daley supporters cheered on the new mayor and his family. Chicago politicians and notables crowded the stage, including Governor Jim Thompson; Congressman Dan Rostenkowski; US Senators Alan Dixon and Paul Simon; Illinois Senate President Philip J. Rock; Cardinal Joseph Bernardin; former mayors Jane Byrne, Michael Bilandic, and Eugene Sawyer; famed author Saul Bellow; and Tim Evans. Cardinal Bernardin gave the invocation.[10]

Many Chicagoans felt relief. But the large dynamics driving change in the city persisted. White ethnics continued to leave the city for the suburbs or other parts of the country. Patronage disappeared, as did the communalism that had marked the old immigrant and ethnic neighborhoods. Jews left the city at an astounding rate, except for the far North Side. The Roman Catholic Church, once a pillar of the Democratic machine, was in disarray. In 1990 a slew of Catholic parishes closed their doors, the beginning of a vast retreat from the inner city. Daley's future seemed hardly secure. His promise of being both a new modern progressive Daley and the upholder of his father's legend put him in a difficult position. During the next twenty-two years, Daley worked through this political paradox with a surprising degree of success, as well as some notable missteps.

A NEW MACHINE?

Like his father, Rich Daley kept a close circle of advisors. His six brothers and sisters, his wife, and his mother stood at the center of that group. Bill Daley, his youngest brother, served as his closest counselor and campaign manager. Harvard-educated John Schmidt, a liberal lawyer, became his first chief of staff. Frank Kruesi, another progressive, researched and wrote several of the measures Daley touted in his campaign. The inner circle included Avis LaVelle and David Axelrod, who directed Daley's broadcast media blitz and wrote his victory speech. Daley sought out progressive advisors and started to form new alliances, including with state Senator Dawn Clark

CHAPTER 11

Netsch, an independent Democrat and a law professor at Northwestern University. Daley knew that Harold Washington's legacy had to be embraced. Indeed, two important groups—the LGBTQ+ community and Latinos—proved vital to his new coalition.[11]

Daley's progressive views on gay rights and abortion rights had helped him solidify support along the liberal lakefront. Gays and lesbians had been a visible part of Washington's constituency and now proved to be an important subset of Daley supporters, despite some early friction between the administration and radical leadership in the LGBTQ+ community.* There had been no openly gay backers of his father's organization, and it would have been unthinkable for the older Daley to march in a Pride Parade, as his son did in 1989.[12]

Daley had promised robust support for issues of deep concern to the LGBTQ+ community. These included a pledge to seek all available funding from the state, federal government, and private sector for AIDS programs and to directly fund LGBTQ+ community organizations that dealt with the disease. He also promised to have completed, within six months of his inauguration, a Health Department strategic plan for AIDS prevention and education. Candidate Daley had urged the creation of a formal advisory council, including representatives of the LGBTQ+ communities, to advise the Department of Health on its policies and programs. He said he would provide leadership to ensure housing resources to people with AIDS and related illnesses, and he vowed to publicly oppose any attempt to retract the city's Human Rights Ordinance, which had banned discrimination on the basis of sexual orientation.[13]

A formidable interest group, the LGBTQ+ community came to resemble in function a traditional ethnic group within Chicago's political structure. Besides making demands on City Hall, the LGBTQ+ community began to leverage political power, as openly gay politicians won offices in the 1990s. In 1994, Thomas R. Chiola

---

* Terminology around gay rights and the gay community has evolved rapidly since the 1970s. By the late 1980s, the term LGB was increasingly used. I have chosen to use the current inclusive term LGBTQ+ to represent the constituency more accurately.

won election to the circuit court, becoming the first openly gay man elected to public office in Chicago. Soon thereafter, voters supported Larry McKeon as the first openly gay member of the state legislature. In 2002, Mayor Daley appointed Tom Tunney as the first openly gay alderman, succeeding Bernie Hansen in the 44th Ward.

Daley continued to pursue LGBTQ+ support by promoting gay rights legislation, making political appointments, and performing significant symbolic gestures. In 1991 he supported the opening of the Chicago Gay and Lesbian Hall of Fame (since 2016, the Chicago LGBT Hall of Fame), the first institution of its kind in the United States. He personally handed out the Hall of Fame's awards to over a dozen recipients. Daley also supported Chicago's gay and lesbian political action committee.[14] Importantly, he signed the measure providing bereavement leave for all city employees (1993) and pushed through the City Council a measure providing equal benefits for same-sex partners of city employees (1997). The mayor's North Halsted Streetscape Project, completed in 1998, recognized gay identity and included rainbow pylons that proclaimed the area Boystown. If there was a critique of Daley's involvement with this community, it lay in the possibility that "gayness" was being equated with Whites and gentrifiers, and that Black and poor gays had been left out of the equation.

The historian Timothy Stewart-Winter notes that Tunney and later other gay aldermen quickly fit into the Daley organization. Tunney, who owned the popular restaurant Ann Sather's, supported the Daley administration's pro-growth policy. Other small business owners within the North Side gay leadership also warmed to the Daley administration. Gay politics provided an organizing focus not only in majority gay areas, but also in other liberal wards, particularly along the lakefront. Gay clout had arrived; Daley knew it and used it politically. In many ways, the LGBTQ+ community provided another communal foundation for a reimagined machine.[15]

A more traditional ethnic group also began to flex its muscles during the Daley years. The tremendous growth of the Hispanic population, especially after 1965, had changed Chicago's ethnic landscape. There had long been a Mexican community in the city, with

CHAPTER 11

many of the earlier immigrants settling in South Chicago and working in the Southeast Side's steel mills. Other Mexican immigrants joined the ethnic mix in the Hull House area and in Back of the Yards, where they labored in the packinghouses. The first Mexican Catholic Church, Our Lady of Guadalupe, opened in the early 1920s in South Chicago, just west of US Steel's massive South Works. The parish became a focal point for the expanding Mexican American community.[16]

Mexicans and other Hispanics often faced prejudice in those neighborhoods. Police treated them differently from White ethnic groups, while politicians ignored them. Polish Chicagoans and Mexicans clashed frequently. In turn, like other ethnic groups, Mexicans looked to their own community to develop a communal response that would protect their families. They established about twenty-three *mutualistas* (mutual aid societies), mostly small working-class organizations, by the end of 1928. Small business owners also formed some of these *mutualistas* or *sociedades mexicanas*. In addition to *mutualistas* and churches, Mexican neighborhoods cultivated businesses, newspapers, cultural centers, and sports organizations. These institutions eventually developed into voting power and thus clout.[17]

At the onset of the Great Depression, the Hoover administration launched what has come to be known as the Mexican Repatriation Program, which continued well into the second Roosevelt administration. The Chicago Mexican population declined dramatically during this period, from roughly 20,000 to 12,500, as Mexican immigrants and Mexican Americans alike were expelled. As Gabriela F. Arrendondo has pointed out, not even citizenship could overcome the barrier of prejudice that racialized people of Mexican descent. Mexicans would face further deportations after World War II, especially after the passage of the 1952 McCarran–Walter Act, which severely limited most immigrants' rights to live in the United States.[18]

Conversely, after the passage of the Immigration and Naturalization Act of 1965, Mexican and Hispanic Chicago witnessed tremendous growth, which helped to offset the city's other population losses. Between 1940 and 1980 the city's overall population declined by close to 400,000 residents. More than 1.5 million Whites left the city. African American migration to Chicago could not by itself compensate for the White exodus. Fortunately, the explosive growth of the Latino community mitigated much of it. By 1970, Chicago had nearly 250,000 Spanish-speaking residents. Mexicans and Puerto Ricans made up the overwhelming majority, accounting for 75 percent of that population, with Mexican Chicagoans numbering 106,000 and Puerto Ricans numbering 79,000. By the 1970s and 1980s, Chicago's political leaders came to realize they should connect with this population.

Mexicans created their largest community in Pilsen and Little Village, an area once known as Czech California (South Lawndale), Anton Cermak's original political base. Puerto Ricans settled largely in the old Polish neighborhood around the intersection of Milwaukee, Division, and Ashland Avenues (West Town), in Humboldt Park, and in Logan Square. While Puerto Ricans held US citizenship and therefore could vote, many Mexicans were not citizens and so could not, and this hindered their growth as a political force.[19]

In the early 1950s, Mexican business and civic leaders organized the Mexican American Democratic Organization (MADO) to create a positive relationship with City Hall for the small business community. They hoped to build goodwill and ease their relationships with non-Latino ward bosses. The elder Daley and his supporters viewed MADO as a loyal, conservative business group. Eventually MADO became part of a larger organization known as Amigos for Daley, which also included the Mexican American Chamber of Commerce, the Azteca Lions Club, and the Illinois Federation of Mexican Americans. The Amigos organization held banquets and other fundraising events for the mayor. The political scientist Wilfredo Cruz has pointed out that originally the community received little in return for their efforts, as the Democrats took their votes for granted.[20]

By the time the younger Daley had captured the mayoralty, however, Latinos had learned to flex their political muscle. They had been an important part of Harold Washington's coalition. Nearly 80 percent of Latino voters cast their ballots for Washington in 1983. The Hispanic voting bloc soon mounted a grassroots campaign to gain power. As a result, Latino candidates challenged the traditional

CHAPTER 11

Democratic machine. Still, fissures within the Mexican and Puerto Rican communities divided the Hispanic electorate, with machine loyalists and independents clashing across the Latino neighborhoods over policy differences. Nevertheless, Latino Chicagoans made great strides politically in the last quarter of the twentieth century.[21]

Harold Washington opened City Hall to Latino Chicagoans. During his administration, Luis Gutiérrez emerged as the leader of an expanding group of Latino aldermen and a spokesman for Washington. In 1987, Washington backed Raymond Figueroa, a Puerto Rican attorney, against Miguel Santiago to become alderman of the 31st Ward. A year later Figueroa became ward committeeman after beating machine loyalist Joseph Berrios. That year, Washington also backed progressive Miguel del Valle, who became the first Latino state senator in Illinois. In 1986, voters elected Jesús "Chuy" Garcia alderman in the 22nd Ward, launching his stellar career.[22]

Washington's politics remained potent as Rich Daley built his own coalition. Daley reached out to Gutiérrez and other Latino leaders in his 1989 campaign. Over the years, as Daley ran successfully for reelection six times, Latino clout intensified. Simultaneously, the clout of older ethnic groups, especially Polish Americans and Jews, waned as Daley's ties to them became less substantive and more symbolic. Daley still attended the annual Polish Constitution Day Parade and erected flagpoles in front of the Copernicus Center; participated in the lighting of the Chanukah menorah in Daley Plaza; and posed with his father's old ally, Judge Abraham Lincoln Marovitz, on Jerusalem Day. But the political power of the traditional White ethnic groups receded, albeit gradually. During Daley's first year in office, the ethnic composition of board and commission appointments proved to be fairly consistent with the Sawyer administration's numbers. At least in his first term, Daley showed no interest in overthrowing the ethnic balance.[23]

As Blacks and Latinos gained political power, the largest White ethnic group in Chicago saw its clout fade during the Daley administration. Polish American politicians such as Rostenkowski, Pucinski, Lipinski, Swinarski, and Kluczynski had long led a citywide Polish political bloc in the Irish-led Democratic Party. Former Democratic renegade Benjamin Adamowski and GOP stalwarts Edmund Kucharski and Edward Derwinski also held sway in the local Republican Party. At one time in the postwar period, Chicago sent four Polish American congressmen to Washington, DC. Certain offices, such as city clerk, were considered "Polish offices" by veteran political observers. While a Polish American never sat in the mayor's chair, the community exerted considerable clout in the Democratic Party. That changed by the late 1990s, as Democrats fought over the 5th Congressional District seat held by the once powerful Dan Rostenkowski, who had been indicted for corruption and then narrowly defeated in the 1994 elections. Nancy Kaszak, a Polish American lawyer and state representative who had been involved in Chicago politics since the Washington administration, hoped to recapture the seat in 1996, but Rod Blagojevich, also a state representative but not of Polish descent, defeated her in the Democratic primary. Once Blagojevich declared that he would run for governor in 2002, Kaszak ran again for the congressional seat. She highlighted her Polish American ethnicity when announcing her candidacy in the King's Hall of the Copernicus Center in the Jefferson Park neighborhood. But she lost the primary election to Rahm Emanuel, Daley's fundraiser and political ally.[24]

The new Daley coalition centered on Mexicans, Puerto Ricans, and other Latinos, as well as the LGBTQ+ community and lakefront independents. The organization also benefited from a slow growth in African American support, as the wounds of the Sawyer era receded. But this was not the only hallmark of the new times. In 1993, Rich and Maggie Daley left Bridgeport, the traditional bastion of the Democratic machine and the longtime home turf of the Daleys. They moved into the South Loop, one of the city's newest neighborhoods, where a diverse group of Chicagoans was becoming the new face of the city. Daley had again broken with the past.

Daley's relationship with the African American community gained strength as a result of his support for Barack Obama's campaigns, first for the US Senate in 2004 and later for the presidency

11.1 Richard M. Daley at the Polish Constitution Day Parade, ca. 2000. Despite the movement of Polish Americans to the suburbs and their loss of clout in the city, Daley still appeared at Polish events. He is pictured here as the Honorary Grand Marshall of the parade commemorating the Polish Constitution of 1791. Courtesy of the Alliance of Polish Clubs.

in 2008. Obama did not fit the image of a machine politician, but he did benefit from the support of the Daley administration. In fact, Daley was the first major politician to support the Hyde Park resident in his presidential quest. Daley knew how to pick a winner, and like Jake Arvey, the powerful machine politician turned anticorruption fighter of decades earlier, Daley supported the "clean" candidate. Obama eventually took on board Daley allies such as Valerie Jarrett, political strategist David M. Axelrod, Rahm Emanuel, CEO of Chicago Public Schools Arne Duncan, and Bill Daley. Jarrett and Axelrod had helped Obama win his Senate seat in 2004. These consultants and supporters who had powered the Daley organization simply moved to Obama's White House. A Chicago mayor had finally helped to place a Chicagoan in the White House, with the added historical significance of Obama being the first Black president of the United States.[25]

A NEOLIBERAL MACHINE

Rahm Emanuel, who had raised a legendary $7,000,000 for Daley's 1989 campaign in just thirteen weeks, directed Bill Clinton's successful presidential campaign in 1992. Emanuel then served as Clinton's assistant for political affairs and senior advisor for policy and strategy. He emerged as a leader of the "New" Democrats, a group who were socially liberal but moderate or conservative on economic issues. They came to dominate the party both nationally and in places like Chicago. Their neoliberalism privatized public-sector functions. Neoliberal policies reduced government involvement in the day-to-day provision of services and pursued public-private partnerships to fill budget gaps through the leasing or outright selling of public assets. The Daley administration, despite its roots in New Deal liberalism and communalism, turned to these ideas, which largely emerged out of the Ronald Reagan years, as a "realistic" way for Democrats to regain and retain power. An example of this could be found in the city's effort to use public-private investment to transform public housing.[26]

Daley was a reluctant neoliberal who had grown up in a neighborhood surrounded by a communal political machine. The Shakman decrees had eroded the traditional patronage base for the Regular Democratic Organization, but Daley and others searched for ways around them. Then the Daley administration got caught. The Hired Truck Scandal, uncovered by *Chicago Sun-Times* reporter Tim Novak in 2004, involved several trucking companies that were paid by the city to do little or no work. The trucking companies had ties to city employees and allegedly had mob connections. Truck owners also paid bribes to participate in the program. Michael Tadin, a friend of Daley's and a De La Salle graduate, owned one such firm. John Daley was Tadin's insurance broker. Privatization fit neatly into the Bridgeport Way as long as politicians could control the various programs. The Hired Truck Program was a classic case of the political machine doling out contracts, including jobs, to the private sector in exchange for political support. The former head of the program,

Angelo T. Torres, was charged with extortion, while others within the Daley orbit were charged with bribery. Daley tried to save face by reforming the program, imposing higher standards on truck owners, and barring any who had been convicted of bid rigging, extortion, syndicated gambling, or other crimes. But the administration had known the program was corrupt since at least 1997; turning a blind eye had made it possible to continue using the program as a political tool to maintain power.[27]

The Hired Truck Scandal led to other damaging developments. Two years later, Daley's ally Robert Sorich, who had headed the Office of Governmental Affairs, was indicted along with three others on federal charges that they had exercised insider political influence to place Daley supporters in city jobs, in violation of the Shakman decrees. Sorich, Timothy McCarthy, Patrick Slattery, and John Sullivan, three of whom lived in Bridgeport, passed around lists to city departments of individuals connected with the Hispanic Democratic Organization (HDO) and the Coalition for Better Government, a White ethnic organization. Daley's machine mobilized racial and ethnic organizations instead of using the old ward system for patronage, a shift only in the mechanisms of political clout. Both the Hired Truck Scandal and the Sorich hiring affair might be characterized as "pinstripe patronage"—that is, favors given to well-connected City Hall insiders, especially those from Bridgeport. In a bit of a twist, the Hired Truck Program was promoted as a cost-cutting measure, while the City Hall hiring preference list brought more women and minority groups into the clout-inspired enterprise.[28]

While scandal haunted Rich Daley's administration, neoliberalism soon began to define it. The administration aimed to privatize many of the services his father's administration would never have touched. The younger Daley reduced the role of government and relied on public-private development. He deployed zoning and other land-use policies to transform public housing and to stimulate real estate markets and gentrification. He promoted the city as an entertainment destination, while displacing low-income people and increasing police surveillance. As Chicago's core gentrified, the city expanded festivals, the convention center, and sports venues such as the United Center, the new Comiskey Park (now Rate Field) for the White Sox baseball team, and a remodeled Soldier Field for the Chicago Bears. Daley embraced Daniel Burnham's 1909 Chicago Plan and put his own spin on it. The creation of a vast museum campus and Millennium Park further transformed the lakefront. According to the political scientists Costas Spirou and Dennis R. Judd, Chicago became a city of spectacle and tourism. This newly reimagined city resulted from an intensive interaction between public and private sectors. This was especially true in the construction of Millennium Park, which replaced an old railyard on the northwest edge of Grant Park in the Loop and topped off Daley's rejuvenated downtown.[29]

Neoliberalism, an ideology of markets and individualism, could not have been more different from the old communalism that had formed the foundation of the Democratic machine in Chicago. Communalism also informed the rationale for the welfare state and Roosevelt's New Deal, with the idea that government can and should look out for people and create a shared common good. Neoliberalism rejected those ideas, removing a traditional sense of morality from the political equation and replacing it with market forces. It hurt the working and lower classes of a city that had celebrated them as its bone and sinew. The "City of the Big Shoulders" would soon turn its back on those core constituents as it looked to a more technocratic future. Fewer social programs and more privatization left many feeling disenfranchised, while those with economic power benefited politically from the shifting paradigm. The old system of patronage had seemed corrupt to reformers, many of whom benefited from the neoliberal model. But neoliberalism hurt the lower middle class, working class, and poor who made up a large part of the city's population and who were increasingly Black and Brown.[30]

During the first ten years of his mayoralty, Daley proved to be a somewhat restrained neoliberal. He privatized hauling and trucking but little else, perhaps given the scandals that surrounded these efforts. Daley's Chicago Public Schools Board President Gery Chico and CEO Paul Vallas backed privatized charter schools. They championed a corporate-style regime and launched new programs and schools. Despite these reforms, the school system continued to shortchange Latino and Black students.

Then, between 2004 and 2008, Daley opened the neoliberal floodgates. He privatized the Chicago Skyway, city-owned parking garages, and city parking meters. He attempted but failed to privatize Midway Airport. The 2008 parking meter deal, which Daley used to plug a budget hole and thus avoid raising property taxes, touched off a maelstrom of criticism. He pushed the infamous proposal through the City Council with hardly any review; only five aldermen voted against it.[31] Former mayors of Chicago, including his father, must have been spinning in their graves as a city asset and its accompanying jobs went up for sale! Ironically, perhaps only Mayor Martin Kennelly, the businessman-reformer, might have approved.

THE DALEY FAMILY

Despite his political success and long tenure as mayor of Chicago, many of those close to Rich Daley claimed he was not a very political person. He did not enjoy the confrontational part of politics. Nor did he like the old precinct captain organization: it faded during his years in office and then largely disappeared except for a few traditionally run wards. A hands-on mayor, like his father, Daley made note of infrastructure issues as he rode around the city in the back of a limousine. Well-read and a frequent traveler, Rich Daley brought new ideas to the office that he seems to have felt a filial duty to occupy. Bill Daley said his brother's involvement in politics and eventually the mayoralty might have had something to do with the Irish idea of primogeniture, "the oldest does it."[32] The Daley family itself provided the core of the administration. His mother and wife exerted a powerful influence on the mayor. His three brothers, John, Michael, and Bill, stood as his most loyal allies.

As a close observer of his father, Rich Daley cultivated a deep devotion to the city and learned to carefully hold his cards close to his chest. He knew when to cut his ties to various groups and when to make strong new ones. That sense of opportunity also influenced his policy decisions. At times it seemed that the new Daley would upend some of the decisions of the old one. Rich Daley saw to the destruction of the public housing high-rise wall, just east of the Dan Ryan Expressway, that had been built during his father's reign. Under the influence of Maggie, he moved away from the modernism espoused by the urban planners of the 1950s to a postmodern approach that embraced the City Beautiful ideas of the Burnham Plan. Daley remade Chicago's streetscapes, installing ubiquitous planters not only downtown but in neighborhoods.

As early as 1990, Daley endorsed a riverwalk and said that the banks of the Chicago River should be a destination for Chicagoans and tourists alike. In 1992 Daley insisted that plans to repave and relight Michigan Avenue must include planters that would hold seasonal flowers and unite Michigan Avenue on both sides of the river from Oak Street to Roosevelt Road. Thirty long concrete planters brimming with chrysanthemums and ornamental cabbages and kale soon lined the street. Eventually tulips and other plants bloomed as the seasons changed. Blair Kamin, the *Chicago Tribune*'s architectural critic, pointed out that despite the rather utilitarian look of the planters, "the importance of greening the city" could not be overemphasized. It softened the hard edges of Chicago. The *Tribune* lauded Daley's plans to spruce up the city and reported that first-time visitors were struck by its beauty. In 1993, the Dutch minister of foreign trade agreed to donate 30,000 tulip bulbs for the planters, every year for three years.[33]

Some ridiculed Daley's plans, but most liked the planters and other improvements, including the restoration of State Street, which had been turned into a pedestrian mall in 1979. Daley's administration turned it back into a vibrant street with the hope of regaining its past glory. In addition, in 1996 Daley's urban planners moved Lake Shore Drive's northbound lanes to the west side of Soldier Field, creating a campus uniting the Field Museum, the Shedd Aquarium, and the Adler Planetarium. This project also linked these institutions to the Art Institute and the Loop colleges. The administration also relocated the Goodman Theatre, another important cultural landmark, and created a new Theater Row in the Loop. Millennium Park,

CHAPTER 11

[Campaign button image: "Discover, Explore, Enjoy! NATURE CHICAGO, RICHARD M. DALEY, MAYOR"]

11.2 Campaign button celebrating the Greening of Chicago. John Daley reminisced that Rich Daley had always loved trees. He recalled that Rich had forced his siblings to plant trees at the Daley weekend home in Michigan. Author's Collection.

Daley's most important achievement in beautifying the city, provided new green space for cultural events.[34] Daley presented himself as an eco-friendly green mayor, even turning the roof of City Hall into a greenspace with a garden.[35]

In an uncharacteristically anti-neoliberal move, Daley abruptly closed Meigs Field Airport in March 2003 and turned the lakefront property into a venue open to the public. Many castigated him for destroying the landing strips in the middle of the night and called it an example of mayoral overreach. When actor Harrison Ford criticized Daley's move, the mayor reacted with a spirited defense:

> I don't want to call him elitist, but he is. He has a jet. He has all these planes and all these toys. And he doesn't understand this economy is tough with people and that lakefront belongs to us.... They'd love to privatize the whole lakefront for a few people. That's not the history of Chicago.... He should read the Burnham

Plan.—But in Chicago, that 100 acres, that lakefront belongs—not to you. It belongs to the people of Chicago. That's the great history of the city.[36]

Maggie Daley's role as an advisor and partner to her husband cannot be overestimated. They loved to travel together, and these experiences inspired several urban beautification ideas. Maggie's dedication to the education of children also shaped many of her husband's policies. She helped to create "After School Matters," a program that provided an opportunity for Chicago teens to explore their passions and develop their talents. In the summer of 1991, Maggie Daley looked to Block 37 downtown as a site to showcase teenage artists. In 1987, Mayor Washington had approved a $24 million subsidy to FJV Venture to redevelop the block. The city had demolished the block, located across State Street from Marshal Field's Department Store, in 1989 with the hope of revitalizing it, but it remained an undeveloped eyesore for years. Frank Kruesi, Daley's advisor, came to the mayor with the idea of turning the location into a studio and exhibit center for student artists from After School Matters. The mayor initially dismissed the idea. When Kruesi explained it was Maggie's idea, Daley smiled and said, "Oh, that's a great idea." Maggie ran it along with Lois Weisberg, Chicago's first commissioner of cultural affairs, and it turned out to be very successful. She also worked with Father Jack Wall to create a new parochial school, Frances Xavier Ward School, in Old St. Patrick's parish on the West Side. Maggie Daley's initiatives not only inspired her husband but directly enriched the city.[37]

Sunday, February 16, 2003, broke as a cloudy, gray day in Chicago with the temperature hovering in the mid- to low 20s. Late that afternoon, after a day spent with her firstborn son, one of his sisters, and several grandchildren, Eleanor Guilfoyle "Sis" Daley, matriarch of one of the most powerful political clans in American urban history, died, just a couple of weeks short of her ninety-sixth birthday. Loyal and civic-minded to the end, she had filled out an absentee ballot, voting for her son, just eight days before her death.[38] Now the Daley family mourned the last member of its founding generation in Chicago. The hearse pulled away from the Daley family abode at 7:50 p.m., marking the last time "the city's guiding light" left her home of over sixty years.[39]

Sis Daley's world centered around family, neighborhood, and church. Her wake at Nativity of Our Lord Catholic Church brought out many Chicagoans who described her as the anchor of her powerful clan. Over twelve hours, thousands of mourners came through the church. Many arrived in expensive cars with low-digit license plates, but many others also came by bus or walked from their Bridgeport homes. Men in Chicago White Sox and Notre Dame hats stood in line with women in babushkas. Some mourners told of a political connection while others knew her from parish bingo games. Bouquets of flowers, including a green Celtic cross and one that spelled "Chicago," lined the entire length of both sides of the church. Mrs. Daley's devotion to her neighborhood brought out Bridgeport's office clerks, factory superintendents, firefighters, and police officers. Dorothy Tweedy, a forty-year resident of Bridgeport, affirmed, "we love her and her son, we're from the neighborhood and we stick together." Another mourner, Mary Romano, exclaimed, "we're all close. You don't have to be in power or political. It's just down-to-earth people."[40]

But those down-to-earth people wielded incredible political power for nearly fifty years. For the Daleys, family came first, and the four sons took on much of the persona of their father. They were also formed by the women of the family as well as by the Catholic Church, the neighborhood, their education, their ethnicity, and the city. They understood the so-called Chicago Way of politics, which could be called the Bridgeport Way. It had emerged out of an immigrant working-class culture that saw patronage as an expression of loyalty and a deserving means of getting "our share," as part of the natural order of things that resulted in clout, real power. The Daleys expected loyalty and punished disloyalty.

Bill Daley, the youngest child, had been nurtured by his father for a role in national politics. Despite never being elected to office, he became an important Democratic operative. After leading his brother's successful mayoral campaign in 1989, he served as the US secretary of commerce during the Clinton administration, as chairman of Al Gore's presidential campaign, and as Barack Obama's White House chief of staff. He also worked in the banking industry. Unlike his father and oldest brother, Bill Daley attended St. Ignatius College Prep and Loyola University, and received his law degree from John Marshall Law School. He practiced law as part of the Daley and George Law Firm, founded by his father, as well as later with Mayer, Brown, & Platt. In 2019 he ran his own unsuccessful campaign for mayor. Unlike Rich, Bill Daley, a reluctant campaigner, never seemed to really be cut out for elected office.[41]

Michael Daley, also a well-connected lawyer, took on his father's much valued "behind-the-scenes" role, leveraging the extensive Daley network. A quiet man who never looked to enter the public arena, Michael maintained a below-the-radar profile. Phil Krone, a political consultant, called him the smartest of the Daley boys, the brains behind the operation and the most fascinating of the four. He received his law degree from DePaul University in 1968 and became a partner in the Daley and George firm in 1970. One observer called his law practice an example of "honest graft" and "quiet clout." He had the skills and connections to give his clients an advantage, especially in zoning and tax appeal matters.[42]

The only brother not to earn a law degree, John Daley, took on one of his father's favorite roles: the neighborhood politician and the good neighbor. A successful insurance broker, he benefited from his family ties and his position in the Cook County Democratic Party. A truly likable person, he succeeded his brother as 11th Ward committeeman in 1980 when Rich won election as Cook County state's attorney. John became a member of the Illinois House representing the Twenty-first District in 1985 when John Vitek resigned for health reasons. Four years later, he moved to the Illinois Senate. In 1992, John became a Cook County commissioner. Today he remains a power on the Cook County Board and as 11th Ward committeeman. Above all else, unlike his other brothers, John Daley remained in Bridgeport, a truly neighborhood guy.

The four Daley brothers assumed different parts of their illustrious father's legacy: mayor, national political operative, local behind-the-scenes influencer, and neighborhood politician. The times had changed, and no one person could be the local and national power broker Richard J. Daley had been. Nevertheless, they took up the tasks that he executed so effectively on both the national and local political scene. The next generation would not be as successful.[43]

THE END OF THE DALEY ERA

In 2010, rumors abounded that Rahm Emanuel, who had given up his seat in the US House to become President Barack Obama's chief of staff, wanted to run for mayor of Chicago. A White House aide denied the rumor, and Daley refused to respond to inquiries about his friend's ambitions. The mayor seemed tired and irritable and suffered low popularity ratings. Maggie had been diagnosed with metastatic breast cancer in 2002, and her struggle with the disease had long been a major concern of Daley's. On January 12, 2010, he canceled his public schedule after his wife suffered an adverse reaction to her treatments. He stayed with Maggie at Northwestern Memorial Hospital for most of the day.[44]

Emanuel praised Daley and urged him to run for a seventh term. Emanuel would not run if Daley did. He had no real organization of his own to support him on the ground in the city, and in particular, little connection to the large Black and Latino populations. Many saw him as Obama's neoliberal water carrier. On top of all of that, he did not fit the traditional profile of a Chicago candidate. Emanuel, a Jew, attended Bernard Zell Anshe Emet Day School in Lakeview and, once his upper-middle-class family moved to Wilmette, attended public schools and New Trier High School. Emanuel's father was a successful pediatrician, one brother worked as a nationally known oncologist, the other as CEO of a thriving entertainment agency in California. Many doubted that Emanuel could win in Chicago.[45]

Speculation continued throughout the year. Finally, on September 7, Daley declared he would not seek reelection. Flanked by his wife, Maggie, daughters Nora and Elizabeth, son Patrick, and son-in-law Sean Conroy, he made his announcement at a City Hall news conference deceptively billed as a major cabinet appointment. He stated simply that the time had come to step down: "I have always believed that every person, especially public officials, must understand when it is time to move on. For me, that time is now." He acknowledged that he had been thinking about leaving office for several months and that he felt comfortable with his decision.

Daley's decision did not come as a total surprise. The mayor's approval rating had fallen to a low of 35 percent after the unpopular parking meter sell-off. The city suffered from a downgraded bond rating and a budget crisis while the murder rate rose. Several scandals had rocked his administration. Family matters did not help: His nephew, Robert G. Vanecko, and son Patrick had questionable deals with the city. Another nephew, Richard J. Vanecko, eventually pleaded guilty to involuntary manslaughter of David Koschman, the result of a drunken brawl in the Rush and Division Street area. Of course, Maggie's illness weighed heavily on him. Yet he insisted that the city's budget crisis, its failed bid to host the 2016 Olympics, and his wife's health issues had nothing to do with his decision. A poll of Chicago voters found that two out of five voters agreed with Daley. Only one out of four disagreed. Another one out of four volunteered an answer that was not even included in the opinion poll: they said it made no difference.[46]

Potential successors quickly began to test the waters. Several names appeared in the press, including Cook County Sheriff Tom Dart, retiring Cook County Assessor Jim Houlihan, Alderman Luis Gutiérrez, and former CPS Board President Gery Chico. City Clerk Miguel del Valle announced almost immediately that he would be a candidate, as did state Senator Rickey Hendon. Former US Senator Carol Moseley Braun, the first Black woman senator, floated the possibility of running. The race promised to be crowded.[47]

Rahm Emanuel claimed that Daley's announcement caught him by surprise. His friend and colleague, White House senior advisor David Axelrod, who had long supported Daley, said that they had both just begun to absorb Daley's decision and that he did not know if Emanuel would run. Emanuel knew he would have to navigate Chicago's racially charged and turbulent politics. Alderman Bernard Stone of the heavily Jewish 50th Ward, where Emanuel probably would be popular, cautioned, "he doesn't have the experience and the know-how—Rahm is a strong arm—and I am not looking for a strong-arm mayor." President Obama chimed in that Emanuel would make a terrific mayor of Chicago. He also expected that Emanuel would stay in the White House until after the midterms.

Candidates had to file for the election between November 15 and November 22 with at least 12,500 valid signatures, and probably more than three times that number if they expected to fend off challenges to those signatures. Almost immediately a "Stop Rahm" movement emerged. Alderman Roberto Maldonado (26th Ward) accused Emanuel of thwarting immigration reform. One unnamed alderman referred to him as a tyrant. US Representative Bobby Rush said that Emanuel's skills could not be transferred to Chicago. Emanuel commissioned his longtime pollster, Stanley Greenberg, to survey Chicagoans about his possible bid. On September 15, Emanuel met with State Representative Jesse Jackson Jr., who also considered running.[48]

Emanuel announced his candidacy on November 13. Before that he had visited neighborhoods across the city on what he called a "listening tour." He declared he would work to generate jobs, improve education, and decrease crime. He entered the race with more than $1,000,000 in campaign funds, high name recognition, and a reputation as a relentless campaigner. Despite the fact that Emanuel owned a home in the Ravenswood neighborhood, his residency was challenged because he had not lived there since leaving to work in the Obama administration. His renter had a lease until mid-2011 and refused to move out. Two days later, Emanuel's lawyer, Michael Kasper, filed the candidate's petitions with nearly 91,000 signatures— more than seven times the required number. A February 2012 poll showed Emanuel with a wide lead over his closest competitor, Gery Chico. On February 22, Emanuel won the mayoralty, taking 55 percent of the vote to Chico's 24 percent. A new political era began.[49]

Emanuel had been the preferred candidate of Rich Daley. This did not prevent him, over the next few years, from criticizing some of Daley's moves. Like his father, Rich Daley had tried to build a permanent machine, and like his father's, his organization quickly broke

11.3 Rahm Emanuel at the announcement of his candidacy for Mayor of Chicago, November 13, 2010. Photo by Daniel X. O'Neil, https://www.flickr.com/photos/juggernautco/5172674616/ (CC BY 2.0, https://creativecommons.org/licenses/by/2.0/).

apart after he left the scene. Both men stayed in office too long, and the taint of scandal marred their last years in office. Both men exercised a heavy hand over the City Council, where corruption seemed always to lurk just below the surface. Between the last years of the Richard J. Daley administration and the first two years of the Emanuel administration, thirty-eight Chicago aldermen would be indicted and sent to jail, maintaining a long-standing tradition. Even Bill Daley implied that his brother might have stayed too long in office. He said that staffs get complacent, and the office holder loses his sharpness after a long time in power. Perhaps the same could be said about both Mayor Daleys?[50]

Chicago's uniquely communal brand of politics continued its slow decline after Rich Daley left office. The old pillars of the machine that Cermak crafted, Kelly solidified, and the first Daley perfected soon disintegrated. This disintegration mirrored profound changes in the cultural institutions that had reinforced the old pillars of the machine, not least the Catholic Church, which had long provided a social glue for Chicago politics and now reeled under the unintended consequences of the Second Vatican Council.

The Catholic Church lost influence not only in Chicago, but across the United States. The Church saw its teaching authority diminished by the encyclical *Humanae Vitae* prohibiting artificial birth control. Increased suburbanization and White flight resulted in the closing of a host of city parishes, further loosening the Church's grip. In less than fifty years, the number of priests in the Chicago archdiocese fell by half. By the second decade of the twenty-first century, while Catholics made up the largest denomination in the country, former Catholics made up the second largest group. Some said they made up an even larger number than practicing Catholics. Secularization had attenuated the old ties.[51]

Communal Catholicism, as understood in Chicago in the first part of the twentieth century, had also declined. Novenas and prayers asking for divine intervention, once so popular, disappeared from practice. Pilgrimages to holy sites vanished, along with the celebration of saint's days. Catholic parishes that had once provided neighborhood hubs closed. Assimilation and interethnic marriage resulted in many White ethnics leaving their hereditary cultures behind as they moved to the suburbs. The dominant cultural value of individualism reigned supreme, supplanting the idea of communal solidarity. Old forms of worship disappeared, and with them the sense of community that they reinforced. New immigration patterns emerged. A large portion of Hispanic Catholics converted to evangelical Protestantism, either in their homelands or after immigration, further weakening traditional Catholic cultural ties in the neighborhoods.[52]

Chicago's Jewish population, another major pillar of the old machine, continued to decrease because of the same forces that had reshaped the Catholic population. Jews assimilated and moved from the city to the suburbs, and increased secularization loosened old communal bonds. The old Jewish neighborhoods of the South and West Sides disappeared. New Jewish settlements emerged in the suburbs, particularly the North Shore, but these were wealthier and more individualistic in outlook. The *landsmanshaft* groups largely vanished. The Covenant Club, which once embraced eastern European Jews, sold its Loop property in 1985 and closed entirely in 1986. After more than 150 years, the Standard Club, a bastion of German Jews, closed its doors in 2022.[53]

Two other pillars of the old machine culture had also dissolved or weakened. Patronage jobs declined because of the various Shakman rulings, undercutting a major reason for loyalty to the machine. Also, the old communal ways of interacting with the public basically disappeared in Chicago's neighborhoods. Chicago politicians rarely make evening visits to wakes anymore. Nighttime office hours or open houses, where constituents could register complaints and ask for jobs and favors, have all but vanished. The institution of the 311 telephone system and the City of Chicago website meant that constituents could request everything from tree trimming, new garbage cans, pothole repairs, replacement of damaged trash containers, help with alleys overrun with rodents, and so on directly from the city without going through the alderman's office. While aldermen still held considerable power, the communal interaction between residents and politicians largely evaporated. Furthermore, group participation in traditional organizations such as the American Legion, the Knights of Columbus, and the Veterans of Foreign Wars declined in the city. All of these had once helped bolster the machine as Richard J. Daley knew it. Their influence had lessened by the twenty-first century. They were part of a communalism that seemed to vanish from Chicago's neighborhoods. The tenuous balance between the sacred and the profane faded. Many identified machine politics as corrupt politics. Simply put, the times and people's attitudes had changed.[54]

12

After the Daleys

> We should not be on the fifth floor, and I am speaking with my whole heart. We were not ready because we haven't been in government long enough to know how government runs. . . . And we look real stupid now.
>
> ALDERPERSON JEANETTE TAYLOR,
> December 2023[1]

The infrastructure of the old communal political machine had shown signs of decay in the last years of Richard J. Daley's administration. Corruption abounded and many politicians went to jail. Poverty, racism, and massive income inequality constituted intractable problems. The enormous underfunding of city pensions further tied politicians' hands. Despite these difficulties, Rahm Emanuel seemed almost joyful in taking up the reins. But what would the post-Daley era of Chicago politics look like? And importantly, was there any future for the clout of the traditional, communal political machine in an increasingly neoliberal environment?

On election day, *Chicago Tribune* writer Christopher Borrelli suggested that Emanuel could topple the stereotype of the Chicago politician. His candidacy promised that a trim, Jewish former ballet dancer might be mayor, ending years of legendary pot-bellied politicians and their cigar-chomping precinct captains.[2] The next morning, *Chicago Tribune* columnist John Kass—more cognizant of Emanuel's reputation as a ruthless, foul-mouthed political street fighter—dubbed the fifty-one-year-old mayor-elect "the Rahm-father" and the city's new boss.[3]

EMANUEL TAKES CONTROL

Emanuel prepared to take over City Hall with his usual enthusiasm and energy, despite the overwhelming array of deep-rooted problems, chief among them the city budget shortfalls. Labor costs, unfunded pensions, and rising debt stood at the forefront of concerns. Emanuel also faced a failing school system, crime, political corruption, an understaffed police department, and a rickety transportation system. A possible power struggle between Emanuel and the powerful head of the City Council Finance Committee, Alderman Ed Burke, seemed on the horizon. All of this clouded the new administration's prospects.[4]

Emanuel began his first day as mayor-elect by greeting commuters on the South Side at the 95th Street Red Line Station. The largely Black ridership expressed support, as they lined up to shake his hand, with at least one commuter giving him a hug. Emanuel clearly benefited from his relationship with hometown hero President Barack Obama, who heartily supported him. David Axelrod claimed Obama's endorsement had been critical for Emanuel, who received no support from traditional Black leadership in the city. As it turned out, Emanuel won Black wards across the city, demonstrating the president's influence. In addition, Emanuel had campaigned heavily in African American neighborhoods. He won an impressive 59 percent of the Black vote and carried every African American ward by a ratio of three to one over African American candidate Carol Moseley Braun. Emanuel also demonstrated his skills as a coalition builder, holding his own in Hispanic wards as the two Latino candidates, Gery Chico and Miguel del Valle, split the vote there. Emanuel secured support from the LGBTQ+ community as well as liberals and progressives. City-wide, Emanuel won forty of fifty wards.[5]

Immediately Emanuel faced a clash with the Chicago Teachers Union (CTU), an organization that would play an increasingly powerful role in the post-Daley years. He had been a strong supporter of charter schools, which the CTU opposed, and his plan to keep the school board under his control was anathema to the CTU and its membership. He moved to block a 4 percent pay raise for teachers and sought a longer school day and school year. He threatened to go to the state legislature to mandate them.[6]

Emanuel also faced a possible clash with the firefighters' and police unions, who had both backed Chico. Both groups feared that they might have to pay more into their pension funds under Emanuel. The mayor-elect had been the only candidate who did not rule out cutting pension benefits for city employees. The deputy director of the American Federation of State, County, and Municipal Employees Council 31, Roberta Lynch, said there was a good deal of unease among the rank and file. She promised that the union would not be anyone's doormat. Emanuel also said that the high absentee rate for workers in city departments was unacceptable. City workers had long made up a large part of the Democratic machine's support. Now they felt threatened by the neoliberal perspective of City Hall.[7]

Chicago's non-Black ethnic groups had mixed responses to Emanuel. Jewish Chicagoans, a group that had lost much of its historical clout, celebrated the election of one of their own. Conversely, the clout of Hispanics swelled as both their population numbers and voters increased across the city, but they had little to celebrate. In 1993, Al Sanchez, who headed Rich Daley's Streets and Sanitation Department, and Victor Reyes, Daley's political chief, founded the Hispanic Democratic Organization (HDO). By 2002, HDO could claim to have helped elect fifteen aldermen, twelve state representatives, and six state senators. By the election of Emanuel, however, the organization was defunct. In fact, Sanchez was sentenced to thirty months in prison shortly after the election for rigging hiring to reward political supporters and violating the Shakman decrees. Sanchez claimed he was only doing his job and trying to advance Latino Chicagoans. To any old-time communal Chicagoan, this explanation sounded familiar. Sanchez had acted like a traditional ethnic boss, but those days were over.[8]

On May 16, 2011, Rahm Emanuel was sworn in as the city's forty-sixth mayor in the Pritzker Pavilion in Millennium Park. Cardinal Francis George, along with Protestant, Jewish, and Muslim leaders, asked for God's help in solving the city's problems as once again the sacred and the profane harmonized, at least temporarily. Emanuel's inaugural speech tackled the budget deficit head-on. He told city workers, residents, and business owners to be prepared to sacrifice for the greater good. After spending his first day shaking hands and greeting well-wishers in the mayor's office, Emanuel put on his reformer's hat and signed six executive orders to strengthen the city's ethics rules, an effort to address the penchant for scandals.[9]

Emanuel reconfigured a corporate-dominated promotional group, World Business Chicago, into the city's economic think tank. His connections with the business community shaped his policies and eventually earned him the dubious title of "Mayor 1%." Like mayors before him, he focused on creating a business-friendly climate with the hope of luring new companies to Chicago. World Business Chicago reported that the high-tech sector, along with machinery and chemicals, grew under the Emanuel administration. His policies certainly attracted several corporations to Chicago, as did the city's growing contingent of young urban professionals. United Airlines expanded and extended its lease in Willis Tower (formerly Sears Tower) in 2012, providing a major coup for Emanuel. The Loop bustled with activity, even as the rest of the country slowly recovered from the Great Recession of 2008. Unfortunately, neighborhoods, especially on the South and West Sides, continued to suffer from deindustrialization and disinvestment.[10]

Emanuel soon found himself in conflict with the various labor unions that represented city workers. Unlike many of his predecessors, he had never been seen as a friend of organized labor, especially after the role he played in the passage of the North American Free Trade Agreement (NAFTA) during the Clinton Administration. NAFTA resulted in the elimination or reduction of trade barriers between the United States, Mexico, and Canada. Unions blamed it for the loss of industrial jobs in the United States, particularly to Mexico.[11]

Facing a huge budget deficit, Emanuel looked to cut spending. Since payroll was such a large part of the city's budget, he looked to slash labor costs. But about 90 percent of city workers belonged to organized labor. In late June 2011 Emanuel picked a fight with the unions, particularly in the trade unions that had traditionally supported Democratic mayors, such as those representing carpenters, plumbers, electricians, and others. Emanuel wanted them to agree to work rule changes; if they didn't, he said the city would lay off 625 workers. Union leaders resented this betrayal of the communal pact between labor and government and complained that Emanuel did not even negotiate. Ultimately, the unions and City Hall agreed on cost-saving work rule changes. Other workers faced more changes, especially those who picked up garbage and plowed streets, as Emanuel threatened to privatize recycling and garbage pickup.[12]

More skilled as a strategist than as a retail politician, Emanuel's public demeanor lacked warmth and friendliness. He had a tough-guy reputation, and many ordinary Chicagoans considered him aloof from their concerns. His continuing public relationship with business leaders contributed to this image. In many ways, the Emanuel administration ushered in the final victory of the profane over the sacred, of Loop power brokers over neighborhood people.

THE SACRED VS. THE PROFANE IN ENGLEWOOD

During the first Emanuel administration, Englewood residents clashed with the Norfolk Southern Railroad, which operated a major railyard in the largely Black South Side neighborhood. In 2013 the railroad wanted to expand its busy 140-acre intermodal yard, bounded by 47th Street on the north, Wallace Avenue to the west, Stewart Avenue to the east, and Garfield Boulevard to the south. Norfolk Southern representatives claimed that the expansion was vital to increasing the efficiency of operations and reducing congestion in Chicago's vast rail system. The railyard handled about 480,000 intermodal containers per year, and the company claimed it had not been able to keep up with demand. Rahm Emanuel wanted to sell 105 city-owned lots in the area to the railroad for $1,100,000. This would pave the way for a $285,000,000 expansion south of Garfield Boulevard, adding eighty-four acres. The company claimed that the ten-year project would create about 400 jobs and have an economic impact of $1.6 billion by 2030. Residents protested that the development would vastly increase toxic fumes in a neighborhood that already faced heavy pollution, as well as poverty, poor schools, disinvestment, and violence. Residents demanded a series of concessions to cut back on pollution from trucks, locomotives, and construction and freight-handling equipment, and they wanted the City Council to hold up the sale in the meantime. The railroad promised to meet with neighborhood groups and address their fears, and the city planned to move ahead with the sale of the vacant lots.

On March 25, 2011, the Norfolk Southern got the go-ahead to purchase the city lots, over the objections of Englewood residents and environmental groups. The company had already been buying and demolishing homes in the area. The City Council Housing and Real Estate Development Committee approved Emanuel's plan after the railroad promised to contribute $3,000,000 toward transportation improvements as well as thousands of dollars to area schools. It would also donate an abandoned rail spur to be developed as an elevated bicycle and walking trail. These promises did not satisfy residents.

Englewood's 20th Ward alderman, Willie Cochran, argued in favor of the railyard expansion, stating that it would strengthen the city as a national hub of rail and freight. Cochran cautioned that environmental concerns had to be put in perspective. A large number of his constituents disagreed. The Environmental Law and Policy Center, using a model provided by the US Environmental Protection Agency, determined that pollution from the additional diesel exhaust would exceed federal safety levels in an area bounded by 43rd and 63rd Streets on the north and south and by State and Halsted to the east and west. This area was, of course, long accustomed to pollution, but community activists had had enough. In August 2011, in a surprise move, the mayor's appointed Chicago Plan Commission sided with residents and delayed a vote on the financing that would support the expansion. But in September, the commission approved the plan. The Norfolk Southern did agree to take more aggressive steps to clean up diesel fumes, but it simply had more clout than Englewood residents.[13]

In 2015, the Norfolk Southern faced a new obstacle, when some residents refused to sell their property for the expansion. The homes sat surrounded by lots that had already been cleared. What had been vibrant blocks filled with homes now stood hollowed out. The railroad wanted to complete its purchase of more than 500 parcels of property, but Steven Rogers, Deborah Payne, and twenty other residents resisted. For Rogers, a Harvard Business School lecturer, his house represented the generational struggle of his family to climb into the middle class. By January 2016, however, only ten holdouts remained. More than 400 Black American families were displaced by the multi-billion-dollar freight company.

Under state regulations, railroads and public utilities could invoke eminent domain for projects deemed for public use. The Norfolk Southern decided to use that power and begin construction in February. Rogers continued to fight the railroad, but he, like his neighbors, had little success. They did, however, put up a long and protracted fight. It was not until February 2023 that the City Council agreed to vacate alleys and streets in the area for the expansion.[14] As with the construction of the University of Illinois at Chicago Circle, when neighborhood interests clashed with downtown interests, the neighborhood lost. The profane won and the sacred simply disappeared.

A SECOND EMANUEL ADMINISTRATION

In 2015 Emanuel ran for a second term. He seemed to be the heavy favorite over Jesús "Chuy" Garcia, his main opponent in the now nonpartisan primary. Despite his low favorability ratings, Emanuel was able to muster a long list of wealthy donors to his campaign. The *Chicago Tribune* claimed that his list of fundraisers was the most potent in Chicago history. The funders, in turn, benefited from the relationship with Emanuel, receiving lucrative city contracts, permits for numerous projects, zoning changes, pension work, board appointments, regulatory help, and endorsements by the mayor.

CHAPTER 12

Over a two-year period, Emanuel either appeared with or met privately with donors 376 times. Roughly 20 percent of Emanuel's business meetings with non-staff members involved a campaign donor. He had raised over $30,000,000 for his campaigns since 2010. The tradition of "pay to play" appeared to be as important as ever.[15]

Chicago Teachers Union President Karen Lewis, a prominent mayoral critic, emerged as a possible Emanuel rival. The CTU had been organizing more aggressively in the political arena, especially since the 2012 teachers' strike. They had also been energized in 2013 when Emanuel had controversially closed fifty neighborhood schools and community mental health centers. Unfortunately, Lewis was diagnosed with a malignant brain tumor in October 2014. She threw her support and the support of the CTU behind Garcia.

Emanuel's opponents claimed he was callous about street violence, which continued to plague many neighborhoods. Chicagoans disapproved of his handling of crime. Both Garcia and 2nd Ward Alderman Bob Fioretti, also a candidate, accused the mayor of failing to make good his pledge to hire 1,000 new police officers. The state of public schools and crime remained major problems for Emanuel.[16]

On February 5, 2015, the mayoral candidates faced off in a debate. Emanuel found himself under constant attack, but he responded calmly, noting that his first term saw no property, sales, or gas tax increases. His opponents—Garcia, Fioretti, businessman Willie Wilson, and community activist William "Dock" Walls—condemned Emanuel for his wealthy donors, public school closings, red light cameras, and other questionable sources of city revenue, but they seemed to gain little ground.[17]

Emanuel had agreed to five debates, which appeared to work in his favor. The debates revealed his opponents' flaws more than his own shortcomings. In the February 28 primary, Emanuel was not popular enough to take a majority of the votes, but the field was narrowed to a runoff with Garcia. That ended in an Emanuel victory with 56 percent of the vote. The forced runoff marked a significant turn. The Democratic establishment had backed the incumbent, but he had not closed the deal in the primary. Progressive unions and burgeoning grassroots organizations backed Garcia, while narratives around inequality in the city's economy and top-down governance seemed to resonate with many Chicagoans. And it turns out that the 2013 school closings drove many to the polls and to Garcia, with 63 percent of his voters saying public education was the most important issue to them and that Emanuel had been wrong on the school closings.[18]

The most significant challenge to Emanuel had already happened, but no one knew it. It lay, as it had all too often before, in the problem of police brutality. Back on October 20, 2014, just as Emanuel's second campaign had been ramping up, Chicago Police Officer Jason Van Dyke shot and killed a Black teenager, Laquan McDonald, on the Southwest Side. Officers had responded to a call about someone breaking into cars. The officers later alleged that the seventeen-year-old was armed with a knife and had threatened them. Witnesses claimed the boy was "shying away" from police and that an officer shot him several times while he lay wounded on the ground. The Civil Rights Accountability Project of the University of Chicago's Mandel Legal Aid Clinic, along with Invisible Institute—an investigative organization focused on public accountability—raised questions about the police account. The clinic was refused access to the police dashcam video of the incident. The Independent Police Review Authority continued to investigate the incident. *Chicago Sun-Times* columnist Mary Mitchell reported the story and called for the police to answer questions.

Shortly after Emanuel was reelected, the City Council was asked to authorize a $5,000,000 settlement of the case, even though McDonald's family had not filed a wrongful-death lawsuit. The city still refused to release the dashcam video, which continued to frustrate investigators, including the FBI.[19] In mid-April, Alderman Howard Brookins, the chairman of the City Council's Black caucus, demanded the tape's release in the name of justice. Another Black alderman, Carrie Austin, feared its release might lead to rioting. Jeffrey Neslund, an attorney, saw the video and described it to Mary Mitchell as an execution.

The standoff continued for months. By November 2015 reports circulated that Cook County State's Attorney Anita Alvarez planned to charge Officer Van Dyke with murder. Such a charge against an on-duty police officer would be historic. Jesse Jackson called for a complete shake-up of the police department and for Alvarez to step down as state's attorney for failing to charge the officer more quickly. Cook County Judge Franklin Valderrama then ordered the release of the videotape just before the Thanksgiving holiday. As five police dashcam recordings of the shooting were viewed across the city and the nation, protests broke out.[20]

The murder of McDonald by a policeman, the subsequent refusal of the city to release the videotape, and police reports that conflicted with the tape all hurt Emanuel politically. Despite widespread calls for his resignation, Emanuel let it be known that he planned to run for a third term and began to raise campaign funds. Soon a host of challengers emerged, and lacking a broad base of support, Emanuel changed his mind. The September 3, 2018, announcement came on the eve of Van Dyke's trial for murder, in which he would be found guilty.

Listed among Emanuel's many accomplishments were property development in the central city and attracting foreign investment and corporate headquarters to Chicago, resulting in the creation of 150,000 new downtown jobs. Manufacturing positions also grew. Private-sector employment jumped from just under 275,000 jobs to 339,441 between 2010 and 2018. Emanuel's policies also expanded technology training for industrial workers and created incubators for tech-oriented and digital manufacturing. Emanuel put the city's budget in better shape and improved public transportation. Yet critics argued that job growth did not benefit outlying, primarily Black and Hispanic neighborhoods.[21]

While the twin issues of street violence and police reform hung over Emanuel's administration, many other challenges and scandals contributed to his fall. He not only struggled to find consistent footing over the issues; he also governed with a perceived arrogance and elitism that left him woefully detached from sources of support in the neighborhoods. His decision to shutter schools and mental health centers haunted him and stimulated a grassroots resistance.

The Democratic Organization, which had stood by Emanuel,

faced catastrophe. Many party regulars had believed that Emanuel would build a strong and permanent organization, bolstered by donors with deep pockets, while energizing the city. Instead, chaos and a new but not improved type of politics had emerged. The neoliberal politics and policies of Mayor 1% were too far a cry from the communalism of traditional Democratic politics in Chicago.[22]

THE LAST GASP OF THE OLD MACHINE: BURKE AND MADIGAN

The fact that men and women do both good and evil is a basic tenet of the Catholic view of human nature. The history of the Chicago Democratic machine is full of examples of this principle. One might even say that all politics, but especially Chicago politics, is a prime example of the Catholic worldview. As the old power structure crumbled around them, both Michael J. Madigan and Edward M. Burke proved the continuing truth of this maxim. Madigan was the longest-serving leader of any legislative body in the history of the United States. Burke held the record as the longest-serving alderman in the history of Chicago. During their careers they both served their constituents well, passing laws that benefited the great majority of Chicagoans and the people of Illinois. They also, however, benefited financially, exercised a tremendous amount of power, instilled fear in their opponents and those who might have crossed them, and suffered from a kind of hubris. They abetted or looked away from corruption within their organizations. In the end, both saw their careers ended by federal indictments for corruption.[23] By 2023 their fall from power symbolized the true end of the communal machine, an institution that had done both good and evil in the city.

Their demise came as a result of their questionable and intertwined political and financial dealings, underscoring the conflicts of interest they faced. A federal probe into the relationship between the Commonwealth Edison Company and the state of Illinois soon expanded into a wide-ranging inquiry into the traditional workings of the machine. The investigation shed light on the long-standing "Chicago Way" of pay-to-play politics. In an attempt to get a lighter sentence for his own misdeeds, Alderman Danny Solis, a close Burke

CHAPTER 12

and Madigan ally, agreed to record his conversations with various politicians. Both Burke and Madigan became targets of the investigation. Federal agents tapped Burke's phone and listened to 9,447 calls over an eight-month period. They raided Burke's office on November 29, 2018, and seized files, computers, and thumb drives.[24]

One of the first strikes against Burke's organization came in January 2018, when Aron Ortiz challenged Burke's brother, State Representative Dan Burke, in the Democratic Party primary. Jesús "Chuy" Garcia introduced Ortiz, a twenty-six-year-old counselor at the Back of the Yards High School and a Chicago Teachers Union member, as one of three progressive Latino candidates he backed. Latinos, and especially Mexicans, increasingly made up the 14th Ward's population. Dan Burke had served in the state legislature for twenty-seven years and seemed assured another term. Few doubted that the powerful Burke organization would deliver on election day. Ortiz condemned Ed Burke's law firm, Klafter & Burke, for representing Donald Trump when he appealed the taxes on his downtown skyscraper. In a district where Trump was hugely unpopular, this emerged as a compelling issue. Ortiz defeated Dan Burke in the primary and took his seat in the State House.[25]

On March 7, 2018, Ed Burke appeared before a sold-out crowd at the City Club of Chicago to celebrate his fifty years in Chicago politics. Fran Spielman of the *Chicago Sun-Times* called Burke's tenure a "remarkable achievement" given his years as a leader of the Vrdolyak 29, several federal investigations, vast demographic changes to his once largely White ethnic ward, and prostate cancer. Former alderman and political scientist Dick Simpson offered a couched compliment: "He's evolved his positions over time and become somewhat more reform-minded.... He's changed, but he always kept his base." Critics complained of Burke's decision to represent dozens of clients, including Trump, who did business with the city while also serving as an alderman and the powerful chair of the Finance Committee. Although the seventy-four-year-old politician simply shrugged off the allegations, this practice of mingling legislative duties with his law practice would come to hurt him.

A progressive organizer and chief strategist for Ortiz's successful campaign, Clem Balanoff, predicted Burke's defeat in the next aldermanic election. Some suggested the alderman might consider retirement. Those who knew him well, however, knew that would not happen. Most also knew that Burke would eventually have to cede more power to his growing Latino constituency. Meanwhile, Chuy Garcia played his political cards shrewdly; in the same election that saw Ortiz's victory over Dan Burke, Garcia supported Michael Madigan, the long-term speaker of the Illinois House. In Chicago's Byzantine politics, the speaker and Garcia needed each other, and they helped each other. Not a single anti-Madigan candidate won that year. In April, Burke decided not to retire but to run again.[26] He won reelection.

Both Burke and Madigan ruled with an iron hand. Madigan wielded his power efficiently and stealthily. Burke commanded authority. They knew the ins and outs of their respective legislative bodies and their buried secrets. Burke's fifty-year tenure made him the dean of the council. His knowledge of the often unfathomable *Robert's Rules of Order* allowed him to control meetings. Both Madigan and Burke were feared in and out of their chambers, the result of years of power consolidation. An army of precinct captains and city employees vowed allegiance to both men. They seemed impregnable behind their extensive political machines. But as history has proven time and time again, hubris often leads to a downfall.

In 2019, the federal government charged Burke and two co-defendants, his aide Peter Andrews and developer Charles Cui, on nineteen criminal counts. The case revealed the blurring of lines between aldermanic responsibilities and private gain. After a lengthy trial in 2023, a jury found Burke guilty on thirteen of fourteen charges of racketeering, bribery, and extortion. Cui was convicted on five counts, including federal bribery, using interstate commerce to facilitate an unlawful activity, and making a false statement to the FBI. (The jury found Andrews not guilty on all charges.) Burke, a 1961 graduate of Quigley Preparatory Seminary, stood just a week shy of his eightieth birthday, facing the possibility of spending the rest of his life in jail. Sentencing was set for June 2024. He was sentenced to two years in prison and fined $2 million.[27]

CHAPTER 12

Michael Madigan, often known as the "Velvet Hammer" for the manner in which he called the State House to order, was not only speaker of the House but chairman of the Democratic Party of Illinois. He could make or break legislation and often clashed with both Republican and Democratic governors; some thought he had more power than any governor. Madigan was well known for his work ethic, intense focus, and political judgment. He protected Chicago's interests in a state where suburban and downstate Republicans and some Democrats were eager to strip the city of power and autonomy. The Velvet Hammer also seemed unbeatable. Madigan seemed to reach his apex of power in the fall of 2018 when J. B. Pritzker won the governorship and Madigan gained a supermajority in the Illinois House.[28]

Madigan had honed his approach toward patronage under the elder Daley, whom he considered his mentor. His 13th Ward Democratic Organization fit the model of the communal machine. This was especially true regarding patronage and private businesses. Like Burke, Madigan made money through his law practice, which specialized in fighting property tax assessments. His powerful position automatically attracted clients to his law firm, Madigan & Getzendanner. He also had a close relationship with his fellow Democrat and Cook County Assessor Joe Berrios, who also chaired the Cook County Democratic Organization. The web of influence proved advantageous to Madigan and his clients. He once claimed he could make $1,000,000 in a particularly good year from his tax business.

In October 2017, in light of the #MeToo Movement social media campaign that raised awareness about sexual harassment, more than 200 women had signed a letter that called for challenging every elected official, every candidate, and every participant in the political process who was culpable. Various accusations of sexual harassment in the Illinois legislature arose. Madigan and Senate President John Cullerton tried to react quickly to the accusations. Madigan introduced a bill that would require sexual harassment training for legislators and staff. Cullerton said that lawmakers would be required to take sexual harassment training.[29]

The first crack in Madigan's organization came that November. In a letter to Madigan, campaign staffer Alaina Hampton accused a 13th Ward staff member, Kevin Quinn—the brother of Madigan's handpicked alderman, Marty Quinn—of sexual harassment. Madigan did not publicly address the issue until February 2018, when Hampton took her complaint to the *Chicago Tribune*. He then fired Kevin Quinn. Picking up on the issue, some called for Madigan to resign as chair of the Illinois State Democratic Party. In fact, Madigan was reelected for a record-setting sixth term as chairman in April. But the sexual harassment scandal involving Madigan's staff was the beginning of a very difficult few years for him.[30]

Madigan had a long-standing friendship with state representative-turned-lobbyist Michael McClain. They had forged their relationship as young lawmakers in the 1970s and 1980s. However, reforms pushed by Democratic maverick and reformer Pat Quinn, a future governor, resulted in the elimination of cumulative voting in 1981. The cumulative voting system had led to the rise of Anton Cermak, Richard J. Daley, and countless other working-class ethnic politicians. Its abolition resulted in the immediate downsizing of the Illinois State House from 177 members to 118. As a result, McClain lost his seat. He returned to Springfield as a lobbyist, and his connections with Madigan made him invaluable. The Commonwealth Edison Company and its parent firm, Exelon, became one of McClain's most important clients. McClain steered lucrative changes in state law that benefited the electric utility giant.[31]

Then, in early 2019, reports surfaced that Madigan was the target of a federal investigation that used Danny Solis as a mole. This had resulted from investigation of a developer who wanted to build a hotel in Chinatown. While Madigan denied any wrongdoing in the hotel development plan and was not initially charged, it soon became apparent that the investigation that had ensnared Burke was larger than initially revealed.[32] In the summer of 2019, federal authorities raided the homes of three of Madigan's longtime associates: McClain, Kevin Quinn, and former Alderman Mike Zalewski. The fall of the House of Madigan had begun. Quinn, of course, had been nominally let go from Madigan's organization because of the sexual harassment scandal. McClain and other lobbyists sent checks to the disgraced

Quinn in September 2018 to help him after his dismissal. Behind-the-scenes efforts to get a job for Zalewski with Commonwealth Edison ensued. A federal jury also subpoenaed Commonwealth Edison regarding its lobbying policies.[33]

Like Burke, Madigan's fall from grace was quick and steep. His connection with McClain and Commonwealth Edison brought to light the relationship between powerful machine politicians and private enterprise. Chicago politicians had long cultivated connections with the private sector, but now the courts and the media exposed the depths of this patronage treasure chest. They also revealed the extensive relationships Madigan had with other politicians in his vast clout network. As Madigan's legal bills grew, donations flowed from other politicians into Madigan's two political committees. From January to July 2019, Madigan spent $453,608 in campaign funds for his legal expenses. Yet since the beginning of July his allies, including labor unions, contributed three-quarters of a million dollars to the Friends of Michael Madigan and the Thirteenth Ward Democratic Organization. State Representative Ann Moeller and others donated the maximum allowed, $57,800, from their own campaign funds. Moeller explained that although she did not ask what the money was for, she regarded it as a regular election-cycle request from the powerful party chair.[34]

In 2020 and over the next few years, the Commonwealth Edison scandal, and the role of Madigan's organization in it, dominated the headlines and the courtrooms. In July 2020, Commonwealth Edison admitted to a multi-year scheme to influence Madigan by giving jobs, contracts, and money to his associates while the company lobbied for legislation. Court documents referred to "Public Official A," and it was obvious that Madigan's indictment was imminent. The government subpoenaed Madigan's office and his political allies. Then, in September, a former Commonwealth Edison vice president who oversaw lobbying pleaded guilty to bribery. Eventually, three top Com Ed executives and McClain were indicted, and in May 2023 they were found guilty. Accustomed to playing offense, the most powerful politician in the state was now on the defensive.

Madigan, still hauling in campaign donations, represented a growing problem for his party. Following the November 2020 election, pressure had already begun to mount on Madigan to step down as party chair. Leading Democrats blamed the swirl of corruption around him for the failure of a progressive tax amendment and the loss of key races. Governor J. B. Pritzker called for Madigan to step down as party chair, as did both of Illinois's US senators, Dick Durbin and Tammy Duckworth. Furthermore, Duckworth demanded that Madigan give up the speakership. When the new legislative session opened in January 2021, three female legislators challenged Madigan for the speakership. Despite backing from the Black caucus, who expected his support for legislative and districting initiatives, Madigan failed to secure the necessary votes, suspended his campaign, and waited for the dust to settle in the hopes of prevailing. But when the dust did settle, the longest-serving legislative leader in the nation had fallen. On January 13, 2021, Emanuel Christopher Welch replaced Madigan as speaker of the House. Soon after, Madigan resigned both the chairmanship of the state Democratic Party and his office as a state representative.[35]

A disciplined operator, long directing a well-oiled machine, Madigan ended up with a rusted-out remnant. Tim Mapes, his longtime confidant and chief of staff, was indicted and convicted of lying to protect his boss. In April 2022, federal prosecutors charged Madigan in an exhaustive bribery and racketeering case, set for trial in 2024. The indictment targeted the "Madigan Enterprise," described as a criminal operation to preserve Madigan's power, financially reward his allies, and generate income for Madigan and others. Corruption had finally overwhelmed the last vestiges of the old communal machine, as Madigan's corporate relationships had demolished whatever base he still had in the neighborhood.[36]

A PROGRESSIVE INTERLUDE:
THE LIGHTFOOT AND JOHNSON ADMINISTRATIONS

Even before Emanuel announced that he would not seek a third term, ex–Chicago Public Schools CEO Paul Vallas, past head of the Police Board and former assistant US attorney Lori Lightfoot, and urban planner and attorney Amara Eniya announced that they would challenge the mayor. Once Emanuel declared his intentions in September 2018, several more candidates emerged, including Cook County Board President Toni Preckwinkle, State Comptroller Susana Mendoza, Gery Chico, and Bill Daley. Eventually, an astonishing twenty-one mayoral candidates entered the fray. In December 2018, the FBI raid of Ed Burke's offices upended the field. The criminal complaint against Burke included an attempt to direct a $10,000 donation to Preckwinkle's campaign, which hurt her. Lightfoot's campaign highlighted the ties between several of the candidates, especially Preckwinkle, Mendoza, Chico, and Daley, and allegedly corrupt public officials. Her candidacy took on an anti-machine air. Preckwinkle then challenged all the petitions of her African American and Latino opponents, but not those of White candidates, thereby antagonizing the African American community.

Election day brought an upset as Lightfoot led the field with 17.5 percent of the vote. Preckwinkle came in second with 16 percent. Bill Daley—perhaps the last scion of the last machine—came in third. This set the stage for an April 2019 runoff election between the two African American candidates, both of whom emphasized their progressive reputations. Her relationship with Burke continued to haunt Preckwinkle's campaign, while Lightfoot, a political novice, collected a wave of endorsements. In the general election, Lightfoot won an overwhelming 74 percent of the vote and all fifty wards. A massive change in the City Council also took place, as reformers seemed to rule the day.[37]

Even before her inauguration, the CTU, which had backed Preckwinkle, sent a warning message to the mayor-elect to settle the teachers' contract quickly. Also, CTU teachers at five privately run charter schools planned to strike on May 1, along with more than 400 school clerical and technical workers. Like her predecessor Rahm Emanuel, Lightfoot faced labor problems, budget issues, and a rise in shootings and murders. Also, as an inexperienced politician, Lightfoot faced a wary City Council. Her trip to Washington, DC, after the election brought aldermanic criticism. One veteran council member said, "She should have been here spending more time reaching out to aldermen." The fifty aldermen did not have a clear read on Lightfoot, including how she planned to interact with the council or handle chairmanships. Lightfoot declared that her overwhelming victory demonstrated that the public wanted change.[38]

On May 20, 2019, Lori Lightfoot was sworn in as the city's first Black woman mayor and its first openly gay mayor. Joining her were twelve new aldermen. Having campaigned on an anti-corruption platform, Lightfoot warned City Council members during her inaugural speech that she intended to put an end to "shady back room deals." She promised to challenge the tradition of aldermanic prerogative that had given councilmen sovereignty in their wards. Under the old regime, Richard J. Daley had been able to control aldermen because he wielded tens of thousands of patronage jobs. After the Shakman decrees, mayors found it easier to gain aldermanic loyalty by allowing them to have control over their own wards, almost making them mini-mayors. Lightfoot threatened to divest aldermen of that privilege, fulfilling a promise to her better-government supporters. Most aldermen, at least publicly, agreed with the new mayor, although grumbling could be heard.[39]

In her first act as mayor, Lightfoot signed an executive order that curtailed aldermen's power to have the final say over building and other permits, business licenses, and zoning in their wards. Lightfoot's order targeted the pay-to-play tradition that had led to Burke's indictment. It also struck at the heart of the old communal machine, with its intricate network of connections, relationships, handshakes, and reciprocity. Lightfoot claimed that aldermen would still have a good deal of control over their wards in order to provide constituent services, but she intended to end their unchecked prerogative: "Aldermen will have a voice, but not a veto." Now it remained to be seen how much reform the new mayor could accomplish and how much of the progressive agenda she would support.[40]

According to the political scientists Marco Rossi and Dick Simpson (the latter a former alderman), two key coalitions supported the Lightfoot campaign and hoped to bring about change in city government. One coalition consisted of good-government reformers eager to dismantle what was left of the old Democratic machine. This group was committed to robust ethics reform. The other coalition encompassed progressives who hope to encourage focus on neighborhood development. They hoped to resuscitate Harold Washington's priorities and wanted to see a revival of outlying communities, especially on the South and West Sides. Although many saw these coalitions as compatible, in practice fulfilling both sets of goals would be difficult for someone new to the way the city worked. While Lightfoot pleased many of her good-government supporters with her early ethics reforms, it became more difficult to hold the progressive coalition together. Rossi and Simpson suggest that this was due largely to Lightfoot's view of mayoral control. Her heavy-handed exercise of political power could be effective in curbing clouted aldermen, but it ran counter to the progressive goal of participatory democracy.[41]

Furthermore, the COVID-19 pandemic, the nationwide racial reckoning following the murder of George Floyd, and Chicago's rising murder and crime rates hampered the Lightfoot administration. Despite some early support during the initial months of the pandemic, she proved to be unpopular with large segments of the population. Importantly, she alienated many in the City Council who, perhaps unfairly, considered her too combative. Even her efforts at government reform faltered, as evidenced by her increasingly frosty relationship with the inspector general. As the next election approached, her opponents criticized the manner in which she ran her signature program investing in South and West Side Black and Brown neighborhoods, but also promised to increase those investments, thereby taking away one of her major campaign issues. When voters went to the polls on February 28, 2023, they rebelled against the incumbent. Lightfoot finished third behind Paul Vallas and Brandon Johnson, a Cook County commissioner relatively unknown in Chicago politics. Since neither had captured 50 percent of the vote, a runoff election followed. Vallas attracted support from the business community and hoped to dominate both the White and Latino wards. Most considered him the frontrunner.[42]

On April 4, 2023, Cook County Commissioner and Chicago Teachers Union (CTU) organizer Brandon Johnson won election as mayor. Johnson, a leftist candidate, received overwhelming support

After the Daleys

not only from the CTU but from the Service Employees International Union (SEIU) Locals 1 and 73, and the American Federation of State, County, and Municipal Employees (AFSCME) Council 31. These unions provided an army of highly motivated volunteers who flooded the wards his campaign felt he had a chance to win. Launching a massive "get out the vote" effort, these union representatives replaced the army of precinct captains and patronage workers that had traditionally delivered votes for the old communal machine. Paul Vallas did have the backing of more conservative trade unions like the plumbers and electricians, but his organization paled before the unions that supported Johnson. Johnson won all of the African American wards and many liberal lakefront wards, and basically split the Latino vote with Vallas. Young people rallied behind the commissioner: at least 6,000 more Gen Z and younger millennial voters turned out for the runoff election than had voted in the earlier contest. Many older voters stayed home, diminishing Vallas's numbers. Considering the sharp ideological differences between the two candidates, citywide voter turnout was moderate. Latino turnout disappointed both camps.[43]

In the immediate aftermath of the upset, some observers referred to the CTU as the new machine. This of course raises the perennial question of how to define "machine." If it simply means an organized political operation, then maybe the new labor alliance, if it lasts, could be termed a machine. My definition of that label embodies other essential characteristics, including sustainability over the long term as well as cultural and social coherence.

While Johnson might not head a machine, his victory introduced a structure that suddenly dominated the city's politics. He received the support of Cook County Board President Toni Preckwinkle, who was also chair of the Cook County Democratic Party. She has managed to move the influential county apparatus in a more progressive direction, though she also maintains alliances with some former members of the Rich Daley and Rahm Emanuel administrations. If Preckwinkle's organization can maintain support for Johnson's administration, and combine it with continued progressive union support, then a new machine based on social class and progressive policies is a possibility. Political pundits might point to the rocky first year of Johnson's administration to suggest that the new CTU-centered operation is not comparable to the traditional communal Democratic machine, but history will be the better judge.[44]

CONCLUSION: THE END OF THE COMMUNAL MACHINE

Mayor Richard J. Daley said that good government was good politics. He understood that when elected officials deliver for their constituents—services, jobs, mutual aid, community support, and so on—those people will give their votes in return. As long as the neighborhoods and the political machine maintained the social contract forged over the years, the clout-driven system worked in a mutually beneficial manner. Communal relations, often grounded in cultural affinities, governed local politics; cultivated over long periods of time, the relationships sustained political success. Corruption fueled by hubris, however, frequently poisoned this relationship. Another constant threat was the tug of war between the sacred and the profane, between the communal neighborhood based on local relationships and the downtown corporate city center with its monied interests. In that contest, neighborhoods often came out on the short end, though as long as residents enjoyed the benefits of the machine through patronage and favors, they did not revolt. When the relationship became too strained and inequitable, revolt did take place, such as on the Near West Side in the early 1960s or in the more recent struggle between Englewood residents and the Norfolk Southern Railroad. In both cases, the communal neighborhood lost.

Especially in the years after Daley's death in 1976, the communal neighborhood continued to struggle. Both Richard M. Daley's and Rahm Emanuel's focus on downtown meant that neighborhoods felt neglected. Emanuel's school closures devastated Black and Brown neighborhoods. Even if a profane economic rationale for downsizing the school system made sense to some, the wrenching of neighborhood fabric was sinful to others. Similarly, Emanuel's handling of the McDonald murder ruptured trust with the Black community, while his aggressive neoliberal decisions rallied broad opposition to him.

Lightfoot failed to maintain the coalition of progressives and good-government reformers that had swept her into power in the wake of the investigations into Ed Burke's organization. At the same time, the indictment of Burke and Michael Madigan, as well as some of their close allies, signaled something profoundly flawed in the old communal machine and the neighborhood-based exercise of clout. If the traditional Chicago political machine had its roots in the aspirations of groups who had been on the outside of establishment Chicago politics—immigrants, ethnics, African Americans, working people, Catholics, Jews—then the corrupt weaknesses of the machine's modern leaders heralded an abandonment of local communalism in favor of a more corporate goal.

Brandon Johnson faces the challenge of not only articulating but also implementing a compelling ideology to hold his coalition of progressives and unions together. In the first year of his administration, complaints surfaced about Johnson's inexperience and his administration's lack of transparency. Longtime *Chicago Tribune* political columnist Laura Washington wrote, "nearly eight months in, Johnson has not established himself as a leader of a viable coalition that can govern." Like Lightfoot who faced the COVID-19 pandemic, Johnson faced an unexpected crisis for which the city was ill prepared: migrants who crossed the southern border of the United States have been sent by the busload to Chicago and other Democratic-run cities by Republican Texas Governor Greg Abbott. The administration looked inept handling the emergency, failing to collaborate with neighborhood groups and alderpersons to plan shelters for the newcomers or spending millions on flawed contracts for "winterized base camps." The lack of transparency hurt the new mayor. Also, Johnson clashed with Governor Pritzker over the issue, revealing little kinship between the two Democrats. On the eve of Johnson's first anniversary as mayor, a *Chicago Sun-Times* editorial exhorted the mayor to work for "more successes and fewer blunders."[45]

The old foundations of the machine's power have continued to disappear. Working-class and middle-class White ethnics continue to leave the city, as now African Americans do as well. Patronage continues to decline as a source of power for politicians. The once highly sought position of Democratic Party ward committeeman now seems to be a hollow prize. Committeemen no longer wield the power they once did, and the Democratic Party finds it increasingly difficult to fill the position. Most Chicagoans do not even know what a committeeman does, according to a 2024 *Block Club Chicago* report.[46] The establishment of the 311 telephone system, and its web portal counterpart, further decreased their dependence on aldermen and the Regular Democratic Organization. The communal machine, based on local working-class interests and often held together by neighborhood places of worship and sociability, has disappeared.

Chicago is no longer a city dependent on its industrial might. Today it is a global city transformed by vast economic, cultural, and demographic shifts. The old communal machine, often too tribal, could not adjust to these changes. Weakened by the forces of change, it fell under the weight of corruption. In tracing the historical rise and fall of the Chicago political machine, I have argued that the historical context, especially potent from 1930 to 1970, is the defining force shaping the rise and fall of this fabled institution. The communal Chicago machine should not be conflated with a generic political operation, nor with any future machine that might arise from a new historical context. Has clout disappeared from Chicago politics? Hardly. Neither has the struggle between the sacred and the profane, between neighborhood and downtown business interests. Who exercises clout? How is it exercised? On whose behalf? And how effectively? A future history of Chicago politics will tell that story.

Acknowledgments

Many historians, sociologists, and urbanists have helped to shape this book. I am most grateful for the outstanding work of my former graduate school officemate and friend, Roger Biles, on the biographies of several Chicago mayors. His work has not only informed me but also inspired my approach to understanding "clout" in its Chicago version. The late Perry Duis, Paul Barrett, Arnold Hirsch, Raymond Mohl, and Peter McLennon have also influenced this book through years of conversation and friendship. It is to them that this book is dedicated. Dennis McClendon provided his usual meticulous cartography work and furnished the maps. He passed away just as this manuscript entered its final preparation. This study draws upon the work of the late sociologist Andrew Greeley and the historian Garry Wills, whose studies of American Catholicism helped me to better understand the impact of late twentieth-century reforms on the Catholic Church and society.

Peter McLennon, Charles Shanabruch, Michael O'Keeffe, and Ellen Skerrett read parts of this manuscript and offered suggestions and much-needed corrections. Skerrett also suggested photographs, including one of the 1924 graduating class of De La Salle Institute that featured her father. Iris Cochran and David Terry of De La Salle Institute provided photographs. Daniel Pogorzelski gave advice and suggested sources. Mark Dobrzycki offered his photographs as well as his encouragement. Ted Karamanski, Eileen McMahon, Ann Durkin

Keating, and Nelson Hathcock cheered me on during the usual trying times of writing a book.

I would especially like to thank Daniel Harper and his colleagues in the Special Collections Department of the University of Illinois Chicago. Ellen Keith and Lesley Martin of the Chicago History Museum also aided this project, as did the special collection staffs of both the Newberry Library and Loyola University. Vice Provost for Global Engagement Neal McCrillis, Professor Robert D. Johnston, and History Department Chair Kevin M. Schultz of the University of Illinois Chicago nominated and welcomed me as an affiliated faculty member. Their critical support facilitated my research, especially during the COVID pandemic restrictions. Hannah Landsman, Graduate Program & Human Resources Coordinator in the UIC History Department, helped me to jump various bureaucratic hurdles.

Tim Mennel and Alan Thomas of the University of Chicago Press have not only encouraged my work but also proven their friendship time and time again. Mennel, in particular, guided this project with a steady and patient hand and edited the final manuscript. I am grateful to him for balancing his constructive criticisms with unwavering support. I am also indebted to the anonymous peer reviewers, whose critiques greatly improved the final manuscript. Andrea Blatz skillfully shepherded the manuscript to publication. Elizabeth Ellingboe oversaw the copyediting of this manuscript. Evan Young copyedited the final version. June Sawyers provided the index and corrected several mistakes.

I want to thank my spouse and best friend, Kathleen Alaimo, a fine historian in her own right, who also edited *Clout City*. Over the last forty-five years she has always encouraged and made possible my work. My two children, Johanna and Beatrice, both successful women, have always listened to my stories and cautioned me when I became too enthusiastic. I am grateful to them as well. Finally, I alone am responsible for this manuscript and for any errors or misinterpretations. This has been a long journey of exploration and fascination with a city I call my own.

Abbreviations

CFLPS	Chicago Foreign Language Press Survey
CHHNL	Carter H. Harrison IV papers, Newberry Library
DROSLUC	Dan Rostenkowski Papers, Loyola University Chicago Archives and Special Collections
MABIUIC	Michael A. Bilandic Collection in Special Collections at the University of Illinois at Chicago
MHKUIC	Martin H. Kennelly Collection, Special Collections at the University of Illinois at Chicago
PADOCHM	Polish American Democratic Organization Collection, Chicago History Museum
PUCCHM	Roman C. Pucinski Papers, Chicago History Museum
RJDORALUIC	Richard J. Daley Oral History Collection, University of Illinois at Chicago
RJDUIC	Richard J. Daley Collection, Special Collections at the University of Illinois at Chicago
RMDORALUIC	Richard M. Daley Oral History collection, University of Illinois at Chicago
RMDUIC	Richard M. Daley Collection, University of Illinois at Chicago

Notes

INTRODUCTION

1. Richard J. Daley Quotes, BrainyQuote.com, BrainyMedia Inc., https://www.brainyquote.com/quotes/richard_j_daley_134298, accessed April 3, 2023.
2. *Chicago Tribune*, March 1, 2023; Sarah Schulte, "After Brandon Johnson Elected Mayor, Some Wonder if the CTU Is Chicago's New Political Machine," ABC7 Eyewitness News, April 5, 2023, https://abc7chicago.com/chicago-election-brandon-johnson-teachers-union-political-machine/13091274/.
3. Bessie Louise Pierce, *A History of Chicago*, vol. 3, *The Rise of a Modern City* (Chicago: University of Chicago Press, 1957), chapter 9.
4. For an interesting take on the cumulative voting system, see Robin Tholin, "'One Person, Three Votes': Illinois' 110-Year Experiment with Cumulative Voting," BA thesis, Departmental Honors from the College of Social Studies, Wesleyan University, April 2012, https://digitalcollections.wesleyan.edu/object/ir-514.
5. Interview with Daniel Pogorzelski, May 25, 2020.
6. Garry Wills, *Bare, Ruined Choirs: Doubt, Prophecy and Radical Religion* (Mahwah, NJ: Paulist Press, 1971), is one of the best sources for the trials and tribulations of the Catholic Church both pre– and post–Vatican Council II.
7. Christian Brothers, *Elements of Practical Pedagogy by the Brothers of the Christian Schools* (New York: La Salle Bureau of Supplies, 1905), 1–3.
8. Douglas Bukowski, *Big Bill Thompson, Chicago, and the Politics of Image* (Urbana: University of Illinois Press, 1998); Lloyd Wendt and Herman Kogan, *Big Bill of Chicago* (Indianapolis and New York: Bobbs-Merrill, 1953).

9 Alex Gottfried, *Boss Cermak of Chicago: A Study of Political Leadership* (Seattle: University of Washington Press, 1962).

10 Roger Biles, *Big City Boss in Depression and War: Edward J. Kelly of Chicago* (DeKalb: Northern Illinois University Press, 1984); Peter Joseph O'Malley, "Mayor Martin H. Kennelly: A Political Biography," PhD thesis, University of Illinois at Chicago Circle, 1980.

11 Roger Biles, *Richard J. Daley: Politics, Race, and the Governing of Chicago* (DeKalb: Northern Illinois University Press, 1995); Adam Cohen and Elizabeth Taylor, *American Pharaoh, Mayor Richard J. Daley: His Battle for Chicago and the Nation* (New York: Back Bay Books, 2000); Mike Royko, *Boss: Richard J. Daley of Chicago* (New York: Signet, 1971).

12 James L. Merriner, *Grafters and Goo Goos: Corruption and Reform in Chicago, 1833–2003* (Carbondale: Southern Illinois University Press, 2003); Thomas M. Guterbock, *Machine Politics in Transition: Party and Community in Chicago* (Chicago: University of Chicago Press, 1980); Dick Simpson, *Rogues, Rebels, and Rubber Stamps: The Politics of the Chicago City Council from 1863 to the Present* (New York: Perseus Books, 2001).

13 Biles, *Richard J. Daley*, 222.

14 Roger Biles, *Mayor Harold Washington: Champion of Race and Reform in Chicago* (Urbana: University of Illinois Press, 2018); Gary Rivlin, *Fire on the Prairie: Chicago's Harold Washington and the Politics of Race* (New York: Henry Holt, 1992); Paul Kleppner, *Chicago Divided: The Making of a Black Mayor* (DeKalb: Northern Illinois University Press, 1985).

15 Keith Koeneman, *First Son: The Biography of Richard M. Daley* (Chicago: University of Chicago Press, 2013).

16 Wilfredo Cruz, *Latinos in Chicago: Quest for a Political Voice* (Carbondale: Southern Illinois University Press, 2022); Lilia Fernandez, *Brown in the Windy City: Mexicans and Puerto Ricans in Postwar Chicago* (Chicago: University of Chicago Press, 2012); Gina M. Pérez, *The Near Northwest Side Story: Migration, Displacement, and Puerto Rican Families* (Berkeley: University of California Press, 2004); Timothy Stewart-Winter, *Queer Clout: Chicago and the Rise of Gay Politics* (Philadelphia: University of Pennsylvania Press, 2016).

17 Kari Lydersen, *Mayor 1%: Rahm Emanuel and the Rise of Chicago's 99%* (Chicago: University of Chicago Press, 2013), chapter 7.

18 *Chicago Tribune*, March 28, 2023; *Chicago Sun-Times*, February 1, 2020, March 8, 2023, April 6, 2023, April 10, 2023; Greg Hinz, "The Case Against Ed Burke: Here's What the Feds Say He Did," *Crain's Chicago Business*, May 30, 2019, https://www.chicagobusiness.com/greg-hinz-politics/case-against-ed-burke-heres-what-feds-say-he-did. For a look at Madigan and his organization, see Ray Long, *The House That Madigan Built: The Record Run of Illinois' Velvet Hammer* (Urbana: University of Illinois Press, 2022).

Notes to Pages 19–30

CHAPTER 1

1. Quoted in Richard C. Lindberg, *Quotable Chicago* (Chicago: Wild Onion Books, 1996), 10.
2. Donald Miller, *City of the Century: The Epic of Chicago and the Making of America* (New York: Simon & Schuster, 1996), 161–62; Karen Sawislak, *Smoldering City: Chicagoans and the Great Fire, 1871–1874* (Chicago: University of Chicago Press, 1995), 46–48, 29; Carl Smith, *Urban Disorder and the Shape of Belief: The Great Chicago Fire, the Haymarket Bomb, and the Model Town of Pullman* (Chicago: University of Chicago Press, 1995), 19, 22, 47.
3. Bessie Louise Pierce, *A History of Chicago*, vol. 3, *The Rise of the Modern City* (Chicago: University of Chicago Press, 1957), 300–301.
4. Ann Durkin Keating, *The World of Juliette Kinzie: Chicago Before the Fire* (Chicago: University of Chicago Press, 2019), 79–82, 90–91, 157–64.
5. Pierce, *History of Chicago: The Rise of the Modern City*, chapter 9; Keating, *Juliette Kinzie*, 144–45.
6. Robin Tholin, "'One Person, Three Votes;' Illinois' 110-Year Experiment with Cumulative Voting," BA thesis, Departmental Honors from the College of Social Studies, Wesleyan University, April 2012, 14, 70–71, https://digital collections.wesleyan.edu/object/ir-514.
7. *Fulton* (MO) *Sun*, April 27, 1897, in CHHNL, Clippings, Volume One, 1852–1897.
8. Claudius O. Johnson, *Carter Henry Harrison I: Political Leader* (Chicago: University of Chicago Press, 1928), 3–4, 13–21; Willis John Abbot, *Carter Henry Harrison: A Memoir* (New York: Dodd, Mead & Co., 1895), 41.
9. Abbot, *Carter Henry Harrison*, 40–48.
10. Quoted in Abbot, 49.
11. Abbot, 55–69; Johnson, *Carter Henry Harrison I*, 65; Adolph Kraus, *Reminiscences and Comments: The Immigrant, the Citizen, a Public Office, the Jew* (Chicago: Toby Rubovits, Inc., 1925), 22–23, 47; Abbot, *Carter Henry Harrison*, 81.
12. *Chicago Tribune*, February 9, March 9, March 10, March 16, March 23, 1879; Abbot, *Carter Henry Harrison*, 93–95, Johnson, *Carter Henry Harrison I*, 69, 138; Richard C. Lindberg, *The Gambler King of Clark Street: Michael C. McDonald and the Rise of Chicago's Democratic Machine* (Carbondale: Southern Illinois University Press, 2009), 3.
13. Kraus, *Reminiscences and Comments*, 29–30, 49.
14. Johnson, *Carter Henry Harrison I*, 66, 99, 149; *Chicago Tribune*, April 10, 1879.
15. *Chicago Tribune*, January 11, January 27, 1882.
16. Lindberg, *The Gambler King*, 3–5; Perry Duis, *The Saloon: Public Drinking in Chicago and Boston, 1880–1920* (Urbana: University of Illinois Press, 1983),

10, 28–29, 63–64; "Hannah & Hogg," Rogers Park and West Ridge Historical Society, https://rpwrhs.org/w/index.php?title=Hannah_%26_Hogg, accessed April 17, 2020; "Chapin and Gore: Kings of the Chicago Saloon," Those Pre-Pro Whiskey Men (blog), July 9, 2013, http://pre-prowhiskeymen.blogspot.com/2013/07/chapin-and-gore-kings-of-chicago-saloon.html; *Chicago Tribune*, July 13, 1879.

17 Letter to Major Clifton P. Williamson from Carter H. Harrison IV, n.d., Series 7: Writings, S, Box 15, Folder 715, CHHNL.

18 *Chicago Tribune*, May 25 and May 30, 1882; *Illinois Staats-Zeitung*, July 15, 1881.

19 *Chicago Tribune*, April 1, 1881; Harrison quoted in Johnson, *Carter Henry Harrison I*, 202–3.

20 *Chicago Tribune*, November 6, 1876, July 5, 1879; *Illinois Staats-Zeitung*, March 27, July 7, December 24, 1879; *Dir Westen*, April 3, 1881, CFLPS.

21 *Die Fackel*, June 22, 1879; *Chicagoer Arbeiter Zeitung*, August 30, 1880; *Illinois Staats-Zeitung*, August 26, 1879, July 2, 1881, CFLPS.

22 *Svornost*, March 26, 1883, CFLPS.

23 *Chicago Tribune*, September 7, October 26, 1882.

24 Abbot, *Carter Henry Harrison*, 122–25.

25 *Chicago Tribune*, December 6, 1883; Richard Lindberg, *Chicago by Gaslight: A History of Chicago's Netherworld, 1880–1920* (Chicago: Academy Chicago Publishers, 1996), 53, 66; Duis, *The Saloon*, 52, 126; Johnson, *Carter Henry Harrison I*, 42; Lindberg, *The Gambler King*, 103–4, 115–27.

26 Abbot, *Carter Henry Harrison*, 140–43, 242; Johnson, *Carter Henry Harrison I*, 182–85; Richard Schneirov, *Labor and Urban Politics: Class Conflict and the Origins of Modern Liberalism in Chicago, 1864–1897* (Urbana: University of Illinois Press, 1998), 168–73; Dominic A. Pacyga, *Chicago: A Biography* (Chicago: University of Chicago Press, 2009), 90–99.

27 Johnson, *Carter Henry Harrison I*, 206–11; Abbot, *Carter Henry Harrison*, 141–48, 151, and for his world tour see chapter 7.

28 Johnson, *Carter Henry Harrison I*, 73–74; Abbot, *Carter Henry Harrison*, 191–97.

29 Abbot, *Carter Henry Harrison*, 198f.; letter to Major Clifton P. Williamson from Carter H. Harrison IV, n.d., Box 15, Folder 715, CHHNL; *Chicago Tribune*, January 30, 1892, March 1, 1893; *Skandinaven*, March 25, 1893; *Dziennik Chicagoski*, February 11, February 14, July 18, 1892, April 5, 1893; Chicago City Council, *Journal of the Proceedings*, April 17, 1893, 40–41.

CHAPTER 2

1 Mike Royko, *Boss: Richard J. Daley of Chicago* (New York: Signet, 1971), 33.

2 For the attack on Leigh's Farm, see Ann Durkin Keating, *Rising Up from*

Indian Country (Chicago: University of Chicago Press, 2012), 98–100. See also Bessie Louise Pierce, *A History of Chicago*, 3 vols. (Chicago: University of Chicago Press, 1937), 1.26.

3   Charles Fanning, *Finley Peter Dunne and Mr. Dooley: The Chicago Years* (Lexington: University Press of Kentucky, 1978).
4   Finley Peter Dunne, *Mr. Dooley and the Chicago Irish: The Autobiography of an Ethnic Group*, ed. Charles Fanning (Washington, DC: Arno Press, 1976), 33.
5   Dominic A. Pacyga and Ellen Skerrett, *Chicago: City of Neighborhoods* (Chicago: Loyola University Press, 1986), 452–58.
6   *Chicago Tribune*, November 30, 1859, March 5 and September 12, 1862.
7   *Chicago Tribune*, August 22, 1872.
8   *Chicago Tribune*, August 3, 1859, April 26, 1860, June 11, 1861, March 11, July 26, and December 29, 1862.
9   For the early history of Bubbly Creek and the smells emanating from the packinghouses, fertilizer plants, etcetera, see Louise Wade, *Chicago's Pride: The Stockyards, Packingtown, and Environs in the Nineteenth Century* (Urbana: University of Illinois Press, 1987), chapter 8.
10 Harold L. Platt, *Sinking Chicago: Climate Change and the Remaking of a Flood-Prone Environment* (Philadelphia: Temple University Press, 2018), 15; *Chicago Tribune*, February 25, February 28, 1871.
11 *Chicago Tribune*, April 3, 1877.
12 *Chicago Tribune*, September 8, September 9, February 5, 1857, February 10, October 9, 1858, October 5, 1868. For Irish county rivalries and clashes in Bridgeport, see Fanning, *Finley Peter Dunne & Mr. Dooley*, 48. For Irish clannishness, see James R. Barrett, *The Irish Way: Becoming American in the Multiethnic City* (New York: Penguin Publishing Group, 2013), 39.
13 *Chicago Tribune*, May 19, 1858, November 28, 1860, March 23, 1861, April 24, 1886; Lawrence J. McCaffrey, "The Irish American Dimension," in Lawrence J. McCaffrey, Ellen Skerrett, Michael F. Funchion, and Charles Fanning, *The Irish in Chicago* (Urbana: University of Illinois Press, 1987), 4.
14 For a description of Bridgeport's early labor movement, see Richard Schneirov, "The Knights of Labor in the Chicago Labor Movement and in Municipal Politics, 1877–1887" (PhD diss., Northern Illinois University, 1984), 161–76, 406–7.
15 Barrett, *The Irish Way*, 39.
16 Eugene Kennedy, *Himself! The Life and Times of Mayor Richard J. Daley* (New York: Viking Press, 1978), 31–32.
17 Rev. Msgr. Harry C. Koenig, S.T.D., ed., *A History of the Parishes of the Archdiocese of Chicago*, 2 vols. (Chicago: Archdiocese of Chicago, 1880), 1.145–51; Rev. Msgr. Harry C. Koenig, S.T.D., ed., *Caritas Christi Urget Nos: A History of the Offices, Agencies, and Institutions of the Archdiocese of Chicago*, 2 vols. (Chicago: Archdiocese of Chicago, 1981), 2.903, 925.

18 Edward R. Kantowicz, "The Ethnic Church," in Ellen Skerrett, Edward R. Kantowicz, and Steven M. Avella, *Catholicism, Chicago Style* (Chicago: Loyola University Press, 1993), 8–10; for Catholic settlements, see Deborah A. Skok, *More Than Neighbors: Catholic Settlements and Day Nurseries in Chicago, 1893–1930* (DeKalb: Northern Illinois University Press, 2007).
19 Quoted from *Chicago Evening Post*, November 28, 1896, in Fanning, *Finley Peter Dunne & Mr. Dooley*, 48.
20 *Chicago Tribune*, November 3, 1857, March 2 and March 4, 1858.
21 Michael F. Funchion, "The Political and Nationalist Dimensions," in McCaffrey et al., *The Irish in Chicago*, 61; *Chicago Tribune*, April 21, April 23, April 27, 1863.
22 Funchion, "The Political and Nationalist Dimensions," 71; James R. Barrett, "An Interethnic Paradox: Chicago's Irish and Everyone Else," *Journal of the Illinois State Historical Society* (Spring 2022): 10, 19.
23 For an excellent discussion of the battle between the Irish and the traditional Anglo-Saxon elite, especially on the political front, see Terry Golway, *Machine Made: Tammany Hall and the Creation of Modern American Politics* (New York: Liveright, 2014).
24 For an interesting look at the machine, see James L. Merriner, *Mr. Chairman: Power in Dan Rostenkowski's America* (Carbondale and Edwardsville: Southern Illinois University Press, 1999).
25 *Chicago Tribune*, May 20, 1889.
26 Christian Brothers, *Elements of Practical Pedagogy by the Brothers of the Christian Schools* (New York: La Salle Bureau of Supplies, 1905), 62–66; *Rules of the Brothers of the Christian Schools* (Paris: The Mother House, 1905), 16–17, 20–21.
27 Christian Brothers, *Elements of Practical Pedagogy*, Preface, 1–3.
28 *Rules of the Brothers*, viii; W. J. Battersby, *De La Salle: A Pioneer in Modern Education* (London, New York, Toronto: Longmans, Green and Company, 1949) is a good starting point for understanding the life and religious philosophy of St. John the Baptist De La Salle and the Christian Brothers.
29 *Rules of the Brothers*, 2–5; Brother Jerome L. Cox, F.S.C., "The History of De La Salle Institute, 1889–1969: A Chronicle of a Creative Vision" (Masters thesis, De Paul University, Chicago, 1969), 17–19; Kennedy, *Himself*, 38. I have heard these stories of Bro. Adjutor of Mary's physical prowess in raising money from various Christian Brothers. They were obviously handed down over the years.
30 Battersby, *De La Salle*, 4–9.
31 Cox, "The History of De La Salle," 30–36.
32 *Rules of the Brothers*, 17–18; Brothers of the Christian Schools, *Management of the Christian Schools* (New York: La Salle Bureau of Supplies, 1893), 17–18, 121.

33 Andrew M. Greeley, *The Communal Catholic: A Personal Manifesto* (New York: Seabury Press, 1976), 14, 27–28, 42; Barrett, *The Irish Way*, 7, 57.

34 Ferdinand Tönnies, *Community and Society* (New York: Routledge, 1963). This is the English translation of *Gemeinschaft und Gesellschaft*. See C. H. Cooley, R. C. Angell, and L. J. Carr, *Introductory Sociology* (New York: Charles Scribner's Sons, 1933), 55–56; Avery Dulles, S.J., *Models of the Church* (New York: Doubleday, 1974), 52.

35 Marc R. Foster, "Clericalism and Communalism in German Catholicism," *Infinite Boundaries* (1998): 55–76, https://digitalcommons.conncoll.edu/histfacpub/24/; Dominic A. Pacyga, *American Warsaw: The Rise, Fall, and Rebirth of Polish Chicago* (Chicago: University of Chicago Press, 2019), see especially chapter 2.

36 Gerald D. Suttles, *The Social Construction of Communities* (Chicago: University of Chicago Press, 1972), chapter 2; Greeley, *The Communal Catholic*, Chapter 8; Andrew M. Greeley, *Neighborhood* (New York: Seabury Press, 1977), 24, 32, 38. *Neighborhood* is a rather romanticized depiction of Chicago neighborhoods, but it contains some important insights. Greeley calls neighborhoods a Catholic invention, which is extremely debatable, unless seen within the context of the Irish parish system.

37 Stephen J. Denig, C.M. and Anthony J. Dosen, C.M., "The Mission of the Catholic School in the pre–Vatican II Era (1810–1962) and the post–Vatican II Era (1965–1995): Insights and Observations for the New Millenium," *Catholic Education: A Journal of Inquiry and Practice* (December 2009): 135–56.

38 Ellen Skerrett, "The Catholic Dimension," in McCaffrey et al., *The Irish in Chicago*, 44; James W. Sanders, *The Education of an Urban Minority: Catholics in Chicago, 1833–1965* (New York: Oxford University Press, 1977), 40–41; Dominic A. Pacyga, *Polish Immigrants and Industrial Chicago: Workers on the South Side, 1880–1922* (Chicago: University of Chicago Press, 1991, 2003), 144–45.

39 For an explanation of the Cult of the Saints, see Peter Brown, *The Cult of the Saints: Its Rise and Function in Latin Christianity* (Chicago: University of Chicago Press, 1981), chapter 3. While Brown deals primarily with the early centuries of Latin Christianity, much what he writes is appropriate for my understanding of pre–Vatican II Catholic beliefs. See also the Introduction to David Hugh Farmer, *The Oxford Dictionary of Saints*, 3rd edition (Oxford: Oxford University Press, 1992), ix–xxiv. See also Rosalie Marie Levy, *Heavenly Friends* (Boston: Pauline Books & Media, 1954, 1984), 199–200, 297–300; Farmer, *Dictionary of Saints*, 271. For an exploration of the devotion to St. Jude, see Robert A. Orsi, *Thank You St. Jude: Women's Devotion to the Patron Saint of Hopeless Causes* (New Haven, CT: Yale University Press, 1996).

40 For the role of the Virgin Mary in Western religious thought, see Jaroslav

Pelikan, *Mary Through the Centuries* (New Haven, CT: Yale University Press, 1996). For St. Mary as intercessor, see Marina Warner, *Alone of All Her Sex: The Myth and Cult of the Virgin Mary* (New York: Knopf Doubleday Publishing Group, 1983), part 5; Brown, *Cult of the Saints*, 56.

CHAPTER 3

1 Charles Leroux and Ron Grossman, "Newcomers Enter the Mix of Neighborhoods, Politics Series: Chicago, A Work in Progress. The Issues Facing the Next Mayor," *Chicago Tribune*, February 10, 1999.
2 Ellen Skerrett, "Creating Sacred Space in an Early Chicago Neighborhood," in *At the Crossroads: Old St. Patrick's and the Chicago Irish*, ed. Ellen Skerrett (Chicago: Wild Onion Books, 1997), 21–38.
3 Ellen Skerrett, "The Irish of Chicago's Hull-House Neighborhood," *Chicago History* (Summer 2001): 22–63. Reprinted from Charles Fanning, ed., *New Perspectives on the Irish Diaspora* (Carbondale: Southern Illinois University Press, 2000); Irving Cutler, *The Jews of Chicago: From Shtetl to Suburb* (Urbana: University of Illinois Press, 1976), 73–74.
4 Ellen Skerrett, Edward R. Kantowicz, and Steven M. Avella, "Introduction," in *Catholicism, Chicago Style* (Chicago: Loyola University Press, 1993), xvii–xix.
5 Edward R. Kantowicz, "The Ethnic Church," in Skerrett et al., *Catholicism, Chicago Style*, 8–11.
6 Ellen Skerrett, "Sacred Space: Parish and Neighborhood in Chicago," in Skerrett et al., *Catholicism, Chicago Style*, 139–40, 156, 162; Bill Granger and Lori Granger, *Lords of the Last Machine: The Story of Politics in Chicago* (New York: Random House, 1987), 6.
7 Kantowicz, "The Ethnic Church," 5–6.
8 Christopher Robert Reed, *The Rise of Chicago's Black Metropolis 1920–1929* (Urbana: University of Illinois Press, 2011), chapter 6, is an excellent synopsis of the African American religious experience during the first wave of the Great Migration. See also St. Clair Drake and Horace R. Cayton, *Black Metropolis: A Study of Negro Life in a Northern City*, 2 vols. (New York: Harcourt, Brace, and World, 1970), 1.381.
9 Mathew J. Cressler, *Authentically Black and Truly Catholic: The Rise of Black Catholicism in the Great Migration* (New York: NYU Press, 2017), 20–39; Rev. Monsignor Harry C. Koenig, S.T.D., ed., *History of the Parishes of the Archdiocese of Chicago*, 2 vols. (Chicago: Archdiocese of Chicago, 1980), 1.149, 248–49.
10 Drake and Cayton, *Black Metropolis*, 1.121–22.
11 Cutler, *The Jews of Chicago*, 9–15. For the creation of another important Jewish congregation, see Tobias Brinkmann, *Sundays at Sinai: A Jewish Congregation in Chicago* (Chicago: University of Chicago Press, 2012), 11–20.

12 Irving Cutler, "Jews," in James R. Grossman, Ann Durkin Keating, and Janice L. Reiff, *The Encyclopedia of Chicago* (Chicago: University of Chicago Press, 2004), 436–38; Cutler, *The Jews of Chicago*, 74–75; Carole Krucoff, *Rodfei Zedek: The First Hundred Years* (Chicago: Congregation Rodfei Zedek, 1976), 5–6; Sidney Sorkin, *Bridges to an American City: A Guide to Chicago's Landsmanshaften, 1870 to 1990* (New York: Peter Lang, 1993), xi–xvi.

13 Quoted in Cutler, *The Jews of Chicago*, 59; Cutler, "Jews," 436; Louis Wirth, *The Ghetto* (Chicago: University of Chicago Press, 1956), 248.

14 Cutler, "Jews," 437.

15 Kantowicz, "The Ethnic Church," 7–8.

16 Ernest Poole, "A Mixing Bowl of Nations," *Everybody's Magazine*, October 1910, 554–55.

17 Perry Duis, *The Saloon: Public Drinking in Chicago and Boston, 1880–1920* (Urbana: University of Illinois Press, 1983), 118–21; quoted in Norman Hayner, "The Effect of Prohibition in Packingtown" (M.A. thesis, University of Chicago, 1920), 17.

18 On McDonald, see Richard C. Lindberg, *The Gambler King of Clark Street: Michael C. McDonald and the Rise of the Democratic Machine* (Carbondale: Southern Illinois University Press, 2009). For John Coughlin and Michael Kenna, see Lloyd Wendt and Herman Kogan, *Bosses of Lusty Chicago: The Story of Bathhouse John and Hinky Dink* (Bloomington: Indiana University Press, 1971); Duis, *The Saloon*, chapter 4, 247–48.

19 For an interesting contemporary account of the saloon, see E. C. Moore, "The Social Value of the Saloon," *American Journal of Sociology* 3, no.1 (July 1897): 1–12.

20 Ray S. Baker, "Hull House and the Ward Boss," *The Outlook* 58, no. 13 (March 26, 1898): 769–71.

21 Humbert S. Nelli, "John Powers and the Italians: Politics in a Chicago Ward, 1896–1921," *Journal of American History* 7, no. 1 (June 1970): 67–68; Humbert S. Nelli, *The Italians in Chicago, 1880–1930: A Study in Ethnic Mobility* (New York: Oxford University Press 1970), 93–96; Florence Kelley, "Hull House," *New England Magazine* 18, no. 5 (July 1898): 565.

22 Jane Addams, "Ethical Survival in Municipal Corruption," *International Journal of Ethics* 8, no. 3 (April 1898): 273–91. A shorter version of this paper appeared in *The Outlook*. See Jane Addams, "Why the Ward Boss Rules," *The Outlook* 58, no. 14 (April 2, 1898): 879–82.

23 Skerrett, "The Irish of Chicago's Hull-House Neighborhood," 60–62; Nelli, "John Powers and the Italians," 79; Nelli, *The Italians in Chicago*, 95.

24 Bernard Neistein interview in Milton L. Rakove, *We Don't Want Nobody Nobody Sent: An Oral History of the Daley Years* (Bloomington: Indiana University Press, 1979), 59, 62.

25 Thomas M. Guterbock, *Machine Politics in Transition: Party and Community in Chicago* (Chicago: University of Chicago Press, 1980), 231–32.

NOTES TO PAGES 87–88

26 Letter from Dan Rostenkowski to Mr. and Mrs. Bielinski, June 28, 1968, Folder: Citizenship, 1959–1960, Box 925, DRosLUC; letter from Rostenkowski to Katherine Rudnick, July 22, 1959, Rostenkowski to Michael Z. Nowicki, September 30, 1959, Folder: Immigration General, 1957–1969, Series 4, DRosLUC 1995–2001, Box 925; correspondence between Gerald Gidwitz and Rostenkowski, June 1986, Folder: Labor/Management, 1985–1986, 1995–2001, DRosLUC Box 935; letter from Rostenkowski to Walter J. Stachnik, Secretary-Treasurer, Beef Boners and Sausage Makers Union, Local 100, Folder Agriculture: General, 1959–1983 DRosLUC, Box 918; letter from Rostenkowski to George S. Waldron, June 7, 1961, Folder: General, 1959–1969, 1995–2001, DRosLUC, Box 922; letter from Rostenkowski to Bertha Quinn, April 17, 1964, Folder: Economy: General, 1960–1983, DRosLUC, Box 921; letter from Rostenkowski to Jayne A. Swiatek, October 14, 1980, letter to Umberto Balolocchi February 2, 1960, Folder, General, 1980–1983, DRosLUC, Box 922; letter from Rostenkowski to Steven C. F. Hugh, April 4, 1984, Folder: Employment General, 1984, DRosLUC, Box 936; letter from Rostenkowski to Leslie J. Bajak, June 18, 1982, Folder: General, 1980–1983, DRosLUC, Box 922. See also Tip O'Neill and Gary Hymel, *All Politics Is Local: and Other Rules of the Game* (New York: Crown Publishing, 1993).

27 Various letters about Poland Millennium stamp issue, relations with Poland, Western or "Lost" territories: Rostenkowski to Dean Rusk, January 17, 1969, Rostenkowski to Hon. Al Ullman, August 22, 1975, Rostenkowski to Aloysius A. Mazewski, September 13, 1977, Rostenkowski to Lucyna Migala-Wieclaw, June 30, 1976, Folder: Poland: General 1963–1985, DRosLUC, Box 929; Rostenkowski to Robert Lewandowski, April 17, 1969, Rostenkowski to Mrs. Alma Lawton, October 29, 1968, Folder, Poland: General 1963–1985, DRosLUC, Box 929; Rostenkowski to Joseph Wiewora, August 12, 1976, Folder: Slavic Americans Data Collection, H.J Res, 1047, DRosLUC, Box 926.

28 Rostenkowski to Rev. John T. Richardson, C.M., October 14, 1980, August 26, 1980, Rostenkowski to Raymond Baumart, S.J., June 2, 1982, Folder: General, 1980–1983, DRosLUC, Box 922. For letters to various school principals, see Folder: General, 1980–1983, DRosLUC, Box 922, Rostenkowski to Sister Mary Evariste, October 28, 1963, Folder contains correspondence with other principals, Folder: President Kennedy Chicago Visit, 1963, DRosLUC, Box 919; Rostenkowski letter to Brother Barry, C.S.J., June 1, 1965, Folder: Lyndon Johnson Chicago Visit, 1965, DRosLUC, Box 919.

29 *Chicago Tribune*, June 23, October 7, November 1, November 29, 1973. For a more complete picture of the role Pucinski played in Chicago politics, see James S. Pula, "Roman Pucinski: A Visionary Congressional Leader," *Polish American Studies* 89, no.1 (Spring 2022): 35–57; Dominic A. Pacyga, "Roman C. Pucinski: Chicago Alderman and Polonia Leader," *Polish American Studies* 79, no. 1 (Spring 2022): 75–93.

30 *Chicago Tribune*, October 6, 1987, February 10, 1999; Roger Fross, "Shakman

Decrees," in James R. Grossman, Ann Durkin Keating, and Janice L. Reiff, eds., *The Encyclopedia of Chicago* (Chicago: University of Chicago Press, 2004), 749.

31 *Chicago Tribune*, November 26, 1973.
32 Memo: Margaret Esposito, Deceased, Folder 1820, Box 107, MABiUIC; 11th Ward Request Forms, Folder 1822, Box 107, MABiUIC; Request Form, May 9, 1969, Paul J. Kemmer, Memorandum, July 22, 1969, Complaints about a tavern at 3133–37 S. Halsted, Memorandum from M.A.B., 11th Ward Request Forms, Folder 1841, Box 108, MABiUIC; various day-to-day aldermanic issues, request, etc., Box 109, MABiUIC; letter from Bilandic to Dr. Deton J. Brooks Jr., October 8, 1970, Folder 1871, Box 109, MABiUIC.
33 Len O'Connor, *Clout: Mayor Daley and His City* (New York: Avon, 1975), 12.
34 Edward C. Banfield, *Political Influence: A New Theory of Urban Politics* (New York: The Free Press, 1961), 74–75, 84; Mike Royko, *Boss: Richard J. Daley of Chicago* (New York: Signet, 1971), 68–69; Adam Cohen and Elizabeth Taylor, *American Pharaoh: Mayor Richard J. Daley, His Battle for Chicago and the Nation* (New York: Little, Brown and Company, 2000), 40–45; Bernard Neistein interview in Rakove, *We Don't Want Nobody Nobody Sent*, 61; interview with Roseanne Bonoma, October 3, 2014 transcript, RJDOralUIC, 11; interview with Ed Burke, RJDOralUIC, accessed March 9, 2022, 5; interview with Ed Burke, August 5, 2014, RJDOralUIC, 2, 8; inter-office communication, November 29, 1961—Knauss petition 1961, Folder SIss 1 B46-5, RJDUIC.
35 Mark H. Haller, "Organized Crime in Urban Society: Chicago in the Twentieth Century," *Journal of Social History* 5, no. 2 (Winter 1971): 210–34.
36 Older members of my family had fond memories of John Oberta in Back of the Yards. *Chicago Tribune*, October 11, December 24, 1928; May 4, 1929; March 23, March 30, 1930; November 19, 1960.
37 Joe Kraus, *The Kosher Capones: A History of Chicago's Jewish Gangsters* (DeKalb: Northern Illinois University Press, 2019), chapter 4.
38 Leroux and Grossman, "Newcomers Enter the Mix."

CHAPTER 4

1 *Chicago Tribune*, December 17, 1893.
2 Carter H. Harrison, *Stormy Years: The Autobiography of Carter H. Harrison* (New York: The Bobbs-Merrill Company, 1935), 57–62.
3 "The Harrison Brothers," *The Journalist*, December 15, 1894; "The Chicago Times Change of Management," no citation, in Harrison Scrapbook, vol. 1, CHHNL; Harrison, *Stormy Years*, 18, 31–33.
4 Richard Allen Morton makes this argument in his two books on Sullivan and Hopkins. Although I do not agree with many of Morton's interpretations, these two books fill an important gap in the historical narrative. Richard

NOTES TO PAGES 100–107

Allen Morton, *Roger C. Sullivan and the Making of the Chicago Democratic Machine, 1881–1908* (Jefferson, NC: McFarland & Company, 2016), and *Roger C. Sullivan and the Triumph of the Chicago Democratic Machine* (Jefferson, NC: McFarland & Company, 2019).

5   Morton, *Sullivan and the Making of the Chicago Democratic Machine*, 17–18.
6   *Chicago Inter Ocean*, October 8, 1881, *Chicago Tribune*, December 7, 1881, January 25, 1882; *Charter and By-Laws of the Iroquois Club of the City of Chicago* (Chicago: Iroquois Club, 1882); Edwin F. Mack, *Old Monroe Street: Notes on the Monroe Street of Early Chicago* Days (Chicago: Central Trust Company of Illinois, 1914), 70; Morton, *Sullivan and the Making of the Chicago Democratic Machine*, 21.
7   *Chicago Tribune*, March 5, March 12, March 14, March 15, March 16, 1882, April 15, 1883; *Annual Banquet of the Iroquois Club, March 15, 1882, at the Palmer House* (Chicago: Culver, Page, Hoyne and Company, 1882).
8   *Chicago Tribune*, October 31, November 1, December 28, 1883.
9   Morton, *Sullivan and the Making of the Chicago Democratic Machine*, 21–25; *Chicago Tribune*, December 3, 1893.
10   *Chicago Tribune*, December 2, 1893, December 14, December 17, 1894; Morton, *Sullivan and the Making of the Chicago Democratic Machine*, 39–43.
11   *Chicago Tribune*, December 28, December 29, 1893.
12   Stanley Buder, *Pullman: An Experiment in Industrial Order and Community Planning, 1880–1930* (New York: Oxford University Press, 1967), chapters 13 and 16; Carl Smith, *Urban Disorder and the Shape of Belief: The Great Chicago Fire, The Haymarket Bomb, and the Model Town of Pullman* (Chicago: University of Chicago Press, 1995), 193–200; John F. Hogan, *Chicago Shakedown: The Ogden Gas Scandal* (Charleston, SC: History Press, 2018), e-book edition, locations 737, 747/2196; James Gilbert, *Perfect Cities: Chicago's Utopias of 1893* (Chicago: University of Chicago Press, 1991), 162–63.
13   Morton, *Sullivan and the Making of the Chicago Democratic Machine*, 45–47.
14   *Chicago Tribune*, February 19, 1895.
15   Hogan, *Chicago Shakedown*, location 147/2196; Ray Ginger, *Altgeld's America: The Lincoln Ideal Versus Changing Realities* (New York: New Viewpoints, 1973), 172–73; Lloyd Wendt and Herman Kogan, *Bosses of Lusty Chicago: The Story of Bathhouse John and Hinky Dink* (Bloomington: Indiana University Press, 1971), 118–20.
16   *Chicago Tribune*, March 11, 1895; Wendt and Kogan, *Bosses of Lusty Chicago*, 120–21.
17   *Chicago Tribune*, April 9, September 16, September 22, 1895, November 26, 1918; Hogan, *Chicago Shakedown*, location 160/2196, 2058/2196, 2090/2196, 2109/2196.
18   For a discussion of the Czech-Polish alliance, see Dominic A. Pacyga, *American Warsaw: The Rise, Fall, and Rebirth of Polish Chicago* (Chicago: University of Chicago Press, 2019).

19 Frank B. Zdrubek, *Dejiny Czesko-Narodniho Hrbitova v Chicagu, Illinois* (Chicago: Tiskem A. Geringera, 1902).

20 James R. Grossman, *Land of Hope: Chicago, Black Southerners, and the Great Migration* (Chicago: University of Chicago Press, 1989), 74–79, 123–30, 143–53; Alan H. Spear, *Black Chicago: The Making of a Negro Ghetto, 1890–1922* (Chicago: University of Chicago Press, 1967), 11, 14–20, 44–46, 130; St. Clair Drake and Horace C. Clayton, *Black Metropolis*, 2 vols. (New York, 1970) 1:61–62; William Tuttle, *Chicago in the Red Summer of 1919* (Chicago: University of Chicago Press, 1972), 96–97, 159.

21 Daniel Burnham and Edward H. Bennett, *Plan of Chicago* (Chicago: The Commercial Club of Chicago, 1908). For an interpretation of the plan in its larger historical context, see Carl Smith, *The Plan of Chicago: Daniel Burnham and the Remaking of the American City* (Chicago: University of Chicago Press, 2006).

22 *Chicago Tribune*, July 3, September 3, 1896; Harrison, *Stormy Years*, 70, 73.

23 "We Never Had a Better Show," "Trude Will Not Take It," "May Name Harrison," "Harrison's Stock on the Rise," No Citation, Harrison Scrapbook, vol. 1, CHHNL.

24 *Chicago Chronicle*, February 14, February 17, February 21, 1897; *Chicago Record*, February 18, 1897; *Journal*, February 18, 1897; Harrison Scrapbook, vol. 1, CHHNL.

25 Harrison, *Stormy Years*, 94–100; *Chicago Daily News*, March 10, March 11, 1897; *Chicago Inter Ocean*, March 12, 1897; Harrison Scrapbook, vol. 1, CHHNL; handwritten note from John Peter Altgeld to Carter H. Harrison, April 7, 1897. Another handwritten note from Altgeld to Harrison on April 8, 1897 congratulated him on his mayoral victory, Box 2, Folder 47, CHHNL.

26 *Chicago Inter Ocean*, March 18, 1897; *Chronicle*, March 16, 1897; *Record*, March 25, 1897. Harrison Scrapbook, vol. 1, CHHNL.

27 *Chronicle*, April 1, 1897; *Times-Herald*, March 30, April 6, 1897. Harrison Scrapbook, vol. 1, CHHNL.

28 *Chicago Daily News*, August 9, 1897; *Chicago Tribune*, August 10, 1897, Harrison Scrapbook, vol. 2, CHHNL; letter from William Jennings Bryan to Carter H. Harrison, September 12, 1914, Box 2, Folder 88, CHHNL.

29 *Chicago Tribune*, August 13, 1897; *Chicago Daily News*, August 17, August 19, 1897; *Chicago Record*, August 30, 1897, Harrison, Scrapbook, vol. 2, CHHNL.

30 *Chicago Daily News*, September 8, 1897; *Chicago Tribune*, September 9, 1897, September 30, October 2, 1898; *Chicago Inter Ocean*, September 9, 1897, Harrison Scrapbook, vol. 2, CHHNL; Harrison, *Stormy Years*, 284–85; Kraus, *Reminiscences and Comments*, 134.

31 *Chicago Tribune*, March 7, 1898; Kraus, *Reminiscences and Comments*, 134–45.

32 Alan R. Lind, *Chicago Surface Lines: An Illustrated History* (Park Forest, IL:

349

Transport History Press, 1979), 8; David M. Young, *Chicago Transit: An Illustrated History* (DeKalb: Northern Illinois University Press, 1998), 36–37; Greg Borzo, *Chicago Cable Cars* (Charleston, SC: History Press, 2012), 78, 81–88.

33 Harrison, *Stormy Years*, 109–10; Lloyd Wendt and Herman Kogan, *Bosses of Lusty Chicago* (Bloomington: Indiana University Press, 1971), 39, 171–99.

34 Edward R. Kantowicz, "Carter Harrison II: The Politics of Balance," in *The Mayors: The Chicago Political Tradition*, ed. Paul M. Green and Melvin G. Holli (Carbondale: Southern Illinois University Press, 2013), 16–32. Perhaps the best overall look at the transit issue and technological change in Chicago is Paul Barrett, *The Automobile and Urban Transit: The Formation of Public Policy in Chicago, 1900–1930* (Philadelphia: Temple University Press, 1983).

35 Carter H. Harrison IV, "Wet-Dry Speech," 1910, Box 15, Folder 706, HHNL.

36 Kantowicz, "Harrison II," 24–25; letter from G. J. Barry to Carter H. Harrison, July 7, 1900, Box 2, Folder 67, HHNL; letter from Rev. M. J. Fitzsimons to Carter H. Harrison, May 12, 1914, Box 3, Folder 173, HHNL; John F. Hogan, *Chicago Shakedown: The Ogden Gas Scandal* (Charleston, SC: History Press, 2018) is a recent look at the events surrounding the scandal.

37 Carter H. Harrison IV Address for the Unveiling of the Goethe Monument, June 13, 1914, Box 13, Folder 668, HHNL; letter from Carter H. Harrison to S. G. Woodhall, March 15, 1915, Box 9, Folder 537, HHNL.

CHAPTER 5

1 Quoted in Lloyd Wendt and Herman Kogan, *Big Bill of Chicago* (New York: The Bobbs-Merrill Company, 1953), 171.

2 Douglas Bukowski, *Big Bill Thompson, Chicago, and the Politics of Image* (Urbana: University of Illinois Press, 1998), 11.

3 *Chicago Tribune*, January 19, January 23, 1898; January 8, January 18, 1899; May 27, 1900.

4 *Chicago Tribune*, October 26, 1890; February 17, March 29, 1900; December 20, 1901; July 13, 1908; Bukowski, *Big Bill Thompson*, 14; Wendt and Kogan, *Big Bill*, 32–33.

5 Bukowski, *Big Bill Thompson*, 14–15.

6 *Chicago Tribune*, December 20, 1901, February 3, 1902; Bukowski, *Big Bill Thompson*, 14–15; Wendt and Kogan, *Big Bill*, 42, 47, 49–51.

7 Wendt and Kogan, *Big Bill*, 73–79; Joel Arthur Tarr, *A Study in Boss Politics: William Lorimer of Chicago* (Urbana: University of Illinois Press, 1971), 266.

8 *Chicago Tribune*, January 31, 1915, Bukowski, *Big Bill Thompson*, 29.

9 Tarr, *Boss Politics*, 313; *Chicago Tribune*, February 4, February 5, February 10, 1915; Bukowski, *Big Bill Thompson*, 19, 22.

10 *Chicago Tribune*, February 24, February 28, March 1, March 4, 1915.

11 *Chicago Tribune*, April 7, 1915.

12 Bukowski, *Big Bill Thompson*, 29.
13 Wendt and Kogan, *Big Bill*, 95, 107–11.
14 *Defender*, April 3, May 1, May 8, May 22, June 15, September 18, 1915.
15 *Chicago Tribune*, July 25, 1915.
16 *Chicago Tribune*, October 5, October 6, October 8, 1915; *Svenska Kuriren*, October 7, 1915, CFLPS.
17 *Defender*, October 9, October 16, 1915; Bukowski, *Big Bill Thompson*, 43.
18 *Chicago Tribune*, October 6, October 8, 1915.
19 *Denní Hlasatel*, October 6, October 11, October 14, October 20, 1915, CFLPS.
20 *Denní Hlasatel*, November 1, November 8, 1915, CFLPS.
21 Wendt and Kogan, *Big Bill*, 132.
22 *Chicago Tribune*, March 2, April 3, 1916, Wendt and Kogan, *Big Bill*, 141–43; Bukowski, *Big Bill Thompson*, 51.
23 Melvin G. Holli, "The Great War Sinks Chicago's German Kultur," in *Ethnic Chicago*, ed. Melvin G. Holli and Peter d'A Jones (Grand Rapids, MI: William B. Eerdmans Publishing Company, 1984), 460–511; Pacyga, *American Warsaw*, 136–40.
24 *Denní Hlasatel*, April 27, April 28, April 30, 1917; May 1, 1907, CFLPS.
25 *Denní Hlasatel*, May 18, May 23, May 26, July 21, August 31, 1917; Pacyga, *American Warsaw*, 137–38.
26 Samuel A. Ettelson, *Opinion of Samuel A. Ettelson, Corporation Counsel of the City of Chicago Rendered September 18, 1917 Regarding the Action of Mayor William Hale Thompson in Permitting the Meeting of the People's Council of America for Democracy and Terms of Peace* (Chicago: Champlin Law Printing Company, 1917); *Chicago Tribune*, June 25, September 2, September 3, October 16, November 11, 1917; Bukowski, *Big Bill Thompson*, 62–63; Wendt and Kogan, *Big Bill*, 158–59, 161–62.
27 Bukowski, *Big Bill Thompson*, 80–81.
28 *Abendpost*, February 26, March 28, April 2, 1919, CFLPS; *Onze Toekomst*, March 28, 1919, CFLPS; Wendt and Kogan, *Big Bill*, 168–71; Bukowski, *Big Bill Thompson*, 81–83.
29 The classic study of the riot is William M. Tuttle Jr., *Race Riot: Chicago in the Red Summer of 1919* (New York: Oxford University Press, 1979); Dominic A. Pacyga, "Chicago's 1919 Race Riot: Ethnicity, Class, and Urban Violence," in *The Making of Urban America*, 2nd edition, ed. Raymond Mohl (Wilmington, DE: SR Books, 1997), 187–207.
30 Wendt and Kogan, *Big Bill*, 184–93; Jeff Nicholls, "The Chicago Police Department Once Published a Magazine Featuring Crime-fighting Tactics—and Casserole Recipes," *Reader*, August 26, 1916.
31 Wendt and Kogan, *Big Bill*, 199–204; Bukowski, *Big Bill Thompson*, 140.
32 This section is based upon John R. Schmidt, *The Mayor Who Cleaned Up Chicago: A Political Biography of William E. Dever* (DeKalb: Northern Illinois University Press, 1989), the best biography of Dever. Schmidt's chapter

"William E. Dever: A Chicago Political Fable," in *The Mayors: The Chicago Political Tradition*, ed. Paul M. Green and Melvin G. Holli (Carbondale: Southern Illinois University Press, 1995), 82–98 is a synopsis of his book.
33 Wendt and Kogan, *Big Bill*, 233.
34 *Chicago Tribune*, December 11, 1926.
35 *Chicago Tribune*, February 15, 1927; Thompson quoted in Wendt and Kogan, *Big Bill*, 247–49.
36 *Chicago Tribune*, February 23, March 26, March 27, March 29, 1927; Wendt and Kogan, *Big Bill*, 249–50.
37 *Chicago Tribune*, March 12, March 14, March 29, 1927; Wendt and Kogan, *Big Bill*, 252; John Landesco, *Organized Crime in Chicago: Part III of the Illinois Crime Survey, 1929*, second edition (Chicago: University of Chicago Press, 1979), 40–41.
38 *Chicago Tribune*, March 23, 1927.
39 *Chicago Tribune*, April 6, 1927.
40 Wendt and Kogan, *Big Bill*, 268–71.
41 Landesco, *Organized Crime in Chicago*, 126–28; Humbert S. Nelli, *The Italians in Chicago, 1880–1930: A Study in Ethnic Mobility* (New York: Oxford University Press, 1970), 225–26; *Chicago Tribune*, March 22, March 27, April 20, 1928.
42 Wendt and Kogan, *Big Bill*, 310–17.
43 *Chicago Tribune*, April 8, 1931; Wendt and Kogan, *Big Bill*, 329–32; Bukowski, *Big Bill Thompson*, 236.

CHAPTER 6

1 Cermak in response to William Hale Thompson's attack on his Czech origins, quoted in Alex Gottfried, *Boss Cermak of Chicago: A Study in Political Leadership* (Seattle: University of Washington Press, 1962), 226.
2 Joseph Chada, *The Czechs in the United States* (Washington, DC: SVU Press, 1981), 10, chapter 6; Vlasta Vraz, ed., *Panorama: A Historical Review of the Czechs and Slovaks in the United States of America* (Cicero, IL: Privately published, 1970), 6.
3 John J. Reichman, "Czechoslovaks and the Development of Chicago," in John J. Reichman, ed., *Czechoslovaks of Chicago: Contributions to a History of a National Group* (Chicago: Czechoslovak Historical Society of Illinois, 1937); 6, Jan Habenicht, *History of Czechs in America* (St. Paul, MN: Czechoslovak Genealogical Society International, 1996), 385.
4 Jan Habenicht, *Dějiny Čechův Amerických* (St. Louis: Hlas Publishing Company, 1910), 566–67; Alice G. Masaryk, "The Bohemians in Chicago," *Charities: A Review of Local and General Philanthropy* 131, no. 10 (December 3, 1904): 206; Joseph Slabey Roucek, "The Passing of American Czechoslovaks," *American Journal of Sociology* 39, no. 5 (March 1934): 612.

5   For a short history of Czech California and the early years of Pilsen Park, see Dominic A. Pacyga, "Chicago's Pilsen Park and the Struggle for Czechoslovak Independence," in Leo Schelbert and Nick Ceh, *Essays in Russian and East European History: A Festschrift for Edward C. Thaden* (Boulder, CO: East European Monographs, 1995), 117–29.
6   For more on the relationship between Czechs and Poles, see Dominic A. Pacyga, "Czechs and Poles in Chicago: Pan-Slavism and the Origins of the Cermak Democratic Machine, 1860–1931," *Studya Migracyjne—Przegląd Polonynich*. 4 (2015): 55–68.
7   Gottfried, *Boss Cermak*, 38–39, 66.
8   Pacyga, "Czechs and Poles in Chicago," 58.
9   Gottfried, *Boss Cermak*, 3–18, 29, 46.
10 Gottfried, 49–53.
11 Maureen A. Flanagan, "The Ethnic Entry into Chicago Politics, the United Societies for Local Self-Government and the Reform Charter of 1907," *Journal of the Illinois State Historical Society* 75, no. 1 (Spring 1982): 2–3; Perry Duis, *The Saloon: Public Drinking in Chicago and Boston, 1880–1920* (Urbana: University of Illinois Press, 1983), 258–60; *Abendpost*, May 24, 1906, CFLPS; *Dziennik Chicagoski*, May 28, 1906, CFLPS.
12 Gottfried, *Boss Cermak*, 53–54; Maureen A. Flanagan, *Charter Reform in Chicago* (Carbondale: Southern Illinois University Press, 1987), 33–34; Thomas R. Pegram, *Partisans and Progressives: Private Interest and Public Policy in Illinois, 1870–1922* (Urbana: University of Illinois Press, 1992), 110; *Chicago Tribune*, May 28, May 31, June 3, June 20, 1906; *Abendpost*, May 24, 1906, CFLPS.
13 Pegram, *Partisans and Progressives*, 109–10; Flanagan, "The Ethnic Entry into Chicago Politics," 4–6; *Illinois Staats-Zeitung*, February 17, 1914, CFLPS; *Abendpost*, February 10, 1908, CFLPS.
14 *Proceedings of the Chicago Charter Convention, City Council Chamber, December 6, 1906* (Chicago: Chicago Charter Convention, 1906), 189–90.
15 Pegram, *Partisans and Progressives*, chapter 4; Flanagan, *Charter Reform in Chicago*, 73, 133–34; Laura M. Westhoff, *A Fatal Drifting Apart: Democratic Social Knowledge and Chicago Reform* (Columbus: The Ohio State University Press, 2007), 252–56; *Chicago Tribune*, December 4, December 10, 1906.
16 Flanagan, *Charter Reform in Chicago*, 137.
17 *Denní Hlasatel*, May 26, 1913, May 27, 1918, CFLPS.
18 *Abendpost*, May 24, 1909, CFLPS; *Denní Hlasatel*, February 3, May 27, 1918, CFLPS.
19 Gottfried, *Boss Cermak*, 62–69; *Chicago Tribune*, April 1, April 4, 1909.
20 *Denní Hlasatel*, April 11, June 3, September 4, 1911; February 1, 1912, CFLPS.
21 Gottfried, *Boss Cermak*, 77–78; *Denní Hlasatel*, November 3, May 26, 1913, CFLPS.
22 Gottfried, *Boss Cermak*, 81–90; *Abendpost*, editorial, November 1, 1918,

CFLPS; Pacyga, "Chicago's Pilsen Park,"; *Denní Hlasatel,* June 18, 1917; September 26, October 24, 1918.

23 Gottfried, *Boss Cermak,* 91–97; the December 2, 1917 parade is detailed in *Denní Hlasatel,* December 3, 1917, CFLPS; *Chicago Tribune,* July 13, October 16, October 22, 1918.

24 *Chicago Tribune,* February 26, 1919; Gottfried, *Boss Cermak,* 98–100, 109–13, 120.

25 *Chicago Tribune,* January 4, January 7, February 11, July 12, 1922; *Denní Hlasatel,* March 5, March 6, March 20, 1922, CFLPS; Gottfried, *Boss Cermak,* 115–19.

26 *Denní Hlasatel,* April 1, October 4, October 6, October 17, November 5, 1922, CFLPS.

27 *Chicago Tribune,* September 19, October 16, 1922; Gottfried, *Boss Cermak,* 126.

28 Gottfried, *Boss Cermak,* 128–32.

29 Gottfried, 143–62.

30 *Chicago Tribune,* August 1, August 2, August 3, August 4, August 8, August 9, 1928.

31 *Chicago Tribune,* August 15, August 17, August 18, August 24, August 25, 1928.

32 Gottfried, *Boss Cermak,* chapter 10.

33 Douglas Bukowski, *Big Bill Thompson, Chicago and the Politics of Image* (Urbana: University of Illinois Press, 1998), 232; *Chicago Tribune,* January 16, February 22, February 25, 1931.

34 John M. Allswang, *A House for All Peoples: Ethnic Politics in Chicago, 1890–1936* (Lexington: The University Press of Kentucky, 1971), 55–56; Gottfried, *Boss Cermak,* 234–37.

35 Mary J. Herrick, *The Chicago Schools: A Social and Political History* (Beverly Hills, CA: Sage Publications, 1971), 187–90, 193–215; *Chicago Tribune,* July 16, July 22, August 18, 1931; *Chicago Daily News,* November 16, November 21, 1932; Gottfried, *Boss Cermak,* 238–87.

36 For a complete discussion of these political moves, see Gottfried, *Boss Cermak,* chapter 13.

37 Gottfried, *Boss Cermak,* 288–335.

38 Edward R. Kantowicz, *Polish American Politics in Chicago, 1888–1940* (Chicago: University of Chicago Press, 1975), 193–95; see also Dominic A. Pacyga, *American Warsaw: The Rise, Fall, and Rebirth of Polish Chicago* (Chicago: University of Chicago Press, 2019), 169–73.

CHAPTER 7

1 *Chicago Tribune,* March 15, 1933.

2 Roger Biles, *Big City Boss in Depression and War: Mayor Edward J. Kelly of*

Chicago (DeKalb: Northern Illinois University Press, 1984), 15. This is the definitive biography of Edward J. Kelly.
3   *Chicago Tribune*, March 1, 1933.
4   *Chicago Tribune*, March 15, March 16, 1933.
5   Biles, *Big City Boss*, 18.
6   Biles, 6–8.
7   *Chicago Tribune*, February 16, March 7, April 14, 1933.
8   *Chicago Tribune*, January 1, April 15, 1933; Biles, *Big City Boss*, 19.
9   *Chicago Tribune*, April 16, April 22, 1933.
10 *Chicago Tribune*, May 17, May 18, 1933; *Abendpost*, November 2, 1930, CFLPS.
11 Dominic A. Pacyga, *American Warsaw: The Rise, Fall, and Rebirth of Polish Chicago* (Chicago: University of Chicago Press, 2019), 172; Edward R. Kantowicz, *Polish-American Politics in Chicago, 1888–1940* (Chicago: University of Chicago Press, 1975), 193–94, 183–84; Don Hayner and Tom McNamee, *Streetwise Chicago: A History of Chicago Street Names* (Chicago: Loyola University Press, 1988), 106; *Chicago Tribune*, May 7, May 29, July 16, July 18, July 23, July 28, October 12, 1933.
12 *Chicago Defender* (National Edition), January 1, April 29, May 20, June 6, September 16, 1933.
13 Biles, *Big City Boss*, 92–94; Dempsey J. Travis, *An Autobiography of Black Politics* (Chicago: Urban Research Press, Inc., 1987), 121–23.
14 Ovid Demaris, *Captive City* (New York: Lyle Stuart, Inc., 1969), 171; Biles, *Big City Boss*, 89–90.
15 The most complete description of the Policy Game is included in St. Clair Drake and Horace R. Cayton, *Black Metropolis: A Study of Negro Life in a Northern City*, revised edition, 2 vols. (New York: Harcourt, Brace, & World, 1970), 2.chapter 17. See also Travis, *Black Politics*, 174–77; and Harold F. Gosnell, *Negro Politicians: The Rise of Negro Politics in Chicago* (Chicago: University of Chicago Press, 1935), 122–35.
16 Biles, *Big City Boss*, 89–90.
17 Travis, *Black Politics*, 138; *Defender*, March 2, March 9, March 30, 1935.
18 Biles, *Big City Boss*, 97–99; Travis, *Black Politics*, 147–48; *Defender*, June 8, September 7, September 28, 1935; January 4, 1936; January 27, 1940.
19 *Defender*, November 4, 1939; Travis, *Black Politics*, 154–56, 198; Biles, *Big City Boss*, 100–101; Len O'Connor, *Clout: Mayor Daley and His City* (New York: Avon, 1975), 115; Nicholas Lemann, *The Promised Land: The Great Black Migration and How It Changed America* (New York: Alfred A. Knopf, 1991), 74.
20 Travis, *Black Politics*, 170–74.
21 Dominic A. Pacyga, *Chicago: A Biography* (Chicago: University of Chicago Press, 2009), 253–54; *Chicago Tribune*, August 6, 1934.

22   For the impact of the New Deal on Tammany Hall, see Terry Golway, *Machine Made: Tammany Hall and the Creation of Modern American Politics* (New York: Liveright Publishing Corporation, 2014), 266–67, 270–71, 294. For Chicago, see Biles, *Big City Boss*, 74–80.
23   Biles, *Big City Boss*, 27–30; *Chicago Tribune*, September 8, 1933.
24   Biles, *Big City Boss*, 77–78.
25   Robert A. Slayton, "Labor and Urban Politics: District 31 Steelworkers Organizing Committee, and the Chicago Machine," *Journal of Urban History* 23, no. 1 (November 1996): 47–48.
26   For the development of the neighborhood organizations in Back of the Yards, see Robert A. Slayton, *Back of the Yards: The Making of a Local Democracy* (Chicago: University of Chicago Press, 1986), and Thomas J. Jablonsky, *Pride in the Jungle: Community and Everyday Life in Back of the Yards Chicago* (Baltimore, MD: Johns Hopkins University Press, 1993). For South Chicago's Russell Square Community Committee, see Dominic A. Pacyga, "The Russell Square Community Committee: An Ethnic Response to Urban Problems," *Journal of Urban History* 15, no. 2 (February 1989): 159–84. For the rise of the CIO in meatpacking, see Roger Horowitz, *Negro and White, Unite and Fight!—A Social History of Industrial Unionism in Meatpacking, 1930–1990* (Urbana: University of Illinois Press, 1997), as well as Rick Halpern and Roger Horowitz, *Meatpackers: An Oral History of Black Packinghouse Workers and the Struggle for Racial and Economic Equality* (New York: Monthly Review Press, 1999). Also see Dominic A. Pacyga, *Slaughterhouse: Chicago's Union Stockyard and the World It Made* (Chicago: University of Chicago Press, 2019).
27   Slayton, *Back of the Yards*, chapter 1; Dominic A. Pacyga, *Polish Immigrants and Industrial Chicago: Workers of the South Side, 1880–1922* (Chicago: University of Chicago Press, 2003), chapters 2 and 3.
28   *Chicago Tribune*, June 9, 1937.
29   Slayton, "Labor and Urban Politics," 39–44; *Chicago Tribune*, June 17, June 18, July 23, 1937; Pacyga, "The Russell Square Community Committee," 170–72.
30   Pacyga, *Chicago: A Biography*, 267–68.
31   Biles, *Big City Boss*, 116; Perry Duis and Scott La France, *We've Got a Job to Do: Chicagoans and World War Two* (Chicago: Sewall Company, 1992), 34–35; Pacyga, *Chicago: A Biography*, 273–75.
32   Duis and LaFrance, *We've Got a Job to Do*, 52–53; *Chicago Tribune*, February 8, 1944; a photo of the B-29 bomber is in Folder 15 of the Roman Pucinski Collection, Polish Museum of America; Irving Cutler, *The Jews of Chicago: From Shtetl to Suburb* (Urbana: University of Illinois Press, 1996), 131.
33   Duis and LaFrance, *We've Got a Job to Do*, 53–58; Pacyga, *Chicago: A Biography*, 284–85.
34   Biles, *Big City Boss*, 4–5, 12.

CHAPTER 8

1 "De La Salle Fight Song—Chicago, IL," YouTube video, 1:09, July 1, 2010, https://www.youtube.com/watch?v=0B7pNVByigs.
2 Richard J. Daley Quotes, BrainyQuote.com, BrainyMedia Inc., 2020, https://www.brainyquote.com/quotes/richard_j_daley_134305, accessed May 15, 2020.
3 Dominic A. Pacyga, *American Warsaw: The Rise, Fall, and Rebirth of Polish Chicago* (Chicago: University of Chicago Press, 2019), 206; Jacob M. Arvey interview, in Milton L. Rakove, *We Don't Want Nobody Nobody Sent* (Bloomington: Indiana University Press, 1979), 12.
4 Statement of Martin H. Kennelly to the Members of the Democratic City Central Committee, December 20, 1946, Folder 1 Mayoral Campaign 1947—Press Releases 1–10, Box 1 of 295, MHKUIC.
5 To City Editor, Picture Editor, Political Editor from The Greater Chicago Committee, Martin H. Kennelly for Mayor, February 27, 1947, Folder 4, Mayoral Campaign 1947—Press Releases 31–40, Box 1 of 295, MHKUIC; Bridgeport—advance, Martin H. Kennelly for Mayor Campaign, 7 S. Dearborn St. Release Thursday, AM-PM, Folder 1 Mayoral Campaign 1947, Box 1 of 295, MHKUIC.
6 Radio Address of Martin H. Kennelly, Democratic Candidate for Mayor, Station WLS, 7:30 pm, Wednesday January 22, 1947, Folder 1, Mayoral Campaign 1947—Press Releases 1–10, Box 1 of 295, MHKUIC.
7 Release to Sunday Papers, Feb. 3 and Thereafter, Folder 3, Mayoral Campaign 1947—Press Releases 21–30, Box 1 of 295, MHKUIC; For Release to All Papers of Sunday, March 16, 1947, Martin H. Kennelly Collection, Folder 7, Box 2 of 295, MHKUIC; Mayoral Campaign 1947—Press Releases 61–70; Release to A.M. papers Tuesday March 4 and Thereafter, Folder 4, Mayoral Campaign 1947—Press Releases 31–40, Box 1 of 295, MHKUIC; For Release to Afternoon Papers of Friday, March 7, 1947, Folder 5, Mayoral Campaign 1947—Press Releases 41–50, Box 1 of 295, MHKUIC; Telegram from Polish Roman Catholic Union of America, March 6, 1947, MHKUIC.
8 Address of Martin H. Kennelly, Wednesday February 5, 1947, Station WLS, Folder 1 Mayoral Campaign 1947—Press Releases 1–10, Box 1 of 295, MHKUIC; Address of Martin H. Kennelly, Wednesday, February 19, 1947, Radio Station WLS—7:30 p.m., Folder 2, Mayoral Campaign 1947—Press Releases 11–20, Box 1 of 295, MHKUIC; For Release to Afternoon Papers of Thursday, March 13, 1947, Folder 7, Mayoral Campaign 1947—Press Releases 61–70, Box 2 of 295, MHKUIC.
9 Peter Joseph O'Malley, "Mayor Martin H. Kennelly: A Political Biography," PhD thesis, University of Illinois at Chicago Circle, 1980, 45–46, 60.
10 Inaugural Address of Mayor Martin H. Kennelly, Council Chambers, City Hall, April 15, 1947, 8:00 P.M., Folder 13-342, Box 13 of 295, MHKUIC.

11 O'Malley, "Mayor Martin H. Kennelly," 65–66; Address of Mayor Martin H. Kennelly, New York City, Friday October 24, 1947, Folder 384, Box 17 of 295, MHKUIC.
12 O'Malley, "Mayor Martin H. Kennelly," 70–76.
13 Inaugural Address of Mayor Martin H. Kennelly, April 19, 1951, Folder 13-343, Box 13 of 295, MHKUIC.
14 O'Malley, "Mayor Martin H. Kennelly," 171–72.
15 Press Release, Greater Chicago Committee for the Reelection of Mayor Martin H. Kennelly, January 17, 1955; Address of Mayor Kennelly, WGN-TV, January 16, 1955, 5:30 P.M.; Address of Mayor Martin H. Kennelly, WGN-TV, February 6, 1955, Folder 6-59, Box 6 of 295, MHKUIC.
16 Press Release, Greater Chicago Committee for the Reelection of Mayor Martin H. Kennelly, February 10, 1955; Press Release, Greater Chicago Committee for the Reelection of Mayor Martin H. Kennelly, no date, Folder 6-59, Box 6, MHKUIC. Various other GOP endorsements are all in this file: for labor endorsements see Press Release, Greater Chicago Committee for the Reelection of Mayor Martin H. Kennelly, February 10, 1955; Press Release, Greater Chicago Committee for the Reelection of Mayor Martin H. Kennelly, January 10, 1955.
17 Various correspondence concerning the De La Salle cartoon flyer, Folder 28-507, Box 28 of 295, MHKUIC.
18 *American*, February 16, 1955; *Chicago Daily News*, February 17, 1955. For a full list of candidates, see *Chicago Tribune*, February 17, 1955.
19 Summary of Gambling Arrests Made for the Year of 1951; Summary of Gambling Arrests for the Year 1952; Summary of Gambling Raids for the Year 1953; Summary of Gambling Raids for the Year 1954, Folder 56-1134, Martin H. Kennelly Collection Box 56, MHKUIC; *Chicago Daily News*, February 16, February 18, 1955.
20 Note Cards with 1st Ward Precinct Workers Names and Addresses, Martin H. Kennelly Collection, Box 84 of 295; *Chicago Daily News*, February 23, 1955; Letter from Mrs. E. W. Stubbs to Martin H. Kennelly, March 13, 1955, expressing thanks for Kennelly's neutrality; Letter from Ella J. Daly to Martin H. Kennelly, March 17, 1955, encouraging Kennelly to return to the Democratic Party, Folder 28-506, Box 28 of 295, MHKUIC.
21 "Quotes of Famous People," https://quotepark.com/quotes/1871222-richard-j-daley-good-government-is-good-politics-and-politics-is-g/, accessed May 12, 2022.
22 Michael J. Daley Draft Board Registration Card, September 12, 1918, Ancestry.com; Roger Biles, *Richard J. Daley: Politics, Race and the Governing of Chicago* (DeKalb: Northern Illinois University Press, 1995), 21. Biles's book is the best biography of Richard J. Daley.
23 Mike Royko, *Boss: Richard J. Daley of Chicago* (New York: Signet, 1971), 38.

24 Len O'Connor, *Clout: Mayor Daley and His City* (New York: Henry Regnery, 1975), 18–20.
25 *Chicago Tribune*, February 17, 2003; *Chicago Sun-Times*, February 17, 2003; for Irish courtship habits, see Charles Fanning, *Finley Peter Dunne and Mr. Dooley: The Chicago Years* (Lexington: University Press of Kentucky, 1978), 51.
26 Biles, *Richard J. Daley*, 22–24; Adam Cohen and Elizabeth Taylor, *American Pharaoh: Mayor Richard J. Daley, His Battle for Chicago and the Nation* (Boston: Little, Brown and Company, 2000), 56–63.
27 O'Connor, *Clout*, 13, 104–5.
28 Cohen and Taylor, *American Pharaoh*, 73–87.
29 Form letter Irish Fellowship Club to Members, undated, Folder SIss 1B36–8, RJDUIC; Table List for Irish Fellowship Dinner, March 14, 1959, Folder SIss 1B33–11, RJDUIC.
30 "St. Patrick's Day in Chicago," *Chicago Tribune*, March 18, 1862, https://chicagology.com/irishinchicago/stpatricksday, accessed June 15, 2022.
31 Employment requests appear throughout the collection: see as an example Folder SIss 1 B53–6, RJDUIC; particularly Memo from Don Shinnick to Mayor Richard J. Daley, Subject Board of Health Pending Requisitions, April 6, 1966, Rev. James L. Mollohan Correspondence with Richard J. Daley, December 15, 19, 1966; Memorandum from Raymond F. Simon to Mayor Richard J, Daley, Subject Rep. Peter Miller, N.D.; Note Frances G. Foster to Helen McCabe, February 16, 1962, Folder SIss 1 B44–11, RJDUIC; Letter from Joe Plunkitt to Mayor Richard J. Daley, August 24, 1965, Folder SIss 1 B52–3, RJDUIC; Shinnick Correspondence Folder SIss 1 B55–1, RJDUIC.
32 Note from Richard J. Daley to Lewis Hill, October 1, 1965, Folder SIss 1 B52–1, RJDUIC; Letter from Ray Spaeth to Richard J. Daley, May 18, 1966, Folder SIss 1 B53–1, RJDUIC. Requests for the mayor's intervention are found throughout the Daley Collection at the University of Illinois at Chicago: examples cited are letter from Richard J. Daley to Eric Oldenburg, April 15, 1965; letter from Eric Oldenburg to Richard J. Daley, April 16, 1965; letter from Stephen O'Callaghan Jr. to Richard J. Daley, Folder SIss 1 B52–1 RJDUIC; Margaret A. Reid to Richard J. Daley, October 21, 1963, Folder SIss 1 B48–2, RJDUIC.
33 Letter from Brother Eugene Gaffney to Richard J. Daley, July 13, 1967, and letter from Richard J. Daley to Ferd Kramer, July 19, 1967, Folder SIss 1 B57–7, RJDUIC; letter from Anne Leonhardt to Richard J. Daley, November 19, 1965, letter from Richard J. Daley to Charles Swibel, November 30, 1965, letter from Richard J. Daley to Charles Swibel, September 13, 1965, letter from David Karsh to Richard J. Daley, June 15, 1965, letter from Richard J. Daley to David Karsh, June 22, 1965, letter from Richard J. Daley to Charles Swibel, June 22, 1965, Folder SIss 1 B52–6, RJDUIC; letter from Albert

Musto to Richard J. Daley, March 25, 1965, letter from Walter Poranski to Richard J. Daley, February 5, 1965, Folder SIss 1 B52—3, RJDUIC; letter from Brother Lambert Thomas to Richard J. Daley, March 26, 1966, memorandum from Jack Reilly to Richard J. Daley, April 1, 1966, Folder SIss 1 B52—16, RJDUIC.

34 For example, see Lester Bernstein to John Baily, June 1, 1966, letter from Gerald Blaine to Richard J. Daley, June 6, 1966, Folder SIss 1 B52—16, RJDUIC; letter from Leo J. Meehan to Richard J. Daley, February 2, 1965, letter from Thomas A. McGloon to Richard J. Daley, February 8, 1965, Rev. Louis Pisano to Richard J. Daley, June 10, 1965, Folder SIss 1 B52—4, RJDUIC.

35 Letter to Frank Whiston from Richard J. Daley, March 25, 1966, memo from James G. O'Donohue to Richard J. Daley, March 23, 1966, letter from Richard J. Daley to Frank Whiston, July 8, 1966, letter from Richard J. Daley to Frank Whiston, September 13, 1966, Frank Whiston to Richard J. Daley, September 22, 1966, letter from Richard J. Daley to Frank Whiston, February 24, 1966, Folder SIss 1 B53—1, RJDUIC.

36 On a personal note, my ward committeeman once offered me a job with a private firm, something I did not pursue.

37 Biles, *Richard J. Daley*, 20.

38 The classic studies of the Daley machine are Milton Rakove, *Don't Make Waves—Don't Back No Losers: An Insider's Analysis of the Daley Machine* (Bloomington: Indiana University Press, 1975), and his *We Don't Want Nobody Nobody Sent: An Oral History of the Daley Years* (Bloomington: Indiana University Press, 1979).

39 Statement of the CIO to the Nominating Committee of the Democratic Party of Cook County, December 16, 1954, Folder SIIss 1 30-3, RJDUIC.

40 Correspondence between Peter Tomczak and Richard J. Daley, February 6, 1959, Folder SIss 1B34—24, RJDUIC; Lists of Union Men (Leaders), their office held and their addresses, phone numbers (1961), Folder SIss 1 B39—10, RJDUIC.

41 Royko, *Boss*, 26; Biles, *Daley*, 53.

42 Form Letter, Richard J. Daley to Democratic Precinct Captains, undated but probably 1955, Folder SIIss 1 30-6, RJDUIC; Form Letter, "Richard J. Daley News" N.D.t Workers, March 25, 1954, form letter, Clayton F. Smith to 33rd Ward Precinct Captains & Members, November 1, 1954, Folder SIIss 1 B22-9, RJDUIC; Edwin A. Lahey, "Hail the Precinct Captain," *Chicago Daily News*, undated, Folder SIIss 1 B22-17, RJDUIC.

43 Your Precinct Canvas Book; Democratic Voters That Have Moved from Precinct 7 of the 37th Ward: Revised List of Precinct Captains, 33rd Ward, September 25, 1953, Folder SIIss 1 B22-17, RJDUIC; Card from Precinct Captain Ralph F. Gross, 15th Precinct, 31st Ward, Folder SIIss 1 30-6, RJDUIC; Letter from Henry S. Feit to Richard J. Daley, March 21, 1959; Letter from Henry J. Schultz to Richard J. Daley, March 21, 1959, Folder SIIss 1 34-28, RJDUIC;

Folder enclosed 45th Ward Precinct Captain; letter from F. G. Foster to Pail T. Wigoda, March 11, 1959, Folder SIIss 1 34-10, RJDUIC.

44 For a definition of the Church Triumphant, see Msgr. M. Francis Mannion, "The Church: Triumphant, Militant and Suffering," Simply Catholic, https://www.simplycatholic.com/the-church-triumphant-militant-and-suffering, accessed June 2, 2022. Chicago's cardinals received the No. 1 auto license plate as early as 1938. *Chicago Tribune*, January 26, 1938; John Aranza, *De La Salle Institute Centennial History, 1889–1989* (Chicago: De La Salle Institute, 1989), 104–20.

45 Program, 58th Annual Banquet of the De La Salle Alumni Association, November 19, 1953, Folder SIss 1 B14–5, RJDUIC.

46 *The De La Salle Alumnus Magazine*, September 1954; Letter from Brother Patrick to De La Salle Alumni, July 8, 1954; Press release from De La salle Expansion Campaign, March 14, 1954, Folder SIss 1 B14–5, RJDUIC.

47 Binder, De La Salle 70th Anniversary Building Fund Campaign: Laying of the Cornerstone Program, Letter from Morgan F. Murphy to Richard J. Daley, May 12, 1961; Letter from Morgan F. Murphy to Arthur Ward, May 10, 1961, Folder SIss 1 B39–1, RJDUIC.

48 *Chicago Tribune*, May 5, July 31, October 13, 1955.

49 Various letters acknowledging Daley's fundraising are in Folder SIss 1B34–20, RJDUIC; Letter from Richard J. Daley to Mr. Harry J. O'Haire, May 31, 1960, Folder SIss 1B37–86, RJDUIC; Letter from Sister Mary Josetta to Richard J. Daley, August 25, 1960, Folder SIss 1B37–6; RJDUIC; *Chicago Tribune*, January 8, 1989; "Mayor Daley Pays a Tribute," *Chicago Tribune Magazine*, August 6, 1961, Folder SIss 1B38–8, RJDUIC.

50 Letter from Sister M. Huberta to Patrick O'Malley, March 18, 1962; Letter from Sister M. Huberta to John C. Duba, March 26, 1962; Letter from Sister M. Huberta to Mrs. Frank J. Lewis, February 19, 1962; Folder SIss 1 B44–11, RJDUIC.

51 Richard J. Daley Collection, Series 1, Sub-Series 1, SIss 1 B44 Folder SIss 1 B44–15 contains various letters outlining Daley's participation in the fundraising campaign. Handwritten and typed lists of donors to the Nativity school campaign, Folder SIss 1 B40–1, RJDUIC.

52 *Chicago Tribune*, August 31, 1957, May 1, 1979.

53 Lists of Donors; Letter from Stephen M. Bailey to Mathew J. Danaher, December 11, 1961; letter from Judge James J. McDermott to Rev. Michael J. Conway, December 19, 1961, Folder SIss 1 B40–1, RJDUIC.

54 F. Richard Ciccone, *Daley: Power and Presidential Politics* (Chicago: Contemporary Books, 1996), chapter 6; Biles, *Richard J. Daley*, 72–74.

55 *Time*, March 15, 1963, 24–35.

56 An overall look at the decision-making process is George Rosen, *Decision-Making Chicago-Style: The Genesis of a University of Illinois Campus* (Urbana: University of Illinois Press, 1980).

57 Cohen and Taylor, *American Pharaoh*, 224–25.
58 Cohen and Taylor, *American Pharaoh*, 225–28.
59 Royko, *Boss*, 126–27.
60 Rosen, *Decision-Making Chicago-Style*, 114–15; *Chicago Tribune*, February 13, February 14, 1961.
61 *Chicago Tribune*, May 11, 1961.
62 Biles, *Richard J. Daley*, 74–75.

CHAPTER 9

1 Quotation from Al Raby's Soldier Field speech, James R. Ralph and Mary Lou Finley, "In Their Own Voices: The Story of the Movement as Told by the Participants," in *The Chicago Freedom Movement: Martin Luther King Jr. and Civil Rights Activism in the North*, ed. Mary Lou Finley, Bernard Lafayette Jr., James R. Ralph, and Pan Smith (Lexington: University Press of Kentucky, 2015), 47.
2 Roger Biles, *Richard J. Daley: Politics, Race, and the Governing of Chicago* (DeKalb: Northern Illinois University Press, 1995), 80–83.
3 *Time*, March 15, 1963, 34.
4 Arnold R. Hirsch, *The Making of the Second Ghetto: Race and Housing in Chicago, 1940–1960* (Chicago: University of Chicago Press, 1998), 93–99; Arnold R. Hirsch, "Massive Resistance in the Urban North: Trumbull Park, Chicago 1953–1966," *Journal of American History* 82, no. 2 (September 1995): 522–50.
5 James R. Ralph Jr., *Northern Protest: Martin Luther King, Jr., Chicago, and the Civil Rights Movement* (Cambridge, MA: Harvard University Press, 1993), 12–13.
6 Christopher Robert Reed, *The Chicago NAACP and the Rise of Professional Black Leadership, 1910–1966* (Bloomington: Indiana University Press, 1997), 162–67, 182–91; Ralph, *Northern Protest*, 12; Adam Green, *Selling the Race: Culture, Community, and Black Chicago, 1940–1955* (Chicago: University of Chicago Press, 2007), 182, 186, 195–96.
7 Nicholas A. Juravich, "Wade in the Water: The NAACP Youth Council, the Sit-In Movement, and the Rainbow Beach Wade-Ins in Chicago, 1960–1961," *Chicago Studies* (2008): 43–106.
8 *Chicago Defender*, June 28, July 3, July 11, 1961; *Chicago Tribune*, June 18, June 28, 1961; Juravich, "Wade in the Water," 90–92.
9 *Chicago Tribune*, July 5, 1963.
10 Resolution by Chicago Urban League Board of Directors Submitted to the Chicago Board of Education, October 13, 1961, Series 1, Sub-Series 1, Folder SIss 1 B45—9, RJDUIC.
11 Memorandum to Edwin C. Berry from Harold Baron, December 5, 1961, Folder SIss 1 B45—9, RJDUIC.

12 Letter from Edwin C. Berry to Richard J. Daley, January 6, 1962, Folder SIss 1 B45—9, RJDUIC.
13 *Chicago Defender*, September 23, 1963.
14 *Chicago Tribune*, July 30, 1963.
15 *Chicago Tribune*, September 5, 1963; September 11, September 20, 1965; October 6, October 17, 1963; Ralph, *Northern Protest*, 20.
16 *Chicago Tribune*, October 18, 1963; Fannie Rushing and Patrick Jones, "Chicago SNCC and the Black Freedom Movement," *OAH Magazine of History* 26, no. 1 (January 2012): 56.
17 Christopher Robert Reed, "Towards the Apex of Civil Rights Activism: Antecedents of the Chicago Freedom Movement, 1965–1966," in Finley et al., eds., *The Chicago Freedom Movement*, 108.
18 *Chicago Defender*, July 11, 1964.
19 *Chicago Defender*, August 17, August 20, 1964.
20 Examples of these letters include Judy Nau to Richard J. Daley, September 20, 1964; Michael Blackburn to Richard J. Daley, August 20, 1964; Henry and Marie Neely to Richard J. Daley, August 20, 1964; Telegram, Carl R. Davenport to Richard J. Daley, August 22, 1964; Rudy Frank, University of Illinois Young Democrats to RJD, undated; George W. Beadle to Richard J. Daley, August 19, 1964 (includes Albert Haus, father to George W. Beadle), August 17, 1964. This file contains many others in Richard J. Daley Collection as well as Memo to Raymond F. Simon, Mayor's Administrative Officer, from Albert A. Raby, August 20, 1964, Folder SIss 1 B568—1, RJDUIC. More letters are filed in Folder SIss 1 B567—7, RJDUIC.
21 *Chicago Defender*, August 24, July 30, August 11, September 12, 1964; Adam Cohen and Elizabeth Taylor, *American Pharaoh: Mayor Richard J. Daley, His Battle for Chicago and the Nation* (Boston: Little, Brown, and Company, 2000), 321; William L. Colman to Richard J. Daley, September 17, 1964, Folder SIss 1 B567—7, RJDUIC.
22 *Chicago Defender*, October 10, December 5, 1964.
23 Telegram, Albert Raby to Richard J. Daley, December 12, 1964; Al Raby to Richard J. Daley, January 8, 1965, Folder SIss 1 B567—7, RJDUIC; *Chicago Defender*, September 22, 1965.
24 Proclamation, Mayor Richard J. Daley, March 2, 1960, Folder SIss 1B37—13, RJDUIC; for the Summerdale Scandal, see Greg Hoffman and Anne D. Kroemer, "Remembering Summerdale: A Scandal That Reformed Policing," *International Journal of Peace and Development Studies* 12, no. 1 (January–June 2021): 38–45, https://academicjournals.org/journal/IJPDS/article-full-text-pdf/53B4A4567064, accessed July 12, 2022; William J. Bopp, "In Quest of Police Profession: A Biography of O. W. Wilson," EdD diss., Florida Atlantic University, 1975, 185–206.
25 *Chicago Defender*, January 23, January 25, 1964.
26 *Chicago Tribune*, August 17, August 18, August 20, 1964.

27 *Chicago Tribune*, August 14, 1965; *Chicago Defender*, August 14, August 16, 1965; Amanda I. Seligman, *Block by Block* (Chicago: University of Chicago Press, 2005), 216–17.
28 *Chicago Tribune*, August 17, 1965.
29 Ralph, *Northern Protest*, 83.
30 *Chicago Tribune*, April 2, April 4, April 6, 1965.
31 *Chicago Tribune*, April 17, 1965.
32 Erik S. Gellman, *Troublemakers: Chicago Freedom Struggles Through the Lens of Art Shay* (Chicago: University of Chicago Press, 2020), 94–95, 125–28.
33 *Chicago Tribune*, June 10, July 7, July 8, July 11, 1965.
34 *Chicago Tribune*, July 24, July 25, 1965.
35 Ralph, *Northern Protest*, 7, 21–22; Mary Lou Finley, Bernard Lafayette Jr., James R. Ralph Jr., and Pam Smith, "Introduction," in Finley et al., eds., *The Chicago Freedom Movement*, 1; Robert B. McKersie, *A Decisive Decade: An Insider's View of the Chicago Civil Rights Movement During the 1960s* (Carbondale: Southern Illinois University Press, 2013), 69; *Chicago Tribune*, December 25, 1965.
36 *Chicago Tribune*, January 8, 1966.
37 Ralph, *Northern Protest*, 76–80; *Chicago Tribune*, January 13, April 18, 1966.
38 *Chicago Tribune*, March 25, March 26, 1966.
39 *Chicago Tribune*, May 27, July 7, 1966.
40 Ralph, *Northern Protest*, 105–7.
41 Seligman, *Block by Block*, 217–20; Ralph, *Northern Protest*, 109–12.
42 *Chicago Tribune*, August 6, August 11, August 19, 1966; Ralph, *Northern Protest*, 123.
43 *Chicago Tribune*, September 1, 1966; Leon M. Despres, *Challenging the Daley Machine: A Chicago Alderman's Memoir* (Evanston, IL: Northwestern University Press, 2005), 98; Seligman, *Block by Block*, 218–21.
44 Biles, *Richard J. Daley*, 177–80; Cohen and Taylor, *American Pharaoh*, 501–3, 513–15.
45 Telegrams from Arnold Levin to Richard J. Daley, August 21, 1968; David D. Dellinger, Dr. Sidney Peck, Rennie Davis to Richard J. Daley, August 22, 1968; John de J. Pemberton Jr. to Richard J. Daley, August 22, 1968; Earl Spencer to Richard J. Daley, August 21, 1968; Richard J. Daley to Eugene McCarthy and George McGovern, August 16, 1968; Edward A. McDermott to Richard J. Daley, August 19, 1968, all in Folder SIss 1 B83—12, RJDUIC.
46 Richard J. Daley to Gov. Samuel H. Shapiro, August 19, 1968, Folder SIss 1 B84—5, RJDUIC; Executive Order, Gov. Samuel H. Shapiro to the Adjunct General of Illinois, August 20, 1968, https://www.ilsos.gov/departments/archives/online_exhibits/100_documents/1968-gov-call-national-guard.html, accessed March 20, 2022.
47 For a look at events leading up to and during the convention, see David Farber, *Chicago '68* (Chicago: University of Chicago Press, 1988). For Daley's

private reaction, see Frank Sullivan, *Legend: The Only Inside Story About Mayor Richard J. Daley* (Chicago: Bonus Books, Inc., 1989), 49, 50, 54.
48 Daniel Walker, *Rights in Conflict: Convention Week in Chicago, August 25–29, 1968* (New York: Signet, 1968); Sullivan, *Legend*, 52.
49 Judge William J. Campell to Richard J. Daley, August 29, 1968; Peter M. Shannon to Richard J. Daley, September 6, 1968; Richard J. Daley to Mr. and Mrs. John McCuddy, September 11, 1968. Many such letters may be found in Folder SIss 1 B84—5, RJDUIC, and Folder SIss 1 B85—3, RJDUIC.
50 *Chicago Tribune*, October 25, October 29, November 3, 1970; February 20, March 5, April 20, 1971.
51 *Chicago Tribune*, July 8, September 2, October 21, October 25, 1971; January 12, 1972; Michael L. Shakman et al. etc. v. The Democratic Organization, October 14, 1971, Folder SIss 1 B98—1, RJDUIC.
52 *Chicago Tribune*, February 23, April 21, May 6, 1972.
53 *Chicago Tribune*, July 29, September 12, October 7, 1972, October 28, 1972.
54 *Los Angeles Times*, June 8, 1969, clipping "Daley Statement Before the McGovern Commission," Folder SIss 1 B91—3, RJDUIC; *Chicago Tribune*, June 7, June 8, June 9, 1969.
55 Angelo G. Geocaris to Richard J. Daley, August 15, 1969; Adlai Stevenson III to Richard J. Daley, August 20, 1969; George McGovern to Richard J. Daley, August 21, 1969; Folder SIss 1 B92—1, RJDUIC; George McGovern to Richard J. Daley, June 20, 1969, Folder SIss 1 B91—3, RJDUIC.
56 George McGovern to Richard J. Daley, September 15, 1969, Richard J. Daley Collection; Jay S. Wertheimer to Richard J. Daley, September 15, 1969; Richard J. Daley to Jay S. Wertheimer, September 19, 1969, Folder SIss 1 B92—1, RJDUIC.
57 F. Richard Ciccone, *Daley: Power and Presidential Politics* (Chicago: Contemporary Books,, 1996), 281f.; Biles, *Richard J. Daley*, 190–94; Box 106, Folder 1812, MABiUIC. There is much material in the Daley papers, especially in boxes Series 2, Sub-Series 1, SIss 1 B99, B100, B101, B102, B103, RJDUIC.
58 Memo from E. B. to Mayor Richard J. Daley, July 13, 1972, Statement by Mayor Richard J. Daley, July 13, 1972, Folder SIss 1 B99—1, RJDUIC; for letters both supporting Daley and attacking him for supporting McGovern, Folder SIss 1 B105—1, RJDUIC; Folder SIss 1 B107—1, B107—2, B107—3, RJDUIC; Election November 7, 1972, Cook County, Illinois, Section 1: Registration and Applications for Ballots, Total Votes for Candidates by City of Chicago Wards, Folder SIss 1 B104—1-2, RJDUIC; Biles, *Richard J. Daley*, 195.
59 *Chicago Tribune*, January 17, January 27, 1971; May 1, 1970; July 9, July 10, September 26, December 7, 1971; Walker, *The Maverick and the Machine*, 112–23.
60 *Chicago Tribune*, November 9, November 10, 1972; Thaddeus S. Lechowicz to Richard J. Daley, September 29, 1972, Folder SIss 1 B106—9.

61 Walker, *The Maverick and the Machine*, 225; Sullivan, *Legend*, 204; Biles, *Richard J. Daley*, 195–96.
62 Cohen and Taylor, *American Pharaoh*, 526–27; Dick Simpson, *Rogues, Rebels, and Rubber Stamps: The Politics of the Chicago City Council from 1863 to the Present* (Boulder, CO: Westview Press, 2001), 138–39.
63 Biles, *Richard J. Daley*, 197–201.
64 Cohen and Taylor, *American Pharaoh*, 536, 540–43; Biles, *Richard J. Daley*, 189, 200–205.

CHAPTER 10

1 *Daily News*, December 21, 1976.
2 *Back of the Yards Journal*, April 2, 1975; Black Votes, Election Files, 1975; Results of the Municipal Election, April 1, 1975, Folder SIss 1 B118-4, RJDUIC.
3 Adam Cohen and Elizabeth Taylor, *American Pharaoh: Mayor Richard J. Daley, His Battle for Chicago and the Nation* (New York: Little, Brown and Company, 2000), 548–49; various letters of support are in Folder SIss 1 B118—1, RJDUIC; *Chicago Tribune*, September 20, September 27, October 4, October 28, 1975.
4 Office of the State Board of Elections, Springfield Illinois Certificate of Election, Certified election on March 16, 1976, Richard J. Daley (Stevenson) was elected delegate to the National Nominating Convention for the Democratic Party from the 5th Congressional District, May 5, 1976, Folder SIss 1 B122—11, RJDUIC; Cohen and Taylor, *American Pharaoh*, 552–53.
5 Frank Sullivan, *Legend: The Only Inside Story About Mayor Richard J. Daley* (Chicago: Bonus Books, Inc., 1989), 237–41; Roger Biles, *Richard J. Daley: Politics, Race, and the Governing of Chicago* (DeKalb: Northern Illinois University Press, 1995), 222; *Chicago Tribune*, December 21, 1976. The *Chicago Tribune* covered the day's events extensively, as did the other Chicago papers.
6 *Chicago Tribune*, December 21, December 23, 1976; *Daily News*, December 21, 1976.
7 Call for a Special Meeting of the City Council of the City of Chicago, Folder 126-2125, MABiUIC; *Chicago Tribune*, December 22, 1976; *Daily News*, December 21, 1976.
8 *Daily News*, December 27, December 28, December 29, 1976.
9 Mayor's Office Press Release, December 29, 1976, Statement by Mayor Michael A. Bilandic, January 5, 1977, 118-1999, MABiUIC; Biles, *Richard J. Daley*, 233; *Daily News*, December 29, December 30, 1976.
10 *Chicago Tribune*, December 29, December 30, 1976; January 15, January 21, January 24, February 1, 1977; Dominic A. Pacyga, "Roman C. Pucinski:

Chicago Alderman and Polonia Leader," *Polish American Studies* 79, no. 1 (Spring 2022): 75–93. This entire issue is dedicated to a study of Roman Pucinski, his family, and their impact on Chicago.
11 *Chicago Sun-Times*, April 18, 1979.
12 William J. Grimshaw, *Bitter Fruit: Black Politics and the Chicago Machine, 1931–1991* (Chicago: University of Chicago Press, 1992), 144–45; *Chicago Tribune*, April 20, 1977; for an excellent look at the primary race, see Joseph Zikmund II, "Mayoral Voting and Ethnic Politics in the Daley-Bilandic-Byrne Era," in Samuel K. Gove and Louis H. Masotti, *After Daley: Chicago Politics in Transition* (Urbana: University of Illinois Press, 1982), 37–40, 42–50; Paul Kleppner, *Chicago Divided: The Making of a Black Mayor* (DeKalb: Northern Illinois University Press, 1985), 96–103.
13 *Daily News*, December 30, 1976; *Chicago Tribune*, October 2, 1977.
14 *Chicago Tribune*, January 14, January 15, 1979; *Chicago Sun-Times*, January 14, January 15, 1979.
15 Call for a Special Meeting of the City Council of the City of Chicago, February 1, 1979, 64-1370, MABiUIC; Resolution February 1, 1979, Substitute Resolution February 6, Press Release "National Task Force Created to Study How Rapid Transit Systems Can Cope with Snow and Ice Emergencies," February 22, 1979, Folder 157-2551, MABiUIC.
16 *Chicago Tribune*, January 16, January 17, January 18, January 19, 1979.
17 *Chicago Tribune*, January 19, January 21, January 31, February 1, February 2, February 3, February 5, 1979.
18 *Chicago Tribune*, January 21, January 25, January 28, January 29, February 2, February 16, 1979; *Chicago Sun-Times*, January 14, January 16, January 18, 1979.
19 See the series of handwritten notes dating from January 13, 1979, through January 21, 1979, Folder 160-2666, MABiUIC; *Chicago Sun-Times*, February 27, February 28, 1979.
20 Melvin G. Holli, "Jane M. Byrne: To Think the Unthinkable and Do the Undoable," in Paul M. Green and Malvin G. Holli, *The Mayors: The Chicago Political Tradition*, revised edition (Carbondale: Southern Illinois University Press, 1995), 168–78.
21 William J. Grimshaw, "The Daley Legacy: A Declining Politics of Party, Race, and Public Unions," in Samuel K. Gove and Louis H. Masotti, *After Daley: Chicago Politics in Transition* (Urbana: University of Illinois Press, 1982), 57–87; Holli, "Jane M. Byrne,"170; "Jane Byrne," Chicago Stories, WTTW, https://interactive.wttw.com/chicago-stories/jane-byrne/video, accessed January 23, 2023.
22 *Chicago Tribune*, June 17, 1984.
23 Grimshaw, "The Daley Legacy," 69–71.
24 *Chicago Tribune*, June 17, 1984.

25 Grimshaw, "The Daley Legacy," 81–85; Holli, "Jane M. Byrne," 170–73. Rose is quoted in Holli, "Jane Byrne"; Jane Byrne, *My Chicago* (Evanston, IL: Northwestern University Press, 2003), 330.
26 "Jane Byrne," Chicago Stories.
27 *Chicago Sun-Times*, January 1, December 13, December 20, December 31, 1981; January 16, October 22, October 23, November 4, November 5, 1982.
28 *Chicago Sun-Times*, November 2, November 11, 1982.
29 Quoted in Kleppner, *Chicago Divided*, 177.
30 Kleppner, *Chicago Divided*, 193–96, 210–11 (examples of racist handbills are reproduced on pp. 212 and 213); Don Rose, "How the 1983 Election Was Won," in *The Making of the Mayor: Chicago 1983*, ed. Melvin G. Holli and Paul M. Green (Grand Rapids, MI: William B. Eerdmans Publishing Company, 1984), 113.
31 *Chicago Tribune*, April 29, 1983; Gary Rivlin, *Fire on the Prairie: Chicago's Harold Washington and the Politics of Race* (New York: Henry Holt and Company, 1992), 207. Perhaps the most balanced look at Washington and his administration is Roger Biles, *Mayor Harold Washington: Champion of Race and Reform in Chicago* (Urbana: University of Illinois Press, 2018).
32 *Chicago Tribune*, April 17, April 19, October 10, 1983.
33 Melvin G. Holli and Paul M. Green, *Bashing Chicago's Traditions: Harold Washington's Last Campaign* (Grand Rapids, MI: William B. Eerdmans Publishing Company, 1989), 27, 31–34, 111; Biles, *Mayor Harold Washington*, 228–29; *Chicago Tribune*, May 4, 1986; April 7, 1987.
34 *Chicago Tribune*, April 19, June 18, November 19, November 26, 1987.
35 *Chicago Tribune*, November 28, November 11, December 1, 1987.
36 For the rivalries that exploded after Washington's death, see Rivlin, *Fire on the Prairie*, chapter 22.
37 *Chicago Tribune*, November 29, December 2, December 3, 1987; Holli and Green, *Bashing Chicago's Traditions*, 195.
38 *Chicago Tribune*, December 24, 1956; December 20, 1951.
39 Mark S. Massa, S.J., *The American Catholic Revolution: How the Sixties Changed the Church Forever*, Kindle edition (New York: Oxford University Press, 2010), preface.
40 *Chicago Tribune*, October 23, November 11, 1962; Massa, *American Catholic Revolution*, 1–2, 134.
41 Garry Wills, *Bare Ruined Choirs: Doubt, Prophecy, and Radical Religion* (Garden City, NY: Paulist Press, 1972), chapter 3, 70–71; *Chicago Tribune*, October 16, 1963; Massa, *American Catholic Revolution*, 71. I was told this version of the history of Catholicism by a parish priest as a student in a Chicago parochial school class in the 1950s and early 1960s.
42 Andrew Greeley, *The Catholic Myth: The Behavior and Beliefs of American Catholics* (New York: Charles Scribner's Sons, 1990), 133; Massa, *American*

Catholic Revolution, chapter 2; *Chicago Tribune*, May 16, August 25, October 4, 1964; *Chicago Sun-Times*, March 1, 1965.
43 *Chicago Sun-Times*, March 7, March 8, 1965.
44 Quoted in Massa, *American Catholic Revolution*, 77.
45 Massa, 82–84.
46 *Chicago Sun-Times*, January 22, August 15, 1964; January 10, January 11, October 9, 1965.
47 Suellen Hoy, *Good Hearts: Catholic Sisters in Chicago's Past* (Urbana: University of Illinois Press, 2006), 125, 139–41.
48 *Chicago Tribune*, March 23, June 13, August 10, 1965; Suellen Hoy, *Good Hearts*, 143–48.
49 Massa, *American Catholic Revolution*, chapter 6; Wills, *Bare Ruined Choirs*, 125–32, chapter 10.
50 *Chicago Tribune*, October 20, 1966; March 20, August 2, 1967; March 29, November 3, 1968.
51 Greeley, *The Catholic Myth*, 13, 17.

CHAPTER 11

1 Quoted in the *Chicago Sun-Times*, February 20, 2003.
2 David Axelrod, interview transcript, February 21, 2018, 8, RJDOralUIC; *Chicago Sun-Times*, December 6, 1988; for the Skrebneski photo, see Inaugural Program, City of Chicago, April 24, 1989, Folder 1-13-8, RMDUIC.
3 *Chicago Tribune*, December 6, 1988; *Chicago Sun-Times*, December 8, 1988.
4 Keith Koeneman, *First Son: The Biography of Richard M. Daley* (Chicago: University of Chicago Press, 2013), 116; *Chicago Sun-Times*, December 10, December 12, 1988.
5 *Chicago Sun-Times*, December 11, December 12, December 16, December 20, December 30, 1988.
6 *Chicago Tribune*, February 2, February 8, 1989; *Chicago Sun-Times*, February 7, February 8, 1989.
7 *Chicago Tribune*, February 27, February 28, 1989.
8 Paul M. Green, "The 1989 Mayoral Primary Election," in *Restoration 1989: Chicago Elects a New Daley*, ed. Paul M. Green and Melvin G. Holli (Chicago: Lyceum Books, Inc., 1991), 3–32; *Chicago Tribune*, March 1, 1989.
9 Paul M. Green, "The 1989 General Election," in Green and Holli, *Restoration 1989*, 33–53; *Chicago Tribune*, March 2, March 13, April 5, 1989.
10 *Chicago Sun-Times*, April 25, 1989; *Chicago Tribune*, April 25, 1989.
11 *Chicago Tribune*, April 6, 1989; Koeneman, *First Son*, 65–66.
12 Timothy Stewart-Winter, *Queer Clout: Chicago and the Rise of Gay Politics* (Philadelphia: University of Pennsylvania Press, 2016), chapter 6, 209–13.
13 "Mayor Daley's Campaign Promise to the Gay and Lesbian Community"

(undated, but 1989–1991 folder), Folder 1-8-1, RMDUIC.; Daley-Conroy, Nora Interview, Transcript, February 21, 2018, 8, RMDOralUIC.

14   Thom Dombkowski to Richard M. Daley, July 2, 1991; Marie Kula to Richard M. Daley, July 1, 1991; Judith Johns to Richard M. Daley, July 2, 1991; Tom Tunney and Nancy Pakieser to Richard M. Daley, May 3, 1991, Folder 1-8-1, Box 1-8, RMDUIC.

15   Stewart-Winter, *Queer Clout*, 161, 208, 210–11, 220–23.

16   Msgr. Harry C. Kornig S.T.D., ed., *A History of the Parishes of the Archdiocese of Chicago*, vol. 1 (Chicago: Archdiocese of Chicago, 1980), 691–95; for the history of the Mexican steel mill community, see Michael Innis-Jiménez, *Steel Barrio: The Great Mexican Migration to South Chicago, 1915–1940* (New York: New York University Press, 2013).

17   Garbriela F. Arrendondo, *Mexican Chicago: Race, Identity, and Nation, 1916–1939* (Urbana: University of Illinois Press, 2008), 50, 54–58, 66, 70, 73–74, 76; Wilfredo Cruz, *Latinos in Chicago: Quest for a Political Voice* (Carbondale: Southern Illinois University Press, 2022), 7.

18   Arrendondo, *Mexican Chicago*, 105–6; Mike Amezcua, *Making Mexican Chicago: From Postwar Settlement to the Age of Gentrification* (Chicago: University of Chicago Press, 2022), chapter 2.

19   Lilia Fernandez, *Brown in the Windy City: Mexicans and Puerto Ricans in Postwar Chicago* (Chicago: University of Chicago Press, 2012), 4–5; Gina M. Pérez, *The Near Northwest Side Story: Migration, Displacement, and Puerto Rican Families* (Berkeley, CA: University of California Press, 2004), 130–31; Cruz, *Latinos in Chicago*, 12.

20   Cruz, *Latinos in Chicago*, 12–13.

21   Fernandez, *Brown in the Windy City*, 264–65; Amezcua, *Making Mexican Chicago*, 198–99.

22   Cruz, *Latinos in Chicago*, 48–49.

23   Carole Bialczak to Donald Smith, January 5, 1991, Richard M. Daley Collection, Series 1 Box 1-3, Folder 1-3-4; Myron M. Cherry to Richard M. Daley, December 21, 1990, Folder 1-21-8, RMDUIC; see photo Folder 1-13-5, RMDUIC; To: Richard M. Daley, From: MarySue Barrett, Reason: Statistics on Board and Commission Appointments, November 28, 1990, Folder 1-21-2, RMDUIC.

24   Dominic A. Pacyga, "Losing Clout: Nancy Kaszak Versus Rahm Emanuel and the Decline of Polish American Politics in Chicago," in Wendy Everham, *Probing the Past: Festschrift in Honor of Leo Schelbert* (New York: Peter Lang, 2015), 119–30.

25   Koeneman, *First Son*, 275–78; David B. Cohen, Karen M. Hult, and Charles E. Walcott, "The Chicago Clan: The Chiefs of Staff in the Obama White House," *Social Science Quarterly* 93, no. 5 (December 2012): 1101–26.

26   Euan Hague, Michael J. Lorr, and Carolina Sternberg, "Introduction: Chicago A Neoliberal City," in *Neoliberal Chicago*, ed. Larry Bennett, Roberta Garner, and Euan Hague (Urbana: University of Illinois Press, 2017), 2.

Notes to Pages 294–301

27 *Chicago Tribune*, January 28, 2004; *Chicago Sun-Times*, January 26, 2004.
28 Larry Bennett, *The Third City: Chicago and American Urbanism* (Chicago: University of Chicago Press, 2010), 79–82.
29 Hague, Lorr, and Sternberg, "Introduction," 5–7. For the creation of Chicago as a city of spectacle and tourism, see Costas Spirou and Dennis R. Judd, *Building the City of Spectacle: Mayor Richard M. Daley and the Remaking of Chicago* (Ithaca, NY: Cornell University Press, 2016), chapter 3; Timothy J. Gilfoyle, *Millennium Park: Creating a Chicago Landmark* (Chicago: University of Chicago Press, 2006), is an important account of the park and its development.
30 Roberta Garner, Black Hawk Hancock, and Kenneth Fidel, "Class and Race-Ethnicity in a Changing City," in Bennett et al., *Neoliberal Chicago*, 17–46.
31 Larry Bennett, "Contemporary Chicago Politics: Myth, Reality, and Neoliberalism," in Bennett et al., *Neoliberal Chicago*, 85–86, 90. For a discussion of public school reforms and neoliberalism, see Pauline Lipmann, "Chicago School Reform: Advancing the Global City Agenda," in *The New Chicago: A Social and Cultural Analysis*, ed. John P. Koval, Larry Bennett, Michael I. J. Bennett, Fasil Demassie, Roberta Garner, and Kiljoong Kim (Philadelphia: Temple University Press, 2006), 248–58.
32 John Daley, interview transcript, September 14, 2018, 4, 7, RMDOralUIC; Axelrod interview, 17, 23; William Daley, interview transcript, February 21, 2018, 2, 11–12, RMDOralUIC.
33 John Daley, interview, 17–18; *Chicago Tribune*, March 13, 1990; September 15, November 21, 1993; June 17, 1994; May 15, 1995.
34 Daley-Conroy Interview, *Chicago Tribune*, June 16, 1996, 19–20.
35 Richard A. Devine to Paul Toback, March 26, 1992; memo from Karen Nowacki to Paul Toback, December 11, 1990; Paul Toback to Richard M. Daley, "Reason Landscape Ordinance," January 25, 1991, Folder 1-17-2, Box 1-17, RMDUIC; Daley-Conroy interview, 19; John Daley, interview, 18.
36 *Chicago Sun-Times*, January 14, 2010, April 2, 2023.
37 David Mosena, interview transcript, October 27, 2017, 2, RMDOralUIC; Axelrod interview, 23; Mary Carol Vanecko, interview transcript, February 21, 2018, 10–11, 26, 23, RMDOralUIC; Frank Kruesi, interview transcript, April 24, 2018, 31, RMDOralUIC; Daley-Conroy interview, 10–11.
38 *Chicago Tribune*, February 17, 2003; *Chicago Sun-Times*, February 17, February 27, 2003.
39 *Chicago Sun-Times*, February 17, February 18, 2003.
40 *Chicago Tribune*, February 18, 2003; *Chicago Sun-Times*, February 20, 2003.
41 Carol Felsenthal, "Brother Bill: A Look at William Daley," *Chicago Magazine*, January 4, 2011, https://www.chicagomag.com/chicago-magazine/february-2005/brother-bill-a-look-at-william-daley/.
42 Carol Fesenthal, "Michael Daley, the Smartest Daley Brother You've Probably Never Heard About," *Chicago Magazine*, May 11, 2011, https://www.chicago

371

mag.com/chicago-magazine/felsenthal-files/may-2011/michael-daley-the-smartest-daley-brother-youve-never-heard-of/.
43 *Chicago Sun-Times*, January 1, 2006, May 19, 2002, May 19, 2003.
44 *Chicago Sun-Times*, January 5, January 12, 2010.
45 *Chicago Sun-Times*, January 11, 2010. For a look at the Emanuel family, see Ezekiel J. Emanuel, *Brothers Emanuel: A Memoir of an American Family* (New York: Random House, 2013).
46 *Chicago Sun-Times*, September 7, 2010, September 8, 2010, September 10, 2010, September 11, 2010.
47 *Chicago Sun-Times*, September 8, September 21, 2010.
48 *Chicago Sun-Times*, September 8, September 9, September 14, September 15, 2010.
49 *Chicago Tribune*, November 13, November 14, 2010; *Chicago Sun-Times*, November 15, November 18, November 20, 2010; February 10, February 22, 2011.
50 Thomas J. Gradel and Dick Simpson, *Corrupt Illinois: Patronage, Cronyism, and Criminality* (Urbana: University of Illinois Press, 2015), 61–62; William Daley interview, 15.
51 Mary Ann Ahern, "Major Overhaul Will Leave Chicago Archdiocese With 123 Fewer Parishes by July," February 8, 2022, NBC News Chicago, https://www.nbcchicago.com/top-videos-home/major-overhaul-will-leave-chicago-archdiocese-with-123-fewer-parishes-by-july/2753245/.
52 *Chicago Tribune*, January 4, 2019.
53 *Chicago Tribune*, December 4, 1985, March 5, 2020; *The Forward*, November 23, 2020.
54 Interview with Ed Burke, July 22, 2014, 11–13, RMDOralUIC.

CHAPTER 12

1 "Alderwoman Jeanette Taylor—As She Sees It," The Ben Joravsky Show, December 2023, https://open.spotify.com/episode/2eHPBVqejLk8a0hezhUeji?si=aafa4f7a31cd4cff&nd=1&dlsi=9b5111001894436d.
2 *Chicago Tribune*, February 22, 2011.
3 *Chicago Tribune*, February 23, 2011.
4 *Chicago Tribune*, February 23, 2011; *Chicago Sun-Times*, February 23, 2011.
5 *Chicago Sun-Times*, February 23, February 25, 2011; *Chicago Tribune*, February 24, February 27, 2011.
6 Steven K. Ashby and Robert Bruno, *A Fight for the Soul of Public Education: The Story of the Chicago Teachers Strike* (Ithaca, NY: Cornell University Press, 2016), see chapter 7.
7 *Chicago Tribune*, February 24, 2011; *Chicago Sun-Times*, April 4, 2011.
8 *Chicago Tribune*, February 24, 2011; *Chicago Sun-Times*, March 11, 2011.

9 *Chicago Sun-Times*, May 16, May 17, 2011.
10 Larry Bennett, Roberta Garner, and Euan Hague, "Conclusion: Beyond Neoliberal Chicago," in *Neoliberal Chicago*, ed. Larry Bennett, Roberta Garner, and Euan Hague (Urbana: University of Illinois Press, 2017), 262; Kari Lydersen, *Mayor 1%: Rahm Emanuel and the Rise of Chicago's 99%* (Chicago: Haymarket Books, 2013), 198–99.
11 For a study of the process of NAFTA, deindustrialization, and its impact on American workers, see Chad Broughton, *Boom, Bust, Exodus: The Rust Belt, The Maquilas, and a Tale of Two Cities* (New York: Oxford University Press, 2015).
12 *Chicago Tribune*, June 30, 2011; Lydersen, *Mayor 1%*, 90–93.
13 *Chicago Sun-Times*, March 26, August 16, September 19, September 20, November 13, 2013; *Chicago Tribune*, June 17, September 20, 2013.
14 *Chicago Tribune*, March 30, 2015, March 3, 2016; *Chicago Sun-Times*, March 7, 2017, February 1, 2023; Atavia Reed, "Norfolk Southern Continues Englewood Expansion—But Will the Company Meet Community Demands?," *Block Club*, February 1, 2023, updated February 2, 2023, https://blockclubchicago.org/2023/02/01/norfolk-southern-railway-will-continue-its-englewood-expansion-but-will-the-company-meet-community-demands/.
15 *Chicago Tribune*, February 1, February 2, 2015.
16 *Chicago Tribune*, February 3, February 6, 2015.
17 *Chicago Tribune*, February 6, 2015.
18 *Chicago Tribune*, February 8, February 25, April 8, 2015; "Rahm Emanuel: Another Chicago Politician?," *Harvard Political Review*, October 22, 2013, https://harvardpolitics.com/rahm-emanuel-another-chicago-politician/; Christina Maza, "Chicago Surprise: Why Rahm Emanuel Faces a Runoff—and Can He Survive It?," *Christian Science Monitor*, February 25, 2015, https://www.csmonitor.com/USA/USA-Update/2015/0225/Chicago-surprise-Why-Rahm-Emanuel-faces-a-runoff-and-can-he-survive-it/; Amisha Patel, "How Chicago's Grassroots Movements Defeated Rahm Emanuel at the Polls," *In These Times*, March 5, 2015, https://inthesetimes.com/article/chicago-grassroots-movements.
19 *Chicago Sun-Times*, December 10, 2014, April 11, 2015.
20 *Chicago Sun-Times*, April 14, November 23, November 26, 2015.
21 Kari Lydersen and Daniel Bliss, "2011–2019, Rahm Emanuel—Chicago in Change and Crisis," in Dick Simpson and Betty O'Shaughnessy, *Chicago's Modern Mayors from Harold Washington to Lori Lightfoot* (Urbana: University of Illinois Press, 2024), 111, 122.
22 *Chicago Sun-Times*, December 14, 2015; *Chicago Tribune*, September 4, 2018.
23 The best study of the Madigan affair is Ray Long, *The House That Madigan Built: The Record Run of Illinois' Velvet Hammer* (Urbana: University of Illinois Press, 2022); *Chicago Tribune*, January 3, 2019.

24 *Chicago Tribune*, January 30, 2019.
25 *Chicago Sun-Times*, January 4, February 16, 2018.
26 *Chicago Sun-Times*, March 6, March 7, March 21, March 23, April 16, 2018.
27 *Crain's Chicago Business*, May 30, 2019; "Ex-Alderman Ed Burke, Developer Charles Cui Found Guilty in Chicago Corruption Trial," *The Real Deal: Real Estate News*, December 21, 2023, https://therealdeal.com/chicago/2023/12/21/ex-alderman-ed-burke-developer-charles-cui-found-guilty-in-chicago-corruption-trial/; *Chicago Sun-Times*, December 21, 2023; *Chicago Tribune*, June 25, 2024.
28 Charles N. Wheeler III, "Foreword," in Long, *The House That Madigan Built*.
29 *Chicago Tribune*, October 26, November 2, 2017.
30 *Chicago Tribune*, February 13, 2018; *Chicago Sun-Times*, April 23, 2018.
31 Long, *The House That Madigan Built*, 16, 213.
32 *Chicago Sun-Times*, January 29, January 31, 2019.
33 Long, *The House That Madigan Built*, 214; *Chicago Tribune*, July 14, 2019.
34 *Chicago Sun-Times*, July 18, 2019.
35 Long, *The House That Madigan Built*, 220–37; Hannah Meisel, "Madigan Suspends Campaign for Speaker After Falling Short on Votes, But Isn't Officially Out," *NPR Illinois*, January 11, 2021, https://www.nprillinois.org/statehouse/2021-01-11/madigan-suspends-campaign-for-speaker-after-falling-short-on-votes-but-isnt-officially-out.
36 *United States v. Madigan*, 22 CR 115 (N.D. Ill. Mar. 9, 2022), https://s3.documentcloud.org/documents/21317892/madigan-indictment.pdf.
37 Marco Rosaire Rossi and Dick Simpson, "2019–2023 Lori Lightfoot's Two Coalitions," in Simpson and O'Shaughnessy, *Chicago's Modern Mayors*, 143–45.
38 *Chicago Tribune*, April 25, May 13, 2019.
39 *Chicago Tribune*, April 26, May 20, 2019.
40 *Chicago Tribune*, May 20, 2019.
41 Rossi and Simpson, "Lori Lightfoot's Two Coalitions," 141, 151.
42 Heather Cherone, "Analyzing Lori Lightfoot's Legacy: A Combative Mayor Whose Reform Push Faltered Amid Pandemic Woes, Self-Inflicted Wounds," WTTW News, May 10, 2023, https://news.wttw.com/2023/05/10/analyzing-lori-lightfoot-s-legacy-combative-mayor-whose-reform-push-faltered-amid.
43 *Chicago Tribune*, March 28, 2023; *Chicago Sun-Times*, April 6, April 10, 2023.
44 *Chicago Sun-Times*, February 1, 2020, March 8, 2023; *Crain's Chicago Business*, May 30, 2019, https://www.chicagobusiness.com/greg-hinz-politics/case-against-ed-burke-heres-what-fedssay-he-did.
45 *Chicago Tribune*, January 8, 2024; Editorial, *Chicago Sun-Times*, March 24, 2024.

46 *Chicago Sun-Times*, January 16, 2024; Quinn Myers, "Ward Committee People Are on the Ballot This March. What Exactly Do They Do?," *Block Club Chicago*, March 12, 2024, https://blockclubchicago.org/2024/03/12/ward-committeepeople-are-on-the-ballot-this-march-what-exactly-do-they-do/.

Index

Page numbers in italics refer to illustrations.

Abbott, Greg, 331
Abbott, Robert S., 178
Abner, Willoughby, 225
Abrahams, Manny, 93
abstinence movement, 155
Adamowski, Benjamin, 173, 202–3, 205, 223, 291
Addams, Jane, 8, 83, 94
African Americans, 75, 79, 123, 127, 129, 132, 143–44, 170, 178, 198, 204–5, 219, 226, 236, 248, 255, 268, 275, 282, 284, 291–92, 310, 315, 326, 331; Black Belt, 179–80; Black Democratic sub-machine, 224–25, 234, 274; Black Muslims, 237–38; Black schools, overcrowding in, 227–28; Bridge Builders, 260–61; and Chicago Fire Department, 233; Democratic Party and, tension between, 241; and Great Depression, 180; Great Migration, 72–73, *74*, 107, 194; Lincoln Jubilee Exposition, 130; 1919 race riot, 148; and police violence, 232, 234; and Policy Kings, 180–82, 185, 202; and policy wheel, 179–80; and political machine, taken for granted by, 264–65; population growth of, in Chicago, 107–8, 137, 148; public school boycott, 228–30; and racism, 180; and Republicans, 108, 167; residential segregation, 148, 224; school board and, conflict between, 229; social change, 237–38; as unassimilable outsiders, 148

African Methodist Episcopal (AME) Church, 72–73
Agnew, Spiro, 244
Allen Law, 118, 120
Alliance of Central East European Nations, 259
Altgeld, John Peter, 110
Alvarez, Anita, 317–18
American Dream, 198
American Federation of Labor (AFL), 188–89, 203
American Federation of State, County, and Municipal Employees (AFSCME), 328–29
American Protective Association, 109
American Railway Union, 104
Americanism, 51, 136, 161; and Protestantism, 51
Americanization, 72
Amigos for Daley, 289
anarchism, 26, 34
Ancient Order of Hibernia, 50, 123
Anderson, Charles P., 131
Andrews, Peter, 321
Anixter, Julius "Lovin'" Putty, 94
Anti-Prohibition League of Illinois, 164
Anti-Saloon League, 153–54, 164
Arrendondo, Gabriela F., 288
Arvey, Jacob "Jake," 79, 94, 162–63, 167, 171–72, 198, 201, 205, 292
assimilation, 6, 16–17, 78, 155, 275, 306
Austin, Carrie, 317

377

INDEX

Austin Coming Together (ACT), 233–34
Axelrod, David, 282, 285, 292, 310

Badovinac, Peter, 132
Baker, Doris, 228
Baker, Ray Stannard, 82
Balanoff, Clem, 320–21
Baron, Harold, 227–28
Barzyński, Vincent, 69
Battle of Halsted Street, 46–47
Bauler, Mathias "Paddy," 204
Bellow, Saul, 285
belonging, 61, 77–78
Benner, Matt, 31
Bennett, Edward, 109
Bernardin, Joseph, 285
Berrios, Joseph, 290, 322
Berry, Edwin C., 227
Berwyn (Illinois), 173
Bevel, James T., 235, 237, 239
Bianchi, Raymond, 221
Bilandic, Michael A., 15, 88–89, 257–58, 259–60, *260*, 261, 265, 284; background, 262; as machine candidate, 263; and New Year's Eve blizzard, 263–64
Birth of a Nation, The (film), 130
Bismarck, Otto Von, 135
Bittner, Van A., 190–91
Black, Timuel, 225–26, 230
Black Panther Party, 240–41
Black Power movement, 239
Blagojevich, Rod, 291
Blaine Club, 128
Bloom, Lawrence, 273, 283–84
blue laws, 11, 132–33, 154, 164
Bohemia, 135, 148–49
Bohemian immigrant communities, 111, 129, 164
Bohemian Saloonkeepers Association, 158
Bonfield, John, 35–36
Borovský, Karel Havlíček, 152
Borrelli, Christopher, 309
Boston, 9
Bowler, James, 172
Bradley, Mamie, 225
Brand, Rudolph, 34
Braun, Carol Moseley, 303, 310
Breen, James, 144–45
Brennan, George, 139, 144, 158, 165–67, 169
Bridgeport, 7, 12–15, 32, 39, 41, *49*, 53–54, 62, 105, 165, 167, 174, 198–99, 205–7, 210, 236, 257, 260, 268, 281–82, 284, 291, 301; agency, 47; Archer Avenue (Archey Road), 42–43, 45, 48; boundaries of, 42; Bridgeport Industrial Institute, 48; "Bridgeport stench," 43–44; Bridgeport Way, 300; Catholic character of, 48; as communal in nature, 61; communal social activities, 50; corrupt politics, known for, 11; culture of poverty and alcoholism, 46; Five Points neighborhood, equivalent of, 45; flooding, 45; as hardscrabble neighborhood, 42, 45; health concerns, 44–45; Irish in, 11, 42–43, 45, 47, 51, 65; joining city of Chicago, 50; mass strikes in, 46–47; as microcosm of city, 52; Old Timers of Bridgeport Association, 199; packinghouses in, 43–44; patronage, as expression of loyalty, 300; as political powerhouse, 175–76; questionable political practices, reputation for, 50–51; and race, 63; racial tensions in, 226; Richard J. Daley Library, 283; "Shanty" Irish, 208; slaughterhouses in, 44; violence in, 45–46; youth gangs, 63
Brookins, Howard, 317
Bryan, William Jennings, 110, 114; "Cross of Gold" speech, 109
Burke, Bobbie, 113, 115
Burke, Dan, 320, 321
Burke, Edward M., 1, 9, 15–16, 18, 255, 257, 266, 271, 274, 282, 310, 319–20, 322, 324, 326; indictment and trial, 321, 327, 331; prison sentence, 321
Burkhardt, William, 133
Burnham, Daniel, 109; Chicago Plan, 295, 298–99
Bush, Earl, 244, 253
Busse, Fred, 156–57
Butler, Josetta, 216
Butler, Thaddeus J., 53
Byrne, Alfred, 177
Byrne, Jane, 15–16, 262–64, 269–70, 273–74, 285; conflicts with labor, 266–67; Daley family, united against, 268; Democratic machine, victory over, 265; public attitude toward, 268; reformers, shutting out, 266; and sexism, 268; and strikes, 267

Callaghan, P. O., 155
Calumet High School, 232–33
capitalism, 34, 105, 210–11, 215; and individualism, 59, 61

Index

Capone, Al, 92, 145; and Thompson campaign, 142, 144
Carey, Archibald J., 72
Carey, Archibald J., Jr., 225
Carey, Bernard, 241, 254, 264–65
Carroll, H. M., 182
Carter, Jimmy, 257
Carter H. Harrison Associations, 37
Cary, Eugene, 32
Cathedral of the Holy Name, 31
Catholic Church, 16, 42, 47, 51, 68, 87, 89, 98, 105, 107, 208, 234, 276, 279, 285, 305, 361n44; "Church Militant," 214; "Church Triumphant," 214, 217–19, 275; expansion of, 71–72; Hyde Park–Kenwood Urban Renewal Project, opposition to, 219; Irish model, 60; loss of influence, 306; loyalty, waning of, 279–80; parishes, 64–65, 71–72; saints, 64; sense of belonging, 61
Catholic culture: agency, 79; communal loyalty, 60; parish church and parochial school, as center of community, 60
Catholicism, 4, 45, 275, 278; African Americans' conversion to, 75; Catholic communalism, 5, 8–9, 11–12, 16, 275; communal, 5, 11–12, 63, 306; cult of the saints, 11, 64–65; folk religion of, 7, 11–12; obligation and interdependence, 63; unity of, 79–80; view of human nature, 319
Cayton, Horace R., 73
Century of Progress, 175–76, *176*, 187–88
Cermak, Anton, 2, 9, 14, 129, 132–33, 146–47, 152–54, 157–59, *159*, 160, 163, 171–73, 175–78, 180, 189, 202, 204–6, 208, 215, 253, 257, 289, 305, 323; anti-German attitude toward, 162; anti-Prohibition, 164; assassination of, 13, 169–70; Czech independence, in favor of, 162; defense of personal freedom, 164; as first and only immigrant mayor, 168; as hard drinker and brawler, reputation of, 151; "House for All Peoples," 7, 241; legacy of, 170; "little guys," representing, 161; national politics, interest in, 169; policy wheel, 179; as president of Cook County Board, 165–66; Thompson, mayoral campaign against, 167–68
Cervenka, John, 133, 157–60
Chalmers, Mr. and Mrs. W. J., 20
Chapin, Gardner Spring, 29
Chapin & Gore, 29
Chesbrough, Ellis Sylvester, 44

Chicago, 6, 8, 11, 16, 63, 130, 134, 136, 146, 201–2, 218, 247, 250, 297, 331; African Americans, as divided, 185; anti-Catholic and anti-immigrant hysteria, 26; anti-Japanese incidents, 193–94; anti-war movement, 242; as birthplace of skyscraper, 4; Black activist movement, 235, 237; Black population, 107–8, 148, 186; boodle, 100, 118; cable cars, 117; cardinals, 361n44; as Catholic and Jewish city, 148; changing demographics, 17, 23, 25–26, 123, 125, 148, 155, 167–68, 195, 224, 287–89; Chicago Tammany Hall, goal of, 167; Chicago Way of politics, 300, 319; as city of spectacle and tourism, 295; class divide, 26; clout, 160, 188; clout, and immigrant communities, 39; as collection of small communities, 67; communal frame, 47; communal phase, 68; communal societies, 42; decline as industrial city, 4; Democratic National Convention (1968), 242–44; gentrification of core, 294–95; as German city, 147; as global city, 4, 332; during Great Depression, 168; as haven for European immigrants, 107; home rule, 155–56; Human Rights Ordinance, 286; immigrants, collective mobility of, 60; isolationism, 191; labor troubles, 34–35; LGBTQ+ community, 286; malleable borders of neighborhoods, 42; Millennium Park, 295; New Deal, impact on, 187–88; 1919 race riot, 108, 137, 198; organized labor, 188–89, 191; political dynasties, 12; political machine, 41; political transformation of, 18; progressive reforms, 108–9; public housing, 198; public school boycott, 228, 229; public school segregation, 227–28; racial tensions, 194–95, 219, 225–26, 232–33, 239, 267–68; riots, 239; ruling elites, 51; saloons, 29, 41; social contract between voters and politicians, 5; social services mentality, 5; suburbanization, 306; 311 telephone system, 332; traction franchise, 118; transit strikes, 34–35; Trumbull Park Homes race riot, 204; and Vietnam War, 241–42; war effort, 192–93; ward committeeman, clout of, 158–59; White flight, 306; as wild place, 10; as Yankee-dominated city, 10, 21–22. *See also* Chicago neighborhoods; Chicago wards

INDEX

Chicago Area Friends of the Student Nonviolent Coordinating Committee (Chicago-SNCC), 229
Chicago Athletic Association, 126
Chicago Baptists, 72–73
Chicago Charter Committee, 153
Chicago City Railways, 117
Chicago Crime Commission, 144, 204
Chicago Defender (newspaper), 225, 230–31, 234
Chicago Evening Post (newspaper), 43
Chicago Federation of Labor (CFL), 156–57, 162, 176, 266–67
Chicago Federation of Settlements and Neighborhood Centers, 230
Chicago Freedom Movement (CFM), 228, 237, 239–40
Chicago Hebrew Institute, 78
Chicago Housing Authority (CHA), 89, 268
Chicago Inter Ocean (newspaper), 118–19
Chicago Maternity Center, 78
Chicago neighborhoods: Auburn-Gresham, 232–33; Austin, 132, 239, 275; Back of the Yards, 11, 42, 68–69, 71, 81, 92, 164, 189–90, 288; Beverly, 171; Brighton Park, 174; Bronzeville, 75, 92, 108, 142–43, 180–82, *184*, 186, 190, 203, 218–19, 226; Canaryville, 11, 53, 71; Czech California (now Little Village), 13, 107, 131, 150, 153, 162, 164, 170, 289; Douglas Park, 11, 53–54, 93; East Garfield Park, 239; Englewood, 224, 282, 313–15, 330; Garfield Park, 93, 220, 222, 239; Hegewisch, *81*; Humboldt Park, 282, 289; Hyde Park, 68, 102–3, 132, 269, 282; Lake View, 132; Lawndale, 160, 239; Little Italy, 222; Little Prague, 107; Little Village, 13, 289; Logan Square, 289; Marquette Park, 239; Maxwell Street, 76–77, *77*, 93; McKinley Park, *62*; North Lawndale, 78, 93, 150, 233–34, 237, 275; Pilsen, 13, 46–47, 107, 131–32, 149–52, 160, 164, 289; Ravenswood, 304; Saugansh, 268; South Chicago, 42, 68–69, 93, 189–90, 209, 211, 287–88; South Lawndale, 150, 170; South Loop, 291; South Shore, 210; Uptown, 93; West Garfield Park, 239; West Town, 42, 289; Woodlawn, 132. *See also* Bridgeport
Chicago Plan Commission, 314
Chicago Teachers Union (CTU), 267, 310–11, 316, 328; as new machine, 329–30
Chicago Times (newspaper), 97–99

Chicago Tribune (newspaper), 51, 103, 145–46
Chicago Turners, 31
Chicago Turngemeinde Annual Old Settler's Festival, 31
Chicago Urban League, 227
Chicago wards: 1st Ward, 15, 32–33, 81, 98, 111, 119, 127, 205, 266; 2nd Ward, 126–27, 129, 137, 182–83, 185, 316; 3rd Ward, 171, 182, 185; 4th Ward, 50, 114; 5th Ward, 206, 283; 6th Ward, 51, 274; 10th Ward, 160; 11th Ward, 15, 88, 199, 208, 258, 284, 301; 12th Ward, 13, 158, 160, 162–65; 13th Ward, 9, 283, 322–23; 14th Ward, 9, 255, 320; 17th Ward, 139, 172–73; 18th Ward, 82; 19th Ward, 9, 82–83, 85, 138, 171; 20th Ward, 145, 314; 24th Ward, 171–72; 26th Ward, 271, 284; 29th Ward, 81–82, 94, 269; 31st Ward, 290; 32nd Ward, 86, 111; 33rd Ward, 274; 34th Ward, 257–58; 41st Ward, 88; 44th Ward, 287; 46th Ward, 265, 283; 49th Ward, 273; 50th Ward, 303–4
Chicago West Division Railway Company, 35
Chico, Gery, 295, 303–4, 310–11, 326
Chinese immigrant communities, 111, 191, 193
Chiola, Thomas R., 286–87
Christian Brothers, 7–9, 11, 14, 48, 52–58, *58*, *59*, 203, 209, 214–15
Cicero (Illinois), 164, 173
Cities and Villages Act, 117
City Council, 44, 103, 114–15, 121, 136, 153, 163, 170–71, 173, 201–2, 228, 231, 252, 257, 272, 282, 315, 317, 326, 328; Chicago Commission on National Defense, 191–92; "Council Wars," 271; Gray Wolves, 22, 118; Joint Committee on Streets and Alleys, 119; liquor laws, 156; Lyman bill, 119–20; power of, 22; racial infighting, 271; traction franchise, 117–18; ward redistricting, 271
civil rights movement, and Democratic Party politics, 224
Civil Service Commission, 115–17
Civil Service Law, 113, 116
civil service reform, 113
Civil War, 21–22, 26, 28–29, 34, 51, 97; "bloody red shirt," 27
Clan na-Gael Guards, 53
Clark, John, 28
Clark, John S., 166, 171–73
Clark, Mark, 240
Clay, Henry, 25
Cleveland, Grover, 36, 97–99, 102–3

380

Index

Clinton, Bill, 293, 300–301, 312
clout, 1–2, 6, 11, 86, 123, 148, 160, 188, 222, 309, 324, 331–32; agency, 39; communalism, 205; financial gain, 105; gay clout, 287; Hispanic clout, 311; honest graft and quiet clout, 301; immigrant communities, 39; Latino clout, 290; Mexican clout, 288; national, 218; patronage, 113; political influence, 47; Sain scandal, 264; social contract, 330. *See also* political clout
Coalition for Better Government, 294
Cochran, Willie, 314
Cody, John, 238–39, 254, 257
Coleman, Charles E., 131
Coleman, Slim, 283
Coleman, William L., 231
Collins, Morgan A., 143
Colosimo, Big Jim, 133
Comite Contra El Eje (Anti-Axis Committee), 193
Commonwealth Edison, 210, 217, 319, 323–24
communal machine, 325, 327, 331; communal politics, 259, 268, 274; corruption, 332; disappearance of, 332; sociability, 332; 13th Ward, as model of, 322
communalism, 2, 8, 12, 42, 47, 63, 113, 158, 202, 203, 285, 293, 319; and clout, 186, 205; collective identity, 61; communal response, 211; dark side of, 94–95; decline of, 306–7; floundering of, 17, 254; foundation for clout, 6; individualism, triumphing over, 280, 306; and labor movement, 69, 71; and loyalty, 252; protection, need for, 67–68; and racial prejudice, 241; reciprocal, 94; social contract, 252; welfare state, rationale for, 295
Congress of Industrial Organizations (CIO), 188–91, 211
Congress of Racial Equality (CORE), 228–29, 236
Conlisk, James B., Jr., 244, 253
Connelly, Hugh "Babe," 199
Conroy, Sean, 302
Conway, Michael J., 217
Coogan, Thomas J., Jr., 256
Cook County Democratic Club (CCDC), 101
Cook County Democratic Party, 13, 33, 83, 158, 193, 198, 208, 245, 249, 258, 267, 271
Cooley, Charles H., 61
Coordinating Council of Community Organizations (CCCO), 228, 234, 235–37
Copperheads, 51

Corbett, James J., 111
Corr, Frank J., 171–73
corruption, 1–2, 17, 22, 44, 83, 146, 200, 232, 253, 262, 265, 291–92, 305, 309–10, 319, 325, 330; anti-corruption, 156, 205, 327; bribes, 106, 111, 128, 180, 293; communal machine, 332; Levee vice district, 28, 30, 33, 122, 127, 143; loyalty, 252; patronage, 113; police, 203; public, 105; as transactional, 6; as tribute to community leaders, 5
Cosmopolitan Electric Company, 105–6
Coughlin, "Bathhouse" John, 81, 103, 110–11, 115, 118–22, 127, 172
Coughlin, Charles E., 186
Covelli, Daniel, 249, 252
Covenant Club, 307
COVID-19 pandemic, 328, 331
Cregier, DeWitt C., 36–37
Croatian immigrant communities, 52, 193
Crowe, Dorsey R., 144
Crowe, Robert, 138, 142–45, 165
Cui, Charles, 321
Cullerton, Edward F., 82, 119
Cullerton, John, 322
Cuthbertson, William, 114
Czarnecki, Anton, 135
Czech Democratic Organization of Cook County, 160
Czech immigrant communities, 10, 13, 31–32, 34, 39, 52, 71, 130, 132–35, 144, 148, 150–51, 154, 157–58, 161–63, 166, 191; first wave of immigration, 149; Freethinkers faction, 107, 149; Irish and, tensions between, 155; political power of, 160; 12th Ward, loyalty toward, 160
Czech National Alliance, 134

Daley, Bill, 285, 292, 296, 300–301, 305, 326
Daley, Eleanor "Sis" (née Guilfoyle), 206–8, 256, 263, 268, 281, 283, 300; death of, 299
Daley, Elizabeth, 302
Daley, John, 251, *260*, 293, 296, *298*, 301
Daley, Lillian, 205–6
Daley, Maggie, 281–83, 291, 297, 302–3; as advisor and partner, 299; "After School Matters," 299; Block 37, 299
Daley, Michael (son of Richard J. Daley), 256, 296, 301
Daley, Michael J. (father of Richard J. Daley), 205–6, 252
Daley, Nora, 302

INDEX

Daley, Patrick, 302
Daley, Richard J., 1–2, 7–9, 15, 58, *90*, 165, 187, 197, 199–200, *200*, 203, 207, *207*, 214, 216, 224–29, 235–36, 241, *243*, 245–46, 250, 258, 260–61, 264, 266–68, 278, 282, 289, 296–97, 300, 304–5, 307, 309, 322–23, 327; background, 205–6; Black vote, 223, 253–55; Black vote and White ethnic vote, straddling of, 232; campaign ad, *213*; canvas booklets, 212–13; construction projects, 212, 218; crosstown expressway, 251; death of, 256–57, 262, 263, 274, 284, 330; Democratic Convention delegates (1972), 248–49; Democratic National Convention (1968), 242; dying Chicago River green, 209; good government as good politics, 330; hierarchy, attitude toward, 234; Irish American organizations, ties to, 208–9; King, meeting with, 238; as kingmaker, 218; and labor unions, 211–12; legacy of, 301–2; loyalty of, 14, 205, 215, 217; McGovern, meeting with, 247–48; and Mississippi Freedom Democratic Party, 230–31; national clout of, 218; national reputation, as tarnished, 244; nepotism, charges of, 251–52; New Deal, embracing of, 14, 215, 293; open housing, 240; as organizer, 217; as patron saint of patronage and clout, 210; patronage system, defender of, 208–9; and police violence, 232; race riots, reaction to, 234, 239; sacred and profane, blending of, 215; scandals, 251–53; Summer Jobs for Youth Committee, 210; and University of Illinois, 219–22
Daley, Richard M., 8, 16–17, 251–52, 260, *260*, 266, 269, 273, 281, 289, 292, *292*, 301–5, 311, 329–30; Chicago Skyway, privatization of, 296; and City Beautiful ideas of Burnham Plan, 297; coalition of, 290–91; as eco-friendly green mayor, 298; and gay rights legislation, 287; Greening of Chicago, 297, *298*; Hired Truck Program, 293–94; Meigs Field Airport, closing of, 298–99; parking meter deal, 296; progressive views of, 286; as reluctant and restrained neoliberal, 293, 295–96; as rightful heir, 268; and riverwalk, 297; victory of, 284–85; Washington coalition, 282–83
Daley and George Law Firm, 301
Damen, Arnold, 69
Danaher, Matt, 253–54

d'Andrea, Anthony, 138
Darrow, Clarence, 20
Dart, Tom, 303
Davis, Danny, 269, 283
Davis, Rennie, 242
Dawson, William L., 183, *184*, 189, 203–4, 224–25, 231, 234; clout of, 185–86; Dawson Boosters Basketball Team, 182
De Grazia, Victor, 250
De La Salle, John Baptist, 53, 55, 59, 64
De La Salle Institute, 8–9, 11, 14–16, 41, *54*, *58*, 61, 105, 199, 200, *204*, 206–8, 210, 214, 218–19, 252, 279; *The Common Rules*, 59; corporal punishment, prohibiting of, 59; curriculum, 57–59; Democratic machine, shaping of, 7, 60; fight song, 197; fundraising campaign, 215–16; growth of, 215; middle-class Catholic virtues, instilling of, 59; opening of, 52–53; as political incubator, 7; simultaneous method, 55–56; teaching of Latin, 57–58
De Priest, Oscar, 130, 132–33, 143, 182
deindustrialization, 6, 17, 266, 312
del Valle, Miguel, 290, 303, 310
Dellinger, David, 242
Democratic Party, 7–8, 11, 14, 26, 29, 32, 34, 39, 47, 104–5, 123, 130, 138–40, 157, 161, 163, 166, 168–70, 172, 179, 188, 215, 230, 247, 254, 322; and African Americans, 178, 180–83, 241; as "Big Tent," 248; Catholic loyalty, waning of, 279, 280; Central Committee, 159–60; Civil Service Law, 113–14; Cook County Democratic Party, 13, 33, 83, 158, 193, 198, 208, 245, 249, 258, 267, 271; Credentials Committee, 249; Democratic National Convention (1968), 242–44; divisions in, 109–10, 194–95; factionalism, 171; Gold Democrats, 102, 109–10; hyper-local organizations, 214; and immigrants and ethnic groups, 12; independent Democrats, rise of, 15; and organized labor, 190; as "Party of Revolution and Robbery," 27; political machine, 99, 125; progressive wing, 250; Regular Democratic Organization, 4, 15, 37, *90*, 165, 173, 183, 201–3, 205, 250, 255–56, 261–62, 266, 269–71, 274–75, 293, 332; Shakman decree, 246; Silver Democrats, 102, 109–10; Star League revolt, 115
Deneen, Charles, 145
Derwinski, Edward, 291

382

Index

Despres, Leon, 240
Dever, William E., 139, 140, 142–44, 165
Dickerson, Earl, 183, 185
Dickerson, Spencer C., 178
Ditka, Mike, 283
Dixmoor (Illinois), 233
Dixon, Alan, 285
Dorney, Maurice J., 7–8, 53, 71
Dorsey, Thomas A., 73
Douglas, Paul, 185, 198, 201, 230–31
Dovre Club, 129
Doyle, Tommy, 206
Drake, St. Clair, 73
Drucci, Vincent "The Schemer," 144
Dry Chicago Federation, 131
Duba, John G., 216–17
Duckworth, Tammy, 325
Duffy, John, 171
Duis, Perry, 193
Duncan, Arne, 292
Dunne, Edward F., 122, 139, 158
Dunne, Finley Peter, "Mr. Dooley" character, 43, 50
Dunne, George W., 7, 258–59
Durbin, Dick, 325
Dutch immigrant communities, 13, 23, 82

Eastland disaster, 130–31, *131*
Eckert, Joseph, 75
Eibler, Henry, 45–46
Eller, Morris, 93
Emanuel, Rahm, 291–93, 302–3, *305*, 314–15, 319, 325–26, 329; accomplishments of, 318; arrogance and elitism, perceptions of, 318; CTU, clash with, 310–11; listening tour, 304; as Mayor 1%, 17, 312, 319; McDonald murder, mishandling of, 317–18, 330; neoliberal decisions, 330; public demeanor of, 313; "Rahm-father," 309–10; reputation of, 309–10; residency, challenging of, 304; school and mental health centers, closings of, 316–18, 330; unions, picking fight with, 313
Eniya, Amara, 325–26
Epton, Bernie, 270
Equal Employment Opportunity Commission, 88
Esposito, Joseph "Diamond Joe," 145
Europe, 12–13, 34, 63, 76, 123, 138, 148, 155, 161–62, 191, 193
Evans, Timothy, 273–74, 282–85

Everleigh Club, 122
Exelon, 323. *See also* Commonwealth Edison

Fagin, Mike, 46
federalism, 17
Feehan, Patrick Augustine, 53, 122
Figueroa, Raymond, 290
Fioretti, Bob, 316
First Ward Democratic Party Organization, 28
Fitzmorris, Charles C., 138
Fitzsimmons, Robert J., 111
Floyd, George, 328
Ford, Gerald, 256
Ford, Harrison, 298
Foy, Michael, 132
Franz Joseph (emperor), 130
Fraser, Donald M., 247
fraternal organizations, 5, 50, 75, 80, 131, 150, 153
Freedom Clubs of Illinois, 230–31
Friend, Hugo, 145–46
Frost, Wilson, 15, 257–59
Funston, Frederick, 135

Gabinski, Terry, 274
Gahan, Thomas, 110
Gale, Stephen F., 126
Galena and Chicago Union Railroad, 22
Gallego, Joseph, 221
Galler, Roberta, 229
gambling, 28–30, 33, 81, 85, 92–94, 109–11, 122, 179–81, 202, 204–5, 294
gangsters, 93–94; communal friendship and ethnic loyalty, 91–92; gambling, 92; liquor and beer trade, 138; upward mobility, 91
Garcia, Jesús "Chuy," 273, 290, 315–16, 320–21
Garfield, James, 113
gemeinschaft, 42; communal values of, 61
Gemeinschaft und Gesellschaft (Tönnies), 60–61
Geocaris, Angelo G., 248
George, Francis, 312
German American Bund, 186
German immigrant communities, 6, 10, 12, 23, 31–32, 34, 37, 48, 52, 71–72, 82, 101, 105, 111, 123, 129–30, 132–33, 137, 144, 154–55, 157, 161, 167–68, 176–77; Cahenslyism, rise of, 63
German Sharpshooter Society, 31
Germano, Joe, 211–12
Germany, 76, 87, 123, 134, 191

383

INDEX

gesellschaft, 42, 61
Gestefeldt, Theodore, 30
Getter, Howard D., 278
Getz, George F., 166
Gilbert, Charles C., 155
globalism, 17
Goethe Monument, 123
Goldberger, David, 246
Goldwater, Barry, 231
Gore, Al, 300–301
Gore, James Jefferson, 29
Gorecki, Roman, 177
Goslin, Patrick J. (Brother Adjutor of Mary), 57; "clout in a cassock," 57; fundraising skills of, 56–57; Jesse James anecdote, 56
Gottfried, Alex, 152
Graham, Gilbert, 257
Granady, Octavius, 145
Great Britain, 147
Great Chicago Fire, 3–4, 6, 10, 19, 26, 34, 39, 43, 69, 71, 125, 130–31, 149–50; "Burnt District," 20–21; Irish blamed for, 21
Great Depression, 13, 91, 146, 168, 180, 187–88, 193–95, 288
Great Recession, 312
Greece, 193
Greek immigrant communities, 111, 193
Greeley, Andrew, 276, 279, 343n36
Green, Adam, 225
Green, Dwight H., 188
Greenback-Labor Party, 26
Greenback movement, 26
Greenberg, Stanley, 304
Gregory, Dick, 236
Griffith, D. W., 130
Grimshaw, Jackie, 283
Grogan, Barney, 82
Grossman, Ron, 67
Grudzinski, Louis, 69, 71
Guardians of Liberty, 129–30
Guiteau, Charles, 113
Gunther, William F., 127
Gutiérrez, Luis, 271, 282, 284, 290, 303

Haderlein, John, 132
Haider, Donald, 271
Hamburg Athletic Association, 14, *62*, 63, 206–7, *207*, 211
Hamer, Fannie Lou, 231
Hampton, Alaina, 322–23
Hampton, Fred, 240
Hannah, Alexander Donnan, 29

Hanrahan, Edward, 240–41, 246, 253
Hans Christian Andersen Monument Association, 37
Hansen, Bernie, 287
Hansen, Mary F., 19
Harding, George, 146
Harken, Daniel, 153–54
Harlan, John Maynard, 122
Harold Washington Party, 283
Harrington, Cornelius J., 236
Harris, Cass, 132
Harrison, Carter H., III, 6, 10, 12, 26, 33, 99–102, 109, 110, *112*, 125–26; assassination of, 11, 19–20, 97, 103–4, 113, 150, 172–73; background of, 23, 25; Catholic sensibilities, exposure to, 122; "the Eagle," 27–28, 111; eight-day hour movement, support of, 35; ethnic card, playing of, 123; funeral procession of, *38*; German community, relationship with, 31; as hands-on mayor, 121; Irish vote, courtship of, 32; labor rights, support of, 34; language fluency, 37; "live and let live" attitude, 28; as orator, 27; "Our Carter," 28, 30, 34, 36, 39; popularity of, 36; retentive memory, 37; and saloons, 28, 30; and traction franchise, 117
Harrison, Carter H., IV (Young Carter), 10–12, 25, 97, 99, 109–10, *112*, 125, 130, 139, 150–52, 157–61, 163, 167, 199; background, 98; balancing act of, 123; Catholic Church, relationship with, 98, 122; Civil Service Law, enforcing of, 116; civil service reform, 112–16; Coughlin and Kenna, break with, 122; ethnic card, playing of, 111, 123; as first Chicago-born mayor, 111; as hands-on mayor, 121; Levee, breaking up of, 122, 127; patronage, 113; primary defeat, 122, 129; as progressive reformer, 121; as reform political boss, 121; Star League, revolt against, 114–15; and traction franchise, 112, 117, 119, 121; as "Wet," 122
Harrison, William Preston, 20, 36, 97
Hartigan, Neil, 256
Harvey (Illinois), 233
Harvey, William H., 185
Hasidism, 76–77
Hayes, Charles, 230
Haymarket Affair, 35–36, 47
Healey, Charles C., 131–32
Heaney, Thomas, 278–79
Heath, Monroe, 31

384

Index

Hebrew Theological College, 78
Heil and Heil, 251
Hendon, Rickey, 303
Henry, Aaron, 231
Hesing, Washington, 37, 39
Hill, John J., 278–79
Hill, Lewis, 209
Hired Truck Scandal, 293–94
Hispanic communities, 287–88; Catholic, 306; clout, 311; voting bloc, 289–90. *See also* Mexican immigrant communities; Puerto Rican immigrant communities
Hispanic Democratic Organization (HDO), 294, 311
Hitler, Adolf, 191
Hoffman, Julius, 236
Hogg, David, 29
Holman, Claude, 252
Holy Cross Brothers, 56
Holy Family Church, 21, 31, 65
Holy Family Parish, 69
Holy Guardian Angel Church, 221
Honoré, Henry H., 25–26
Hoover, Herbert C., 165–66, 288
Hopkins, John P., 12, 99–100, 102–6, 115, 125, 347n4
Horejs, Mary, 152
Horner, Henry, 169, 178, 187, 199
Houlihan, Jim, 303
Howlett, Michael, 256
Hull House, 83, 288
Humanae Vitae, 306
Humphrey, Hubert, 247
Humphrey, John, 118
Hyde Park–Kenwood Urban Renewal Project, 219

Igoe, Michael J., 166, 169
Illinois, 6, 22, 25, 33–34, 57, 118, 121, 168, 171–72, 187, 193, 218, 230–31, 250, 319, 322
Illinois and Michigan Canal, 42–43
Illinois Blue Law, 131
Illinois Club for Catholic Women, 278
Illinois House Charter Committee, 156
Illinois Solidarity Party, 271
immigrants, 7, 11, 13, 25, 29, 31, 34, 37, 43, 52, 69, 94, 101, 103, 107, 122, 138, 147–48, 151, 189, 197, 287–88, 331; assimilation, 155; attacks on, 109, 153, 168; clout and agency, 39; collective mobility of, 60; and communalism, 12; and cult of saints, 64; Democratic Party, as protector of, 47; making fun of, 111; organized crime, and upward mobility, 91–92; ward bosses, as friend and protector of, 86; working class, 51. *See also individual immigrant communities*
Immigration Act (1924), 148
Immigration and Naturalization Act (1965), 288
Independence League, 157
individualism, 6, 8, 12, 59, 61, 68, 280, 295, 306
Industrial Revolution, 41, 51–52
Industrial Workers of the World (IWW), 189
industrialization, 68
Ireland, 83, 85, 137, 147; "penny-a-week" collections, 69; potato famine, 51
Irish immigrant communities, 4, 10–13, 23, 27, 32, 34, 42–43, 52, 68–69, 71, 82–83, 85, 92, 101, 105, 111, 123, 165–66, 169, 171, 174, 176–77, 198, 210, 266, 275; as America's first social problem, 46; Czechs, Poles, and, tension between, 155; famine, 48, 51; Irish Catholics, pinnacle of power, 214, 254; "Irish Gold Coast," 57; "Lace Curtain" Irish, 208; organizations, 208–9; "Pig Shit" Irish, 45, 167, 175; as political brokers, 7; primogeniture, Irish idea of, 296; "Shanty" Irish, 45, 208; violence associated with, 45
Iroquois Club, 101, *101*, 102–3; as silk-stocking club, 100
Italian immigrant communities, 7, 13, 34, 52, 61, 82, 111, 129, 133, 137–38, 144, 157, 193, 222

Jackson, A. L., 182
Jackson, Daniel M., 142
Jackson, Jesse, 15, 238, 249, 258–59, 283–84, 318
Jackson, Jesse, Jr., 304
Jackson, Joseph H., 226–27, 238
Jackson, Robert R., 143, 182
Jankowski, Lester, 278
Janovsky, Felix B., 160
Japanese Americans, 194
Jarecki, Edmund K., 139
Jarrett, Valerie, 292
Jarrett, Vernon, 264–65, 282
Jesuits, 56, 58, 69
Jewish communities, 7, 10, 13, 32, 52, 75–76, 82, 93, 107, 111, 129, 137, 146, 150, 166–67, 189, 193, 285, 311, 331; agency, claiming of, 79; and anti-Semitism, 78; commu-

INDEX

Jewish communities (*continued*)
nalism, decline of, 275; Jewish People's Institute, 78; Jewish Training School, 78; *landsmanshaften verein* (fraternal groups), 61, 77–78, 306–7; political clout, 79; population decline, 306–7; waning of, 290; Yiddishkeit, steeped in, 77
Joffre, Joseph, 134–35
John XXIII (pope), 276
Johnson, Brandon, 1, 18, 328–30; inexperience and lack of transparency, 331; and migrant crisis, 331
Johnson, Lyndon B., 15, 87, 223–24, 230–31, 242
Johnson, Wallace, 264–65
Johnson–Reed Act, 148
Johnston, Olin D., 226
Joint Committee to End Patronage Abuse, 245
Jones, Jesse H., 186
Jones brothers, 181–82
Judaism, 275; as communal, 63; Reformed, 78
Judd, Dennis R., 295

Kamin, Blair, 297
Kantowicz, Edward R., 121
Karabasz, Francis, 69, 71
Kasper, Michael, 304
Kass, John, 309–10
Kaszak, Nancy, 291
Keane, Tom, 253
Kearns, Robert M., 278
Kehilath Anshe Ma'ariv (Congregation of the Men of the West) (KAM), 76
Kelly, Ed (park commissioner), 256, 282
Kelly, Edward J., 2, 9, 14, 177–78, 182–83, 186, 189–90, 192, *192*, 193, 199, 202, 204–5, 208, 215, 305, 354–55n2; African Americans, championing of, 194, 198; background, 174–75; Blacks, popularity among, 181; fraudulent tax returns, 187; Kelly–Nash machine, 13, 176, 181, 185, 187–88, 191; "Let's Go Chicago Week," 176; machine politics and New Deal attitudes, embracing of, 194; Mayor's Committee on Race Relations, 194; and public schools, 179; "stick and slug" motto, 175; submachines, 195
Kenna, Michael "Hinky Dink," 81, 110, 118–22, 127
Kennedy, John F., 87, 217–18, 275; assassination of, 223, 230
Kennedy, Robert F., 242
Kennedy, Ted, 257

Kennelly, Martin H., 14, *200*, 201, 203, *204*, 210–11, 215, 218, 296; African Americans, loss of support, 204–5; attacks on patronage, 202; background, 198–99; communalism and clout, disbelief in, 205; gambling, attack on, 202; nonpartisan image, 198; racism, accusation of, 204; Railroad Fair, 202; as reformer, 199–200; tourism, encouraging of, 202
Kenner, Tyrone, 264
Kerner, Otto, 162, 239, 253
King, A. D., 236
King, Martin Luther, Jr., 15, 224, 235; assassination of, 240, 242; Chicago visit, 236–40; Daley, meeting with, 238; in North Lawndale, 237; open housing march, 239–40
King, William E., 182–83, 185
Kinzie, John, 22
Kinzie, Juliette, 22
Kiołbassa, Piotr, 37, 39
Kipley, Joseph, 114
Klaus, Frank, 160
Kluczynski, John, 290–91
Knights of Columbus, 50, 129
Knights of Labor, 47
Know-Nothing movement, 64
Korshak, Marshal, 217
Koschman, David, 303
Kosciuszko, Thaddeus, 135
Kramer, Ferdinand, 209
Kraus, Adolph, 26–27, 31–32, 37, 39, 98, 103, 112–14, 116, 150–51
Krone, Phil, 301
Kruesi, Frank, 285, 299
Kucharski, Edmund, 291
Kunz, Stanley, 103
Kupcinet, Irv, 282

La France, Scott, 193
La Guardia, Fiorello, 192–93
labor movement: eight-hour day strike, 47; labor unions, 11, 14, 32, 80, 195, 205, 211–12, 312, 324. *See also individual unions*
Lahey, Edwin A., 212
Lakeside Bank, 209
Lally, Luke, 46
Landau, George, 133
Landry, Lawrence, 230
Lange, John, 71
Lapp, John A., 203
Last Hurrah, The (O'Connor), 9
LaVelle, Avis, 282, 285

Index

Law and Order League, 153
Lee, William A., 266–67
Leo XIII (pope), 47, 215
Leroux, Charles, 67
Lessing, Gotthold Ephraim, 177
Levy, Julian, 219
Lewis, James H., 169
Lewis, John L., 188–89
Lewis, Karen, 316
Lightfoot, Lori, 17–18, 325–26, 331; aldermanic prerogative, challenging of, 327; coalitions of, 327–28; pay-to-play tradition, targeting of, 327; as unpopular, 328
Lincoln, Abraham, 22, 97, 129
Lincoln, Bob, 265
Lincoln Park, 107, 123
Lipinski, William, 290–91
Lithuanian immigrant communities, 48, 52, 71, 137, 193
Litsinger, Edward R., 142–43
Loeffler, William, 150–51
Long, Huey, 186
Lorimer, William, 128–29; "the Blond Boss," 127
Los Angeles, Watts riots, 234
Louis, Joe, 179, 181
Loveland, Catherine, 46
Lowden, Frank, 136
loyalty, 6, 59, 85, 128, 162, 170, 181, 195, 205, 214–17, 231–32, 247, 249; aldermanic, 327; Catholic, 7, 279–80; communal, 60, 280; communalism, based on, 198; and corruption, 252; ethnic, 91; neighborhood, 240, 281; party, 185, 270; patronage, as expression of, 113, 300, 307; and political machine, 89, 94; reciprocal, 208; and urban politics, 14; ward boss, 86
Loyola University Chicago, Institute for Urban Life, 88
Lucas, Robert, 236
Lueder, Arthur, 139–40
Lundin, Fred, 127–29, 137, 139–40; Lundin-Thompson machine, 138
Lurie, Paul M., 244–45
Lutzenkirchen, Henry, 115–16
Lyle, John H., 163–64
Lyman, W. H., 119
Lynch, Mike, 46
Lynch, Roberta, 311

machine politics, 2, 4–5, 8, 9, 75, 188; independent voting bloc, growth of, 17; nepotism, 252; as phrase, 1; racism of, 274; restoration of, 284; war effort during WWII, 193. *See also* political machine
Mack, Michael, 45–46
Mackin, Joseph Chesterfield "Oyster Joe," 32–34
Madigan, Michael J., 9, 18, 283, 319–21, 323–24; clout network, 324; indictment of, 325, 331; patronage, approach to, 322; resignation of, 325; "Velvet Hammer," 322
Madigan & Getzendanner, 322
Maldonado, Roberto, 304
Mapes, Tim, 325
Marovitz, Abraham Lincoln, 245–47, 290
Marshall, John, 25
Marshall, Lewis, 25
Masotti, Louis, 265
McAndrew, William, 142
McCaffrey, Lawrence, 46
McCarran-Walter Act, 288
McCarthy, Eugene, 242
McCarthy, M. Huberta, 216
McCarthy, Timothy, 294
McClain, Michael, 323, 324
McCormick, Cyrus Hall, Jr., 100
McCormick, J. Medill, 136
McCormick, Robert R., 174–75
McCormick Harvesting Machine Company, 100
McCormick Reaper Works, 35, 151
McDermott, Edward C., 242
McDermott, James J., 217
McDermott, John A., 238
McDevitt, Bernard "Barney," 99
McDonald, Laquan, 17, 317–18, 330
McDonald, Michael Cassius "King Mike," 28–30, 32–34, 81, 109–10, 179
McDonough, James "Big Jim," 162–63
McDonough, Joseph, 14, 165, 205–6, 208, 215
McGann, Lawrence E., 115–16
McGill, Nathan K., 178
McGillen, John, 103
McGovern, George S., 242, 249–50; Daley, meeting with, 247–48
McGovern-Fraser Commission, 247–49
McKenna, James, 48
McKeon, Larry, 287
McKinley, William, 109
McManus, Frederick R., 276
McMullen, Jay, 265
Medill, Joseph, 26–27, 44; Mayor's Bill, 21
Mell, Richard, 274

387

INDEX

Mendoza, Susana, 326
Mercy Hospital, 89, 215–16
Merriam, Robert, 204–5, 208
#MeToo Movement, 322
Mexican American Democratic Organization (MADO), 289
Mexican Americans, 288
Mexican immigrant communities, 193, 287, 289, 291, 320; clout, 288; *mutualistas* (mutual aid societies), 288
Meyer, Albert Gregory, 277
Michael Reese Hospital, 78, *79*
Michaelson, Albert A., 133
Mikva, Abner, 250
Miller, Al, 93
Miller, Davey: gang of *shtarkers* (Jewish toughs), 93; as Judah Maccabee, 93; political clout of, 94
Miller, Jake, 103
Miller, Harry, 93
Miller, Hirschie, 93
Miller, J. K., 27
Miller, Max, 93
Mississippi, 28, 224, 225, 230, 231–32
Mississippi Freedom Democratic Party (MFDP), 230–32, 248–49
Mitchell, Arthur, 182–83, 185
Mitchell, Mary, 317
modernization theory, 61
Moeller, Ann, 324
Molitor, Joseph, 69
Moore, Phil, 230
Morgan Park High School, 178–79
Morton, Richard Allen, 99, 347n4
Moses, Robert, 231
Mother McCauley Liberal Arts High School, 216
Mueller Law, 121
Mullen, Catherine, 46
Mullen, Patrick, 46
Mundelein, Cardinal, 75
Municipal Airport (Midway Airport), 187, *192*
Municipal Tuberculosis Sanitarium, 133, 136–37, 140; "Sachs Machine," 134
Municipal Voters League, 110, 121, 158, 162
Murphy, Big Tim, 93
Murphy, Morgan F., Sr., 210, 216–17

Nash, Patrick, 13, 167, 170, 172–75, 183, 195
National Army Aid Association, 162
National Association for the Advancement of Colored People (NAACP), 225–28, 238
National Conference of Brewers, Distillers, and Liquor Dealers, 30
nativism, 29, 47–48
Nativity of Our Lord Church, 207, 257–58, 300
Nativity of Our Lord Parish, 47–48, 217
Nectar Club, 102–3
Negro American Labor Council, 225–26
neighborhoods, 208, 252, 315, 318, 343n36; communal Catholicism, 5; communal phase, 68–69; communal ways, disappearing of, 307; downtown, clash with, 4, 221, 315, 330, 332; as economic engines, 68; folk religion of, 11–12; and gangsters, 91; loyalty to, 215; parish pastors, 69; sacred and profane, interaction between, 239, 332; as sacred space, 4; as small towns, 67; and social contract, 330; and social segregation, 60; spatial integration of, 60; as sub-machines, 195. *See also* Chicago neighborhoods
Neistein, Bernard, 94–95
neoliberalism, 293–96, 309, 319, 330
Neslund, Jeffrey, 317
Netsch, Dawn Clark, 285–86
Newhouse, Richard, 253
New York, 6–7; Five Points neighborhood, 45
Nixon, Richard, 218, 233, 247
Noonan, Edward T., 155
Norfolk Southern Railroad, 313–15, 330
North American Free Trade Agreement (NAFTA), 312
North Riverside (Illinois), 173
Norwegian immigrant communities, 13. *See also* Scandinavian immigrant communities
Novak, Tim, 293

Obama, Barack, 291–92, 300–302, 304, 310
Oberman, Martin J., 258, 265, 268
Oberta, Johnny, 93; as Robin Hood character, 92
O'Brien, Billy, 81
O'Brien, Martin J., 166
O'Connell, William, 157
O'Connor, Edwin, 9
Ogden, William B., 22
Ogden Gas Company, 105–6
Ogden Gas Scandal, 105
Ogilvie, Richard B., 233, 251, 269
Oglesby, Richard J., 34
Old St. Mary's Church, 73, 276–77
O'Leary, Big Jim, 81–82

Index

Oliver Westcott Vocational School, 232
Olivet Baptist Church, 73, *74*
Olson, Harry, 128–29, 136, 161
O'Neill, Tip, 87
Orr, David, 273
Ortiz, Aron, 320–21
O'Shaughnessy, Thomas, 69
Oswald, Lee Harvey, 223
Our Lady of Guadalupe Church, 288

Packinghouse Workers Organizing Committee (PWOC), 190
Palmer, John M., 109
Palmer, Potter, 104
Palmer House, 100
Parks, Rosa, 224
Parsons, Albert, 35
patronage, 5, 108, 136, 202, 208–9, 245, 284–85, 295, 322, 327; and clout, 113, 210; decline of, 331; as expression of loyalty, 300; pinstripe, 294; and political clout, 102; and political machine, 330; in private sector, 210
Paukstis, John L., *243*
Payne, Deborah, 315
Payne, John Barton, 109–10
Peck, Sidney, 242
People's Council of America for Democracy and Terms of Peace, 136
Peoples Gas, Light, and Coke Company, 106. *See also* Ogden Gas Company
Peterson, Charles S., 164
Philip, James "Pate," 246
Pietraszek, Adeline, 281
Pike, Gene, 126
Pilgrim Missionary Baptist Church, 73, 209
Pius XII (pope), 217
Plotkin, Robert, 246
Poland, 87, 135, 193
Polish American Political League, 259
Polish immigrant communities, 7, 10, 13, 31–32, 34, 37, 48, 52, 71, 87, 105, 107, 129–30, 133–35, 137, 144, 157, 162–63, 166–67, 178, 191, 193, 260, 262, 288; Irish and, tension between, 155; *rodacy*, 61; Roosevelt, betrayed by, 197–98; Polish Solidarity movement, 271; waning of, 290–91
Polish Independent Church movement, 63
Polish National Catholic Church, 63
Polish Roman Catholic Union, 201
political clout, 7, 85, 94, 103; of Bridgeport, 62; of Democratic Party, 206; and honest graft, 105–7; of Jewish community, 78–79; of neighborhoods, 72; and patronage, 101–2, 294; ward committeemen, 158–59. *See also* clout
political machine, 2, 4, 7, 39, 91, 113, 122, 201, 223, 250–51, 254, 262, 274, 304, 321, 332; African American votes, 264; assimilation and individualism, promoting of, 6; canvas booklets, 212; Catholics, as significant portion of, 275, 285; as citywide organization, 176, 210; clout, 210; collective network of, 12; communal Catholicism, 11–12; as communally based, 6, 41; decline of, 15, 309; disappearing of, 331; disintegration of, 305–6; as distinctive institution, 1; ethnicity, obsessed with, 51; fissures in, 257; as hierarchical, 89; machine politics, as corrupt politics, 307; and New Year's Eve blizzard, 263; parlor politics, 22, 41; and patronage, 284, 330; pillars, dissolving of, 307; racial issues, threat to, 219; slow death of, 254; and social contract, 330; as stalled, 270; undermining of, 17; weakening of, 247; worldview and moral code of, 89
Populism, 26
Populist Party, 110
Porter, John H., 278
Powell, Paul, 250
Power, Joseph, 241
Powers, John, 81–82, *84*, 110–11, 113–15, 118–19, 138, 180, 221; corruption of, 83; franchises, authorizing of, 83; Irishness of, as shaping his politics, 83; "The Mourner," 85; "Prince of Boodlers," 83
precinct captains, 9, 206, 214, 296, 321; canvas booklets, 212–13; union representatives, 329
Preckwinkle, Toni, 326, 329–30
Prendergast, Patrick Eugene, 19–20, 113
Preston, Sophonisba, 10, 25
Pritzker, J. B., 322, 325, 331
Progressive (Bull Moose) Party, 129
Prohibition, 92–93, 122, 138, 140, 143, 153, 163, 187–88; "Drys," 155; raids on 12th Ward, 164–65; "Wets," 164, 169
prostitution, 92, 122
Protestant churches, 79; Protestantism, and Americanism, 51; public schools, as Protestant in nature, 64; race and migration, 72
public sphere, 80

389

INDEX

Pucinska, Lydia, 193
Pucinski, Aurelia, 271, 273
Pucinski, Roman C., 88, 193, 258, 260, *261*, 262, 267, 270, 272–73, 290–91; communal politics of, 259; "Vrdolyak 29," 271
Puerto Rican immigrant communities, 289, 291
Pulaski, Casimir, 177

Quinn, James, 172–73
Quinn, Kevin, 322–24
Quinn, Marty, 322–23
Quinn, Pat, 323

Raby, Al, 223, 228, 230–31, 234–38
Race with the Sun, A (Harrison), 36
racism, 108, 204, 225, 234, 274
Ragen, Frank, 206
Ragen's Colts, 206
Rainbow Beach, "wade-ins," 226
Reagan, Ronald, 293
Reid and Sherwin packing plant, 44
Reilly, Jack, 256
Republic Steel, Memorial Day Massacre, 190–91
Republican Party, 10–11, 22, 26–27, 29, 33–34, 51, 100, 103, 113, 127–28, 129, 137–39, 142, 145, 156, 160, 165–66, 171–72, 181, 183, 198, 204; and African Americans, 108, 167, 179; and patronage, 245–46; and political machine, 123, 125, 144, 146
Rerum Novarum, 47, 215
Reyes, Victor, 311
Ridgeway, Hamlet C., 141–42
Riordan, Daniel J., 75
riots: Airport Homes, 224; Dixmoor, 233; North Lawndale, 233–34; Peoria Street, 224; Trumbull Park, 224
Robertson, John Dill, 133–34, 140, 142–43
Robinson, Bill "Bojangles," 181
Robinson, Renault, 259
Roche, John A., 36
Rochford, James, 253
Rock, Philip J., 285
Rockefeller, Nelson, 257
Rodgers, Ella, 48
Rogers, Steven, 315
Romano, Mary, 300
Romiti, Philip J., 241
Roosevelt, Franklin D., 175–77, 186, 191–93, 195; assassination attempt, 169–70; New Deal, 8, 14, 17, 178, 187–88, 194, 197, 215, 293, 295
Roosevelt, Theodore, *101*
Rose, Don, 265, 268
Rossi, Marco, 327–28
Rostenkowski, Dan, 86–87, 217, 285, 290–91; "good politics," 88
Rostenkowski, Joseph, 86–87
Roti, Fred, 15, 266
Royko, Mike, 41, 255, 271
Rush, Bobby, 240, 304
Rutherford, Kathryn, 128
Ryan, Dan, 7, 171, 173, 215

Sabath, Adolph J., 79, 133, 150–51, 160
Sachs, Theodore J., 133; spoils system, 134
Sain, Kenneth, 258, 263–64
saloons, 28, 33, 43, 47, 68–69, *81*, *84*, 142, 155, 164–65; anti-saloon factions, 156, 161; barkeeper, as political power, 52, 81; Black owners, 132; "blind pigs," 29; bum boats, 29–30; communal solidarity, as places of, 50, 82; face-to-face communications, 80; free lunch, 32; license fees, 153–54; as meeting place, 52; and political machine, 41; saloon keepers, betrayal of, 132; sample rooms, 29; as social club for working class, 80; special permits, 153–54; Sunday closings, 30, 131–34, 153. *See also* Anti-Saloon League
Saltis, Joe "the Polak," 93
Sanchez, Al, 311
Santiago, Miguel, 290
Sawyer, Eugene, 274, 282–85, 290–91
Scala, Florence, 221
Scandinavia, 147
Scandinavian immigrant communities, 23, 32, 39, 82, 144. *See also* Norwegian immigrant communities; Swedish immigrant communities
Scanlon, John F., 53
Schaldenbrand, Mary A., 279
Schiller, Helen, 283
Schmidt, John, 285
Schneirov, Richard, 46
Scola, Italo, 221
Scott, Maurice, Jr., 278
Scottish immigrants, 23
Sears, Barnabas F., 241
Sears, Nathanial C., 111
segregation: de facto, 178; of neighborhoods,

Index

108; of public schools, 219; racial, 108; residential, 148; social, 60
Serritella, Daniel A., 144–45
Service Employees International Union (SEIU), 328, 329
settlement houses, 49, 139
Severinghaus, Albert H., 135
Sexton, William H., 172
Seyferlich, Arthur R., 177
Shakman, Michael L., 244–47
Shakman decrees, 16, 88, 261, 284, 293–94, 307, 311, 327; machine politics, 247
Shapiro, Samuel, 242
Sheet Metal Workers Union, 211
Sherman, Francis Cornwall, 51
Simon, Paul, 250–51, 285
Simpson, Dick, 252, 258, 265, 320, 327–28
Singer, William, 15, 253, 265
Sisters of Charity of the Blessed Virgin Mary, 48
Sisters of Mercy, 215–17
Sisters of St. Joseph Carondolet, 48
Sisters of the Blessed Sacrament for Indians and Colored People, 75
Skrebneski, Victor, 281
Skudera, Matthew, 150
Slattery, Patrick, 294
Slavic immigrants, 82, 107
Slovakian immigrants, 191
Small, Len, 138
Smith, Al, 164–66, 169
Smith, James A., 233
Smith, Sidney, 34
sociability, 332
social contract, 14–15
Society of the Divine Word missionaries, 75
Society of the Veterans of Foreign Wars, 136
Solis, Danny, 319–20, 323
Sorich, Robert, 294
Southern Christian Leadership Council (SCLC), 235, 237, 239
Soviet Union, 193
Spaeth, Ray, 209
spatial integration, 60
Spielman, Fran, 320
Spirou, Costas, 295
Spotswood, Stephen G., 226
St. Bridget Catholic Church, 43, 48, 49, 50, 207–8
St. Francis of Assisi Parish, 69
St. Gabriel's, 53

St. Ignatius, 56
St. Jarlath's, 31
St. Mel School, 203
St. Michael's Church, 71
St. Patrick's Academy, 56
St. Patrick's Church, 21, 48, 68; Celtic-inspired stencils and window, 69
St. Stanislaus Kostka Parish, 87
St. Valentine's Day Massacre, 146
St. Xavier College, 215–17
Stalin, Josef, 193, 197
Standard Club, 307
Star League, 114–15
Stearns, Marguerite E., 36
Steel Workers Organizing Committee (SWOC), 190–91
Steffens, Lincoln, 19
Stege, John, 179–80
Stevenson, Adlai, II, 198
Stevenson, Adlai, III, 248, 250
Stewart-Winter, Timothy, 287
Stone, Bernard, 303–4
Store, The (saloon), 28, 33
Storey, Wilbur Fisk, 29
Strauss, Robert, 257
street gangs, 50, 63
Strike Relief Committee, 104
strikes, 46–46; Great Railroad Strike, 26, 46–47; meatpacking, 211; Pullman, 97, 104–5
Students for a Democratic Society (SDS), 241
suburbanization, 6, 17, 306
Sullivan, Frank, 244
Sullivan, John, 294
Sullivan, Roger C., 12, 99–100, 102–3, 105–6, 115, 125, 139, 152, 158–61, 208, 347n4;
Sullivan-Brennan machine, 163
Swabian Cannstadter People's Festival, 31
Swanson, John A., 145
Swedenborgians, 30–31
Swedish immigrant communities, 7, 13, 48, 72, 129, 137. *See also* Scandinavian immigrant communities
Sweitzer, Robert, 122–23, 129–30, 136, 161
Swift, George Bell, 99, 103
Swinarski, Donald T., 90–91
Szymczak, M. S., 177, 186–87

Tadin, Michael, 293
Taylor, Graham, 139
Taylor, Jeanette, 309
Teamsters Union, 176

INDEX

Thistle, The (saloon), 29
Thompson, Floyd E., 165
Thompson, James, 253, 256, 285
Thompson, Patrick Daley, 9
Thompson, William Hale, Sr., 126
Thompson, William Hale "Big Bill," 2, 123, 125, 131, 133, 139–40, 145, 161, 163–65, 182, 202; African American community, courting of, 13, 127, 129–30, 132, 137, 143–44; America First movement, *141*, 142; anti-Catholic card, 129; attacks on, 134; background, 126; "Big Bill" moniker, 126; Capone, support of, 142, 144; Cermak, mayoral campaign against, 167–68; home rule for Ireland, 137; "I Will" spirit, 129; mayoral loss, 146; 1919 race riot, 137–38; patriotism, questioning of, 135; patronage, 136–37; political machine, creating of, 12; political oratory, 127; pro-German, accusations of, 134–36; signature cowboy hat, 141–42; upper-class Chicagoan, playing part of, 126; White Anglo-Saxon Protestant rule, 13; and women voters, 129
Thomson, Charles M., 128
Thornton, Charles S., 113
Thorp Elementary School, 210
Till, Emmett, 225
Tillman, Dorothy, 283
Tittinger, Joseph E., 183
Tolton, Augustus, 75
Toman, John, 157–58, 163–64, 173
Tomczak, Peter, 211
Tönnies, Ferdinand, 60–61
Torres, Angelo T., 293–94
Torres, Manuel, 271
traction franchise, 117, 120; boodle, 118
Travis, Dempsey, 226
tribalism, and agency, 160
Trude, Alfred S., 103, 109–11
Truman, Harry S., 218
Trump, Donald, 320
Tunney, Tom, 287
Tweedy, Dorothy, 300
Twyman, Willie, 104

Uhlir, J. Z., 158
Union League, 100
Union Steel Company, 51
United Steel Workers of America, 211
Union Stock Yard, 43, 82, 104, 210–11; 1934 fire, 179; "Stockyard Stench," 190
United Airlines, 312

United Societies for Local Self-Government, 132–33, 155, 158–61, 163, 166; blue laws, opposition to, 154; Chicago Charter, opposition to, 156–57; growth of, 157
United States, 61, 92, 129, 134, 148, 162, 193–94, 214, 277, 306, 312; first English-language Mass, 276; isolationism, 191; public schools, 64
University of Chicago, 219; Chicago Area Project, 69; Civil Rights Accountability Project, 317
University of Illinois at Chicago Circle (University of Illinois Chicago), 221, 315; clout, 222
University of Illinois at Urbana-Champaign, 219
upward mobility, 6, 11, 17, 51, 75, 91, 275

Valderrama, Franklin, 318
Vallas, Paul, 295, 325–26, 328–29
Van Dyke, Jason, 317–18
Vanecko, Richard J., 303
Vanecko, Robert G., 303
Vatican II, 2, 8, 16–17, 65, 276, 305–6; sisterhoods, reform of, 277–78
Vietnam War, 15, 241–42, 279
Vitek, John, 301
Vivian, C. T., 235
Volstead Act, 163
Voting Rights Act, 232
Vrdolyak, Edward, 15–16, 256–57, 258, 266, 269–70, 272–73, 284; "Vrdolyak 29," 271, 320

Walker, Dan, 15, 244, 251, 255–57; walking across Illinois campaign, 250
Walker Report, 244
Wall, Jack, 299
Wallace, George, 228
Walls, Chaka, 240
Walls, William "Dock," 316
Walsh, Frank J., 173
Walsh, J. M., 114
War on Poverty, 235–36
Ward, Jasper D., 26
ward bosses, 82–83, 85–86, 88; and precinct captains, 89–91; ward organizations, as hierarchical, 89
Washburne, Hempstead, 37
Washington, Harold, 16, 260, 262, 269, 272, 272, 274, 290, 299, 328; City Council, struggles with, 271; coalition, 282, 284,

Index

289; death of, 273; legacy of, 283–84, 286; victory of, 270–71
Washington, Laura, 331
Weaver, Robert C., 194
Weil, Milton, 140–41
Weisberg, Lois, 299
Welch, Emanuel Christopher, 325
Wentworth, "Long John," 27
West Side, 68, 93, 102, 138, 171, 189, 223, 234, 275; riots, 239–40; University of Illinois Chicago campus, 220–21; The Valley, 220–21
Western Electric Company, 130, *131*
Whig Party, 22
Whiston, Frank, 210
White, Charles A., 128
White Anglo-Saxon Protestants, 129, 137, 147, 156
White ethnics, 137, 282, 285, 306, 331
White flight, 16, 224, 228, 262, 270, 306
Wiedrich, Bob, 264
Wigoda, Paul, 253
Wilhelm, Kaiser, 130, 135
William Hale Thompson Women's Club, soap opera speeches, 128
Williams, Hosea, 235
Willis, Benjamin, 227–29, 233, 235, 237, 278; Willis Wagons, 227
Wilson, Orlando W., 232

Wilson, Willie, 316
Wilson, Woodrow, 123, 162
Wimbish, Christopher, 185
Winnetka (Illinois), 237
Wirth, Louis, 78
Wolfe, Richard, 140–41
Wood, Elizabeth, 198
Woodlawn Organization, The (TWO), 235–36
World Business Chicago, 312
World War I, 12–13, 92, 107, 125, 134, 148, 150, 161, 211
World War II, 13, 87, 194–95, 224, 288
World's Columbian Exposition, 19, 30, 36–37, *176*

Yarrow, Philip, 131
Yates, Richard, 117
Yattaw, "Black Jack," 30
Yerkes, Charles Tyson, 112; *Chicago Inter Ocean*, purchase of, 118–19; London "Tube," construction of, 120; "Transit King," 117, 119
Yiddish theaters, 78
Youngstown Sheet and Tube, 190

Zalewski, Mike, 323–24
Zangara, Giuseppe, 170, 175
Zikmund, Joseph, 262
Zoldaks (Czech social club), 152